D0982683

The Philosophy of John Locke

Twenty-four of the most important
publications on Locke's philosophy
reprinted in sixteen volumes

Edited by
Peter A. Schouls
The University of Alberta

A GARLAND SERIES

Locke's Writings and Philosophy

Historically Considered

Edward Tagart

Garland Publishing, Inc.
New York & London
1984

For a complete list of the titles in this series
see the final pages of this volume.

This facsimile has been made from a copy in
the Yale University Library.

Library of Congress Cataloging in Publication Data

Tagart, Edward, 1804–1858.
Locke's writings and philosophy historically considered.

(The Philosophy of John Locke)
Reprint. Originally published: London : Longman,
Brown, Green, and Longmans, 1855.
1. Locke, John, 1632–1704. 2. Hume, David, 1711–1776.
I. Title. II. Series.
B1297.T27 1984   192 83-48578
ISBN 0-8240-5613-2 (alk. paper)

The volumes in this series are printed on
acid-free, 250-year-life paper.

Printed in the United States of America

LOCKE'S

WRITINGS AND PHILOSOPHY.

LOCKE'S

WRITINGS AND PHILOSOPHY

HISTORICALLY CONSIDERED,

AND

VINDICATED FROM THE CHARGE OF CONTRIBUTING
TO THE SCEPTICISM OF HUME.

BY

EDWARD TAGART, F.S.A., F.L.S.

LONDON:

LONGMAN, BROWN, GREEN, AND LONGMANS.

1855.

"I know not how men, who have the same idea under different names, or different ideas under the same name, can in that case talk with one another."—LOCKE.

"I rejoice in your quotations from Locke. That great man has done more for the enlargement of the human faculties, and the establishment of pure Christianity, than any author I am acquainted with."—BISHOP WATSON.

PREFACE.

—◆—

THE Work now presented to the reader supposes careful students of the philosophy of the mind, with access to the books which profess to treat of it. It is a plea for English Philosophy and its great masters. It consists of two parts. The first is a vindication of Locke from prevalent misrepresentations, and especially from the charge of encouraging scepticism in religion and morals, showing, by a somewhat careful examination of Hume's metaphysical writings, that Hume neither built nor affected to build on any principles peculiar to Locke, and placing Locke in just relation to Descartes, Berkeley, Gassendi, and Leibnitz. The second contains a view of the progress of English philosophy, properly so called, from Bacon, through Hobbes, Locke, and Hartley, to more modern thinkers, such as Bentham, Mill, and Austin. It aspires to give such a view of the contents of the 'Essay on the Human Understanding' as may facilitate the pro-

fitable study of it, and give to the reader a clear perception of its excellencies and defects. The second
part arose naturally out of the first. Not having
been originally contemplated, some slight repetitions
of sentiment occur, which yet may not be unpleasing
or useless to the reader.

Brought up in a school in which Locke was the
object of traditional veneration,—a veneration height-
ened and justified by reading, reflection, and experience,—I have seen with mingled astonishment and
pain the attempts recently made to depose the master
from his seat of honour, among those from whom better things were to be expected. But it is one thing
to be convinced of the futility of the common objections to Locke's philosophy, of the ignorance in which
they originate, and of the injustice of the insinuations
against its character and tendency—another to display that futility, that ignorance, that injustice before
the eyes of an impartial inquirer by an elaborate picture of the condition of mental and moral science before and about his time, and a truthful representation
of its progress since. Learned men, as well as others,
are oftentimes hard to be convinced of the falsehood
of an opinion once embraced by them; " nor will they
yield," says Lardner, " till they are overwhelmed by a
heap of reasons."

In addition to the observance of the excellent rules
laid down by Locke for remedying the imperfection
and abuse of words,—first, that words should be applied, as near as may be, to such ideas as common use
has annexed them to; secondly, that they should be
made, when doubtful or obscure, as clear as possible
by explanation or definition, that is, by enumerating,
in the case of terms significant of complex ideas, the
several simple ones which enter into the complexity;
and thirdly, that there should be constancy in adherence to the same meaning;—writers touching on the
history of metaphysics should also observe a fourth
rule, namely, that of "faithful quotation." They
should never attempt to give the opinions of authors
whom they criticize and controvert in words other
than those which the authors themselves have used.
Writers and thinkers worthy of attention express their
notions in language deemed by them the fittest; a
language not to be changed with advantage to their
sentiments, except in so far as they have themselves
supplied correction. Mr. Dugald Stewart, like most
other writers on the mind, in his 'Dissertation on the
Progress of Metaphysical Philosophy,' is very defective in this respect. To that dissertation I must acknowledge myself indebted for opening many paths
of interesting inquiry, though the result of inquiry

has led me, for the most part, to conclusions very different from my guide's.

In a work of this nature, surveying so wide and difficult a field, no doubt errors will be detected; some oversight of matters worthy of attention, some instances of bad reasoning, and of that laxity of phrase against which it is so difficult to guard. Such errors I shall rejoice to see corrected, being anxious only for the fullest investigation of the subject, for the advancement of mental and moral science. My wish is to be one of those combatants whom Locke describes " as a champion for knowledge, truth, and peace ; not a slave to vainglory, ambition, or a party." " Rational metaphysics," to translate a passage of D'Alembert in the admirable preliminary discourse to the ' Encyclopédie,' where he speaks of Locke as the Newton of the mind, "like experimental physics, can only consist in gathering with care all the facts, reducing them to a body, explaining some by others, and distinguishing those which ought to hold the first rank, to serve as the common basis."

E. T.

Wildwood, Hampstead, May, 1855.

CONTENTS.

—◆—

OUTLINE OF THE PROGRESS OF ENGLISH PHILOSOPHY.

APPENDIX.

LOCKE'S

WRITINGS AND PHILOSOPHY

HISTORICALLY CONSIDERED.

DESIGN OF THE WORK.

THE writings of Locke cannot be appreciated, unless
they are studied. They will not be studied with the
careful attention which they deserve, while unfounded and hurtful prejudices indispose any considerable
number of readers from looking into them with the
hope of satisfactory result; while the opinion is in-
dustriously propagated that they do not contain the
elements of a sound philosophy of the mind, but, on
the contrary, that they encourage a scepticism fatal to
true science, to the intellectual progress, the moral
improvement, and the lasting happiness of mankind.

To remove or soften these prejudices, and to vindicate their scientific worth, is the object of the present
Work; and in whatever degree success attends it, and
truth accompanies, in that degree something will be
done for the progress of correct thought, and to pro-

B

mote the use of intelligible language concerning the operations and powers of the human understanding. The path will be smoothed for future inquirers; the prospect of possible additions to our knowledge of human nature in its deepest and darkest recesses may be brightened; for in mental, no less than in physical science, it is desirable to know how to observe and what to observe, in order to attain substantial and satisfactory results. A patient and minute attention to works and authors very much forgotten, and when not forgotten, much misrepresented, will be necessary; and although to extract from a multitude of metaphysical books the modicum of valuable and practical sense and reasonable logic which they contain, is like cleansing the Augean Stable or disentangling Neæra's net, yet to uphold the just authority of one of the greatest and purest of English philosophers, to add one votive offering to his honoured memory, is a duty of gratitude and a labour of love. Some future historian of the literature and philosophy of the eighteenth century, continuing Mr. Hallam's labours, may be assisted with materials for a useful chapter. Could I indulge the faintest hope of being remembered in some distant day, I could wish it to be in connection, humble but not unworthy, with the name of Locke.—" Magnus veri sacerdos*."—" The incomparable man, who emancipated human reason from the yoke of mystery and jargon; the greatest and best of philosophers †."—" The father of the

* The poet Gray.　　† Professor Austin, in his Jurisprudence.

modern logic*" and " of rational criticism."—" First master of intellectual truth! without whom those who have taught me would have been as nothing†."— Such grateful praise has been given by disinterested and competent judges. It may be added, that he was the most distinguished champion of England's toleration and religious liberty; foremost among those who endeavoured to make the purest reason compatible with benevolent religious faith—knowledge instrumental to devotion, and who considered the elucidation and defence of truth the first office of benevolence—the noblest service of mankind.

In pursuing this subject, it is desirable at the outset to adduce some evidence of the nature and prevalence of the prejudices which I endeavour to remove. The less-prepared reader will then judge how far there is real occasion for the present Essay. I shall then proceed to trace the origin and inquire into the reasonableness of these prejudices. In doing this, it will be necessary to enter fully and carefully into an examination of Hume's principles and reasonings, in order to show that the statements which I endeavour to refute, are prejudices for which the authors have neither produced, nor in most instances pretended to adduce, any evidence whatsoever. This examination will prepare us for the remarks, with which I shall venture to conclude, on the present condition of

* Sir Humphry Davy; and in what sense true, will be shown hereafter.

† Jeremy Bentham's Works, vol. x., Bowring's edition.

mental and moral science, and on the means by which
the study of it may be improved, and relieved from
many embarrassments. In following this plan, much
minute, but not unimportant literary history will of
necessity demand attention; but it may be hoped that
its general accuracy, combined in some cases with
novelty, as well as its sincerity of purpose, on a subject of the highest moment, will repay whatever attention may be given.

MODERN OPINIONS CONCERNING LOCKE.

1. Mr. Dugald Stewart, in the Dissertation prefixed to the Encyclopædia Britannica, after mentioning
some communications which took place by letter between Dr. Butler, the author of the ' Analogy of
Natural and Revealed Religion with the Constitution
and Course of Nature,' and David Hume, expresses
himself as follows:—" Dr. Butler was, I think, the
first of Mr. Locke's successors, who clearly perceived
the *dangerous consequences likely to be deduced from
his account of the origin of our ideas, literally interpreted.* And although he has touched on this subject but once, and that with his usual brevity, he
has yet said enough to show that his opinion with
respect to it was the same with that formerly contended for by Cudworth, in opposition to Gassendi
and Hobbes, and which has since been revived by
the ablest of Mr. Hume's antagonists. With these
views, it may be reasonably supposed that he (*i. e.*

Butler) was not displeased to see the consequences of Locke's doctrine so very logically and forcibly pushed to their utmost limits, as the most effectual means of rousing the attention of the learned to a re-examination of this fundamental principle."

The whole passage in Mr. Stewart's dissertation has reference to Hume's 'Treatise of Human Nature;' and it implies that in that Treatise some important doctrine of Locke's was logically pushed to its utmost limits. It is worthy of notice, if only as a specimen of Mr. Stewart's mode of treating these subjects, that what Dr. Butler really alludes to, in the Essay on Personal Identity, is *not Locke's account of the origin of our ideas*, about which Butler says nothing, and to which I am not aware that he ever made objection, but certain expressions and suppositions concerning personal identity; of which Locke himself modestly says, " Did we know more of the thinking thing within one, we might see the absurdity of some of those suppositions I have made*."

2. Monsieur V. Cousin, in his ' Cours d'Histoire de la Philosophie Morale,' speaks of ' sensualisme' and the ' Ecole sensualiste,' as represented by Locke, Condillac, Helvetius, Saint-Lambert, and of idealism as associated with the Scotch, with Kant and Fichte; and he makes certain criticisms on Locke, which, if not hereafter noticed, will only be passed over because they have been sufficiently animadverted upon by an excellent American writer, Mr. Bowen, in his ' Meta-

* Essay on Understanding, b. ii. ch. 27, and Stewart's Dissertation, p. 217.

physical Essays.' The terms 'sensualisme' and 'sensualiste' are not found in ordinary French dictionaries.
They sound harshly to the English ear as expressive of
a philosophical theory, especially when connected with
the name and principles of Locke, who was as little of
a sensualist, in the common English meaning of that
term, as man could be. His taste, his principles, his
habits, were in the highest degree remote from any
tendency to the grosser indulgences of sense. Habitually an invalid, an exquisite refinement, a delicacy
almost painful, pervades the expression of his countenance, as the common engravings and busts have transmitted it to us; and the grave lines which we now
trace therein would have been deepened, or perhaps
have relaxed into a smile, by the momentary suggestion
that in future times his principles and his authority
would come to be associated with any of the less pure,
less worthy, and less elevated enjoyments, pursuits,
and attributes of human nature. It could hardly
have been intended by Monsieur Cousin to charge
upon Locke any personal leaning to what in England
would be most readily understood by a sensualist;
but he takes no care to discuss an abstract philosophical question upon its merits, and to sever the
simple matter of fact and of principle from the delu-
sive mixture of motive and of consequences, from what
Bentham aptly calls dislogistic phraseology. The applause of his audience seduces him into declamation,
when he should tax the understanding with patient
analysis. But it is pleasanter to gather flowers which

may be thrown away tomorrow, than to cut out steps in a hard rock, which, when once made, may thenceforth serve for easier ascent and wider views.

3. After Cousin, as an additional evidence of the state of thought on metaphysical subjects among the students of France, C. Rémusat may be referred to, in whose third Philosophical Essay, under the head of 'Reid,' the following sentiment occurs :—" Sensualism however was not the only result of the philosophy of Locke. One and the same error may produce different errors— may sometimes give authority to contrary errors. Thus from a philosophy which exaggerates the part played by sensation, it was doubtless natural to conclude the reference of all reality to that which is perceived by sense (*senti*),—a conclusion which drives us to consider only body in the universe. But as sensation taken alone, despoiled of the beliefs which accompany it and make it fruitful, reveals nothing but itself alone, it was equally possible, in following Locke, to see only in external objects the sensation which they occasion, to annihilate their proper existence, and to rest the boldest doubt on the humblest empiricism. Thus that doctrine which sacrifices mind to sensation might give birth alike to the negation of mind,—that is, materialism ; and to the negation of matter,—that is, idealism ; in fine, the negation of both, universal negation or scepticism. Of all these errors, the least unreasonable appears to be materialism,—that is the error of the French. Idealism without scepticism, or dogmatic on one side, and on the other, scepticism with prefe-

rence for materialism, the two doctrines or rather two subtle views, two paradoxical speculations, which could not make a school, are represented in England by two philosophers without disciples, Berkeley and Hume. After Locke, Hume and Berkeley have been the immediate adversaries of Reid; and we shall soon see how he combated them. But their doctrines were little adapted to the English genius : it is on the soil of Germany speculations of this sort flourish*."

4. Mr. J. D. Morell, in an 'Historical and Critical View of the Speculative Philosophy of Europe in the Nineteenth Century' has the following remarks:— "The principles of Locke's celebrated Essay we have already criticized at some length, and shown, we trust sufficiently, the dangerous readiness which it manifested to regard experience as the sole basis on which any system of truth could be erected." "The scepticism which arose out of the school of Locke, we find, in fact, to be the most deeply grounded in its principles, the most logical in its arguments, and the most sweeping in its conclusions, of any which the history of philosophy has recorded; and the name of David Hume, its great advocate, will ever be remembered as associated with all that is bold and comprehensive in the attacks which have been made against the validity of human knowledge."

"Hume united in himself, to a high degree, the observing power of sensationalism with the faculty of abstract reasoning that has generally belonged pecu-

* 'Essais sur la Philosophie,' by Rémusat, vol. i. pp. 183–4.

liarly to idealism, and knew perfectly what had been found unsatisfactory in the one system, as well as what was inconclusive in the other. He came, properly speaking, from the school of Locke, and adopted throughout the fundamental axioms of that philosophy for his own; but he could equally well employ the rationalistic method of Descartes whenever it suited his purpose, in order to strengthen the grounds of his startling unbelief." "To the first principles, from which he took his start, no one at that time could very strongly demur, as it was then generally admitted that Locke's account of the origin of our ideas was correct, and that the whole of our knowledge might really be traced to sensation and reflection as its source. Hume in fact did little more than change the current phraseology, when he said that all our mental phenomena consist of *impressions* and *ideas ;* including under the former our direct perceptions, and by the latter, meaning the *signs* of them, which by virtue of memory, association, etc., remain after the impression has ceased. In addition to this, he was only following Aristotle, the scholastic philosophers, Descartes, Malebranche, and Locke himself, when he assumed as indisputable the representationalist theory of human knowledge, and took for granted, that by the idea of any real outward existence we are to understand the representation or copy of it actually existing within our own minds, this copy being the sole means by which we can attain to the knowledge of the objective*."

* Morell's Philosophy, vol. i. p. 272.

There is more to the same purpose and in a similar spirit in Mr. Morell's volumes. His taste seems to have been formed upon French models, and in the school of Cousin, more than upon a patient study of the solid writers of his own country. Such use of the terms 'sensationalism,' 'idealism,' 'rationalistic,' 'representationalist,' is somewhat new to the English student; its value, with that of the correctness and precision of the whole statement, will be tested in some degree by that examination of Hume which lies before us.

I throw into an Appendix some additional quotations from an Italian writer, Vincenzo Gioberti, from an American writer, a Mr. Rowland, and from a reviewer in the 'Westminster and Foreign Quarterly,' and some other writers, which will illustrate still further the very extensive prevalence of these views of the influence of Locke. It is not worth while to detain the reader with their perusal here.

It may be added that, partly by the reflex action of continental writers upon English opinion and taste, partly by the fear of social changes and of those reforms, ecclesiastical and educational, which are favoured by a clear, practical, and benevolent philosophy, the high estimation of Locke, as the founder of a true theory of the mind, as the leading discoverer in that important field of observation and inquiry, has of late years been declining in England, except among a few of the more independent and sober thinkers. Professor Sedgwick, in his 'Dis-

course on the Studies of the University of Cambridge,'
Dr. Whewell, in his recent 'History of Moral Philosophy,' though acknowledging the great merits of
Locke in many respects, are upon the whole unfavourable to him, and do not encourage the opinion that he
furnishes the brightest light, and leads the way as our
best guide, in the dark and intricate paths of metaphysical research. It is even more to be regretted
that other English writers and thinkers, freer in position than the Professors in our Universities, who might
be expected to appreciate the rare intellectual and
moral qualities of the author of the 'Essay on the
Human Understanding,' and to own their inestimable
obligations to him, have lent a hand to the destruction of his fame and influence,—an influence already
sufficiently dreaded by the lovers of darkness, and
the favoured beneficiaries of exclusiveness and intolerance.

Taking the evidence now adduced of the nature
and prevalence of those impressions concerning Locke,
the justice of which is to form the subject of our examination,—evidence the readiest to my hands, though
not perhaps the most important, which the literature
of later days supplies, we may pass to that minute inquiry into the real influence of Locke's philosophy
upon his immediate successors, and into the exact nature of that philosophy, which will test their correctness, and account for their origin and prevalence.
This examination will prove a salutary philosophical
exercise, of some value in itself, and of the highest

importance in its results, in proportion to the completeness and fidelity of the inquiry.

HIGH ESTIMATION OF LOCKE IN THE FIRST HALF OF THE EIGHTEENTH CENTURY.

"Towards the close of the eighteenth century, it became fashionable sometimes to accuse Locke of preparing the way for scepticism—a charge which, if it had been truly applicable to some of his opinions, ought rather to have been made against the long line of earlier writers, with whom he held them in common; sometimes, with more pretence, to allege that he had conceded too much to materialism; sometimes to point out and exaggerate other faults and errors of his Essay; till we have seemed to forget that it is perhaps the first, and still the most complete chart of the mind which has been laid down; the most ample repertory of truths relating to our intellectual being; and the one book which we are compelled to name as the first in metaphysical science."

Such is Mr. Hallam's language in the third of his delightful and instructive volumes on the History of the Literature of Europe, and it will not be disregarded by any one capable of following in the paths which he has trodden. It will be found, on a close examination of writers on the philosophy of the mind subsequent to Locke, worthy of the discrimination and judgment of its venerated author.

For the first half of the eighteenth century the

writings of Locke stood high in public estimation. His ' Essay on the Human Understanding*' had been early adopted as a text-book at the Universities. It became the " Novum Organum" of mental science, and pushed aside all previous works on that capital portion of the field of human knowledge. Continental writers of the highest eminence acknowledged its vast importance. Le Clerc gave it deserved rank, by his review and account of it in the ' Bibliothèque Choisie' (tom. vi., 1706), preceded by Locke's own abridgment of it in the ' Bibliothèque Universelle,' 1688, and followed by an *éloge* of Locke, after his death,—earnest and affectionate, but not extravagant, —the tribute of a friend and a philosopher†.

The eminent and gifted Leibnitz early published some short reflections on it, which, while expressing considerable diversity of opinion, showed his high

* First published in 1689, and abridged by Mr. Wynne, 1695, for University use.

† Locke did what he could to induce Le Clerc to settle in England, and to provide for that eminent scholar a living in the English Church. But it could not be brought about. One wishes that, as in the case of Erasmus, England had had the honour of sheltering and gladdening in his declining years a man of so much learning and accomplishment as Le Clerc,—

  " Who scorned delights, and lived laborious days."

The only notice of Locke which I trace in Gibbon is honourable and in connection with Le Clerc, who had given Locke's method of a commonplace book, in the 'Bibliothèque Universelle,' of which method Gibbon observes, "The exactness and perspicuity of that great man are seen in that trifle." See Locke's Familiar Correspondence with Molyneux, and Gibbon's Miscellaneous Works, in one vol., p. 433.

sense of its importance and of the merits of the author. And he commented upon it at length, in 'Nouveaux Essais sur l'Entendement humain,' in 1703. It was speedily translated into French by the admiring hand of Mons. Coste. A Latin translation appeared in 1701*. At home, writers of all classes united to extol and recommend it. The learned Bentley, in the Boyle Lectures against Atheism, in 1693, built upon Locke's principles, and "vented his notions from the pulpit †." Addison infused into his 'Spectators' a spirit of practical wisdom, and a refinement of feeling and taste, caught from the great philosopher, whom he delighted to mention with honour. His name was venerated, not merely as a synonym for intellectual sagacity, but for the pure and dispassionate love of truth, combined with a rational piety and calm religious faith; as that of a man who had done perhaps more than any living individual to dissipate prejudices, to stimulate inquiry, to secure the liberties, and, by an example of intellectual and moral greatness, to promote the highest honour and happiness of his country. The friend of Somers and of William the Third, of Molyneux, of the first Shaftesbury, of Pembroke, of Newton, and an inmate in the house of the daughter of Cudworth, he enjoyed and

* Mr. Stewart observes "that we everywhere trace the influence of Locke's doctrines in Crousaz's 'Treatise of Logic.'" If the 'Art of Thinking,' by Crousaz, translated in 1724, be meant, the fact is otherwise: much of Locke's language is misapplied, and his authority scarcely recognized.

† See Locke's Letter to Molyneux, Feb. 22, 1697.

used the finest opportunities for intellectual accomplishment, and for social influence the most beneficial and the most extensive. Who can read Coste's Character of Mr. Locke without sympathizing in its raptures of admiration for *his "virtue, capacity, and the excellency of his writing"?*

The high estimation in which Locke was held, about the middle of the last century, especially at Cambridge, when Law and Gay were also there as visitors or residents, associated in common studies, is shown by the beautiful address to the philosopher, which the poet Gray introduces into the fragment of a metaphysical poem, entitled, 'De Principiis Cogitandi,' designed to embody the philosophy of Locke.

> " Nec dedignare canentem,
> O decus ! Angliacæ certè ô lux altera gentis !
> Si quà primus iter monstras, vestigia conor
> Signare incertâ, tremulâque insistere plantâ.
> Quin potius duc ipse (potes namque omnia) sanctum
> Ad limen, (si ritè adeo, si pectore puro,)
> Obscuræ reserans naturæ ingentia claustra.
> Tu cæcas rerum causas, fontemque severum
> Pande, Pater ; tibi enim, tibi, *veri magne Sacerdos*,
> Corda patent hominum, atque altæ penetralia mentis."

This invocation of Locke by Gray is the more impressive, because there was hardly any branch of learning except the pure mathematics in which Gray had not acquired a mastery, and he had paid particular attention to metaphysical and moral science, ancient and modern.

From the whole character of the metaphysical philosophy prevalent in England and at the Universities, at the period when Gray wrote, it is evident that not only had Shaftesbury lapsed into comparative oblivion, but that other writers also, who were opposed to Locke, such as Stillingfleet, and the less-remembered Norris, the Platonist, and Lee, and Lowde, who wrote on the Nature of Man, and drew forth some comments from Locke in the later editions of the Essay, had sunk into the same condition.   Then Warburton* and Conybeare spoke of Locke as " the honour of this age, and the instructor of the future," and of the Essay on the Human Understanding as " one of the noblest and most original books in the world."

REID, THE FIRST WHO CHARGES LOCKE WITH LEADING TO SCEPTICISM.

But after the writings of Berkeley and of Hume appeared, a different tone began to be in vogue.   The depreciation of Locke, and the connection of his name with sceptical principles, came from the North, and the first who set the fashion was Dr. Thomas Reid, Professor of Moral Philosophy in the University of Glasgow, who published, in 1764, an ' Inquiry into the Human Mind, on the principles of Common Sense.'   I say the first, because Shaftesbury's unwar-

---

* See the Dedication to the Free-thinkers prefixed to the ' Divine Legation,' with the striking remarks on the treatment of Locke by Collins and by Shaftesbury: Warburton's Works, vol. i. p. 163, edit. 1811.

rantable attack on Locke's Essay, which has of late been frequently quoted, and may be found in Stewart's Dissertation (p. 118) mentioned with praise, as putting the question about innate ideas in a right light, although it really changes that question entirely, is a mere piece of rodomontade, passed over at the time as unworthy of its author. 'To throw truth and virtue out of the world,' is happily not within the scope of any man's powers; and to speak thus of such a work as Locke's, can only be regarded as a hasty ebullition of temper, which its author upon the least reflection must have repented. There is a severe and contemptuous notice of Shaftesbury in the Letters of the poet Gray : it is at the close of a letter addressed to Mr. Stonhewer, dated Cambridge, August 18, 1758, and may be given in a note*.

* "You say you cannot conceive how Lord Shaftesbury came to be a philosopher in vogue. I will tell you. First, he was a lord. Secondly, he was as vain as any of his readers. Thirdly, men are very prone to believe what they do not understand. Fourthly, they will believe anything at all, provided they are under no obligation (? *rational obligation*) to believe it. Fifthly, they love to take a new road, even when that road leads nowhere. Sixthly, he was reckoned a fine writer, and seemed always to mean more than he said. Would you have any more reasons ? An interval of above forty years has pretty well destroyed the charm. A dead lord ranks but with commoners. Vanity is no longer interested in the matter, for the new road has become an old one. The mode of free-thinking is like that of ruffs and farthingales, and has given place to that of not thinking at all; once it was reckoned disgraceful half to discover and half to conceal the mind, but now we have been long accustomed to see it quite naked ; primness and affectation of style, like the good breeding of Queen Anne's Court, has turned to hoyden-

C

"I acknowledge," says Dr. Reid, in the dedication
of his 'Inquiry into the Human Mind,' "that I never
thought of calling in question the principles commonly
received with regard to the human understanding,
until the 'Treatise of Human Nature' was published
in the year 1739. The ingenious author of that Treatise *upon the principles of Locke*, who was no sceptic,
hath built a system of scepticism which leaves no
ground to believe any one thing rather than its contrary. His reasoning appeared to me˙ to be just;
there was therefore a necessity to call in question the
principles or to admit the conclusion*." Dr. Reid
expresses himself still more strongly to the same effect
at the conclusion of his work. After intimating that
Locke's principles concerning ideas were in some important particulars *identical with those of Descartes*,
and that Berkeley's system is founded upon Cartesian
principles, he says :—"Thus we see† that Descartes
and Locke take the road that leads to scepticism
without knowing the end of it; but they stop short
for want of light to carry them further. Berkeley,
frighted at the appearance of the dreadful abyss, starts
aside, and avoids it. But the author of the 'Treatise

ing and rude familiarity."—The above is followed, in Mason's 'Gray,'
by some pertinent strictures on the writings of Lord Bolingbroke,
and his attack on the 'Moral Attributes of the Deity.'

* 'Inquiry into the Human Mind,' by Dr. Reid.   Dedication,
p. 5, edit. 1769.

† Conclusion of the 'Inquiry,' p. 374.   Compare also various passages relating to Descartes, Malebranche, and Locke, in the Introduction to the same work, p. 10.

of Human Nature,' more daring and intrepid, without turning aside to the right hand or to the left, like Virgil's Alecto, shoots directly into the gulf :—

> "Hîc specus horrendum, et sævi spiracula Ditis
> Monstrantur : ruptoque ingens Acheronte vorago
> Pestiferas aperit fauces."

Dr. Reid's work reached a third edition in 1769. It was exceedingly well received.   Being Professor of Philosophy in a Scotch University, the Doctor's opinions and statements were influential from his position ; and without examination (for how few would examine Descartes and Malebranche for themselves) they gained credit and were repeated.   Mr. Dugald Stewart, in his account of the life and writings of Dr. Reid, published in 1802, declares that the idea of prosecuting the study of the Human Mind on the plan of Lord Bacon and his followers in physics, if not first conceived, was at least first successfully carried into execution by Dr. Reid*.   Dr. Reid was soon followed by two other writers in the same track, namely, Dr. Oswald, who published an 'Appeal to Common Sense in behalf of Religion,' a second edition of which came out in 1768, and Dr. James Beattie, more famous as a poet, who became Professor of Philosophy in Marischal College, Aberdeen, in 1760, and first published his 'Essay on Truth' in 1770, an essay which went through five editions in as many successive years—an evidence of the fluctuation of taste and fashion in literature.   Thus we see that reputations flourish like

* Stewart's Account, 4to, p. 40.

c 2

plants or weeds. They that grow most rapidly and are decked most gaily, for the most part decline also the soonest. The growth of the monarchs of the forest is slow and unnoticed; but year after year they spread out their glories, and stand for ages, the object of ever-renewed admiration. So is it with the greatest productions of human intelligence: they bear fruit for successive generations, and fill the air season after season with the perfume of their blossoms.

These three writers, the Curiatii of the North, were not allowed to flourish their trumpets and claim a victory, without meeting an antagonist. A champion for England's superior sense against their common sense soon descended into the lists. They were sharply attacked and roughly handled by Dr. Priestley, who published an examination of them in 1774. It has been said that the flippant and sarcastic style which the Doctor assumed in his 'Examination' was disapproved even by his own friends. If this be true, it may be readily imagined that those who were already unfriendly were deterred from looking into his pages, and found in the manner a sufficient excuse for undervaluing and disregarding the matter.

Dr. Campbell, in his 'Philosophy of Rhetoric,' is particularly hard upon it*. He says:—"The attack was made in a manner which no man who has any regard to the name either of Englishman or of philosopher, will ever desire to see imitated in this or in any other country." Yet there is that vigour, pur-

---

* See vol. i. pp. 94–97, edit. 1808.

pose, and clearness in Dr. Priestley's work, which keeps the reader awake, and relieves the dryness of metaphysical disquisition. And Dr. Campbell's note proves that he also, candid and scholarly as upon the whole he was, could be blind to the real question at issue, in zeal for his discomfited countrymen. That question was—not the existence of first truths or principles, as Dr. C. states it—this Dr. Priestley never denied; but it was the extent to which Reid and his coadjutors had misunderstood and misrepresented the philosophy of Locke and his school*.

Dr. Priestley, ardent in everything, was the ardent disciple of Locke and Hartley. He thought he had found in these great and sober writers, not only a sufficient preservative from religious scepticism, but the elements of a true philosophy of the human mind. He was astounded and grieved at the manner in which these great masters of metaphysical science had been treated. He saw a modest and candid philosophy, as well as pure religion, endangered, wounded, betrayed, by officious and ill-judging friends. With a courage and energy characteristic of his free and generous nature, he rose up at once and unhesitatingly in their defence. He advanced boldly, and with the first weapons at hand, into the camp of the enemy. He exposed their feeble resources and unworthy manoeuvres. He found their positions weak and untenable; and he

---

* The reader may compare with this Stewart's notice both of Campbell and Priestley in his account of Reid, which may be most conveniently referred to as reprinted in Hamilton's 'Reid,' p. 27.

scrupled not to represent their alliance as virtually a
compact of prejudice and vanity. He denounced their
principles as alike dangerous and false, and their works
as destructive to the progress of sober and scientific
inquiry, and to the proper estimation of writers far
superior to themselves in all the highest attributes of
the mind.

Dr. Priestley's work, however severely animadverted
upon for its tone and temper,—a tone which no doubt
contributed to alienate readers whom it would have
been better, if possible, to conciliate,—readers who,
though refusing to be driven, might not unwillingly
have been led,—was never candidly examined, still less
was it deliberately answered, by any of the parties
whom he attacked. Yet nothing can be more candid
nor more amiable than the letters of Dr. Priestley in
his correspondence with Beattie, appended to later
editions of the 'Examination*.' The present Sir W.
Hamilton, in the notes to his edition of 'Reid,' has
referred to it, admitting and even following up with
confirmatory matter the reasonableness of some of its
exceptions to Reid's statements and language, and
damaging those statements and that language quite
as unsparingly. Yet there are passages where Sir W.
Hamilton might have referred to Priestley with equal
advantage, but has not done so†. Dr. Priestley was
not convicted of misrepresenting the opinions nor mis-

* See Rutt's Priestley, vol. iii.

† Compare Hamilton's 'Reid,' p. 110, with Priestley's 'Examination,' p. 97 ; Reid, pp. 121, 122, with Priestley, pp. 60 and 89.

quoting the statements of those on whom he commented. He was neither corrected nor confuted*. He showed that, far from being original in their views and expressions, with regard to intuition and common sense, the Scotch writers had been anticipated by Dr. Price, who published his 'Review of the Principal Questions in Morals' in 1758; and in some measure also by Mr. Harris, in the 'Hermes.' He might have added, by Father Buffier, in his 'Treatise on First Truths.' But Sir W. Hamilton has, I think, successfully defended Reid from the charge of plagiarism brought against him by the translator of Buffier†.

Now there was a part of the subject which Priestley left untouched, and which it is the chief purpose of this Inquiry to discuss, on account of its connection with the history of philosophy and the current of

* Yet the reader should consult the comments on Priestley in the Notes A to D of Stewart's 'Essays on the Philosophy of the Mind,' first published in 1810.

† The translation was published, with an instructive preface, in 1780. This preface is anonymous. Who was the author? The work was published by Johnson, of St. Paul's Churchyard; and the successor to Johnson, now living, has informed me that he always understood Dr. Priestley to be the author. This has been supposed by other students; but there is no allusion to that authorship in Dr. Priestley's works or letters. It was not like him to publish without his name. The style (though easy) and the spirit are scarcely his. The Rev. W. Turner, jun., of Halifax, a competent judge, has suggested that Berrington, the author of 'Letters on Materialism,' and the correspondent of Dr. Priestley, might possibly be the translator and editor in question. Whoever was the author, there is a severe notice of Hume in his preface (p. x.), which will be found in our Appendix, and justified to a great extent by the matter of the present work.

opinion on speculative points of the highest importance to the present time.   Valuable and suggestive
as Priestley's examination of Reid, Beattie, and Oswald is to the philosophical inquirer, for the acuteness
and earnestness with which it exposes the pretension
and shallowness of their productions, it would have
been more valuable—it would have produced probably a far stronger impression on his contemporaries,
even on the minds of those whom he opposed—had
he examined also the Treatise of Human Nature, and
Hume's Inquiries and principles in general, instead
of contenting himself with referring his readers to his
own ' Institutes of Religion' for an answer to Hume;
and if he had shown or endeavoured to show that
Hume's scepticism, to whatever it amounted, was neither professedly nor legitimately deduced from the philosophy of Locke.   It may therefore be thought, notwithstanding Dr. Priestley's animadversions on these
writers, that Hume did build on Locke's foundations,
and did support himself by Locke's principles; and
that his scepticism is the natural and unavoidable
result and growth of what is now called the ' sensational philosophy.'   This is in fact the current doctrine,
as has been partly shown, in Germany and France,
and more recently in England and America.   It was
Hume, and the opinion that he was unanswered, that
gave rise to the transcendental school, of which the
celebrated Kant was founder, and in which Fichte,
Schelling, Jacobi, and Hegel have since been teachers.
    There is some not unimportant literary history con-

nected with this inquiry. About the time when the Scotch philosophy began to invade the territory of which Locke had hitherto been master, there existed at Aberdeen a society, or club, for the discussion of literary and philosophical subjects, composed of men whose opinions were in many points congenial, and who have all been hailed among the revivers of Scotch literature. It is supposed that the topics which fill the works of Reid, Beattie, Oswald, Campbell, Gregory, and Gerard were first produced, and their merits discussed, in this society, either in the form of an essay or of a question for familiar conversation *.

It is probable that these Scotchmen were alarmed at the bad opinion which Hume's sceptical writings were calculated to diffuse of the nature and tendency of Scotch literature and Scotch philosophy. Their universities, as institutions for education, and their own character and influence as professors, might come to be in very bad repute, if it were supposed that any extensive sympathy existed among the professors of those universities with the views of their countryman —a sympathy which the proverbial national partiality of the Scotch rendered far from antecedently improbable. While therefore Campbell and Gerard devoted

---

* A very interesting account of this Society, called " The Wise Club," is given in the ' Life of Beattie,' by Sir W. Forbes. Without doubt it laid the foundation of the popularity and the influence of Scotch philosophy and literature. With a natural partiality these friends praised each other's " learning and sagacity ;" nor would this be objected against them, if they had done justice to writers and philosophers far superior to themselves.

themselves purely to the theological questions connected with the study and defence of Revealed Religion, and both produced works which the theologian
will highly value—the one in his Dissertations prefixed to the Translation of the New Testament, the
other in his 'Institutes'—as constituting no mean portion of his critical apparatus, the professors of moral
philosophy sought to encounter the sceptic in the
rarer atmosphere of metaphysics, but with infinitely
less success.   The contests of metaphysicians are like
those of Milton's angels.   The sword of logic, even
when tempered, like that of Michael from the armoury
of God, " so that neither keen nor solid might resist
that edge," ever inflicts what the poet calls " *a dis-
continuous wound.*"   The ethereal substance is not
long divisible.   Metaphysicians are " spirits that live
throughout, vital in every part !"—

> "And, as they please,
> They limb themselves, and colour, shape, or size
> Assume, as likes them best, condense or rare."

Even when most discomfited and confounded by an
opposing and overwhelming force, the adherent of the
most atheistic system of metaphysical philosophy con-
soles himself with something like the sentiment of
Satan :—

> " True is, less firmly arm'd,
> Some disadvantage we endured and pain,
> Till now not known, but, known, as soon contemn'd ;
> Since now we find this our empyreal form
> Incapable of mortal injury,

Imperishable, and though pierced with wound
Soon closing, and by native vigour heal'd*."

Those who are familiar with metaphysical writers will feel sufficiently the force of the comparison. The absence of definite meaning in their terms is the torment of the logical thinker—"a limbo broad and large, the paradise of fools." They build a tower of Babel; and trying to scale heaven, the result is a confusion of tongues. No questions of practical utility susceptible of satisfactory solution are kept before the mind. What is Time? What is Space? What is Being? What is absolute existence? What is the absolute in itself †? How are synthetical cognitions *à priori* possible? These are the dark questions that, like the

---

* The admirer of Dante may remember with pleasure that the author of the Inferno, and his guide, after an encounter with the poets, meet in the first region, which appears cheerful enough, with its castle of seven walls and gates, its pleasant stream, its mead with lively verdure fresh, the *philosophic train*—Aristotle, whom he calls, with just appreciation, "the Master of the sapient throng;" "there Socrates and Plato both I marked, Tully, and moral Seneca, Avicen, and him who made that commentary vast, Averroes." The commentators may be left where they were seen; but one would hope, with Zwingle and Augustin, that the merit of the great masters may ultimately save them, though unbaptized.—See Cary's Dante, canto 4.

† The reader may consult Morell's 'History of Philosophy,' vol. ii. p. 62, and consider the following definition of the Absolute given by Rémusat in his account of Kant, p. 407 :—"L'absolu est le caractère ou de la chose prise en soi, et de ce qu'elle vaut intrinsèquement, ou de la chose valable à tous égards et tous les rapports. Ce dont l'opposé est impossible à tous égards et sous tous les rapports (et non pas seulement intrinsèquement impossible) est absolument nécessaire. Tel est le véritable absolu. La raison pur ose s'élever à cet absolu." Why not similar definitions of the 'resolute,' dissolute,

smoke ascending from the first touch of Aladdin's lamp, now meet us at the threshold of metaphysical inquiry, and on which are made to depend the further questions, whether we ourselves are merely accidents of an accident, or subjects of a creative Ruler, whose law we are competent in some measure to interpret and obey.   It is forgotten that, if we could answer such questions to our satisfaction, and supply available definitions to the terms in doubt, little or nothing would be done towards a settlement of those points on which Locke pursued his inquiries, namely, "the original, certainty, and extent of human knowledge, together with the grounds and degrees of belief, opinion, and assent;" "those measures whereby a rational creature, put into that state which man is in this world, may and ought to govern his opinions, and actions depending thereon."   We should still be left to inquire how the mind comes to be furnished with its vast store and endless variety of ideas, with all the materials of reason and knowledge? what are the powers of the understanding, and their limits? whether ideas can be usefully distinguished into those of sensation and reflection? how ideas come to be associated with words, and simple ideas become complex? and whence language derives its significancy and strength, and what are its defects and its perfections as an instrument of

involute, convolute, etc., or any other Latin participle, without meaning except in connection with an object to which it is applied? To this great height the pure reason may dare to lift itself, till it finds an atmosphere too rare for useful and desirable existence.

thought and communication? and what is the quality in an act, or habit, or disposition, or agent, which entitles any one of the four to the epithet virtuous on the one hand, or vicious on the other? and by what methods the mind may be enriched and cultivated, and the dispositions and habits of the individual be improved? Upon these important questions transcendental philosophy seems to throw no light. It even scorns them, as empiricism; but they are the questions which, till recently, chiefly exercised the thoughts and investigations of English thinkers,— such as our Bacon, and Hobbes, and Selden, and Cumberland, and Locke, and Hartley, and Paley, and Law.

This will appear more relevant as we proceed. Many philosophers had inquired into the Human Mind, and with no slight sagacity, before Dr. Reid undertook the task, and published the results of his inquiry in a work which Mr. Dugald Stewart so warmly eulogized as the first successful execution of Lord Bacon's plan of study. If to make bold assertions with complete indifference to the proof,—to appeal to vulgar prejudice, under the title of common sense, in answer to refined and subtle arguments,— to declaim, but not to analyse,—to substitute metaphors, fancies, prophecies, for an examination of nature, fact, and reasoning,—to worship the *idola tribus* or *idola specus;* if this be to execute Lord Bacon's plan of study, then indeed Dr. Reid has executed it. But whoever reads with conscientious care the authors

who preceded Dr. Reid, will be only mortified to find
to how little purpose they had written—how completely their excellencies and their faults were thrown
away on this new candidate for literary distinction
and philosophical discovery.   It would perhaps be
difficult to mention a treatise on any other subject of
scientific investigation less worthy than this ' Inquiry
into the Human Mind' by Dr. Reid, coming from a
source of such repute, and considering the means of
information within the author's easy reach.   It is
manifestly deficient in all the qualities of a careful
philosophical production.   No doubt our best authors
have much improved, since Dr. Reid's time, in power
of metaphysical analysis and closeness of metaphysical reasoning*.   But Reid should be judged by the
standard of those whom he ought to hàve known,
because he professed to study and understand them.
Whoever reads with due attention the third and fourth
chapters of Locke's Essay, Berkeley's ' Principles of

* " We are grown" (says Mrs. Barbauld—' Preliminary Essay to
Selections from the Spectator,' p. 6—speaking of the inaccuracies
and vulgarisms which blemish the pages of Steele) " more accurate
in our definitions, more discriminating in our investigations, more
pure in our diction, more fastidious in our ornaments of style; we
possess standards of excellence of every kind to refer to, books multiply on our hands, and we willingly consign to oblivion a portion of
the old, to make way for the increasing demands of the new." Was
not the first part of this passage truer a few years ago than it is now?
Was it not truer before the ' Edinburgh Review' began to put sober
English authorship somewhat out of countenance by the unfairness
and pretension of anonymous reviewing; and before we began to be
flooded with translations from the Germans and the French by those
who have paid little attention to the English masters?

Human Knowledge,' the first volume of Hume's 'Treatise of Human Nature,' the translation, with notes by Edmund Law, of King's 'Origin of Evil,' some of the earlier propositions of Hartley's 'Observations on Man,' particularly the eighth, tenth, twelfth, thirty-third, and seventy-ninth, and subsequent propositions relating to words and truth; whoever, instead of confining himself to the authors whom Dr. Reid professes to review and correct, looks into the pages of the clear and thoughtful Hobbes, or of writers less immediately concerned—Descartes and Gassendi, Norris and Peter Browne, Jackson and Collins, or into the metaphysical correspondence of Clarke and Leibnitz, all of whom entered into the arena of metaphysical discussion with a zeal and power characteristic of their day, for Locke left behind him an atmosphere glowing with light and warmth long after his sun had set, —such a reader will feel that Dr. Reid's work, whatever its reputation at home or on the continent, entitled an 'Inquiry into the Human Mind,' is altogether unworthy of its title,—that it is, to say the least of it, a very shallow and feeble performance.

An examination of a few pages of the introduction to the Inquiry will be amply sufficient to justify these remarks, and to convince the real student that his language and tone have far more the characteristics of a declaimer—with too little of the show of argument to entitle him to be called a sophist—than of a philosopher, reasoning with antagonists, whose powers and views were to be respected on subjects demanding the nicest investigation, and the most carefully adjusted terms. A vein of sarcasm and badinage runs through his work, destructive to serious reflection, as the influx of water is destructive to the working of a mine and the extraction of valuable ore. A sneer and an apostrophe are his weapons of argument. Vulgar prejudice is enthroned under the form of common sense*.

* Mr. Stewart has defended Dr. Reid against this charge. More recently, Sir W. Hamilton has published an Historical Survey of the Philosophy of Common Sense, appended to his edition of ' Reid ;' and he gives abundant examples of the use of the words from writers prior to Dr. Reid. Hamilton makes much of Locke's own use of them in one passage of the Essay. I have observed them in Descartes, one of his immediate predecessors. But the question is, whether an instance can be produced, before Dr. Reid, of a writer who rested the decision of any refined or difficult question in philosophy, in opposition to thinkers far above the vulgar,—a question which ordinary minds do not entertain or dismiss quickly, from a distaste or incapacity for subtle inquiries,—on an appeal to common sense. And if an instance could be adduced, it would not justify the appeal, nor be a defence for Dr. Reid. Sir W. Hamilton gives up that defence when he says :—" Common sense is like common law. Each may be laid down as the general rule of decision ; but in the one case it must be left to the jurist, in the other to the philosopher, to ascertain what are the contents of the rule ; and though in both instances the common man may be cited as a witness for the custom or the fact, in neither can he be allowed to officiate as advocate or judge. It must be recollected also that in appealing to the consciousness of mankind, we only appeal to the consciousness of those not disqualified to pronounce a decision." Now to appeal from the multitude, who may be blinded by prejudice and passion, to the judge, the interpreter and administrator of the law, is to do the very opposite to that which Dr. Reid did, who appealed from Locke, Berkeley, and Descartes, from the philosopher or judge, to the ' plain man,' his ' plain neighbour,' and even the ' sensible day la-

Examine the fifth section of the first chapter, entitled, "Of Berkeley, of the Treatise of Human Nature, and of Scepticism." It is full of erroneous assertions, bold but unfounded, and frequently repeated in the body of the work. He begins with saying—"His (Berkeley's) arguments are founded upon the principles which were formerly laid down by Descartes, Malebranche, and Locke, and which have been very generally received." He then says, "that Hume proceeds upon the same principles, but carries them to their full length; and as the Bishop undid the whole material world, this author, *upon the same ground*, undoes the world of spirits, and leaves nothing in nature but ideas and impressions, without any subject on which they may be impressed." It would not be easy to find, in a treatise of repute on any other science, an equal amount of misstatement with that contained in these few sentences. There is no pretence to justify it by exact reference to the words or works of the authors in question. The whole is a presumption on the ignorance or indifference of the reader, characteristic of the mode in which metaphysical and moral science is commonly treated.

The principles of Locke are confounded with those of Descartes and Malebranche, without any distinct

bourer.' In proof see the eighth section, p. 112, Hamilton's Reid. There are excellent remarks on common sense in the preface (p. 14) to Whately's 'Logic.' It may be added, that the character of the appeal was made still worse by Dr. Reid's coadjutors, Oswald and Beattie.

D

account of any principles whatsoever. Now Locke
had written fully and expressly against both—certainly
against Malebranche—and it is commonly supposed
that the whole of Locke's first book is directed specially against Descartes. "Locke a combattu Descartes, quoique sans prononcer le nom de ce philosophe,
et le premier livre de l'Essai sur l'Entendement humain
est entièrement dirigé contre un point fondamental de
la philosophie Cartésienne," says Degerando*. And
the following is Mr. Stewart's language in the Dissertation prefixed to the 'Encyclopædia Britannica'† :—
"The extraordinary zeal displayed by Locke at the
very outset of his work against the hypothesis of *innate
ideas*, goes far to account for the mistakes committed
by his commentators in interpreting his account of the
origin of our knowledge. It ought however to be always kept in view, in reading his argument on the subject, that it is the Cartesian theory of innate ideas
which he is here combating, according to which theory,
as understood by Locke, an innate idea signifies something coeval in its existence with the mind to which it
belongs, and illuminating the understanding before the
external senses begin to operate." On the other hand,
Mr. Hallam says (vol. iv. p. 291) :—"It is by no means

* Histoire Comparée des Systèmes, ch. 16.

† P. 115, edit. 1842. Stewart's estimate of the illustrious English philosopher appears to have greatly improved as his own
studies were matured. He speaks of him in the Dissertation in a
very different tone from that which pervades his earlier works.
Nevertheless it contains much to which just exception may be taken,
and the concluding remarks on Hume hereafter to be noticed are
wholly inconsistent with this estimate and unworthy of it. An ob-

evident that Locke had Descartes chiefly, if at all, in his view." Without precise references on Locke's part, we cannot be confident on such a point. But admitting the theory of innate ideas combated by Locke, to be such as Mr. Stewart describes, it is questionable whether it was Cartesian. Locke* speaks in his first book (c. 2, § 14) of the "men of innate ideas," but he does

servation is worth making on a common mistake respecting Locke's taste in poetry, propagated by a note of Mr. Stewart's. He says :— "With the disposition of Locke to depreciate the Ancients was intimately connected that contempt which he everywhere expresses for the study of eloquence, and that perversion of taste which led him to consider Blackmore as one of the first of our English poets." He then quotes Molyneux's expression to Locke :—"All our English poets except Milton have been mere ballad-makers in comparison to Sir R. Blackmore," and makes Locke's reply to this to be :— "There is, I find, a strange harmony between your thoughts and mine." Now it happens that Locke's words in reply have no reference to Blackmore's merits as a poet, as the reader who consults the correspondence will see. Locke's thoughts were not running upon the subject of poetry, so much as upon *building on hypotheses and innate ideas, and agreement of notions in this.* And let not the reader be deterred from looking into Blackmore's poem on Creation, and its suggestive preface, by these depreciatory remarks. Of this poem, published in 1712, Johnson says :—" If he had written nothing more, it would have transmitted him to posterity among the first favourites of the English Muse." This is extravagant praise, but the poem illustrates very remarkably the manner in which Locke's principles and thoughts had taken possession of the general mind, and in which the most devout thinkers of that day considered the *à posteriori* argument for the being of a God drawn from His works of nature all-sufficient for devotion and faith. It is easy to see that Blackmore aspires to be to Locke what Lucretius was to Epicurus.

* We find allusions to Descartes and the Cartesians in Locke, b. iii. c. 4, § 9 and 10; iv. c. 7, § 12 and 13; and in the second reply to the Bishop of Worcester. Had Descartes any distinct theory of

not particularize the individuals in his view, if at the moment of using the expression he had any.   His attention was drawn to Lord Herbert of Cherbury, to whom he alludes especially in the third chapter, after he had written a considerable portion of the Essay.

A posthumous treatise of Locke remains to us, written expressly in confutation of the theory peculiar to Malebranche—a theory which is far more likely to have given occasion to Berkeley's pure idealism than anything to be found in Locke himself, and which is indeed nearly identical with that of Berkeley in metaphysical and moral bearing.   According to Malebranche, " God, being intimately united to the soul, exhibits ideas to it*."   It was Malebranche who led to Collier's disbelief in the existence of an external material world, and that agreement with and anticipation of Berkeley, which we find in the ' Clavis Universalis†.'   That Locke thought it worthy of his industrious pains to enter so fully into the examination and confutation of such a theory,—a theory so likely to die out of itself, and which had so little to support it beyond the merits and talents of its author,—is an encouragement for the present attempt to draw attention to a neglected portion of literary history, and to the sources of prevailing errors in philosophical inquiry.

innate ideas?   And what was its influence if he had?   As this is a question of the greatest nicety and difficulty in the history of mental philosophy, I shall give in a future chapter some notes upon it.

* See Malebranche, l. iii. part 2, c. 1: Locke's Examination, vol. iv. p. 196, 4to edition.

† See ' Memoirs of Collier,' by the Rev. Robert Benson, p. 12.

But it may be said, notwithstanding Locke's opposition to some of the peculiar principles of Descartes
and Malebranche, that there were others which Locke
held in common with them, and on which Berkeley
built.	If there were others, Dr. Reid at least has not
been careful to exhibit them.	No doubt writers like
Descartes, Hobbes, and Malebranche abound in observations on human nature and the mind which are
perfectly accordant with Locke's views, but without
identity in important and peculiar principles.	So all
correct observations on reasoning, on habit, on the
pleasures and pains, the sympathies and affections of
our nature, from Aristotle downwards, are perfectly
accordant with and even illustrative of the theory of
association as developed by Hartley.	So all correct
reasoning had been in Aristotle's mood and figure,
before Aristotle showed it must be so; though it is
often, perhaps commonly, supposed that Aristotle in-
vented the rules which he only expounded.	So all just
observation of nature and nature's laws before Lord
Bacon's time was perfectly consistent with the principles of the ' Novum Organum;' nor is it unpleasing
to observe that Bacon occasionally does some justice
to Aristotle's merits in natural history, and in ethics
and rhetoric, though, with the consciousness of power
to advance human intelligence, and with that impa-
tience for improvements, characteristic of genius, he
was disposed more generally to disparage than to
applaud the efforts and successes of those who had
trod the paths of science before him.

BERKELEY.

But did Berkeley himself build professedly upon the principles of Locke? It is true the ingenious and amiable idealist could not have written his 'Principles of Human Knowledge,' exactly as we find it, had not Locke preceded him in his inquiries into the origin and certainty of all our knowledge; but Berkeley begins his work with something like a sharp attack upon certain portions of the 'Essay on the Human Understanding,'—those portions relating to abstract ideas and general terms found in the last three books of the 'Essay.' The opinion that "the mind hath a power of framing abstract ideas or notions of things" was an opinion which Berkeley found, or thought he found, to be greatly in his way; his criticisms upon Locke's doctrine of abstraction as a mental power, and upon the value of abstract ideas, and the use of general terms, are not only ingenious, but, what is more, they are just. They have helped us to read Locke with greater intelligence, and to discover in him some of those slips, of which writers, even more cautious and more exact than Locke in his 'Essay' professes to be, are seldom, if ever, guiltless. The few pages of introduction to Berkeley's 'Principles of Human Knowledge' form therefore an important step in the history and progress of metaphysical science,—a step in which he has been followed, and for which he has been highly praised, by Hume, and more particularly by Horne Tooke.

And here it is to be observed that Mill's chapter on Abstraction, in his 'Analysis of the Human Mind,' turns almost wholly on the formation of *abstract terms :* the phrase 'abstract ideas' does not occur in it. His previous chapter on Classification has more to do with the mental power usually understood by the word abstraction, which, as a mental power or process, he defines to be, in conformity with its etymology, "separating one or more of the ingredients of a complex idea from the rest*." It is also worthy of observation that the whole of the second volume of Horne Tooke's 'Epea Pteroenta' turns also upon abstraction, and he would drop even the word complex as an epithet for ideas, and confine it wholly to terms. May we not consider that Hartley improves upon Locke, by entirely dropping the word abstract in connection with ideas, and using chiefly the epithets *complex* and *decomplex,* the latter pointing by etymology to the cluster of sensible impressions and states of feeling associated together in one term? Yet for this improvement Locke himself prepared the way.

"Words become general by being made the signs of general ideas," says Locke. "But it seems," says Berkeley†, "that a word becomes general by being made the sign not of an abstract general idea, but of several particular ideas, any one of which it indifferently suggests to the mind." This is true, and it

---

* Mill's 'Analysis,' vol. i. p. 215.

† Compare Locke, book iii. ch. iii. § 6, with Berkeley's Introduction, p. 10.

may be remarked, that when we talk about ideas, whether our own or other men's; when we give them epithets, and speak of compounding and decompounding, enlarging and refining them; turning them on all sides, repeating, comparing, and uniting them,— Locke's too frequent language,—we are always in a region of comparative obscurity; but the nature and force of terms, etymologically considered, is more within our grasp, and this is especially to be regarded when applying terms borrowed from outward things to the supposed operations of the mind, and even from mechanical and chemical processes, endeavouring thereby to explain or describe those operations. This is a part of the history of mental philosophy, as it has been treated, and it may be hoped, improved in England, which has received very little attention. It appears to be utterly neglected by the Continental writers on metaphysical science in the greatest repute. But he who confines himself to the careful study of the great English writers, on the mind and its kindred subjects, will find more than enough to engage his thoughts with eminent advantage, while he makes the necessary and only fitting preparation for estimating at their real worth the writers of other countries, and becomes able to measure both the quantity and value of the ground which has been occupied and cultivated in common *.

* Locke seems never more defective than when speaking of the names of mixed modes and relations, and of the composition and abstraction of ideas, as in the Fifth and Sixth Chapters of his Third

Berkeley repeats his attack upon the doctrine of abstract ideas in the 97th section of his 'Principles,' when he comes to speak of natural philosophy and the mathematics, and the connection of his theory with the principles and truths of those sciences.

"It is indeed an opinion strangely prevailing among men," writes Berkeley, with amusing *naïveté*, "that houses, mountains, rivers, and in a word all sensible objects, have an existence, natural or real, distinct from their being perceived by the understanding." "Is it not plainly repugnant that any one of these, or any combination of them, should exist unperceived?" "If we thoroughly examine this tenet, it will perhaps be found at bottom to depend on the doctrine of ab-

Book. While complaining of "the pudder made about essences and the jargon of the schools," it is evident he could not wholly emancipate himself from it. He even apologizes for his own obscurity, while he labours under "the difficulty of leading another by words into the thoughts of things" (Essay, b. iii. ch. vi. § 43). Thus he speaks of "abstract ideas being the essences of the species, distinguished by general names." Yet he perceived clearly enough, and intimates in other places, that general names were only significant of a combination of simple ideas; and he might have perceived that names—objects—and simple ideas were all with which we were concerned. On this point no criticisms on Locke are more instructive than those of Horne Tooke, who always touches the philosopher with fitting reverence, dissents from him with regret and diffidence, and who defends himself from the imputation of treating two men of the North, Lord Monboddo and Mr. Harris, with too much asperity, by entreating "the generous and grateful reader to recollect the manner in which these gentlemen and *the common-sense Doctors* had treated *the vulgar, unlearned, and atheistical Mr. Locke*, for such are the imputations they cast upon that benefactor to his country."—Epea Pteroenta, edit. 1829, vol. ii. p. 561.

stract ideas." But it may be answered, the belief in
the real existence of sensible objects depends on no
doctrine whatever, least of all a doctrine unknown
and obscure. May it not arise from the constancy
and uniformity of impressions made on us from without, independent of our own wills? May it not be a
part of our mental frame, of which, as no reasoning
gives it, no reasoning can deprive us? In the analysis
of the mind, as in the anatomy of the body, must we
not rest upon certain phenomena or ultimate facts, the
recognition of which constitutes our only valuable
knowledge? and is not this what we call the just interpretation of nature,—when we see the connection of
such facts with the highest law, and an end designed?
The genuine disciple of Locke disputes not the existence of such ultimate facts, and still less the value of
first principles and of primitive beliefs, which arise
out of, and are inseparable from, the early exercises
of reason and speech, and which, when once gained,
become " beliefs of consciousness," if it be thought
proper so to call them; but he is not in haste to call
his facts ultimate, nor his beliefs primitive or intuitive, before he has cautiously investigated their nature
and origin.

There was another distinction of Locke's which
Berkeley with great justice attacked : it was that between the primary and secondary qualities of matter.
" The ideas of the latter—colours, sounds, tastes, etc.
—were acknowledged not to be resemblances of anything but sensations—not of anything without the

mind;" but of the former,—our ideas of the primary qualities, namely extension, figure, and motion,—these were supposed to be "patterns or images of things existing without the mind, and dwelling in an inert senseless substance, called matter." "But it is evident," says Berkeley, "that extension, figure, and motion are only ideas existing in the mind; an idea can be like nothing but another idea." "Hence it is plain that the very notion of what is called matter, or corporeal substance, involves a contradiction in it*."

With these animadversions upon Locke's principles and language before his eyes, and in the utter absence of any pretence elsewhere, on Berkeley's part, to build his theory of the non-existence of matter upon any principles or concessions which were peculiar to Locke, it is evidently a very great misrepresentation, on the part of Dr. Reid, to throw the onus of Berkeley's idealism upon the English philosopher.

But Dr. Reid has done no justice to Berkeley nor to his argument. His advice to the man who finds himself entangled, or *embrangled*, as Berkeley calls it, in metaphysical toils, is to cut the knot which he cannot loose, and curse metaphysic. His comparison of philosophy to a fair lady, who befools her votaries, and is fit only to be sent back to the infernal regions, from which she came, is more worthy of the market-place than the professorial chair†. He would have done

---

* Principles of Human Knowledge, 4th, 5th, and 9th sections.

† The reader will observe also Reid's elegant language upon Hume's doctrine of ideas—"Ideas turned out of house and home into

far better to examine closely Berkeley's argument; had he done so, he might perhaps have detected in it a *petitio principii*. He might perhaps have found, if he had looked carefully, a flaw in the demonstration which appeared so clear. It would have been far more satisfactory, by a faithful and candid representation of Berkeley's statements, to show, if possible, where the fallacy lay, than to indulge in declamations, sneers, and sarcasms, gratifying only to the hasty, the prejudiced, and unreflecting.

After all, has not Berkeley rather assumed than proved the point in question—the non-existence of an external material world? Has he not sometimes attempted to prove too much, or asserted without proof what a reader following his own advice, and " making his words the occasion of his own thinking," will never concede to him? Thus he says, that " the absolute existence of unthinking things are words without a meaning, or which include a contradiction." But the cautious reader will perceive no such absence of meaning,—none of the contradiction which Berkeley assumes. What more contradiction is there in the absolute existence of an unthinking, than the absolute existence of a thinking thing? At other times he overlooks the nature of the argument, and confounds the proof of

the world, without a rag to cover their nakedness;" and his confession, in reference to Berkeley's theory, " that he would rather make one of those credulous fools whom Nature imposes upon, than of those wise and rational philosophers who resolve to withhold assent at the expense of being probably taken up, and clapped into a madhouse."—Hamilton's Reid, p. 184.

an external world, which, as regards spirit, he concedes, with that of a material world, which he denies. " Because we know not how ideas are produced, as he states in the 19th section, " because we are unable to comprehend in what manner body can act upon spirit ;" " hence," he says, " it is evident the production of ideas or sensations in our minds can be no reason why we should suppose matter or corporeal substances." Nor is there any reason why we should deny the fact, and reject the supposition, because we cannot comprehend the manner. He admits there is a cause external to ourselves, which does produce ideas. " We perceive," he says, " a continual succession of ideas : some are new excited, others are changed or totally disappear. There is therefore *some cause* of these ideas, whereon they depend, and which produces and changes them. That this cause cannot be any quality, or idea, or combination of ideas, is clear from the preceding section. It *must* therefore be a substance ; but it has been shown that there is no corporeal or material substance ; it remains, therefore, that the cause of ideas is an incorporeal active substance or spirit." Now this negative was not shown ; the alternative therefore cannot be accepted as the only possible alternative.

Again, in the 29th section, he repeats this :—" As to the hearing and other senses, the ideas imprinted on them are not creatures of my will. There is *therefore* some other will or spirit that produces them."

Thus the strength of Berkeley's argument depends on what is, after all, a mere assumption, namely, that

" the *esse* of things is *percipi**." But this is not to be hastily conceded. To be, and be perceived, are not the same. The *esse* is anterior and subservient to the *percipi*, which depends upon the *esse*, but is not the *esse*. Apply the maxim to the mind, and it will not sustain itself. The Divine Mind exists, as a cause of our perceptions; but it exists independently of those perceptions. It exists indeed as a *percipient*, for percipient power cannot be separated from the thought of mind, and belief in it as mind. Here the *esse* and *percipere* may be considered one and the same; percipiency constituting, if we please, the essence, and entering into our definition of mind. And yet, with regard to finite minds, each act of percipiency, being distinct in itself, is distinct also from the active percipient power, that is, from the being that perceives. But if the *esse*, in respect of mind, be not necessarily *percipere*, still less in respect of matter is it *percipi*. Berkeley admits there is some cause of perception external to ourselves. He is obliged continually to imply a distinction between the organs of sense, and the sensations or ideas arising from or conveyed through them. (See particularly the 90th section of his ' Principles.') He seems not to allow sufficient weight to the constancy and uniformity of certain impressions, ideas, and feelings which accompany us, independent of our desires and wills; that unfailing attendant sense, for

* Beattie perceived this assumption on Berkeley's part, and his use of it, but had not patience to follow it up logically." See Essay on Truth, p. 49, edit. 1778.

instance, of a bodily frame, which is so different from, and so completely the instrument and inlet of those feelings, thoughts, and passions which are peculiar to the mind. Thus solidity and extension are not merely names for affections or states of mind, granting that all ideas associated with words imply such states; they are also significant of external existences giving rise to those affections and states. This is equally true in respect of ideas of the secondary, as with what have been called the primary, qualities of matter. A cause operating from without is necessary to account for the idea.

Can Berkeley be said to prove that such external existences are merely the ideas of another mind or spirit, imparted immediately to ours,—a mode of spiritual action upon our spirit? The total absence of such proof, this great assumption of spiritual action, and of the existence of an Infinite Intelligent mind acting immediately and constantly upon our minds, without any attempt to establish that existence as a fact, is far more likely to have led to Hume's scepticism than anything to be found in Locke, whose chapter on the Being of a God seems at least to be deserving of some attention from a candid and philosophical inquirer. Berkeley struggles to get rid of the abstract ideas of time, space, and motion, and denies the absolute existence of external realities corresponding to them, combating the definitions and distinctions laid down by the great Newton in his treatise of mechanics. These definitions and distinctions are of very great importance in a metaphysical point of view, and deserve the closest attention from the exact inquirer. The acceptance of them, together with Newton's beautiful and profound language on the Deity, at the close of his 'Principia,' constitutes the best refuge and great security from the gross pantheism which, as in the case of Spinoza, refuses to the Supreme cause intelligence—will—design, and of course all moral attributes. Without attempting here to defend Newton's refined distinctions between *absolute* and *relative time*, *true* and *apparent, mathematical* and *vulgar*, may we not say that time, space, and motion are habitually conceived of, and reasoned upon, as independent of all mind, as the subsidiary and necessary elements of all finite existence? Time and space are necessarily excluded in the idea of motion. We do not commonly consider them as created, nor yet are they necessarily conceived of as attributes, still less as parts of the Creator; for these are divisible, or are conceived to be so in relation to human measures of them, while the Creator is *without parts and passions*. It is now customary to call them essential forms of thought, inseparable from our frames, or logical conditions of the understanding and practical reason. But the value of all such accounts or definitions depends upon the use made of them in subsequent reasoning, that is, upon their application to other conclusions; for no one will pretend that the ideas themselves are rendered clearer. Nor is it proved by such accounts that the ideas do not grow out of, and are not suggested by, all our experience; the first—time—out of the succession of our ideas, on which Locke dwells, as the origin and essence of our notion of time; and the second—space—out of the perceived relation of objects one to another, the relation of outness, distance, and position, which accompany almost all the phenomena of sensation, but chiefly those of sight, in a less degree those of touch and hearing, and in least degree, if in any degree, those of smell and taste*.

* *Time, space, motion, God, freedom, immortality*,—with the associated ideas, and their origin,—are now, as they have always been, the battle-field of dissentients in metaphysical speculations and inquiries. And could we ever bring the mystical adherents of transcendental philosophy to the point, or keep them to it, we might perhaps examine, with some hope of satisfaction, the value of their definitions and assertions. But they are emphatically 'children òf the mist.' Like the witches and ghosts in 'Macbeth,' after they have delivered their oracles, they endure no further question, and vanish into thin air,—leaving the questioner aghast. "That the notion of Space is a *necessary condition of thought*, and that *as such it is impossible to derive it from experience*, has been cogently demonstrated by Kant," says Sir W. Hamilton, in a note on Reid, p. 126; and the reader should look also at the notes, pp. 128, 129. But Locke, Hartley, and Mill have demonstrated the contrary, at least of the latter of the two propositions, if we may talk of demonstration in the case. I shall therefore examine hereafter, as briefly as the matter will allow, the so-called demonstration by Kant; not that the admission of one side or the other is of practical consequence, any further than as the discussion of it may throw light on the proper philosophy of the mind, and help the right interpretation of our mental frame. Every idea, with which the mind is furnished after a certain experience, and of which it cannot divest itself,—more especially when, with a word annexed, used as a sign, it comes to be employed in reasoning in support of a fixed conclusion,—may be called, with equal advantage and propriety, *a necessary condition of thought*.

E

"To what purpose is it to dilate on that which may be demonstrated with the utmost evidence in a line or two, to any one that is capable of the least reflection?" asks Berkeley. "It is but looking into your own thoughts, and so trying whether you can conceive it possible for a sound, or figure, or motion, or colour, to exist without the mind, or unperceived. This easy trial may make you see, that what you contend for is a downright contradiction. I am content to put the whole upon this issue."

Berkeley is frequent in applying the term 'contra- diction' to assertions which do not imply it*. Inge- niously as this is worked out, the whole is but a re- petition of this. The answer is, we do perpetually conceive it possible. The perception itself, and a cause of perception, existing without us, are different things. There is an outward agency, uniform and independent, imparting to us certain conceptions; and the belief in external realities, which, not being parts of our own minds, are not necessarily parts of or immediate imprints by another mind, involves in it no such contradiction as Berkeley pretends.

"The things perceived by sense may be termed ex- ternal with regard to their origin, in that they are not generated from within, by the mind itself, but *im- printed by a spirit distinct from that which perceives them*. Sensible objects may likewise be said to be without the mind in another sense, namely, *when they*

* Principles of Human Knowledge, 22nd section; and compare

exist in some other mind. Thus, when I shut my eyes,
the things I saw may still exist, but *it must be* in another mind." (Prin. Hum. Kn. 90th section.) This is
rather assumption than proof. The '*must*' is not the
clear result of any '*why.*' The attentive reader will
also perceive how arbitrary but harmless is Berkeley's
previous account or definition in the 89th section, of
the words thing, being, spirits, and ideas. The former
—spirits—he calls "*active, indivisible substances;*"
the latter—ideas—he calls "*inert, fleeting, dependent beings,*" which subsist not by themselves, but are
supported by and exist in minds or spiritual substances." Again, it may be very true that an idea can
be like nothing but an idea, as Berkeley says; it may
be even further true that it is only in the way of ac-
commodation we can speak of one idea being like
another idea; there being, without some reference to
objects or sensations, no standard or means of distinct comparison. But all this is little to Berkeley's
purpose; for although we cannot conceive or explain
how matter acts upon spirit, or spirit upon matter,—
a difficulty which Berkeley finds or feigns to be greatly
in his favour,—as little can we conceive how spirit
acts upon spirit, directly and without the intervention
of matter, or how an idea, or series of ideas, can pass
from one mind to another by an act of will only. Of
purely spiritual *contact* or *influence*—for we must use
these materialistic terms—we have no more clear conception than of spirit in connection with matter.

From impressions originating in causes without us,

we infer the existence of minds like our own ; and the existence of mind is, no doubt, implied in all consciousness and thought, which cannot be said of the existence of matter. But from these same impressions and signs we are also led to infer external realities, which, as they are not parts of our own minds, are not so obviously and necessarily the mere and direct agency of another mind or spirit, as Berkeley contends, and as Malebranche before him had set forth. And although Berkeley believed that he removed the chief source and support of atheism, when he removed matter from the universe, he seems not to have perecived that his own theory was not wholly free from the embarrassments of pantheism, since it left the argument for the existence of one perfect supreme cause, one infinite, omniscient, benevolent, spiritual Being, precisely where it was ; it even reduced the mind to a mere mirror for the reflection of the imprinted images, or to a recipient of the excited ideas. It may be said however that the existence of such an Infinite mind was an assumption which formed a part, and a necessary part, of his theory.

There is a continual flow of thought, a consciousness of perceptive and reflective power, more or less active and intense, always in the mind in its wakeful state. Images, faint or lively, of absent objects, present themselves to the mind's eye ; remembrances of former impressions, anticipations of the future, more or less vivid, arise within, of which the mind is conscious as something totally distinct from the impressions of that visible, tangible, audible world of sense, which remains outward and unchanged, or subject to certain observed and regular changes, which continue and go on independent of our attention. Thus the book which we hold in the hand, and which suggests so many ideas remote from its own simple character, the room which we occupy, the ground on which we stand, the chair in which we sit, the posture and action, voluntary or automatic, of the body; the whole scenery of nature from the window; all these outward things have a permanent relation to and connection with our whole life and being, which is manifestly different from that inner life, peculiar to the mind itself, that flux or reflux of thought, desire and will, which we never attribute to the objects present to the senses, nor to any consciousness but our own. After all, this constant natural feeling is perhaps the best, if not the only, argument for an external material world, if argument be required for it, and argument it deserves to be called. All our sensations and ideas remaining the same,—our feelings of pleasure and pain, our hopes and fears, being the same with Berkeley's theory and without it,—there is nothing to argue about, but the propriety and philosophical use of certain definitions; and if we define matter, as I believe Faraday does, *a centre of powers,* and if the same definition applies to mind, it is evident that what we are then concerned with is the different character, descriptions, or definitions of these powers, that is, the mixtures and clusters, so to speak, of the sensible impressions and associated ideas.

Here then we must rest; and when logic has done its utmost, we may amuse ourselves with poetry, and betake ourselves to the lines of Arbuthnot, quoted by Beattie, as a summary of the evidence, so far as it is dependent on the phenomena of consciousness.

> " This frame, compacted with transcendent skill,
> Of moving joints, obedient to my will,
> Nursed from the fruitful glebe,—like yonder tree,
> Waxes and wastes ; I call it mine,—not me.
> New matter still the mouldering mass sustains,
> The mansion changed—the tenant still remains,
> And from the fleeting stream repaired by food,—
> Distinct, as is the swimmer from the flood*."

I must now leave this criticism of Berkeley's theory. How far it is adequate or perfect the reader will judge. It might be easily extended, for with the pages of Berkeley open before us, what end is there to notes and comments ? Such as it is, it may help the future and youthful student of metaphysical philosophy to read the skilful and amiable idealist with more advantage than he might otherwise have enjoyed, and with a more wakeful attention to his weak points. In all metaphysical reasonings, the maxim of Horace is

---

* Since the above was written, I have looked into the disquisitions relating to the Philosophy of the Mind, by the late Lord Jeffrey, found in the third volume of his collected Papers. In these the eminent author has gone somewhat carefully into the speculations on the non-existence of matter, and the observations above made accord perfectly with Lord Jeffrey's views : " All beyond our own consciousness," he observes, " is matter of inference ; but it evidently implies no contradiction to suppose that such a thing as matter may exist, and that an omnipotent Being might make us capable of discovering its qualities."

invaluable, '*Principiis obsta.*' There are however several incidental differences between Berkeley's principles and 'those of Locke, not to be overlooked by any one who attempts an exact comparison.

From the principle that the duration of any finite spirit *must* be estimated by the number of ideas or actions succeeding each other in the same spirit or mind*, Berkeley made it a plain consequence that the soul always thinks: contrary to Locke's opinion, who contended that the soul does not always think, that it may exist in a state of sleep, and without actual perceptions.

Berkeley, supposing himself to have shown that the soul is indivisible, incorporeal, unextended, argued that "it is consequently incorruptible,—a being indissoluble by the force of nature,—that is to say, *the soul of man is naturally immortal*†:" contrary to Locke's opinion, who thought that it could not be made out demonstratively by natural reason that the soul is immaterial, nor, consequently, in its own nature immortal, and who rested the hope of a future state, and especially the influence of it in a practical point of view, upon the declared or revealed will of God‡. Berkeley availed himself of Locke's language against the existence, anywhere but in the mind per-

---

* See the 98th section of his 'Principles,' etc., and Locke, b. ii. c. i. § 19.

† Principles, p. 97.

‡ See the 'Second Reply to the Bishop of Worcester,' p. 758, and compare the admirable passages in the 'Essay:' book ii. c. 21, and book iv. c. 4.

ceiving, of what are called the secondary qualities of matter—colours, tastes, and smells,—and turned it against the existence of the so-called primary qualities —*bulk, figure, extension, number,* and *motion;* and so denied matter altogether. But he did not trouble himself specially with Locke's views relating to the separate existence of matter and thought, and to the existence of an eternal, omniscient, omnipotent Being, whether matter be itself eternal or not, which are given in the tenth chapter of the fourth book of the ' Essay*.'

Again, the term Idea was applied by Locke—as, I believe, by Gassendi before him—to whatever could be the subject of thought and of discourse; but to Berkeley it appeared that " the term Idea would be improperly extended to *signify everything we know, or have any notion of*†."

These differences will not be considered of little importance by the careful inquirer. Others may probably be traced. On the whole, it seems evident that Berkeley neither rested his theory, nor pretended to rest it, upon any principles peculiar to Locke. On this point therefore it has been shown that Dr. Reid's inquiry was calculated to give, as no doubt it has given, a very erroneous and mischievous impression.

* An interesting account of a conversation between Sir Isaac Newton, the Earl of Pembroke, and Locke, on the possible creation of matter, extracted from Coste—the French translator and friend of Locke—may be found in the ' Edinburgh Review,' p. 352, No. 138, with comments on Reid's and Stewart's views of Locke's meaning.

† See 89th Section.

HUME.

But how is it with Hume? This is a more tender question. Berkeley's was eminently a religious mind. His amiable enthusiasm called forth warm sympathy and admiration from many of the finest spirits of his age. His ingeniously-woven theory was the fanciful garb of a dreaming philosopher, which shocked none of the prejudices, struck at none of the superstitions of the multitude. Neither priests nor lawyers felt their influence shaken, and their craft exposed, by his elaborate and fine-spun system. They thought he was answered sufficiently by a smile.

> "When Berkeley said, there was no matter,
> It was no matter, what he said."

His theory of vision has taken, and yet retains, a high place in the estimation of metaphysical inquirers, as an important illustration of the manner in which the ideas of one sense are transferred by association to another*. The lover of the Scriptures—the ancient lore of Christendom—is indebted to him for many admirable observations on the excellency and usefulness of the Christian religion; and the devout will concur with him heartily in the opinion that, as in reading other books, so in perusing the volume of Nature, we should propose to ourselves noble views, " such as to recreate and exalt the mind with a prospect of the

---

* The review of this theory, by Mr. Samuel Bailey of Sheffield, published in 1842, has however considerably shaken its authority, and this notwithstanding the defence of it by a Westminster Reviewer.

beauty, order, extent, and variety of natural things; hence, by proper inferences, to enlarge our notions of the grandeur, wisdom, and beneficence of the Creator; and, lastly, to make the several parts of the creation, so far as in us lies, subservient to the ends they were designed for,—God's glory, and the sustentation and comfort of ourselves and our fellow-creatures."

But soon a very different competitor for the rank of philosophic chieftain appeared. The differences between the Irish and Scotch national character are somewhat strongly marked in the lives and tempers of Berkeley and of Hume.

The life and correspondence of David Hume, published by Mr. J. Hill Burton, in 1846, enables us to approach the question whether the philosophy of Locke laid any foundation or furnished any support for the scepticism of Hume, to whatever it amounted, with some means of judgment which previous inquirers could scarcely have enjoyed. Of Hume's boyhood and earlier days, of the domestic influences and the scholastic training under which he grew to manhood, we learn little from these volumes of any interest or importance. The biographer, Mr. Burton, makes the most of some scanty notices by Hume himself of his ancestral estate at Ninewells. Little is added to the few particulars which, in his simple autobiography, he has chosen to give us. Rarely has a life been more destitute of points of domestic interest. He appears to have studied for a time at the University of Edinburgh, but how long cannot be ascertained.

As soon as he had finished his studies there, or while pursuing them, he plunged into the vortex of metaphysical abstractions; and we are called upon at once to inquire into the results of his struggles in that whirlpool, or rather to watch the paths of speculation and research into which his passion for literature hurried him,—a passion which seized him early, and became the ruling passion of his life, and the great source of his enjoyments. It is not clear whether he was acquainted with the person, or had paid attention to the writings, of the eminent Francis Hutcheson, who was Professor of Philosophy at Glasgow from 1729 to 1747. A letter to Hutcheson is given in Burton's Life*, from which it appears that Hume submitted some of the papers of his 'Treatise' to Hutcheson's perusal, and was favoured with his reflections upon them before publication. Yet in the third volume of Hume's 'Treatise of Human Nature,' which came out in 1740, he follows Hutcheson in maintaining that moral distinctions are not derived from reason, but from a moral sense, without mention of Hutcheson's name, or condescending to allude to the 'Inquiry into the original of our Ideas of Beauty and Virtue,' published about fifteen years before. Anxious for the reputation of an original thinker and discoverer, his sense of obligation to preceding thinkers was never strongly marked. Gratitude is not the virtue of usurpers.

A letter to a physician, written at the age of twenty-three, reveals the peculiar character of Hume's mind,

* Vol. i. p. 112.

and the boldness of his temper.   The first part is as follows :—

"After fourteen or fifteeen years of age I was left to my own choice in my reading, and found it incline me almost equally to books of reasoning and philosophy, and to poetry and the polite authors. *Every one* who is acquainted either with the philosophers or critics, *knows that there is nothing yet established in either of these two sciences* *, and that they contain little more than endless disputes, even in the most fundamental articles. Upon examination of these I found a certain boldness of temper growing in me, which was not inclined to submit to any authority in these subjects, but led me *to seek out some new medium, by which truth might be established.* After much study and reflection on this, at last, when I was about eighteen years of age, there seemed to be opened up to me a new scene of thought, which transported me beyond measure, and made me, with an ardour natural to young men, throw up every other pleasure or busi-

---

* We may contrast with this a passage from Gibbon's 'Essay on the Study of Literature :'—" Descartes was not a man of letters, but literature is under deep obligations to him. An intelligent philosopher, who inherited his method of reasoning, thoroughly investigated the true principles of criticism—Le Clerc, in his excellent 'Ars Critica,' and several other works." Gibbon wrote this Essay before he was twenty-two years of age,—a wonderful production for so young a man. What did Hume know of Descartes or Le Clerc at the same age? Gibbon, like Hume, felt early the passion for literary distinction; but he had a mind far more earnest and grateful, far more intent on the honour of literature, and through it the improvement of mankind; notwithstanding a certain grossness of taste from which Hume was free.

ness to apply entirely to it." Thence he determined
to push his fortune in the world by the way of a
scholar and philosopher. He was smit, he tells us,
with the beauties of Cicero, Seneca, and Plutarch; no
great range this even of Classical studies. We nowhere learn from him what English authors he had
read at this period with the slightest interest or profit.
He does not tell us, nor can we gather from his first
work, that he had perused with care and deep attention the works of Bacon, of Hobbes, of Cudworth,
of Clarke, Locke, Cumberland, Law, and others who
might be mentioned, who had gone with a power and
penetration, which successors could not easily hope to
emulate, into the nicest and most abstruse questions
of metaphysical philosophy. He appears to have had
no conception of the care and completeness with which
the most difficult subjects in philosophy, natural religion, history, and mathematics had been investigated
before him by English philosophers and scholars,
and of which the collection of pieces and letters by
Newton, Clarke, Leibnitz, Collins, and other celebrated writers, first published by Des Maizeaux, at Amsterdam, in 1720, may be taken as one of the most
striking evidences; and the very learned dissertation,
published anonymously, but known to be by Dr.
Waterland, on the *à priori* argument for the Being of
a God, in connection with Law's 'Inquiry into our
Ideas of Space and Time' (1734), as another. The
name of Aristotle Hume nowhere mentions; and to
the pages of the speculative Descartes, the learned

Gassendi, and the excursive Leibnitz, he was at this time probably a stranger *.

After leaving the University of Edinburgh, and paying a short visit to Bristol, Hume spent three years in France, from 1734 to 1737, very agreeably. Of the nature of his studies during this period we have no information of the slightest interest, beyond the intimation that intercourse with some members of the Jesuits' College at La Flèche laid the foundation of his scepticism concerning miracles, and that he had paid attention to Butler's ' Analogy of Natural and Revealed Religion,' which came out in the year 1736. We must therefore judge from internal evidence of Hume's fitness to give such a complete and improved view of human nature,—the understanding, the passions, and the foundation of morals,—as he aspired thus early in life to be the author of†. " Never literary attempt was

* It is true that Hume, in the chapter on Knowledge and Probability, refers to the opinions and arguments of Hobbes, Clarke, and Locke, on the subject of cause and effect, in order to confute them; but how carelessly he treated them will be shown hereafter, when I come to examine Mr. Dugald Stewart's extraordinary commendations of the Sceptic. With obstinate determination to yield nothing in favour of a hated conclusion, Hume pretends to invalidate the proposition admitted by all three,—that "whatsoever has a beginning, has also a cause of existence." From the first, it was Hume's determination to put down, if possible, the propositions, "that no creature could come into existence of itself," and "that there must be some one, and but one, necessary and self-existent Being,—the cause of causes;"—these being the received axioms of natural religion. He calls the ancient maxim, "*Ex nihilo nihil fit*," an impious maxim; in the spirit of a Mephistopheles, willing to extinguish the light of reason, rather than admit a ray to show the being of a God.

† Two volumes came forth in 1739; the third, in 1740.

more unfortunate," says Hume in his autobiography, "than my 'Treatise of Human Nature.' It fell dead-born from the press, without reaching such distinction as even to excite a murmur among the zealots*." The indifference with which it was received gave him deep mortification; but it fell from its own natural want of buoyancy. It had no inherent worth to sustain it. Two years after the publication, its author began to feel that he had attempted a task for which he was wholly incompetent, and that in the execution he had only exposed his weakness. The regret which Hume felt for his precipitancy deepened as he advanced in life; and in a letter written to Sir G. Elliot, of Minto, in 1751, we find him thus expressing himself:—

" I believe the ' Philosophical Essays' contain every-thing of consequence relating to the Understanding, which you would meet with in the Treatise; and I give you my advice against reading the latter. By shortening and simplifying the questions, I really render them much more complete. *Addo dum minuo.* The philosophical principles are the same in both; but I was carried away by the heat of youth and invention to publish too precipitately. So vast an undertaking, planned before I was one-and-twenty, and composed before twenty-five, must necessarily be very defective. I have repented my haste a hundred and a hundred times."

* Hume received £50 for the manuscript of this work from an enterprising bookseller. What bookseller would now give a similar sum for a philosophical treatise by an author of no reputation?

The repentance, thus candidly expressed, was perfectly well founded. The 'Treatise of Human Nature' is written neither in philosophical style nor philosophical spirit. Its reasoning is viciously loose; its language miserably inexact. It did not produce —it could not produce any deep impression on the minds of its readers. It tended not to establish—it scarcely even aimed to establish—a single important principle or truth connected with, or growing out of, the study of the constitution of the human mind, of the principles of morals, or the foundations and objects of political society. Full of sentiments and language which it could not have contained, but for the impulse and direction which Locke's 'Essay' had given to metaphysical inquiry, there is no attempt on the part of Hume to fix the knowledge and principles which he owed to Locke, nor to display the additions to that knowledge which he conceived himself capable of making; and this, while touching on the origin of our ideas, on knowledge and probability, on cause and effect, on space and time, on belief and scepticism,—in short, on all those topics, which the masterly intellect of the English metaphysician had recently searched with so much persevering care, and with the success resulting from perfect singleness of purpose—the dispassionate pursuit of truth.

The first and second sections of the first part of the 'Treatise' exhibit the confusion which pervades Hume's method of treating the subject of the mind. The first is entitled, 'Of the origin and composition of ideas.' The second is a division of the subject. In the first, though he had blended into one inseparable mass ideas, impressions, and perceptions, complex and simple, forcible and faint, yet he had laid it down as a leading principle, that "ideas were derived from, and were but the faint images of impressions;" under the last name, however, he comprehended all our *sensations*, *passions*, and *emotions*, as they make their first appearance in the soul. But in the second section he divides our *impressions* into two kinds,—those of sensation, and those of reflection. "*The first kind arises in the soul originally from unknown causes; the second is derived in a great measure from our ideas, and that in the following order.*" The order which he suggests becomes 'confusion worse confounded,' for he speaks of "an idea of pleasure or pain, when it returns upon the soul, producing new impressions of desire and aversion, hope and fear, which may properly be called impressions of reflection, because derived from it; and these again, being *copied* by the memory and imagination, become ideas, which perhaps in their turn give rise to other impressions and ideas." Thus he leaves his reader in a state of painful distraction, at a loss for any distinct impression or correct idea, in a perfect labyrinth of words. Between the two, the understanding is beaten to and fro, like a shuttlecock between two noisy battledoors, and not allowed to settle anywhere. Far from establishing the clear and satisfactory distinction which he undertook to make, he has only destroyed a dis-

F

tinction tolerably good before. He has not shaken the strength nor added to the convenience of the philosophical structure, which Locke had founded on the phenomena of our physical and mental constitution,—the ideas of sensation and of reflection. He has not elicited a fact, nor established a principle peculiar to himself, in any subsequent part of the Treatise, which has been received as valuable by any pupil of eminence in the school of Mental Philosophy *.

But the 'Treatise of Human Nature' was not so wholly overlooked and neglected at its first appearance as Hume's language respecting it implies. On the contrary, it met with the attention of some candid readers and competent judges. This is evident, from the review to be found in the papers published under the title of the ' History of the Works of the Learned,' a periodical which came out in the years from 1738 to 1742 inclusive. The criticism on Hume, found in the numbers for November and December 1739, is

* In a note, p. 13, Hume brings a charge against Mr. Locke of perverting the word idea from its original sense. "I here make use of these terms, impression and idea, in a sense different from what is usual, and I hope this liberty will be allowed me. Perhaps I rather restore the word idea to its original sense, from which Mr. Locke had perverted it, in making it stand for all our perceptions." How far that observation is correct, the reader may be left to judge. The rest of the note is either unintelligible, or he uses the word impression as a synonym for perception, for which, yet, he says, there is no particular name in the English or any other language that he knows of. At the end of the section, p. 21, he professes to give, with an affected air of superiority to preceding philosophers, a clear statement of the question concerning innate ideas, so as to remove all disputes concerning it.

somewhat elaborate, and on the whole much to the purpose. It points out not a few inconsistencies and extravagancies. It marks the love of paradox and the vein of egotism. Far from supposing that Hume had pushed to their legitimate consequences any principles peculiar to Locke, or that he was led to extreme sceptical notions by Locke's method of analysis, the reviewer observes, " that a man who has never had the pleasure of reading Mr. Locke's incomparable Essay will peruse the author with much less disgust than those who have been used to the irresistible reasoning and wonderful perspicacity of that admirable writer." The reviewer with justice speaks of Hume as " *trampling upon Mr. Locke,* and pretending to restore or rectify what he had perverted*." It would be without advantage to

* This review is attributed by Chalmers, in the Biographical Dictionary, and by Mr. J. Hill Burton, to Warburton, afterwards Bishop of Gloucester: I cannot find on what authority, although the opinion seems consistent enough with the internal evidence. I trace no allusion to that authorship in the Life and Letters of Warburton, published by his friend Hurd, amid many criticisms and papers, in which such allusion would seem almost unavoidable, considering the pains bestowed on the review, and the importance attached by Warburton to whatever he did. In 1739, Warburton was busy with his defence of Pope against Crousaz, with notes on Shakespeare, and above all with the ' Divine Legation of Moses.' He speaks also of the whole periodical, under the title of the ' Works of the Learned' in a way somewhat inconsistent with the idea of his being concerned in the production of the papers. " The journal in general is *a most miserable one;* and, to the opprobrium of our country, we have neither any better, nor, I believe, any other." See ' Nichols's Anecdotes of the Literature of the Eighteenth Century,' vol. v. p. 562.

About 1757 or 1758 Bishop Hurd edited some remarks, written

the reader to adduce any considerable number of passages in justification of the opinion that the ' Treatise
of Human Nature' is characterized, to all the extent
common in metaphysical writings, by looseness of expression and inconclusive reasoning.   Such books are
now seldom read, and still less weighed and considered; nor can the inquirer into the proper philosophy of the mind be encouraged with the hope that
it will repay any attention which may be given it, by
additions of value to his stock of thought.   A few instances of arbitrary and unsatisfactory definition may
suffice as samples of his manner.   He defines an opinion or belief, "a lively idea, related to or associated
with a present impression*."   Is not the definition
equally suitable for unbelief,—a lively idea of the
falsehood of a statement?   Are not all present impressions associated with lively ideas?—light, fire,
ice, a throne, a crown? the thousand objects that
awaken apprehension, or kindle hope and desire,—
the sound of a trumpet, the cry of distress?   In the
midst of vague language about the business or affair,
as he calls it, of causes and effects, he defines a cause
to be "an object precedent and contiguous to another,
and so united with it, that the idea of the one determines the mind to form the idea of the other, and

by Warburton on Hume's 'Natural History of Religion,' immediately on the first perusal of that Essay. See Warburton's Works
and Life, vol. i. pp. 65–69, and vol. xii. pp. 239–240.

* Treatise, pp. 167, 172, 188. See also his definition quoted and
criticized by Reid, in his 'Essay, etc., on the Intellectual Powers,'
p. 352.

the impression of the one to form the more lively idea
of the other*." He proceeds to lay down eight rules,
by which to judge of causes and effects, of which the
last is the following, " that an object which exists for
any time in its full perfection *without any effect*, is not
the sole cause of that effect, but requires to be assisted
by some other principle, which may forward *its influence* and *operation*†." What language can be more
indefinite, less satisfactory, or, closely examined, more
absurd? Who now is satisfied that mere precedence
and contiguity constitute the amount and essence of
his notion of cause? If precedence relates to time,
and contiguity to space, how little comparatively does
the latter enter into the notion at all! When

> " Morn, her rosy steps in the eastern clime
> Advancing, sows the earth with orient pearl,"

the dawn precedes, and is contiguous to the rising of
the sun, who " brings the day his bounteous gift."
It is impossible to separate the idea of the one from
that of the other; but is the dawn the cause of its
coming? Is the moon contiguous to the ocean and
the tidal motions? or is the sun contiguous to its
attendant orbs? Is the resolution of the Board of
East India Directors contiguous to the banks of the
Ganges, where the effects of the resolution will be
felt? Yet the root of Hume's scepticism lies in this,
as will be seen when the examination of his more important work—the ' Essays'—comes to be entered
upon; and what pretence is there for the assertion

* Treatise, p. 298.   † Ibid., p. 306.

that anything in Locke suggested or supports this
theory? In regard to our belief in the continued existence of external objects, he has a passage more remarkable for its childishness and confused verbosity,
than for any just and useful discrimination: "All objects to which we attribute a *continued existence* have
a *peculiar constancy*, which distinguishes them from
the impressions whose existence depends on our perception." He had previously made impressions and
perceptions the same; and it is obvious there can be
no impression without a perception; but here he confounds objects with impressions, or rather he makes
the constancy of objects that which distinguishes one
sort of objects from a peculiar class of impressions,
as if the objects and impressions could be thus legitimately compared. He goes on to say that "in the
midst of changes—which even the constancy admits
of—the objects have a coherence and a regular dependence, which produces very reasonably the opinion
of their continued existence." What however are the
constancy, the coherence, the regular dependence, and
the continued existence, but different words for one
and the same opinion and belief? unless you come
to distinguish them by some reference to their etymology or for a practical purpose,—a distinction which
we might hope to find in a good book of synonyms.
A little attention to the first sentence of Aristotle's
categories on common names might have suggested
to Hume the desirableness of more coherence in his
terms, and more dependence in his conclusions.

But the most lively part of the Treatise is the last chapter, on the sceptical and other systems of philosophy, in which he attacks more particularly the modern system* of Mr. Locke. Because we have no idea of the substance of our minds, and cannot point to the particular impression of sensation and reflection that produces that idea, he would have us abandon altogether "the question concerning the substance of the soul, as absolutely unintelligible" (p. 434). He speaks of certain philosophers promising to diminish our ignorance; but, unwilling to point too distinctly to other instructors, he makes no allusion to the controversy between the learned Dr. S. Clarke, Mr. Dodwell, and Collins, on this difficult subject. For him such men had written and thought in vain. He pronounces the maxim, that an object may exist, and yet be nowhere, not only possible; but he asserts that the greatest part of beings do and must exist after this manner; meaning apparently, by objects and beings, merely our own perceptions, which have no necessary relation to one portion of space more than to another. He confounds the possibility of a maxim with the existence of a fact. He then endeavours to show that the hideous hypothesis of Spinoza, that there is only one substance in the world, is " almost the same with that of the immateriality of the soul" †; and " that all the absurdities

* See particularly the fourth section, on the Modern Philosophy, where he agrees with Berkeley, and argues against Locke. Treatise, vol. i. pp. 397–405. † Ibid., pp. 410, 419.

which have been found in the system of Spinoza, may
likewise be discovered in that of theologians" (p. 423).
In the section on personal identity, he decides that
we have no idea of self, such as some philosophers
imagine we are every moment intimately conscious of,
for "if any impression gives rise to the idea of self,
that impression must continue invariably the same
through the whole course of our lives, since self is
supposed to exist after that manner. But there is
no impression constant and invariable; consequently
there is no such idea" (p. 437).

The careful metaphysical inquirer will do well to
compare Mr. Hume's section with Locke's chapter
on Identity and Diversity, and with the dissertation
on personal identity added to Butler's 'Analogy'*
When we summon the philosopher, the divine, and
the sceptic before us, and compare their views and
methods, we shall have no difficulty, in this instance,
in assigning the superiority to the divine in perspicuity and precision. The sceptic, consistent with
himself, concludes in "the *affair*," as he calls it,
"that all the nice questions concerning personal identity can never possibly be decided, and are rather

---

* Locke's chapter, the 27th of his second book, was added in
later editions of the Essay, at the instance of his friend and correspondent Molyneux,—(see Letters between Molyneux and Locke,
vol. iv. p. 292,)—and is by no means a favourable specimen of the
philosopher's care and powers. Butler observes, "he was hasty in
some of his positions," but he appears unusually playful with his subject, as in the story of the ' Parrot of Mariman,' and in the suggestion that the soul of Heliogabalus might be in one of his hogs."

to be regarded as grammatical than as philosophical difficulties." But he had previously suggested that, "as memory alone acquaints us with the continuance and extent of the succession of our perceptions, it is to be considered upon that account chiefly as the source of personal identity." "Had we no memory, we never should have any notion of causation, nor consequently of that chain of causes and effects, which constitute our self, or person." It is easy to see how little the sceptic is in such language consistent with himself. But when least consistent with himself, he often approaches nearest to philosophy and truth. For—let us listen to Mr. Locke—"since consciousness always accompanies thinking, and it is that which makes every one to be what he calls self, and thereby distinguishes himself from all other thinking things; in this alone consists personal identity, that is, the sameness of a rational being; and as far as this consciousness can be extended backwards to any past action or thought, so far reaches the identity of that person*." Again: "As far as any intelligent being can repeat the idea of any past action with the same consciousness it had of it at first, and with the same consciousness it has of any present action,—so far it is the same personal self." Thus memory and consciousness, and the connection of thought with thought, of present with past impressions, play a conspicuous part in giving the idea, and even in constituting the essence of personal identity, according to Mr.

* Locke's Essay, book ii. c. 27, §§ 9 and 10.

Locke.   Butler, with true wisdom, does Mr. Locke
the justice to admit that he has suggested much better
answers than those which he gives in form to the various questions concerning personal identity; for, says
he, "when any one reflects upon a past action of his
own, he is just as certain of the person who did that
action, namely himself, the person who now reflects
upon it, as he was certain that the action was at all
done. Nay, very often a person's assurance of an action
having been done, arises wholly from the consciousness
(*i.e.* present remembrance) that he himself did it."

    " And he who can doubt whether perception by me-
mory can be depended upon, may doubt also whether
perception by deduction and reasoning, which also
include memory, or indeed whether intuitive perception can.   Here then we can go no further.   For it
is ridiculous to attempt to prove the truth of those
perceptions, whose truth we can no otherwise prove,
than by other perceptions of exactly the same kind
with them, and which there is just the same ground
to suspect; or to attempt to prove the truth of our
faculties, which can be no otherwise proved than by
the use or means of those very suspected faculties
themselves."   To such language and sentiments the
sceptic himself must bow, and for these, (with much
more that I do not quote, indicative of nice discrimination, and germane to the matter,) the philosopher
would embrace the prelate as a worthy pupil in his
school, or as a successful fellow-student in the great
school of nature, truth, and Providence.   We see that

all three really place personal identity in one and the same unity of consciousness, of which memory makes a part, or, to express it differently, in the association of present impressions with remembrances of the past and anticipations of the future. Herein consists that unbroken thread of life, of which the Fates—three sisters, according to the ancient poets—hold the destiny. Whether we are satisfied with this account of it or not, whether we agree with it or not, it is something to know how far such writers and thinkers approach each other, and are consistent, first with themselves, and next with the actual phenomena of our being. If Hume had paid due attention to what had been said before him on such topics, aiming less at originality and more at truth, he would have saved himself and his readers trouble, and earned a gratitude which now cannot be felt.

At the conclusion of his chapter, Hume breaks out into that famous and often-quoted passage :—" I am affrighted and confounded with that forlorn solitude in which I am placed, and fancy myself some strange uncouth monster, who, not being able to mingle and unite in society, has been expelled all human commerce and left utterly abandoned and disconsolate. Again, the intense view of the manifold contradictions and imperfections in human reason has so wrought upon me and heated my brain, that I am ready to reject all belief and reasoning, and can look upon no opinion as even more probable or likely than another. Where am I, or what? From what causes do I derive my existence, and to what condition shall I return? . . . I am confounded with all these questions, and begin to fancy myself in the most deplorable condition imaginable, environed with the deepest darkness, and utterly deprived of the use of every member and faculty."

But these sentiments, with the addition that all are certainly fools who reason or believe anything, he pronounces to be the result of spleen and indolence; and he concludes that, "in all the incidents of life we ought still to preserve our scepticism. If we believe that fire warms, or water refreshes, 'tis only because it costs us too much pains to think otherwise. Nay, if we are philosophers, it ought only to be upon sceptical principles, and from an inclination which we feel to the employing ourselves after that manner." One gleam of light, one transient intimation of possible advantage in the midst of this darkness and difficulty, escapes him at last, when he says :—"For my part, my only hope is that I may contribute a little to the advancement of knowledge, by giving in some particulars a different turn to the speculations of philosophers, and pointing out to them more distinctly those subjects, where alone they can expect assurance and conviction. Human nature is the only science of man, and yet has been hitherto the most neglected." The last sentence deserves but a qualified, if any assent. More books have been written, and had been, in Hume's day, on Human Nature, its characteristics and interests, physical and metaphysical,—on man as an individual and a social being, as occupant of earth and heir of heaven,—than on any other subject of scientific investigation.

The dismay and alarm which Hume expresses at the darkness in which he is involved, are often referred to in proof of the baneful and gloomy effects of scepticism on his own and other minds. When we consider the age at which these sentiments were written—when we remember that they exhibit not the permanent characteristics of Hume's temper and feelings—their force as evidence of such effect is much abated. We may agree with Hume in thinking that, after a certain term of life, the character is little influenced by abstract speculations. The habits and the temper generally become fixed. We must therefore judge of the probable or real effects of scepticism partly by an honest appeal to our own hearts and consciousness, partly by a broad survey of the characters which have been formed under the influence of belief and unbelief respectively, so far as we can bring them to any true or desirable tests—to a common standard of virtue and social worth. We may place in contrast the lives and pages of a Milton, Newton, Locke, Boyle, Clarke, Addison, Hartley, and Butler, with those of Bayle, Bolingbroke, Hume, Shaftesbury, Gibbon, Helvetius, Voltaire, Rousseau. Perhaps we may compare the lives of a Wickliffe, a Luther, a Fénelon, a Wesley, a Priestley, with the most virtuous or the most learned of professed unbelievers. The dogmatism and intolerance of the believing are among the chief causes of scepticism, by keeping alive a spirit of antagonism.

Who ever argues against 'faith, hope, and charity,' in the abstract, or is worth listening to, if he does? And who that has tried to 'converse with heaven,' returns not from the effort with a deep consciousness of the inadequacy of the finite to comprehend the Infinite? Then, grateful for the light and strength vouchsafed to him, he gladly descends from the cold and exhausting regions of speculation into the lowly habitable vale of practical enjoyment and utility.

> " Wisdom is ofttimes nearer when we stoop
>   Than when we soar."
> " The primal duties shine aloft like stars ;
>   The charities that soothe, and heal, and bless,
>   Are scatter'd at the feet of man, like flowers*."

Whatever the demerits of the 'Treatise on Human Nature,' it would be gross injustice to lay any stress upon its contents as evidence of Hume's real sentiments, after the decided manner in which he condemned the work, and insisted upon being judged solely by the 'Essays, Moral and Political,' published in 1742. A comparison of the first volume of the Treatise with the Inquiry concerning Human Understanding in the second volume of the Essays, particularly the chapters on Probability and the Idea of Necessary Connection, will show a considerable improvement in the latter in qualities both of matter and style. But much of the original leaven remains ; and to neither will the cautious reader be disposed to award any such share of praise, for ingenuity of thought and

* Wordsworth's ' Excursion.'

subtlety of argument, as it has been customary to bestow upon them among writers north of the Tweed.

The Inquiry concerning the principles of morals,
with the appendix, which we now find in the ' Essays,'
was, in Hume's own opinion, "of all his writings,
historical, philosophical, or literary, incomparably the
best." With the dissertation on the Passions, it fills
about a third of the second volume of the ' Essays,'
and contains all that he thought worth preserving,
or could use to any purpose, of the second and third
volumes of the Treatise. The passages retained are
few, but they are among the best.

It is generally thought that in this Inquiry utility
was first broadly and clearly set forth as the basis of
morals ; advantage to society being made the foundation of merit in actions and of moral approbation in
character. Perhaps it is nowhere more distinctly expressed than in the conclusion of the Essay on Justice.

" The necessity of justice to the support of society
is the *sole* foundation of that virtue ; and since no
moral excellence is more highly esteemed, we may
conclude that this *circumstance of usefulness* has, in
general, the strongest energy, and most entire command over our sentiments. It must therefore be the
source of *a considerable part of the merit* ascribed to
humanity, benevolence, friendship, public spirit, and
other social virtues of that stamp, as it is the *sole
source* of the moral approbation paid to fidelity, justice, veracity, integrity, and those other estimable and
useful qualities and principles."

Yet, after all, this is not very distinct or happy. It is remarkable that Hume nowhere attempts a definition of virtue. If the above passage be compared with another from the appendix, a paper concerning Moral Sentiment, it will be seen how little Hume understood his subject or was consistent with himself. " Now as virtue is an end, and is desirable on its own account, without fee or reward, merely for the immediate satisfaction which it conveys; 'tis requisite that there should be some sentiment which it touches, some internal taste or feeling, or whatever you please to call it, which distinguishes moral good and evil, and which embraces the one and rejects the other."

" Thus the distinct boundaries and offices of *reason* and of *taste* are easily ascertained. The former conveys the knowledge of truth and falsehood; the latter *gives the sentiment* of beauty and deformity, *vice and virtue*." The reader may form his own opinion of the value of this distinction; and of other statements which follow or accompany the above. On consideration he will probably concur in the criticism, suggested no doubt by such passages as these, pronounced by Mr. Austin in his 'Province of Jurisprudence determined.'

" The hypothesis in question (namely that of a moral sense, or that certain inscrutable sentiments of approbation or disapprobation accompany our conceptions of certain human actions, which are not begotten by reflection upon the tendencies of the actions which excite them) has been embraced by sceptics as well as by religionists. For example, it is supposed by David

Hume, in his ' Essay on the Principles of Morals,' that *some* of our moral sentiments spring *from a perception of utility;* but he also appears to imagine that others are not to be analysed, or belong exclusively to the province of taste. Such, I say, appears to be his meaning. For in this Essay, as in all his writings, he is rather acute and ingenious, than coherent and profound; handling detached topics with signal dexterity, but evincing an utter inability to grasp his subject as a whole *.''

The criticism is eminently just, and too closely connected with the subject,—though it be not the history of any theory of morals, but relates to inquiries more strictly metaphysical,—to be omitted.

Our chief business is with the inquiry concerning the Human Understanding. A close comparison of the Treatise with the Essays will show a considerable improvement in the latter. Much of the useless language on cause and effect found in the former is abandoned to its destined oblivion. Sentiments dignified with the name of maxims, but never known as such before, are dropped into the same gulf. In the Treatise the most offensive paradoxes are put forward, for the sake of showing ingenuity in defending them; for instance, that " Reason is, and ought only to be, the slave of the passions, and can never pretend to any other office than to serve and obey them." In the Essays he forbore their repetition. In the Treatise he is a sort of hard, uncompromising necessarian, as-

* Austin's Jurisprudence, pp. 101, 102.

G

serting that "the doctrine of necessity, according to his explication of it, is not only innocent, but even advantageous to religion and morality." In the 'Essays' he is neither libertarian nor necessarian, but as favourable to liberty as to necessity; for he ventures to affirm that the doctrines both of necessity and of liberty, as he explains them, "are not only consistent with morality and religion, but are absolutely essential to the support of them*." He concludes the Essay on liberty and necessity without deciding anything except "the impossibility of arriving at any satisfactory conclusion," which is of course the proper condition of the genuine sceptic. "To reconcile the indifference and contingency of human actions with prescience, or to defend absolute decrees, and yet free the Deity from being the author of sin, has been found hitherto to exceed all the skill of philosophy. Happy, if she be thence sensible of her temerity, when she pries into these sublime mysteries; and, leaving a scene so full of obscurities and perplexities, return with suitable modesty to her true and proper province, the examination of common life, where she will find difficulties enough to employ her inquiries, without launching into so boundless an ocean of doubt, uncertainty, and contradiction†."

* Compare the Treatise, vol. ii. p. 237, with Essays, vol. ii. p. 108, 115. edit. 1764.

† It does not appear that Hume had paid any attention to the controversy and correspondence between Hobbes and Bramhall, Bishop of Dromore, where the question of necessity, if not exhausted, is put perhaps in as clear and strong a light as it can be made to sus-

In the two papers entitled 'Sceptical Doubts,' Mr. Hume does not appear to entertain himself, nor to propose to others, any real doubts about which he desired satisfaction; but he makes many decided and sufficiently dogmatical assertions. Thus: " I shall venture to affirm, as a general proposition, which admits of no exception, that the knowledge of this relation (that is, of cause and effect) is not in any instances attained by *reasonings à priori**, but arises entirely from experience, when we find that any particular objects are constantly conjoined with others." What is meant in these passages by " reasonings *à priori,*" and who had ever contended or conceived that such reasonings gave a knowledge of the relation of cause and effect? Such reasonings were held before Hume's time to be reasonings from a cause, known, assumed, or conceived, to the certain or pro-

tain, and it is easy to see which of the disputants has the mastery. Yet there seems one point in this difficult subject, to which Hobbes has not adverted with a due sense of its importance,—that is, the force of the will, and of steady continued resolution in giving birth to a repeated and protracted series of acts—fixing the habits, and thus influencing the individual life and character for a period indefinitely long. A copy of this correspondence, made valuable by the notes of P. Mallet, Esq., who edited an excellent abridgment of Locke's Essay, and Hobbes' Philosophy, now scarcely to be met with, is in Dr. Williams's Library. I observe with pleasure that Dr. Priestley, of all the writers on Philosophical Necessity, appears best acquainted with the history of opinion on the subject, and his historical references are always correct and instructive. See particularly the preface to his Doctrine of Necessity illustrated.—Rutt's Priestley, vol. iii.

* Compare also subsequent passages, " when we reason *à priori,*" etc., pp. 36, 38, 40.

bable effect. They supposed a knowledge of the relation already to exist, whencesoever the knowledge
might be derived. Whatever Hume meant, it is supposed that he began that fallacious use of the words
à priori, as an epithet for an intuition, or conception,
now so common, under which use a twofold error or
assumption lies concealed: first, that there are intuitions and conceptions in the mind capable of being
expressed in words, which are antecedent to or independent of experience,—that is, of sensation and reflection; secondly, that there are propositions, or conceptions, capable of being expressed in words, into the
evidence of which, even into the meaning of which, we
must not inquire prior to the admission of the reasonings founded upon them, an intuitive certainty being
pleaded or assumed for such propositions. As this
is a point of considerable importance in tracing the
history and appreciating the condition of modern metaphysics, some observations upon it will be submitted
in a future chapter. This proposition Mr. Hume endeavours to establish by a variety of considerations.
The reason is discernible in the following passage,
which covertly contains the real sceptical doubt which
he entertained, and which he designed rather to insi-
nuate than to express.

" Hence we may discover the reason why *no philosopher, who is rational and modest,* has ever pretended
to assign *the ultimate cause* of any natural operation,
or to show distinctly the action of that power which
produces any single effect in the universe. 'Tis con-

fessed, that the utmost effort of human reason is, to reduce the principles, productive of natural phenomena, to a greater simplicity, and to resolve the many particular effects into a few general causes, by means of reasonings from analogy, experience, and observation. But as to the causes of these general causes, we should in vain attempt their discovery; nor shall we ever be able to satisfy ourselves by any particular explication of them. These ultimate springs and principles are totally shut up from human curiosity and inquiry. Elasticity, gravity, cohesion of parts, communication of motion by impulse, these are probably the ultimate causes and principles which we shall ever discover in nature; and we may esteem ourselves sufficiently happy, if by accurate inquiry and reasoning we can trace up the particular phenomena to, or near to, these general principles. The most perfect philosophy of the natural kind only staves off our ignorance a little longer; as perhaps the most perfect philosophy of the moral or metaphysical kind serves only to discover larger portions of our ignorance. Thus *the observation of human blindness and weakness* is the result of all philosophy, and meets us at every turn, in spite of our endeavours to elude or avoid it*."

The covert atheism of the first part of this extract, and the vanity of attempting any exact metaphysical science or truth in the last, constitute the real scepticism which Mr. Hume took such pains to cherish and to instil. If this be so, there is no attempt at solution

* Essays, vol. ii. pp. 38, 39.

in any subsequent remarks. To suppose that we have
in this any legitimate conclusion from principles peculiar to Locke, is to suppose what is utterly contrary
to evidence. Instead of Hume being a disciple of
Locke, with more truth may it be said that Diderot,
who, in 1751, began the French Encyclopédie, was
the disciple or fellow-labourer of Hume. "Strictly
speaking," says Diderot, "there is but one sort of
causes,—that is, physical causes *." We are reminded
of the admirable lines of the author of the 'Dunciad,'
written soon after the appearance of the Treatise!

> "Philosophy, that leaned on Heaven before,
> Shrinks to her second cause, and is no more."

In the second part of the paper entitled, 'Sceptical
Doubts,' our author carries on his sifting humour.
He asks, "What is the foundation of all conclusions
from experience?" and answers negatively, that "they
are *not* founded on reasoning, or any process of the
understanding." But what is a conclusion or an inference? If there be any process to arrive at it, it
must be a process of the mind or understanding. It
is a result of thought,—but who thinks or entertains
ideas without an experience? Mr. Hume, as often as
most other metaphysicians, loses sight of his meaning,
and destroys his argument by changing his terms.

Comment on other passages of the 'Sceptical Doubts'

---

* See the letter of Diderot to the Baron de Grimm, quoted by
Stewart, Dissertation, p. 150; and compare the account of Diderot
in the 'Dictionnaire des Sciences Philosophiques.' Paris, 1845.

may be dispensed with, but it is worth while to observe that the concluding paragraph is too positive to be consistent with any scepticism; and the reader may consider whether the perception and remembrance of sensible qualities—the observation of the present, the memory of the past, and the expectation of the future—are or are not processes of the understanding? While Mr. Hume admits these to be the characteristics of all percipient natures—even peasants, children, and beasts—he would on that account hold them beneath the attention of the philosopher. Thus the most general are made the least important principles. The insignificance of a law is in proportion to its universality! Gravitation, which keeps the worlds in harmony, is subordinate to the explosive power of steam or gunpowder. It is of no moment that men usually walk erect upon the ground, because one man, at a loss otherwise for a subsistence, has been known to walk upon the ceiling with his head downwards.

Where there are really no doubts, there can be no solutions. In the subsequent paper, entitled, ' Sceptical Solutions of these Doubts,' we find chiefly a repetition of the same statements, touching the entire dependence of our knowledge of causes and effects on experience, for which a new term is found, as if it were a new principle, namely, custom. " All inferences from experience, therefore, are effects of custom, not of reasoning." A long but unsatisfactory note follows, on some common distinction between *reason* and *experience;* the result of which is to show

that there is no sufficient distinction, that the one
supposes the other, and that neither is of value without the other.   Much of the subsequent language in
the first part is open to obvious objection, as where he
compares the belief in the existence of the sensible
qualities of objects, and the expectation of effects in
future similar to those experienced in the past, to the
passion of love, when we receive benefits, or hatred,
when we receive injuries, and says, " all these *operations* (!) are a species of *natural instincts*, which no
reasoning or process of thought is able to produce or
to prevent."   How much reasoning and thought, experience and reflection, modify all our beliefs and
passions, and expectations, he did not concern himself
at that moment to inquire, forgetting that this in fact
was the main business and proper purpose of his
Essay, which is an illustration of it.

A rich specimen of confusion of thought and language in an author affecting metaphysical depth occurs
in the concluding section of these papers, where Mr.
Hume proceeds *to examine more accurately* the nature
of this belief, and of the customary conjunction whence
it is derived; from which examination, readers who
have no taste for the abstract sciences, and for such
speculations, are politely warned off.   He gives what
he conceives to be the difference between fiction and
belief.   " The difference," he says, " lies in some sentiment or feeling, which is annexed to the latter, not
to the former, and which depends not on the will,
nor can be commanded at pleasure.   It must be *ex-*

cited by nature, like all other sentiments, and must
arise from the situation in which the mind is placed
at any particular juncture. Whenever any object is
presented to the memory or senses, it immediately,
by the force of custom, carries the imagination *to conceive that object, which is usually conjoined to it;*
and this conception is attended with a feeling or sentiment different from the loose reveries of the fancy.
In this consists the whole nature of belief." In the
subsequent paragraph he attempts not a definition,
but another description of this sentiment or feeling of
belief, although he says it is a term of which no one
is ever at a loss for the meaning. " I say then that
belief is nothing but a more vivid, lively, forcible, firm,
steady conception of an object, than what the imagination alone is ever able to attain. This variety of
terms, which may seem so unphilosophical, is intended
only to express that act of the mind, which renders
realities, or what is taken for such, more present to
us than fictions, causes them to weigh more in the
thought, and gives them a superior influence on the
passions and imagination. Provided we agree about
the thing, 'tis needless to dispute about the terms."

Now, first, belief is not rightly or usefully opposed
to fiction, but to unbelief or disbelief; it relates to
the assent which the mind gives to propositions, or
affirmations, respecting the past, the present, or the
future; for the mind frames for itself propositions
more or less distinct, whenever it forms a judgement
attended with belief. Belief relates to the acceptance

of testimony—first of the senses, and next of other witnesses. It is confidence in the correctness of the inferences which experience leads us to draw from the sensible impressions. Fiction is feigned or false history, as distinguished from true or real history. It is the play of imagination as distinguished from the observation of fact. Liveliness of conception does not distinguish the sentiment or feeling of belief from that (sentiment or feeling) which attends the reveries of fancy. Dr. Brown has well observed this, criticizing these papers of Mr. Hume. The conception, which is present to the mind when perusing the statements of the historian may be very languid and unsteady, while the excitement of the imagination may be great when following the ideal pictures of the poet and the novelist. The fables of Æsop give a far more lively conception than the natural histories and catalogues of Aristotle, Buffon, and Linnæus.

But, secondly, no act of the mind renders realities more present to us than fictions, or causes them to weigh more in the thoughts. This is an obvious error. Surely realities act upon the mind, not the mind upon the realities. Whatever the force of imagination, or internal feeling, and of that pre-occupation of mind, which prevents us occasionally from attending to the presence of sensible objects, in general the continuity and force of the impressions from without are sufficient to make us quite aware of the difference between a fact and a fancy, an object and an idea.

> " Oh, who can hold a fire in his hand,
>   By thinking on the frosty Caucasus?
>   Or cloy the hungry edge of appetite
>   By bare imagination of a feast?"

" Let us then," says Mr. Hume, " take in the whole compass of this doctrine, and *allow that the sentiment of belief is nothing but a conception of an object more intense and steady than what attends the mere pictures of the imagination;* and that this manner of conception arises from a customary conjunction of the object with *something* present to the memory or senses. I believe that it will not be difficult, upon these suppositions, to find other operations of the mind analogous to it; and to trace up these phenomena to principles still more general*."

But who will allow this? The manner of conception does not constitute the difference between a sensation caused by the presence of an object, and the remembrance or idea of that object, or of *something* else not present to the senses. Still less does it constitute the difference between belief and disbelief, fiction and fact. The conception of a centaur or satyr, of Bacchus and Silenus, may be far more lively than that of the personal appearance of the Roman Emperors. The figures on the Elgin marbles may be more distinctly impressed on the mind's eye than the expression on the busts of Cæsar and of Cicero. But belief in the existence of the one and the other as real

---

* Sceptical Solutions, p. 59. Compare Brown's Essay on Cause and Effect, p. 308, edit. 1835.

beings, assent to propositions respecting them, consti-tute a class of sentiments and feelings wholly different from the mere presence or remembrance of visual or audible impressions.

When errors like these pervade Mr. Hume's Scep-tical Solution, it is evident that nothing is solved. No doubt which any man, rational and modest, se-riously entertained, ever was solved, and was believed by Hume to be solved, in any of his remarks. A few passages in the Treatise are preserved in these papers,—one touching the influence of relics on the feelings of the Roman Catholics,—another on the in-fluence of a sensation, such as that caused by the voice or hand-writing of a friend, to call up the idea of his personal appearance. But they affect no phi-losophical question; they help no analysis of mental phenomena; they point no moral. Let them, if they may, adorn a tale.

We come to the 'Essay on the Idea of Necessary Connection,' the most laboured in the collection. There is concentrated the essence of Hume's sceptical phi-losophy, if philosophy it deserves to be called. Of this Essay he has made considerable use, both in the well-known paper on miracles, and the less known but not less remarkable Essay on Providence and a Future State,—remarkable for contemptuous indiffer-ence to all the received principles and ordinary feel-ings of mankind; for how subordinate is the question whether there be evidence for any peculiar, special, and exceptional interpositions of Providence, to the question whether there be an Intelligent and Benignant Providence at all. To the Essay on the Idea of Necessary Connection, the greatest attention must be paid by one who would know the nature and extent of the scepticism of Hume.

The general tenor of the section in the Treatise is preserved in the Essay, but with some improvement in the mode of putting the argument. Yet it is difficult, without minute attention, without thorough acquaintance with Mr. Hume's style and sentiments, and even with it, to discern clearly the proposition which he seeks to establish. It is not clear whether we have or have not the idea in question; nor whether, if we have it, it can be rationally entertained, and made a basis for philosophical reasoning and conclusion. Dr. Reid understood Hume to deny that we have the idea of power. He understood him to deny that we have any idea of power, because there is no one impression to which it can be specifically traced. On the other hand, Dr. Brown contends that this is a mistake of Reid's, that Hume admits and asserts we have it, quoting the sentence: " *This connection, therefore, which we feel in the mind, or customary transition of the imagination from one object to its usual attendant, is the sentiment or impression from which we form the idea of power or necessary connection**.

---

* It seems obvious, that the connection which we feel in the mind is only another term for the idea of connection which Mr. Hume says is formed from a sentiment or impression. Do not the words feeling, sentiment, impression, and idea, signify one and the same subject of thought and reasoning?

*Nothing further is in the case.   Contemplate the sub-
ject on all sides, you will never find any other origin
of this idea *."*   Nevertheless Dr. Reid's mistake was
perfectly natural, at least on a superficial view : it was
founded on the general course of Mr. Hume's argument. Hume makes much use of his peculiar principle,
that we have no idea without its corresponding impression, and because we have no impression of a
power or a cause in what he conceives to be the ordinary sense of those terms, and in the sense in which
some philosophers (though he mentions them not) have
taken them, he concludes or seems to conclude we have
no such idea.

" Upon the whole there appears not, through all
nature, any one instance of connection which is conceivable by us. *All events seem entirely loose and
separate.* One event follows another, but we can never
observe any tie between them : they seem *conjoined*,
but never *connected*.   And as we can have no idea of
anything which never appeared to our outward sense
or inward sentiment, the necessary conclusion *seems*
to be, that we have no idea of connection or power at
all ; and that these words are absolutely without any
meaning, when employed either in philosophical reasonings or common life."

If he had stopped there, Dr. Reid would have been
partially right† ; but he adds, " there still remains
one method of avoiding this conclusion, and one source

---

* Essays, p. 87.

† This passage is referred to by Stewart (Dissertation, p. 214),

which we have not yet examined. When one particular species of event has always, in all instances,
been conjoined with another, we make no longer any
scruple to foretel the one upon the appearance of the
other, and to employ that reasoning which can alone
assure us of any matter of fact or existence. We then
call the one object *cause*, and the other *effect*. We
suppose that there is some connection between them,
some power in the one by which it infallibly produces
the other, and operates with the greatest certainty and
strongest necessity.

" It appears, then, that this idea of a necessary connection amongst events arises from a number of similar instances, which occur of the constant conjunction
of events ; nor can that idea ever be suggested by any
one of these instances, surveyed in all possible lights
and positions. But there is nothing in a number of
instances different from any single instance which is
supposed to be exactly similar, except only, that after
a repetition of similar instances the mind is carried by
habit, upon the appearance of one event, to expect its
usual attendant, and to believe that it will exist*."

Now what Mr. Hume mentions as an exception is
evidently no exception, but a different kind of assertion. The effect of repetition on the mind, the direction in which the mind is carried by habit, adds

and well criticized by Brown ('Essay on Cause and Effect,' part iv.
sect. 7, on Mr. Hume's Theory :) and compare Dr. Reid's First
Essay, on Active Power in general,' ch. iv.

* Essays, p. 86.

nothing to the instances themselves, and varies not their character. In the recapitulation of the argument in the last paragraph of the Essay, where Hume repeats these views, he makes the same mistake; he confounds the different effect of repeated instances upon the imagination, the different degrees of confidence of anticipation in the mind, with a difference or change in the character of the instances themselves.

The real object of all this, it may be presumed, is to pluck up by the roots the common argument in favour of a Supreme Intelligence and Power from the manifestations of intelligence, design, and power in the universe. Because we have had no immediate experience, no impression of the connection between the will of a Supreme Being and any of the events or phenomena of the universe, we ought not to attempt to account for the phenomena by referring them to the existence of such a Being. It is travelling " out of the sphere of our experience," into regions unknown, into questions beyond the grasp of our faculties. Mr. Hume refers to the Essay on the academical or sceptical philosophy*, as exhibiting these results: " While we cannot give a satisfactory reason why we believe, after

* This Essay, like the rest of Hume's writings, abounds with ingenious and useful observations, but with strange inconsistencies. For in the same page (183) he says, " 'Tis only experience which teaches us the nature and bounds of cause and effect, and enables us to infer the existence of one object from that of another. Such is the foundation of moral reasoning, which forms the greatest part of human knowledge, and is the source of all human action and behaviour." Yet shortly after he says, " Morals and criticism are not so

a thousand experiments, that a stone will fall, or fire burn, can we ever satisfy ourselves concerning any determination which we may form with regard to the origin of worlds, and the situation of nature from, and to, eternity ?"

As the whole of Hume's Sceptical Philosophy turns on this point, it is a duty to examine it with some care. And first, there is no pretence for attributing any assertion or thought concerned in his reasoning to Locke. There is neither statement drawn from the pages, nor inference deduced from the principles of the great English metaphysician, to whom Hume pays little attention. His reference to Mr. Locke's chapter on ' Power,' in a note, is short but incorrect. Locke does not say what Hume represents him as saying, " that, finding from experience that there are several new productions in matter, and concluding that there must somewhere be a power capable of producing them, we arrive at last, by this reasoning, at the idea of power." Locke's chapter on ' Power' is one of the least happy portions of his great Essay. He was himself little satisfied with it, as appears by his letter to Molyneux, of July 15, 1693. But his language is not quite so muddy and inconsistent with himself, as Hume represents it. He suggests the only

properly objects of the understanding as of taste and sentiment;" as if our tastes and sentiments were themselves to be excluded from the domain of knowledge, understanding, and criticism. Why did he not remember his own principle, expressed a few sentences before, that our difficulties in these matters " proceed entirely from the undeterminate meaning of words, which is corrected by juster definitions"?

sources whence the idea of power can be derived. He lays it down that the mind, "taking notice of alteration in things without," "how one comes to an end, and ceases to be, and another begins to exist, which was not before; reflecting also on what passes within itself, and observing a constant change of its ideas"— "so comes by that idea which we call power." Such, in consistency with his analytic view of the mind—with his account of the origin of all our ideas, and striking out some useless words in which he has wrapped up his theory,—such is the substance of his account of the origin of our idea of power. He attributes it to no reasoning. "If," he says at the end of the fourth section, "from the impulse bodies are observed to make one upon another, any one thinks he has a clear idea of power, it serves as well to my purpose, sensation being one of those ways whereby the mind comes by its ideas; only I thought it worth while to consider here by the way, whether the mind doth not receive its idea of active power clearer from *reflection on its own operations* than it doth from any external sensation." Mr. Hume, on the other hand, denies that the idea of power can be derived "from the contemplation of bodies in single instances of their operation," and he concludes that neither is it "copied from any sentiment or consciousness of power within ourselves." He especially combats at great length Mr. Locke's position that it is an idea arising chiefly from reflecting on the operations of our own minds, —with what success will hereafter appear.

It is to be regretted that Hume did not take the trouble to represent carefully, in Locke's own language, what Locke really thought. He would then have perceived himself, and his readers have perceived after him, to what extent he did or did not agree with the English philosopher. If the idea of power or necessary connection arises from the contemplation of repeated instances, or many uniform instances of sequence of events, as Mr. Hume, so far as he is intelligible, admits, what is the difference, what the inconsistency, between this and Mr. Locke's " observation of the operation of bodies by our senses"? But the virtue of faithful quotation has been rare among metaphysicians, particularly among those who write for the softest heads, and the applause of a partial audience. How careless and how incorrect Dr. Reid could be in his representation of Locke on this very subject of *power*, active and passive, Sir W. Hamilton has shown in his notes to the late edition of Reid's collected writings*.

Secondly, Mr. Hume makes a great point of a distinction between what he calls a ' constant conjunction' and a ' necessary connection.' But there is no such difference between a junction and a tie in any essential value of these terms, as to enable us to found upon that difference a metaphysical argument or a philosophical truth. The one does not refer any more than the other to any important peculiarities in the phenomena of matter or of mind. Had Hume paid

* See Hamilton's Reid, p. 519.

any salutary attention to the fourth book of Locke's Essay on the connection between language and thought, he would have paused before he laid so much stress upon an arbitrary or imaginary difference between a conjunction and a connection, as if the one implied something in its own nature more casual and less necessary than the other,—as if the one expressed independence of law and a union of events without a cause, while the other expressed dependence and involved more completely the notion of cause and of power.

Thirdly, the stress of his argument evidently lies on the word necessary, which he never explains. Yet he must have known, if accustomed to nice metaphysical and logical distinctions, that the very word necessary had been taken in various senses, or considered in several relations*. To man, whatever happens independently of his own will may be said to be a neces-

* A good and short view of the importance and meaning of the word necessary, with remarks on its introduction and use by the schoolmen, may by found in Waterland's Dissertation 'Upon the argument à priori for proving the existence of a First Cause,' mentioned above. He distinguishes four kinds of necessity,—logical, moral, physical, and metaphysical; and the distinction is well carried out. Those who are conversant with Dr. S. Clarke's ' Demonstration' will remember that he dwells much on a necessity of the last kind, when he argues for " an absolute necessity of existence." The reader, desirous of accurate historical views on such metaphysical points, will be greatly assisted by that Dissertation. Touching on the connection of causes and effects with a masterly hand, and especially on the application of the word necessary to that connection, it claims an attention, which hitherto it does not appear to have received.

sary event, and whatever truth or proposition he cannot but admit without annihilating thought, or contradicting his faculties, is a necessary truth. Its correlatives are the words contingent, voluntary, accidental. Because we know not always what determines the will, and what is the sequence of events arising from unknown causes, we call such events contingent or accidental. Now the constant conjunction on which Mr. Hume lays stress, is in the proper sense of the term necessary to us. Means are as necessarily connected with, as they are constantly conjoined to, ends. Powers are necessary to the production of effects. Antecedents necessarily precede consequents by the force of the terms, which have no meaning but as they imply order in place or sequence in time. In a procession some must go first, and others follow behind. Two distinct bodies cannot occupy the same space. Two persons cannot reason together or syllogize in common without having a common premiss and agreeing in the use of their signs and understanding each other's language. Practically things may be tied together in as many ways as they are joined. They may be bound in paper and string, sown up with thread, nailed, and glued. All these words suggest thoughts, associated with various sensible impressions; and thoughts suppose minds accessible to reasoning, and on which the reasoning is to take effect. For the purpose of the reasoning there is a necessary connection between the words, the thoughts, and the impressions. "Repeated similar instances," says Mr.

Hume, "give rise infallibly to uniformity of expectation, and determine the mind on the perception of
one object to anticipate another." But what is this
determination of the mind? It is a case of indissoluble association. It is a simple illustration of that
great law of thought without which there could be no
reasoning. There is a necessary connection between
the nature and order of our thoughts and the phenomena which give rise or occasion to that order, as
there is between reasoning and the signs or marks employed to connect thoughts together, and impart them
to another mind. When we open our eyes, it is not a
matter of will what objects, forms, or colours we shall
see. When a gun is fired close to the ear, it is not
an arbitrary but a necessary result that we should be
startled or disturbed by the sound. In vain would
you try to persuade workmen to remain within a few
feet of the piece of rock, to which a train of gunpowder has been properly applied for blasting, and
which is about to be exploded. Life—the last possession—is at stake. Their belief in the established,
that is necessary connection between cause and effect,
in the uniformity of sequence, is inseparable from the
exercise of their reason and faculties. Now the first
powerful impression on the senses, such as heat from
fire, or light from flame; and the first conscious exercise of the will in originating muscular motion, or
bringing about a new sequence of phenomena, lays
the foundation for that idea or sentiment of power,
which repeated instances and uniformity of experience

combine to strengthen. There is nothing in the repetition of instances, but the repetition. The uniformity and strength of expectation is conformable to
the uniformity or invariableness of the experience, although the degree and nature of expectations may vary
in different minds in proportion to the amount of observation and reflection, or be in accordance with the
peculiar nature of the casual or acquired associations.
Outward objects continually impress us with the idea
of a sequence, independent of our own wills. The
exertion of the will, the result of desire, is followed by
changes which we feel that we ourselves originate, and
which, without the existence and influence of that will,
we feel and know, as much as we can know anything,
would not exist. Hence the notion of power, first of
specific powers, material and intellectual, which indi-
vidually are known by experience, and afterwards of
power itself; power, an abstract or general term, significant of a complex idea, a convenient abbreviation
for whatever causes change, or involves the notion of
a sequence of phenomena, whether in the world of
matter or of mind. The succession of events in an order independent of our wills, and the existence of will
in ourselves, however limited in its sphere of influence,
enable and compel us to recognize powers out of ourselves, of which we are the subjects, and powers in ourselves, of which we are possessors. The sensible impressions leave traces of their existence in the memory,
and recur to thought with uniform or varying associations. The sensations and ideas become associated

with language according to a certain law; and the miniatures of sensation, to use Hartley's language, blend with the associated ideas, so as to form complex and decomplex ideas. Hence the formation, import, and use of such terms as power, virtue, honour, beauty, goodness, utility, order, law, generosity, philosophy, and so on, through the dictionary. In vain should we seek for any one particular impression in Hume's sense, however indefinite, to account for the ideas attached to these words; but equally vain is it to deny the natural origin of the ideas in sensation and reflection, experience, and consciousness; and to question their connection with the realities and interests of our practical and hourly life. The terms experience and consciousness cover all the phenomena of our perceptive and intellectual being.

Whoever accepts the account now given of the origin and nature of the complex idea of power, will see at once the insufficiency and weakness of Hume's attempt to analyse the idea of necessary connection, and may think further comments on it unnecessary. But as the diligence of readers cannot always be trusted, some further exposure of its fallacies or obscurities may be useful.

He runs the changes upon the words, *influence, force, energy, command,* and *authority,* in connection especially with the human will, without appearing to see that they alike involve the notion of power, if there be any notion of it. It is easy to show that his attempt to prove a negative, to prove that this notion comes neither from observation nor consciousness, is altogether a failure, and is inconsistent with his own statements and admissions.

For example, to prove that "single instances" give no impression of power, he adduces the instance of motion in billiard-balls. " The impulse of one billiard-ball is attended with motion in the second. This is the whole that appears to the outward senses. The mind feels no sentiment or inward impression from this succession of objects." This is untrue. There can be no succession of objects, attracting any attention, without an inward impression; when we are talking of the one, we are talking of the other. Besides, the observation is more complex than Mr. Hume supposes. There is the will of the striker,—directing one ball against another, and success or failure in the effort to give the balls a particular direction. If the observer saw motion arising in the first ball without an apparent mover, the first ball beginning to move and imparting motion to a second, without any apparent cause for the first motion, he would be at a loss to account for such beginning of motion; but he would not the less feel that there was, first, a cause out of himself, for the particular impression on his own mind—his own perception of motion; nor would he the less believe, secondly, that wherever there is motion, there must be a moving power.

Again, Hume says that, "from the first appearance of an object, we never can conjecture what effect

will result from it." But do we ever perceive objects
without effects? We may not conjecture, on perceiving a new object, with whose qualities we are not
familiar, all the effects which it is capable of producing
under conditions not yet observed. But this is no
proof that the objects of nature do not from the first,
from the dawn of intelligence, affect us by their sensible qualities, and that such objects as we do observe,
by the manner in which they affect us, by the uniformly experienced effects, do not give us the notion
of power. In short what does Hume mean by his
"repeated instances," but the observation or impression of a uniformity of sequence? Again, he says,
"there is no part of matter that does ever by its sensible qualities discover (he should have said disclose)
any power or energy." But what are sensible qualities? Are they not the impressions made on our
senses by outward objects? Do not these objects act
upon our senses in a uniform manner, independently
of our volition? Are not form, colour, and smell, in-
separably associated with our idea of the rose? If so,
why is not this subjection of our senses to effects or
impressions uniform and constant, but independent
of our control and volition, an element in our notion
of power? Because we know specific effects only by
experience, and learn to attribute them to specific
causes, or invariable antecedents; because we learn
particular powers, and their exercise, by observation,
and conclude the dependence of the observed effects
upon the observed causes, and derive from the repe-

tition of instances the idea of necessary connection ;
therefore our idea of connection or power does not
arise from the observation of body, or outward changes
and sequences at all. Such, if I understand it, is Mr.
Hume's argument. But the premises seem to hold
a conclusion precisely the reverse of that at which he
has arrived.

Mr. Hume goes on with an attempt to prove that
the idea of power is not an idea of reflection, or consciousness. He examines this pretension—first with
regard to the influence of volition over the organs of the
body—and afterwards to the command of the mind
over itself or its ideas. Again, what are his proofs ?
" The union of soul with body is very mysterious."
" Is there," he asks, " any principle in all nature more
mysterious ?" It may be so. But how does the my-
steriousness of that union help to show that the consciousness which, in a sentence or two before, as he
admitted, attends us every moment,—a consciousness
of the command of the will over the organs of the
body, does not supply the idea of power, the idea of
a necessary connection between that command of will
and the resulting motion. But, secondly, "we are
not able to move all the organs of the body with a like
authority."—" Why has the will an influence over the
tongue and the fingers, and not over the heart and
liver ?" The question implies that we can move some
organs with some authority. The question supposes
that there is an influence within certain limits. That
is enough. Instead of proving that the exercise of

such authority and such influence is not the source of
our idea of power, and of the necessary connection between the will and the deed, it is a virtual admission
of the contrary.   The example of the man suddenly
struck with palsy is little to Mr. Hume's purpose, and
fatal to his own argument.   That we learn the influence of our will from experience alone, does not
disprove such influence to be the true source of our
idea of power.   The influence, the authority, and the
power, are the same thing under different terms.
Thirdly, "we learn from anatomy that the immediate
object of power in voluntary motion, is not the member itself which is moved; but certain muscles, and
nerves, and animal spirits—and perhaps something
still more minute and more unknown—through which
the motion is successively propagated, ere it reach the
member itself, whose motion is the immediate object
of volition.   Can there be a more certain proof that
the power, by which this is performed, so far from
being directly and fully known by an inward sentiment or consciousness, is to the last degree mysterious and unintelligible?"   But does the length of the
chain through which the power is propagated alter
the nature of the power?   A chain must equally be
upheld; the last link must be connected with the first,
whether it consist of two or two hundred links.   The
weight on the last must be maintained by the power
with which the first link is fastened to the beam, and
by the power of the walls to support the beam.   Anatomy cannot alter the metaphysics of muscular motion.

It may reveal a longer or shorter process; it may show the connection of the resulting motion with the will to be more immediate, or more remote; but it does not destroy the necessary connection of the one with the other. It does not alter the consciousness of that connection. It does not show that such consciousness is not one source of our idea of power.

So much, then, for Mr. Hume's attempt to prove that the idea of power is not an idea of reflection. The same observations apply to his remarks on the command of the mind over its ideas. The positions that "this command is limited," and that "our authority over our sentiments and passions is much weaker than that over our ideas," are admissions of the existence of some command and some authority, and therefore rather proofs than disproofs that reflection on what passes within must be one source of all our ideas, and all our knowledge of power, physical or mental, intellectual or moral. Thus, when closely examined, Mr. Hume's arguments afford confirmation of Locke's theory, while they refute himself. They support a conclusion the reverse of that which he was anxious to establish. They even go to show that Mind is the true origin of all motion, as it is the sole inherent possessor of wisdom, order, and law; that it affords the only conceivable explanation of an adjustment of means to ends, or of the pursuit of an object by suitable contrivances. When, therefore, Hume advances to a confutation of the opinion of Malebranche and Berkeley, that everything is full of God,

that to the constant agency of a Supreme Mind,
every power of matter and finite mind must be attributed,—when he contends that such theories are too
bold for the weakness of human reason, and that we
are alike profoundly ignorant of the operation of
bodies on each other, and of minds on body, he forgets the nature and extent of his own admissions. To
argue from our ignorance is to argue from nothing.
The facts we do know, or have admitted, be they few
or many, are the only basis of just reasoning. He
forgets that it is the proper business of the philosopher
to arrive at some great ultimate principles on which
the mind can rest with satisfaction, beyond which it
feels no desire to go, which can be applied to all its
wants, in consistency with all the phenomena of observation and reflection, and ample for the purposes
and government of life.

Having sufficiently confused our idea of necessary
connection, and left us in some doubt whether we
have it or have it not; whether, if we have it, the experience or the repetition of instances on which it
rests, justifies our entertaining it, and reasoning from
it; whether "all events are not really what they seem,
entirely loose and separate" (though this is in fact as
contrary to the appearance as to the reality), Hume
passes on to the section on Liberty and Necessity,
where he intimates that the most sublime and specious reflections are in practice weak and ineffectual;
that no conclusions of the understanding can influence
our natural emotions and affections; and he advances

to the subject of miracles, and of Providence, and a future state. In the one he would destroy the foundation of Revealed, in the other of Natural Religion.

"While we argue from the course of nature, and infer a particular intelligent cause, which first bestowed, and still preserves, order in the universe, we *embrace a principle which is both uncertain and useless.* 'Tis uncertain; because the subject lies entirely beyond the reach of human experience. 'Tis useless, because our knowledge of this cause being derived entirely from this course of nature, we can never, according to the rules of just reasoning, return back from the cause with any new inferences, or, making additions to the common and experienced course of nature, establish any new principles of conduct and behaviour."

Such is Hume's defence of Epicurus; such his indifference to the principle that the order of the universe argues an infinitely wise and benevolent Providence. To Mr. Locke's argument from the existence of knowledge in ourselves, to the existence of "some knowing Being from all eternity," and its beautiful corollaries*, he makes no allusion; to the questions suggested by Hartley†, a summary of all metaphysical possibilities on the subject of Providence, he was most probably a stranger; to Cudworth's noble temple of worship, the 'Intellectual System,' he scorns a reference; and to 'Clarke's Demonstration,' full of pro-

* Essay, book iv. c. xi.   † Proposition, iv. part ii.

found and admirable thoughts, though not felicitous in some of its definitions, he refers only to show how little accurate consideration he chose to give it. But how little was Hume consistent with himself! There are times when he breaks out into acknowledgments which, like flashes of lightning, relieve for an instant the prevailing darkness. Thus he concludes the first appendix concerning moral sentiment, which proposes to ascertain the boundaries and offices of Reason and Taste, with saying, " The standard of the one, being founded on the nature of things, is eternal and inflexible, even by the will of the *Supreme Being :* the standard of the other, arising from the internal frame and constitution of animals, is ultimately derived from that *Supreme Will*, which bestowed on each being its peculiar nature, and arranged the several classes and orders of existence *." His general corollary derived from all considerations on the natural history of religion is, that " though the stupidity of men, barbarous and uninstructed, be so great, that they may not see a *sovereign author* in the more obvious works of nature, to which they are so much familiarized, yet it scarce seems possible that any one of good understanding should reject that idea, when once it is suggested to him. *A purpose, an intention, a design is evident in everything ;* and when our comprehension is so far enlarged as to contemplate the first rise of this visible system, we must adopt with the strongest conviction the idea of some intelligent cause or author. The

* Hume's Essays, vol. ii. p. 369.

uniform maxims too which prevail through the whole frame of the universe, naturally, if not necessarily, lead us to conceive this intelligence as single and undivided, where the prejudices of education oppose not so reasonable a theory. Even the contrarieties of nature, by discovering themselves everywhere, become proofs of some consistent plan, and establish one single purpose or intention, however inexplicable and incomprehensible." "The good, the great, the sublime, the ravishing, are found eminently in the genuine principles of theism." "The universal propensity to believe in invisible, intelligent power, if not an original instinct, being at least a general attendant of human nature, may be considered as a kind of mark or stamp, which the Divine Workman has set upon his work, and nothing surely can more dignify mankind than to be thus selected from all the other parts of the creation, and to bear the image or impression of the Universal Creator*!" "Look out for a people entirely void of religion. If you find them at all, be assured that they are but few degrees removed from brutes."

What more could the most ardent theist require than this? and how much better would Mr. Hume have been employed in endeavouring to purify theological systems from error and inconsistency,—in strengthening the influence of a genuine theism over the sweetest hopes

* These warm sentiments and concessions in favour of Theism were added in the later editions of Hume's Essays. The small volume entitled 'Philosophical Essays concerning Human Understanding,' published in 1748, ends with the Essay of the Academical or Sceptical Philosophy.

I

and most endearing charities of existence, than in persuading himself and his readers of the uselessness of reason, and the inefficacy of every principle against the instincts of nature, amid the tempests of passion, or under the immediate visitations of physical pain! Why should he thicken the obscurity of the region of philosophy into the outer darkness of despair, and spitefully dash down the taper, whose feeble beam affords the only solace in the desolation, the only guidance through the gloom?

The attempt to "ascend the height of this great argument" would lead to paths remote from the purpose of this Essay, the object of which is to show that Hume neither built, nor pretended to build, on any principles peculiar to Locke. Experience Mr. Locke had shown to be the foundation of all our ideas,—it followed from the denial of innate ideas. In experience Mr. Locke included our simple ideas of sensation, such as of colours, sounds, tastes,—the rudiments of intelligence; he included also our more complex ideas of reflection, which imply the exercise of the faculties of the mind, memory, comparison, abstraction, volition; ideas of mental states, and whatever are the phenomena of consciousness. In it was therefore the origin of our idea of causation and of power. But in thus laying down the true chart of the human mind, Locke supplied to Hume, and his coadjutors, the French sceptics, none of the peculiar elements of their dogmatic scepticism*. But he did supply to Bentley,

* No doubt the English deists of the early part of the last century,

Law, Butler, Paley, Hartley, and many others, some of the elements or arguments for their benevolent religious faith. The practice of associating Locke's name with the scepticism of the former, rather than with the eminently religious spirit of the latter, betrays the ignorance and the prejudice of those who indulge in it. It is alike injurious and unjust. Let it be left to those who are aliens by birth and feeling, from the great commonwealth of English sincerity and sense. Let it be repudiated by those who should cherish with gratitude and pride the names and memories of their great chiefs,—of the men who have conquered new

such as Tindal, Collins, and Bolingbroke, sought to shelter themselves under the authority of Locke, whom they held in high esteem. But they pleaded his great name to justify the freedom of their inquiries, and to assert the supremacy of Reason; not pretending nor imagining that Locke's philosophical principles were more peculiarly favourable to their conclusions than those of any other metaphysical school. To these writers must be conceded the merit of being intelligible and practical, of advocating principles which they conceived to be as useful, as rational,—a merit which cannot be conceded, with the utmost stretch of charity, to the writers of transcendental idealism. Descartes, who may be considered as the fountain-head of the modern intuitional school, is, beyond question, far more sceptical, both in the foundations and in the tendency of his philosophy, than Locke. Spinoza began his course by endeavouring to demonstrate, in a geometrical method, the philosophical principles of Descartes. D'Alembert—the best of the writers concerned in the Encyclopédie—in the 'Discours Préliminaire,' has given a splendid and just eulogium of Locke, without intimating or conceiving any connection between his philosophy and either religious or philosophical scepticism. Compare Stewart's Dissertation, pp. 144, 145.

provinces from the domain of ignorance, darkness, and superstition, and secured them for the culture, enjoyment, and improvement of mankind.

But there is another work of Hume's, which enables us to judge of the nature and extent of his scepticism, a work less known, but by no means the least interesting or least elegant,—the 'Dialogues of Natural Religion,'—which, though written as early as 1751, was not published till after his death, which took place in 1776. In acuteness of reasoning, in charm of style, these dialogues have all, and more than all, his characteristic excellence,—the charm, notwithstanding frequent incorrectness, of a graceful ease. Without precision or clearness enough for logic and philosophy, they have the happy turns and sparkling lights that gratify the taste. The speakers are Philo, a materialist of Spinoza's school; Cleanthes, a philosophical theist, on the principles of Natural religion; and Demea, an orthodox Christian, or one who receives the whole scheme of revealed religion, as commonly understood. Demea makes but a poor figure in the conversation, and quits before it is concluded. The weight of the discussion rests upon the first two. "Philo," says Dr. Priestley, "speaks the sentiments of the writer." But Mr. Burton affirms, "It is with Cleanthes the author shows most sympathy, very nearly professing that the doctrine announced by Cleanthes is his own, while it will be found in his correspondence that he admits his having designedly en-

deavoured to make the arguments of that speaker the
most attractive*." This is confirmed by Hume's own
language to Sir Gilbert Elliot of Minto, to whom he
submitted a portion of the manuscript in 1751. " You
would perceive by the sample I have given you, that
I make Cleanthes the hero of the dialogue. Whatever
you can think of to strengthen that side of the argument will be most acceptable to me." The whole
letter is worth attention, unfolding the state of Hume's
mind, and the 'absolute philosophical indifference'
which he flatters himself, not without reason, that he
had reached. But is such indifference peculiarly entitled to the epithet philosophical? Was it the characteristic of the early sages, whose names are like a
trumpet-sound, calling to battle for right and truth?
Are questions relating to Providence and the mind,—
the strength and the weakness of reason,—frivolous,
or to be treated as the playthings of children? Are not
a desire for truth and salutary views, and a desire to
develope the consequences of truths useful to mankind,
equally philosophical? Was Bacon's passion for fruit,
instead of dry leaves, unworthy of a great mind?
Such questions answer themselves. Recurring to the
dialogues, the truth is that Philo and Cleanthes come
in the end nearly to an agreement; and the last chapter, in which they do so, abounds in just sentiments
beautifully expressed, sentiments which can hardly
fail to be read with pleasure and with hearty concur-

* 'Letters to Philosophical Unbelievers:' Priestley's Works,
vol. iv. p. 368, Rutt's edition. Burton's Life of Hume, vol. i. p. 320.

rence by every philosophically religious mind. The
distinction between true religion and religion as it
is commonly found in the world is admirably put.
History and daily life give ample evidence of the unhappy severance of the religious feelings from those
great moral principles and habits, those sterling social
virtues, which, from their connection with the permanent happiness of mankind, the philosopher must ever
regard with chief concern, and associate with the
proper and most acceptable worship of the Deity.
When the orthodox Demea has given vent to the most
extravagant opinions respecting the predominance of
pain and misery in the universe, and departed, unable
to bear the conversation further, Philo addresses Cleanthes in the words, " You are sensible that, notwithstanding the freedom of my conversation and my love
of singular arguments, no one has a deeper sense of
religion impressed on his mind, or pays more profound
adoration to the Divine Being, as he discovers himself
to reason in the inexplicable contrivance and artifice
of Nature. A purpose, an intention, a design strikes
everywhere the most careless, the most stupid thinker;
and no man can be so hardened in absurd systems,
as at all times to reject it."

" The most agreeable reflection which it is possible
for human imagination to suggest," replies Cleanthes,
as the conversation advances, " is that of genuine
theism, which represents us as the workmanship of a
Being perfectly good, wise, and powerful; who created
us for happiness, and who, having implanted in us im-

measurable desires of good, will prolong our existence
to all eternity, and will transfer us into an infinite
variety of scenes, in order to satisfy these desires, and
render our felicity complete and durable. Next to
such a Being himself (if the comparison be allowed),
the happiest lot which we can imagine is that of being
under his guardianship and protection*."

In apology for Hume, we must remember that he
had few encouragements in early life to connect religion with the true honour and perfect happiness of
mankind, with the social graces, with intellectual culture, with active but mild benevolence, and with virtuous self-rule. To him terror appeared its primary
principle; gloom and melancholy, the characteristic of
all devout people. "Among the votaries of religion
(of which number the multifarious fraternity of Christians is but a small part) there seem to be but few—
I will not say how few—who are real believers in his
(the Deity's) benevolence. They call him benevolent
in words, but they do not mean that he is so in reality.
They do not mean that he is benevolent as man is
conceived to be benevolent; they do not mean that he
is benevolent in the only sense in which benevolence
has a meaning. For if they did, they would recognize
that the dictates of religion could be neither more nor
less than the dictates of utility; not a tittle different,
not a tittle less or more. But the case is, that on a
thousand occasions they turn their backs on the principle of utility. They go astray after the strange prin-

* Dialogues of Natural Religion, pp. 228-255.

ciples, its antagonists; sometimes it is the principle of asceticism; sometimes it is the principle of sympathy and antipathy. Accordingly the idea they bear in their minds, on such occasions, is but too often the idea of malevolence, to which idea, stripping it of its own proper name, they bestow the specious appellation of the social motive. Sometimes, in order the better to conceal the cheat, (from their own eyes doubtless, as well as from others,) they set up a phantom of their own, which they call justice, whose dictates are to modify—which, being explained, means to oppose— the dictates of benevolence*."

In England, it is true, there had been writers, not a few, who, before Hume's time, had endeavoured to free religion, natural and revealed, from the reproach of being inimical to philosophical inquiry, to social improvement, to the innocent pleasures and amiable feelings of mankind; not a few, who had endeavoured to associate " Glory to God in the highest," with its scriptural adjuncts, "peace on earth, and goodwill to man." Tillotson had maintained that " the great design of Christianity was the reforming men's natures, and governing their actions, the restraining their appetites and passions, the softening their tempers, and sweeten- ing their humours, and the raising their minds above the interests and follies of this present world to the hope and pursuit of endless blessedness†." Dr. Sa-

---

* See Bentham's 'Principles of Morals and Legislation.' Ben- tham's Works, by Bowring, vol. i. p. 58.

† Birch's Life of Tillotson, p. 551.

muel Clarke* had endeavoured to show that " the practical duties which the Christian religion enjoins are all
such as are most agreeable to our natural notions of
God, and most perfective of the nature and conducive to the happiness and well-being of men." Moral
virtue, he contended, "is the foundation and the
sum, the essence and the life of all true religion; for
the security whereof all positive institution was prin-
cipally designed, for the restoration whereof all revealed religion was ultimately intended; and inconsistent wherewith, or in opposition to which, all doctrines whatsoever, supported by what pretence of reason or authority soever, are as certainly and necessarily
false as God is true." Many divines of the English
church—followers of Arminius and Episcopius—called
Latitudinarians, had, like Fowler, Bishop of Gloucester,
identified religion with true goodness of heart and life;
and no one more earnestly nor more admirably than
the large-minded Joseph Glanvil†, who died comparatively young, but whose writings breathe a spirit, if
not above his age, yet of the highest order of minds.

* Clarke's 'Discourse concerning the unchangeable obligations of
Natural Religion,' etc., p. 113, fifth edition.

† See many admirable passages in his 'Remains,' published in
1681, and his 'Essays,' *passim*. "The great design of religion and the
Gospel is to perfect human nature; and all the acts of worship, which
Christianity binds upon us, tend to our perfection and felicity."
Glanvil was of Oxford, the contemporary of the Cambridge men
mentioned by Burnet (History of his own Time, i. 187), Whichcote,
Cudworth, Wilkins, and Worthington. Why has he been so much
forgotten? Mr. Hallam has done something to revive the impression
of his merits.

Locke had contended for the " reasonableness of Christianity, as delivered in the Scriptures," and given five great reasons for valuing it, which deserve to be deeply graven on the minds of all who desire to be considered rational Christians, and who are grateful for Christian hope. Lady Masham, his friend and disciple, the daughter of Cudworth, had published her tract in reply to the spiritualist John Norris, and to some of the wild and frightful sentiments of Malebranche*. She had placed religion in harmony with practical philosophy, in the regulation of our appetites and passions. She had beautifully contended, in opposition to the ascetic principle, that, " as short-lived flowers, though they ought not to employ the continual care of our whole lives, may yet reasonably enough be found in our gardens, and delight us in their seasons, so the fading things of this life, though not to be fixed on as the ultimate good of eternal beings, yet there is no reason why we may not rejoice in them as the good gifts of God, and find all that delight in them which he has joined with their lawful use." The Honourable Robert Boyle had followed or accompanied in the same path, uniting the most accurate investigation of nature, and the indefatigable pursuit and encouragement of experimental philosophy, with the most

* Such as that " a child (by virtue of its union with the mother) does, whilst in her womb, know and love bodies, consequently therefore is a sinner, and shall be necessarily damned:" mitigated in a note to being eternally deprived of the possession of God. Malebranche, Conversations Chrétiennes, 1685, p. 114. Lady Masham's tract ' On the Love of God' was published anonymously in 1696.

ardent sentiments of devotion. There is also a scarce tract, by Bayes of Tunbridge, ' On the Divine Benevolence, or an attempt to prove that the principal end of the Divine Providence and Government is the Happiness of his Creatures*.' The great Leibnitz had done still more in his ' Theodicy ' to vindicate the wisdom and goodness of the Deity. But such writers have been either unknown or held in little esteem north of the Tweed†. In Scotland, a gloomy and malevolent Calvinism had been the bequest of Knox to his willing followers ;—Knox, a monk and an inquisitor in the Genevan gown. There the Assembly's Catechism fastened its iron band round the head of youth, and formed the bars of a prison-house of thought, beyond which, if the eyes of the poor inmates wandered to view the fair creation without, they were taught instantly to withdraw them with mingled feelings of apprehension and mistrust. In Hume's time, or before it, such men as Bentley, Stillingfleet, and Warburton made the loudest noise in the arena of theological controversy,—men whom neither religion nor philosophy rendered candid, temperate, and patient.

* Of this tract, dated 1731, I possess a copy. The interest of it is diminished to the student by its being merely an answer to a superficial writer, who makes *order*, not happiness, the end of the Deity in creation. It is not a collection of proofs of benevolent design. Paley's chapter on the Goodness of the Deity is far more to the purpose.

† Has not the Principal Campbell, one of the answerers of Hume, the honour of being the first, as he is yet the greatest and best, of the rational critics and moderate theologians whom Scotland has produced?

Captious, petulant, arrogant in their temper and tone, they gave too much reason for the belief that danger to their craft alone inspired their zeal. They had too much of what Glanvil calls the animal religion, too little of the Divine. The Boyle Lectures upon atheism, and the answer to Collins, by the first, though expressly founded on the principles of Locke; the controversial letters of the second, animadverting on those principles, whom Locke laid on his back so gently as not to hurt him; and the addresses to Freethinkers by the last, cannot, by any intellectual superiority, whatever the learning of their authors, compensate for their tone of assumption and bitterness, nor escape the charge of being too plainly deficient in the temper and the taste proper to religion and philosophy.

So many valuable treatises on Natural Theology and the doctrine of a Providence have been written since Hume's time, that it would be quite beyond the limits and purposes of this Essay to attempt a survey of our philosophical and literary wealth on that great topic. But it would be difficult to name a dissertation in English prior to that by the good and learned Dr. Price, which takes up Hume's view of objections and difficulties comparable to it in depth and merit. Dr. Price indeed is not always as logical as a keen disputant wishing for truth on his own side of the question could desire, yet he entrenches himself in many strong and defensible positions. He makes reason tremble on the height to which she rises, in order to survey the vast, the universal scheme, yet he plants his footing on a rock. But while stretching an aching gaze into the infinite expanse, we are compelled to feel that our horizon is still limited.

> " Too, too contracted are these walls of flesh,
>   This vital warmth too cold, these visual orbs,
>   Though inconceivably endow'd, too dim
>   For any passion of the soul, that leads
>   To ecstasy.*."

" Truth," says Cudworth in an admirable passage, " is bigger than our minds, and we are not the same with it, but have a lower participation only of the intellectual nature, and are rather apprehenders than comprehenders thereof. This is indeed one badge of our creaturely state, that we have not a perfectly comprehensive knowledge, or such as is adequate and commensurate to the essences of things ; from whence we ought to be led to this acknowledgment, that there is another perfect mind or understanding Being above us in the universe, from which our imperfect minds were derived, and upon which they do depend." " Nevertheless, because our weak and imperfect minds are lost in the vast immensity and redundancy of the Deity, and overcome with its transcendent light and

---

* A beautiful and refined religious philosophy pervades the poetry of Wordsworth, which shines out nowhere more brightly than in the third and fourth books of the ' Excursion.' That philosophy the mind well seasoned with the theopathetic principles and affections of Hartley's Rule of Life can now best appreciate, and we may hope it is destined to give increasing pleasure as readers of culture multiply.

dazzling brightness, therefore hath it to us an appearance of darkness and incomprehensibility, as the unbounded expansion of light in the clear transparent æther hath to us the apparition of an azure obscurity, which yet is not an absolute thing in itself, but only relative to our sense, and a mere fancy in us *."

What happy effects earlier intercourse with such a mind as Dr. Price's might have produced on Hume's views and feelings, we may judge in part from the account of what passed between them in later days. " Mr. Hume had been so little accustomed to civility from his theological adversaries, that his admiration was naturally excited by the least appearance of it in any of their publications. Dr. Douglas (the late Bishop of Salisbury), Mr. Adams, and Dr. Price were splendid exceptions to this rudeness and bigotry†. Having been opposed by these divines with the candour and respect which were due to his abilities, and which it is shameful should ever be wanting in any controversy, he was desirous of meeting them all together, in order to spend a few hours in familiar conversation with them. Accordingly they all dined by invitation at Mr. Cadell's, in the Strand; and, as might be expected, passed their time in the utmost harmony and good-humour. In a subsequent interview with Mr. Price, when Mr. Hume visited him at his house at Newington Green, he candidly acknowledged that on one point Mr. Price had succeeded in

---

* Cudworth's Intellectual System, p. 639, Birch's edition, 1740.

† Principal Campbell might have been added as another.

convincing him that his arguments were inconclusive; but it does not appear that Mr. Hume, in consequence of this conviction, made any alteration in the subsequent edition of his Essays. It may be added also that in the Dissertation on Miracles, which was intended as an answer to Mr. Hume's arguments against their credibility, Mr. Price had, as he thought, expressed himself improperly, by speaking of the *poor sophistry* of those arguments, and using other language of the same kind. When he sent a copy of his book to Mr. Hume, who was then one of the Under-secretaries of State, he made an apology to him, and promised that nothing of the kind should appear in another edition. He received in consequence a very flattering letter from Mr. Hume, which he regarded more as a matter of civility than as a proof of his own book having wrought any change in the mind of that philosopher. When the work however appeared in a second edition, he fulfilled his promise, and sent him a corrected copy, for which he immediately received an acknowledgment expressive of Mr. Hume's wonder at such scrupulosity in one of Mr. Price's profession*."

The readers who retain, and wish to retain, respect and value for the principles of natural and revealed religion, as received and understood by such men as Newton, Clarke, Leibnitz, and Locke, and who associate transcendental philosophy, not with the forms and expression of it in modern mystics, but with

* Morgan's 'Life of Price,' pp. 16 and 17, as quoted in Monthly Repository of 1815, pp. 580, 581.

those high questions and considerations, susceptible of clear and consistent statement, which affect the practical well-being of man, and the elevation of his moral and intellectual nature, are the only readers likely to be touched and interested by these remarks.

In considering the nature and extent of the scepticism of Hume, it presents itself under two aspects—a religious and a philosophical scepticism; the former throwing clouds of obscurity, difficulty, and doubt over those religious beliefs, even the most simple and rational, which, though not appreciated by the vulgar, the most philosophical minds have ever delighted in; the latter throwing mistrust and scorn over the human faculties themselves. That 'ignorance and blindness are the result of all philosophy,' is a favourite sentiment with Hume. The understanding, according to him, is incompetent to arrive at any substantial or satisfactory truth in morals and religion. Thus we see that those who would prevent mankind from enjoying the waters of life only hope to succeed by poisoning the fountains. They would destroy the very elements of thought. To shut up our books, to close discussion, to amuse ourselves with battledoor and shuttlecock, and descend to the humble level of the animals that crop the food that lies before them, unknowing aught beyond or above,—this is the proper result of Hume's philosophy. But we have seen how little he was consistent with himself.

Before quitting the subject, it is desirable to take a short historical review of the chief discussions which have been given to the world on the subject of causation, and to ascertain, as far as possible, what has been thought and agreed upon respecting it. It has been already intimated, that when Hume is clearest, when he approaches to the principle and statement on which he seems inclined to rest, he does not greatly differ from Locke's Theory of Causation, (so far as Locke can be said to have any theory, and so far as we gather it from his chapter on ' Power,') unless it be by omitting what Locke considered most important. Locke had intimated that we gain our idea of power from two sources, " observation of change in things without, and reflection on what passes in our own minds." Hume declares, " that when one particular species of events has *always*, in all instances, been conjoined with another, we make no longer any scruple to foretell the one upon the appearance of the other, and to employ that reasoning which can alone assure us of any matter of fact or existence. We then call the one object *cause*, and the other *effect*." " It appears, then, that this idea of necessary connection arises *from a number of similar instances*, which occur, of the constant conjunction of these events." Now it seems evident that Hume's " similar instances" is substantially the same with Locke's " *observation of change*." If he adds anything to Locke, it consists in the suggestion of the uniformity, the invariableness, or the perfect similarity, of the sequence.

Dropping all the language about conjunction and connection, or nearly dropping it, Hume has been

K

followed by Brown, in his inquiry into the relation between cause and effect; and by Mr. John Stuart Mill, in his long chapter on Causation. They agree in their view of the uniformity and invariableness of sequence, as constituting the essence or amount of what we know and mean when talking of causation.

The invariable antecedent is by them termed the cause,—the invariable consequent, the effect*.

---

* Mill's Logic, book iii. ch. v. p. 339; and compare Brown's Inquiry, p. 12. It is singular that Mr. Stewart has made no reference in his Dissertation to this work of Brown. Mr. Mill afterwards defines "the cause of a phenomenon to be the antecedent, or the concurrence of antecedents, on which *it* (*i. e.* the phenomenon) is invariably and unconditionally consequent." By unconditional, he means "subject to no other than negative conditions;" or, as he has better expressed it elsewhere, "in the absence of preventing or counteracting causes; an antecedent operating without obstructing conditions." In the headings of the sections, he says, the cause of a phenomenon is "*the assemblage of its conditions;*" and again, the cause is *not the invariable antecedent*, but "the *unconditional* invariable antecedent;" or again, "a cause is the assemblage of phenomena, which occurring, some other phenomenon invariably commences." These variations in the mode of expression seem not very happy, nor is a definite and clear impression left upon the mind.

It is not easy to see why such discussions as those which fill up a large portion of Mr. Mill's volumes, should be introduced into a system of logic. An abridgment of that system, excluding from it the controversial matter, which overlays and obscures it, preserving the definitions and reasonings in concise and simple form, would be useful to students and beginners. It might thus be brought into better and more perceptible harmony with logic, as hitherto received, and considered purely as a science of inference; such as Aristotle, "the master of the sapient throng," and Whately and De Morgan make it. A difference so conflicting as that between Whately, who denies that induction, "so far forth as it is a process of inquiry,"

But this *invariable antecedence* does not satisfy a large, class of metaphysical thinkers as constituting the whole of what we mean by cause. They believe there is something more than this,—not merely sequence, but necessary sequence; and this idea or feeling of necessary connection they consider to be a primitive belief, or ultimate fact of consciousness, a form or law of thought indispensable to all reasoning, and referrible to no ulterior source. At the head of these metaphysicians, among the moderns, perhaps Dr. Reid deserves to be placed, who in his Essays on the intellectual and active powers, discusses at length, and in reply to Hume, the subject of "First Principles of Necessary Truths," and who thus expresses himself:—
"Causation is not an object of sense. The only experience we can have of it is in the consciousness we have of exerting some power in ordering our thoughts and actions. But this experience is surely too narrow a foundation for a general conclusion, that all things that have had, or shall have, a beginning, *must* have a cause." He adds, that it is to be admitted as a first

forms any part of logic; and Mill, who makes it, if not its essence, at least its most important part, shows that philosophers and thinkers have yet much to do in order to understand and approach each other upon the deepest questions; and that there is much to be done, with singleness of aim, in order to bring the highest philosophy and severest logic into harmony with the wants and laws of our intellectual, moral, and religious life. Compare the last sentence of Mill's 6th chapter, book iii., on the Composition of Causes; Whately's Logic, book iv. ch. i.; and De Morgan's Formal Logic, and its most excellent chapter ii., on objects, names, and ideas.

＊ Hamilton's 'Reid,' pp. 452–461. chap. vi. essay 6.

or self-evident principle, for two reasons:—first, the universal consent of mankind; and, secondly, the practice of life being grounded upon it in the most important matters, even in cases where experience leaves it doubtful. After Reid, perhaps Kant may be numbered among the chief thinkers of repute, who adopt a similar view, and who would speak of the idea of causation as "a pure and *à priori* intuition." But are not these merely new phrases of doubtful meaning, by which nothing is gained to reasoning, and something is lost to sense*?

* While this work is passing through the press, a friend has called my attention to an article in the 'Prospective Review' for August, 1853, in which Sir W. Hamilton's philosophy is criticized, and the subject of causality is discussed. In it the following passage occurs: "We never ask for a cause, except to resolve a question of *comparison*,—why *this*, and not *other than this?*" and the function which we demand from it is precisely that of elective determination. Hence, among the assemblage of conditions which are collectively indispensable to a given result, we attach the name "*cause*" distinctively to that *one* which has overset the equilibrium of possibilities, and precipitated the actual fact. Whence this notion of *preferential* agency? To what point does it refer us as the nativity of our causal belief? Can it be denied that, in the exercise of our own will, we are conscious of this very power, of fetching a single fact out of more than a single potentiality? that nowhere else than at this fountain-head of energy *could* this notion be got, requiring access as it does to the occult priorities of action, as well as to its posterior manifestations to the eye? and that only in so far as we interpret Nature by the type thus found, can we recognize there the characteristic element of causality? The will, therefore, we submit, so far from being the solitary exception to a universal rule of necessary causation, is itself the rule which makes all real causation free. Volitional agency is that which the mind originally sees in Nature, as in itself; the opposite term in that dynamic antithesis, on which

Now, were we to admit invariable antecedence and invariable consequence to be a correct and adequate view of what we mean when we talk of causation,— when we turn from the general idea to the particulars, or from the abstract, always more or less obscure, to the concrete, which is always more simple and clear, —when we inquire into the kinds of sequence with which observation and reflection make us acquainted, we may divide these kinds conveniently into two; namely, first, material sequences; and, secondly, mental, or intellectual and spiritual sequences; for by the three last terms I should mean the same phenomena.

the obstructed *nisus* of perception lands us : and never does the inquisitive " whence ?" find repose along the linear ascent of antecedents, till it reaches the only power intrinsically capable of fetching the determinate out of the indeterminate, viz. a *Mind*."

A story is told of a king, who, having had his portrait painted by a fashionable artist, complained that the head was lost in the brilliancy of the flowers by which it was surrounded. So in this article the quantum of needful sense is buried in the excess of metaphor. But the above extract shows a disposition, in quarters where it was not to be expected, to return to the sober English school of thought. Associating the idea of cause with the will or the consciousness of power within, and with election and preference,—terms significant of mental states,—it agrees with Locke in answering in the affirmative the question which Locke puts, when he says, " I thought it worth while to consider here by the way whether the mind doth not receive its idea of active power clearer by reflection on its own operations, than by any external sensation." " The idea of the beginning of motion we have only from reflection on what passes in ourselves, where we find by experience, that *barely by willing it, barely by a thought of the mind*, we can move the parts of our bodies which were before at rest."—Essay on the Understanding, book ii. chap. 21. sect. 4.

With these two different kinds of sequence experience, and experience alone, brings us acquainted, which includes observation of change *without* and reflection on the succession of states *within*. Let us take a very simple case: the water boils when the kettle containing it is placed on the fire, or subjected to the influence of heat: the heat generates steam; and this heat and steam, so essential to our daily domestic comfort, under the name of steam *power*, now performs a most wonderful part in all the *matériel* of our modern civilization. This heat (let chemists make of it what they may, under the name of caloric) is an invariable and uniform, and as we judge, referring it to a law, a necessary antecedent to the desired or expected effects*. By a variety of instances of a like kind it might be shown that an assemblage of material conditions is always conceived of, and believed in, as a *necessary* antecedent to material effects. In arranging the antecedents, so as to bring about these effects, the human will often plays a conspicuous part. But with respect to the grand phenomena and general laws of nature, such as the planetary motions) the course of the seasons, the structure and functions of organized beings, etc.—of these man is only the observer and the registrar.

---

* The classical reader will observe that consequents, results, effects, are terms of Latin origin, signifying the succession of phenomena, *effect* that which is done by an agent. The German language is happy in its term for cause—*Ursache*, originating or first thing; less happy in its term for effect—*Wirkung*, working or operation.

But there is another class of phenomena attributable to mental or volitional antecedents, such as the purpose now fulfilled in this present writing, or the attention given to the requests or commands of a master by the servants of the household and by the members of a family. In every household the arrangements for the day, as well in the established routine as in the variations, depend on the *will* of the governor. The expression of that will leads to its execution ; or it may be silently fulfilled, and a permanent result be attained. Now the social enjoyments—the gratifications of taste, or of a sense of order and beauty—and all the pleasures of amity, depend on the nature and exercise of this will, as modified in each individual by the passions, and by the actively exerted power of reflection and thought. But these mental antecedents and moral consequents are known only by reflection on what passes within : they are a class of antecedents and consequents peculiar to the mind, and perfectly distinct from those which we have called material. Our intellectual, moral, and social or sympathetic pleasures and pains, are made up of such antecedents and consequents, and they differ in character and degree, in proportion as the intellect is developed, and the true social interests are cherished, or morally and religiously pursued. Hence we talk of mental power, meaning the several powers of memory, of imagination, of reflection, of reasoning, of utterance, of volition, affection, and the steady pursuit of chosen ends. But as definition makes not the terms significant of simple ideas of sensation clearer, such as white, black, loud, low, sweet, bitter, and so on, so definition can hardly make the terms significant of certain mental powers and states, known only by consciousness or reflection, clearer, such as memory, will, desire, choice, judgement,—these being the only terms appropriate to the phenomena, interpreted in most cases at once and sufficiently by consciousness, or rather by early and habitual association.

It is of great importance for distinct thinking to keep these two classes of powers distinct, for surely there is a foundation for the distinction, and a use for it, in what we observe and know, both of nature and the human frame or constitution. In observing and laying deep the foundation for this distinction,—in other words, in pointing out the two sources of our idea of power,—it appears to me that Locke has a great advantage over most of those who have discussed the subject after him, but who have not equally kept it in view.

Mr. Mill expressly classes the human will among the *physical* causes; he could hardly say material causes. But where then is the distinction between physical and metaphysical, in the subjects of scientific investigation? The moral sciences, which have special and exclusive relation to the phenomena arising out of, or concerned in, the human will and its functions, and which, according to Mr. Mill, would seem to require a logic of their own, are then reduced to the level of the physical sciences. The phenomena depen-

dent on mental antecedents or conditions, thus become blended with the phenomena confessedly dependent on material conditions, and the old and useful
division of physics and metaphysics is destroyed.   Mr.
Mill's language on the subject of what he calls " permanent causes," or original natural agents ; his decla-
rations against the theory that mind or will is the *sole*
efficient cause of phenomena,—against the theory which
represents efficient causes as capable of being subjects
of human knowledge ; the hints which he has dropped
on the vanity of attempting to arrive at a final or ultimate cause of any phenomena, seem to be largely
affected by his determination to put this distinction
out of sight.   He considers certain material objects of
the universe, such as the planetary bodies and their
motions, permanent causes which cannot be referred
to any higher cause.   "We can give no account," he
says, "of the origin of the permanent causes themselves." "Why these particular natural *agents* existed
originally, and no others, or why they are commingled
in such and such proportions, and distributed in such
and such a manner, is a question we cannot answer."
He calls the opinion or supposition, that all phenomena are produced by the *will* of some sentient Being,
an original Fetichism, and gives a brief history of
what he considers to be " *the original instinctive philosophy of mankind*[*]."

    " *Because among the infinite variety of the pheno-
mena of nature there is one, namely, a particular mode*

[*] Mill's Logic, vol. i. pp. 363, 365, third edit.

*of action of certain nerves, which has for its cause, and
as we are now supposing for its efficient cause, a state
of our mind, and because this is the only efficient cause
of which we are conscious, being the only one of which,
in the nature of the case, we can be conscious, since it
is the only one which exists within ourselves, does this
justify us in concluding that all other phenomena must
have the same kind of efficient cause with that one eminently special, narrow, and peculiarly human or animal
phenomenon* ?"*

Now the stress of Mr. Mill's argument, the vigour
of his answer to those who contend that "volition is
the *sole* efficient cause of all phenomena," seems to
depend very much on the word *all*. But, even admitting that matter is good for some results, that the
permanent causes which he allows of have been from
eternity, or for an indefinite period of time equivalent
to it, are they the sole causes beyond which the mind
cannot go, nor legitimately desire to go? are these
adequate to explain *all* the phenomena? "Volitions
are not known," he says, "to produce anything *directly*, except nervous action, for the will influences
the muscles only through the nerves." Is not this
Hume's old argument from anatomy, introduced to obscure the subject of voluntary agency and mental phenomena? Scarcely anything is more obscure, or less
known and thought of, than what is here called *nervous action*. Be it what it may, be it the *direct* product of volition, still the indirect or ultimate products

* Mill's Logic, vol. i. p: 371, third edit.

are far more important; nay the only products of any importance; nervous action being a very insignificant and subordinate part of the phenomena dependent for existence upon the human *will*. The pleasures and pains, the happiness or misery of inappreciable multitudes for long periods of time, have been and may continue to be affected by the states of an individual *will*, commingled with other assisting conditions. All the interests of our intellectual, moral, and social being are wrapped up, so to speak, in its character and agency. When we look out upon the universe, or turn reflection inward upon ourselves, we feel that material forms, existences, and laws are of no moment or interest, but for the results to animated beings, and for the connected phenomena. It is the subordination of these forms to the various gradations of animated creatures, it is the provision made for the sustenance and succession of the various species, each in their element, each subservient to a purpose beyond itself or conducive to a higher and more interesting result than its individual life, each part of a vast series of phenomena, it is this which demands an originating and presiding intelligent Mind. In short, it is the presence of order and the recognition of law, the manifest and unquestionable adjustment of means to ends, which affects the intellect with its character of resistless power, and the heart, in its purest and happiest moods, at once with a sense of its subjection and dependence, and with an impression of all-pervading rectitude and benevolence.

If we define philosophy to be the *study of causes*,
—and what better can be suggested? for the knowledge of causes has of all knowledge the best title to
be considered emphatically power; and, as Mr. Mill
finely observes, "if we could determine what causes
are correctly assigned to what effects, and what effects
to what causes, we should be virtually acquainted with
the whole course of nature*,"—can we be satisfied
to stop in our search at certain material forms and
motions as the "permanent causes" sufficient for all
effects? Are we precluded from seeking a final or ultimate cause, a first mover, more adequate to account
for all the phenomena and results to which these material forms and motions are subservient, such as the
life of organized beings, perception and thought, and
all the high developments of intellectual and spiritual
life? Can *matter*, when we examine it, be regarded
properly as an agent at all? and even if material
causes be admitted as sufficient antecedents and the
only known antecedents for some material consequents,
the important question still remains, Are there not
still some phenomena referrible only to mind—and a
mind as superior to the human as the heavens are superior to a house? In the acknowledgment of such
a mind, have we not the only adequate Cause for and
explanation of the most impressive phenomena with
which we are concerned? That is the question,
unless I misconceive it, on which what is called the
à posteriori argument for the being of the Deity rests;

* Mill's Logic, vol. i. p. 381, third edit.

and whether we argue from evidence of design and the adjustment of means to an end in nature, or, with Locke, "from the existence of knowledge in ourselves to some knowing being from eternity," the argument is still *à posteriori*, from effect to cause. It is a question which Mr. Mill has not directly touched; nor is it to be lightly assumed that he would answer it in the negative. The argument, as carried out by Paley—its most popular if not its most able advocate—may not be perfectly nor equally satisfactory to all minds. But from Aristotle to Newton it has been the one great resting-place or stand-point of the profoundest thinkers and investigators of nature; and even Hume, as we have seen, was disposed, in later and better days, to yield to the force of the impression. Mr. Mill has referred to Reid, among other comparatively recent writers, as the one *religious metaphysician* whose thoughts and language on the reciprocal action of mind and matter deserved his serious consideration. But in the letters of Sir Isaac Newton to Bentley, in certain portions of Cudworth, Clarke, Locke, and Hartley, in the Theodicy of Leibnitz, which is full of profound and beautiful thought, and in the notes to Price's Dissertations, may be found considerations on the respective powers of matter and mind, touching the nature and province of each, the laws of each, and the phenomena attributable to the one and to the other, far more worthy of the most deliberate and careful attention. These great writers have maintained, with the greatest show of reason, that, be the laws of thought what they may, and howsoever the knowledge of them is arrived at,—be it a knowledge given *à priori*, or learnt by experience,—the recognition of, the highest law ever involves the notion and existence of a supreme, intelligent, percipient, and active Lawgiver or Lawmaker; and let us remember that, without belief in the existence of such a being, we have no longer the benefit of the *religious sanction* for any theory of morals which we may be disposed to form,—a sanction of which even Bentham allowed the great importance. We have no longer an object for those feelings of veneration, nor a foundation for those habits of obedience and submission, and those pure and exalting hopes and aspirations which, however we may trifle with them in hours of ease and speculation, are in life's sore trials the only fountains of refreshment, and without which all the uses and enjoyments of the world become "weary, stale, flat, and unprofitable."

STEWART ON HUME.

The importance which has been attached, and may continue to be attached, in the history of modern metaphysics, to what has been called Hume's Theory of Causation, justifies our attention to it, and this endeavour to understand and explain it. The assertion that his scepticism, to whatever it amounted, is built on the principles of Locke, if not confuted, has been shown at least to require much examination and confirmation before it is credited; and the inquiry, which the reader may be supposed to have made, will prepare him for estimating the justice of some of Mr. Stewart's comments on the sceptic and his extravagant praises of his countryman, comments which have been the chief incitement to the foregoing critical and historical remarks.

To the student and interpreter of nature, the lover of exact science and practical knowledge, there must ever be something trifling in the criticism of a criticism. Idle indeed are the strifes of words, which fill the pages of dissertational metaphysicians, who give us too much of noise without progress, dust without fruit, the whirl and rattle of machinery without the production of any article of value. But so little careful study is bestowed on metaphysical subjects, and so much authority is attributed to a certain class and school of writers, that it can hardly fail to be instructive and useful if I exhibit somewhat in detail the statements to which just exception may be taken in Mr. Stewart's dissertation, not to say the unhappy prejudices and serious errors which he has contrived to heap together within the compass of a few pages, when commenting on Hume and Locke.

First, he observes that "Hume has very great merit in separating entirely his speculations concerning the philosophy of the mind from all physiological hypotheses about the nature of the union between soul and body." It is added, "His works are perfectly free from those gratuitous and wild conjectures, which a few years afterwards were given to the world with so much confidence by Hartley and Bonnet, and in this his example has been of infinite use to his successors in this northern part of the island. I know of no part of Europe where such systems as those of Hartley and Bonnet have been so uniformly treated *with the contempt they deserve* as in Scotland."

The contempt of which Mr. Stewart speaks betrays the narrow and prejudiced character of his own speculations and understanding. He would sacrifice the reputation and estimation of one of the greatest and best of Christian philosophers, the intimate friend and fellow-labourer of Drs. Law, Butler, Warburton, and Jortin, to enhance the merit or screen the ill of the most notorious sceptic of his own country. Hartley was an Englishman. The angelic sweetness of his countenance is a strong recommendation of whatever he thought and believed. Who can look at the engraving of it without feeling it an argument in favour of his religious and amiable philosophy, presenting as it does a singular combination of feminine purity and grace with manly intellectual power*? Heaven is reflected in its soft and ingenuous, yet bright and beaming intellectual expression. Bonnet was a Frenchman. His writings have attracted very little attention in England. It does not appear that there was much ground for classing his speculations with those of Hartley. But to mention the views of such men, and especially of Hartley, in any connection with contempt,

---

* Compare a passage on it in Wakefield's Memoirs.

redounds to the disgrace of a writer who fosters by
such means the most unhappy prejudices in weak
minds,—minds ever too ready to receive them, and
to assimilate their temper to the poison*.

Dr. Hartley's great work, the *Observations* on Man,
was not published till the year 1749. His theory of
vibrations, the nicety and difficulty of which has
blinded Mr. Stewart and many others to the rest of
his system, may or may not be the nearest approach
that has been made to an explanation of the undoubted connection that exists, and which physiological inquiry more and more exhibits and illustrates,
between the peculiar structure of the physical frame
and the developments of intellectual and moral character. It is not my purpose to defend it, if I even
understand it. As its author observed, it is "novel,
intricate, extensive," and remote, therefore, from common apprehension. But it is sufficient to know that
it originated in a suggestion of Sir Isaac Newton, at
the end of his 'Principia' and 'Optics;' that it was
aided by the patient study of the writings of Boer-
haave; that it is carried out with a refinement and
consistency, which only a logical understanding can
in the slightest degree appreciate; that it bears a
near relation to what Descartes and Leibnitz have
advanced concerning animal motion, and that it is in-

---

* If we may trust the article on Bonnet in the 'Dictionnaire des
Sciences Philosophiques,' one of his two great principles was "that
ideas can only be studied in the fibres, which are the organs of
them." This could not be said of Hartley with any justice.

timately connected with another theory—that of association—to the vast importance of which the whole philosophic world, Mr. Stewart included, has been compelled to pay tribute of homage and respect, and which Laplace pronounces the sum of what has yet been done in the science of the mind: it is sufficient to know this, to save it and its author from contempt, if not to attract to both our careful and profound attention. Dr. Priestley's estimate of it, in the very valuable introductory Essays to his edition of a part of Hartley, appears candid and judicious. With what ardour would the Doctor have seized his pen to vindicate the fair fame of the philosopher, whom he considered the Newton of the Intellectual world, from the scorn and the aspersions of these new dilettanti of the north! Mr. Stewart himself admits there is a connection and dependence subsisting between the mind and body, a mutual action and reaction of undoubted constancy and importance. He knew that Descartes and Malebranche dwell upon it at great length; and that Leibnitz had his pre-established harmony between mind and matter. Why then should Hartley and Bonnet be singled out for contempt, in their endeavours to determine the nature and character of the union more nicely and exactly? It seems to be agreed by all physiologists and anatomists that the nerves are the conductors of pleasure and pain to certain nervous centres in the brain. Whatever truth there be, if any, in phrenology, in the phenomena of mesmerism, and of somnambulism,

and what is now called electro-biology,—whatever be
known of the philosophy of sleep and dreams,—
whatever be the physical conditions of the brain preceding and 'accompanying a large and peculiar class
of feelings—involuntary and automatic sympathies
and antipathies, known to every one's consciousness
and experience,—all, that can be considered true or
known upon these and kindred subjects of inquiry,
harmonizes sufficiently well with Hartley's theory,
under which he has introduced the names of vibrations and vibratiuncles for want of other terms, guard-
ing himself against being interpreted with too close
analogy to the comparatively coarse vibrations of visible and tangible strings, and speaking of "an infi-
nitesimal elementary body, intermediate between the
soul and gross body, as no improbable supposition*."
We have now works professing to show how intellectual and moral qualities are hereditary and transmis-
sible. Physicians by profession, who are also metaphysicians, and have leisure and taste for the higher
sciences, as they have peculiar opportunities for observing the functions of nature in the physical frame,
and for tracing the peculiarities of intellectual and
moral development, in connection with those of physical temperament and organic structure, so they give
us from time to time new views and proofs of the
nature of this connection and dependence. Of this
Sir Henry Holland's medical notes and reflections
supply abundant testimony; and Dr. William Car-

* Prop. v. cor. 4, and Prop. xxi. cor. 3.

penter, in his 'Human Physiology,' has given very full and instructive evidence to show how much the intellectual and emotional attributes of our nature are connected with or dependent on peculiar conditions of the brain.

In these matters we are in danger from opposite sources, the Scylla and Charybdis of philosophical inquirers;—on the one hand, of too hasty generalizations from imperfect observation, and on the other, of rejecting phenomena worthy of careful record, because not easily reconcilable with our favourite theories or habitual modes of thought.

Of the pernicious effect of Mr. Stewart's prejudices against Hartley, a striking proof is found in the Life of the late Francis Horner. Recording a conversation with Richard Sharp, in one of the literary parties of London, Horner says of him, " He has paid much attention to metaphysics also, and appears to me to praise the best books, with the exception of Hartley, whom both he and Mackintosh admire extremely, though in Scotland we are prohibited from reading him *by the contempt with which he is spoken of*[*]." The prohibition has evidently extended from Scotland into Germany and France, whence, owing to the cheap translation of foreign works, and the interests of booksellers, many, in this commercial age of literature, are in danger of receiving most erroneous impressions of English literature and philosophy[†]. Thus the article

* Life of Francis Horner, vol. i. p. 240.
† See the remarks on F. Schlegel, in Stewart's ' Dissertations

on Hartley occupies but two pages in the 'Diction-naire des Sciences Philosophiques,' a work with which the authors have taken worthy pains, valuable, and in-deed now indispensable, to the metaphysical inquirer. Not a word is said in it about the theory of asso-ciation, afterwards adopted and illustrated by Brown and Alison and Mill; nor is a hint given of the ad-mirable rule of life, the most complete and beautiful of all the systems of moral philosophy yet in being.

Appended to a pleasing account of some members of the family of Hartley, of Bath, by the Rev. Richard Warner, there is an anecdote worth repeating in this connection. Speaking of his friend David Hartley, the son, an eminent member of Parliament, in the latter half of the eighteenth century, Mr. Warner says of him, "He inherited the placid temperament of his great and good father, the first, perhaps, of our En-glish metaphysicians;—the same clear analytical intel-lect; the same devotion to the pure and single pursuit of truth; the same simplicity and ingenuousness of general character*."

and Philosophy,' p. 214. F. C. Schlosser, in his 'History of the Eighteenth Century, with Reference to Mental Cultivation,' makes Locke an antisupernaturalist! and even asserts that Wollaston, in his 'Religion of Nature,' never mentions, at the end of his book, a future state of rewards and punishments! Could he have read the book?

* He then adds, "The countenance of the celebrated Dr. Hartley beamed with all the lights of his luminous and virtuous mind. Shackleton painted a very correct likeness of him, which was en-graved, and prefixed to his son's quarto edition of his father's great work. David Hartley presented me with a proof impression of the

In the same volume by Mr. Warner are various reminiscences of his friend Parr, who sympathized in
his metaphysical predilections, and to whom we are in
a great measure indebted for the preservation of Dr.
Hartley's Latin tract, modestly entitled 'Conjecturæ
quædam de Sensu, Motu, et Idearum Generatione,'
reprinted, without date, among the Metaphysical
Tracts of English Philosophers of the eighteenth century*.

print. This engraving was once the occasion of some embarrassment
to me. A large party were assembled to breakfast with me, at my
house near Bath. Some branches of the late Earl of Selkirk's family
were among the company. They had brought with them a very
prepossessing young lady from Scotland, whose name, though of
course announced, I had either not heard or had forgotten. She sat
beside me at breakfast. Opposite to us were three portraits; she
looked attentively at them for a few moments, and said, 'Pray,
Mr. W., whose portraits are those to the left hand? The right
hand one I know well, but the central, and that next to it, are new
to me.' 'Oh! the middle one is a print of my friend David Hartley; and that to the right, a print of his great and good father, Dr.
Hartley, author of the well-known Observations on Man, his frame,
his duty, and expectations; one of the most sensible, rational, and
satisfactory metaphysical writers, in my opinion, that ever lived.
By the bye, I have a little quarrel with your Scotch philosophers:
they do not, I think, treat our metaphysicians, Locke, Clarke, and
Hartley, with the respect they deserve. Indeed I am quite hurt that
Dugald Stewart should have spoken so lightly of Dr. Hartley, as he
does, in his admirable Philosophy of the Human Mind.' The excellent girl coloured, and replied, 'I am sure my father would be very
sorry to know that he had written anything which gave Mr. Warner
pain!' She was the daughter of the Scotch Professor."

* This precious volume of Tracts was prepared for the press by
Dr. Parr, and afterwards, as the advertisement informs us, completed
for publication by the assistance of Clement T. Swanston, Esq., of
the Chancery bar. A note in reference to the tract of Hartley,

The present remarks in defence of Hartley may be
fitly closed by a quotation from the second disserta-

with a statement of Dr. Parr's concerning it, occurs in Mr. Stewart's
Dissertation, which cannot be suffered to pass without notice.
"In a letter which I received from Dr. Parr," says Mr. Stewart,
"he mentions a treatise of Dr. Hartley's, which appeared about a
year before the publication of his great work, to which it was meant
by the author to serve as a precursor. Of this rare treatise I had
never before heard. 'You will be astonished to hear,' says Dr. Parr,
' that in this book, instead of the doctrine of necessity, Hartley openly
declares for the indifferency of the will, as maintained by Archbishop
King.' We are told by Dr. Hartley himself, that his notions upon
necessity grew upon him while he was writing his Observations upon
Man, but it is curious (as Dr. Parr remarks) that in the course of a
year his opinions upon so very essential a point should have undergone a complete change." (Stewart's Dissertation, p. 171.) Dr.
Parr's remark does not quite amount to Mr. Stewart's interpretation of it; but I believe the whole passage is without foundation,
and that the truly candid and kind-hearted Parr was for once mistaken. Hartley was employed eighteen years upon his work, and
his opinions were not likely to change suddenly and without deep
thought upon such a subject. The Latin tract is a short but excellent abstract of the great work; and of many of the most interesting
passages, particularly of historical character, it is strictly a translation. I have not found the phrase "*liberum arbitrium*" in it. In
the 'Scholium Generale,' where Hartley sums up the uses of the
doctrine of vibrations and association in his own beautiful spirit,
nothing is said about free-will or necessity.

In this volume of tracts there is an excellent anonymous Essay
(dated 1747, dedicated to the students of the two Universities,) on
the origin of the Human Appetites and Affections, showing how
each arises from association. The editors do not appear to have known
of a second edition of the Essay in 1758, carefully revised, and with
many additions. Of this second edition I obtained a copy, formerly
belonging to the late Walter Wilson, Esq., of Bath. Who was the
author? Could it have been the modest Gay, the friend of Dr. Law,
and author of the Dissertation, also anonymous, prefixed to the Dissertation on the Origin of Evil?

tion of the 'Encyclopædia Britannica,' by Sir James
Mackintosh, which affords an agreeable contrast in its
estimate of his merits, to the hostile language and
contemptuous sneers of Mr. Stewart. "His (Hartley's) style is entitled to no praise but that of clearness, and a simplicity of diction through which is visible a singular simplicity of mind. (*What higher praise
does the pure and philosophic mind desire?*) No book
perhaps exists which, with so few of the common al-
lurements, comes at last so much to please, by the
picture it presents of the writer's character,—a character which kept him pure from the pursuit, often
from the consciousness of novelty, and rendered him
a discoverer in spite of his own modesty. (*It might
be added, by the unsurpassed sublimity and beauty of
the views which it gives of man, his frame, his duty,
and expectations.*) In those singular passages, in
which, amidst the profound internal tranquillity of all
the European nations, he foretells approaching convulsions, to be followed by the overthrow of states and
churches, his quiet and gentle spirit, elsewhere almost
ready to inculcate passive obedience for the sake of
peace, is supported under its awful forebodings by
the hope of that general progress in virtue and happiness which he saw through the preparatory confusion.
A meek piety, inclining towards mysticism, and sometimes indulging in visions which borrow a lustre from
his fervid benevolence, was beautifully, and perhaps
singularly, blended in him with zeal for the most unbounded freedom of inquiry, flowing both from his

own conscientious belief and his unmingled love of truth. Whoever can so far subdue his repugnance to petty or secondary faults as to bestow a careful perusal on the work, must be unfortunate, if he does not see, feel, and own, that the writer was a great philosopher and a good man*."

2. Again, Mr. Stewart goes on to praise Hume's juvenile speculations, for having contributed to forward the progress of our national literature, containing the germs of Lord Kames's historical law Tracts, and Elements of Criticism; and this is followed by a very high estimate of Hume's Treatise, as attended with another important effect in Scotland. "He had cultivated the art of writing with much greater success than any of his predecessors, and had formed his taste on the best models of English composition. The influence of his example appears to have been great and general; and was in no instance more remarkable than in the style of his principal antagonists, all of whom, in studying his system, have caught in no inconsiderable degree the purity, polish, and precision of his diction. Nobody, I believe, will deny that Locke himself, considered as an English writer, is far surpassed, not only by Hume, but by Reid, Campbell, Gerard, and Beattie; and of this fact it will not be easy to find a more satisfactory explanation, than in the critical eye with which they were led to canvass a work, *equally distinguished by the depth of its reason-*

* Dissertation Second, 'Encyclopædia Britannica,' Seventh edition, p. 365.

*ings, and by the attractive form in which they are ex-
hibited."* And this is said of the Treatise of Human
Nature ; than which, especially in the earlier portions,
scarcely any writing can be less pure or precise—more
full of careless repetitions and tautology, where an
argument is often called an *affair* or a *circumstance ;*
where pronouns are continually used without a definite antecedent, and where no useful aim or steady
connection of parts can be traced ; a work with
which the author himself felt justly dissatisfied, and
which he deeply regretted a few years after the publication *.

Mr. Hume's taste was formed far more upon the
model of the French than English writers.   His well-
known criticisms upon the best and greatest of them
in his History speak ill for his judgement, even in
later days.   It does not appear that he had read so
as to appreciate Hobbes and Bacon, whose condensed
strength furnishes perhaps the best model for good
philosophical writing ; and the shades of Shakspeare

---

* I see nothing querulous nor peevish, as Mr. Stewart intimates,
in Hume's remonstrances against being judged by a work upon
which he himself pronounced sentence of condemnation.   It seems
like a wilful perverseness in such writers as Dr. Reid and Mr. Stewart, notwithstanding such condemnation, to attach an importance to
the treatise, which neither intrinsic merits, especially when compared with the essays designed to supersede it, nor its real influence
on the public mind and on the direction of philosophic inquiry, can
ever justify.   The Essays have been frequently reprinted, and constantly admired.   The treatise, I believe, was never called for a
second time : copies of the first and only edition may now be easily
obtained.

and Spenser and Milton have only to arise in their Elysian beauty, to win for them an admiration and a love which the cold Scotchman knew not how to feel.

To turn from Hume's Treatise to the pages of Locke, is like passing from the corrupt air of an over-heated apartment, where one can neither breathe freely nor see distinctly, into the open canopy of heaven, where the atmosphere is fresh and the objects are steady, and where we can hold again that converse with Nature by which, while the senses are gratified, the heart also is improved. The modesty and sweetness of Locke's prefatory matter, his candid account of the origin of the Essay, and submissive appeal to the judgement of the thoughtful and truth-seeking reader, partake scarcely less of the spirit of a saint than the philosopher; and were we making a volume of elegant extracts, we could select from Locke passages far superior to anything which could be found in Hume, distinguished as well for elegance of expression and play of imagination, as for that depth and beauty of religious and moral sentiment, that truth which is the soul's lasting aliment, without which all the rest is vapour. The sweet feeling of Locke is beautifully illustrated by the letters to Sir Isaac Newton, given in Lord King's Life, which brought the great Newton almost at his feet. The annals of philosophy and literature present scarcely any more affecting proof of elevation of sentiment and delicacy of consideration and taste. Whatever may be the speculative merits or defects of Locke's philosophy, now

commonly and somewhat scornfully termed "sensational" (by the French, "*sensualiste*"), its practical
effects upon the mind and temper, as illustrated in his
own life and that of Hartley, to say nothing of many
humbler followers, have been of rare and incomparable order. We see that veneration and hope, a serene
patience, a pure and expansive benevolence, a patriotism unspotted by the smallest taint of venality or any
meaner thought, were its delicious fruits; while the
results of the cold scepticism of Hume are chiefly
manifest in the absence of any glowing admiration for
the great or good, the beautiful or the true, in nature
and in life, in Providence and in man. The deceitful,
narrow-minded, and profligate Stuarts were the heroes
of his historical defence and panegyric: and while he
aimed to seat himself as president in the chair of philosophy, to give a new direction to inquiry, and to
become the arbiter of questions which had divided
Descartes and Gassendi, Hobbes and Malebranche,
Leibnitz and Locke, Clarke and Spinoza, he would
have struck from the mind and from the heart every
sentiment and hope that lifts man above the brutes,
attaches him to the eternal and invisible, and bids
him feel, with our old Daniel, that—

> "Unless above himself he can erect himself,
> How poor a thing is man!"

But mere criticisms on style, however desirable in
works on rhetoric, are of little consequence in histories
of philosophy; nor should I notice these things, but
as illustrations of Mr. Stewart's peculiar and unhappy

national partialities. Even the favourable notice of Addison, found in Hume's later Essays, a notice which Mr. Stewart somewhere quotes, is rather unfortunate for Hume's careful discrimination; for in saying that Addison perhaps will be read with pleasure when Locke shall be entirely forgotten, he himself forgot, or had not observed, that Addison's pages are full of reverential testimony to the merit and influence of that great and good philosopher, from whom, as well as from the many writers of the time who partook of his spirit and sympathized in his views, Addison derived that cheerful, practical wisdom, that happy combination of genial moral sense with hopeful and grateful piety, which form the best antidote, by their own natural recommendations, to the dark and desolating scepticism, whose empire, in his early days, and in his unfortunate treatise, Hume was chiefly employed in maintaining*.

3. Passing over what Mr. Stewart says of the strong leaning of Hume to the idealism of Malebranche and of Berkeley, and of his carrying the sceptical mode of reasoning further than any other modern philosopher with the single exception of Bayle, we come to the remarkable assertion that,—

---

* "Locke is an author whom I observe you frequently quote," says a correspondent in one of the 'Spectators.' The Nos. 62, on Mixed Wit, 64, on the Succession of Ideas, the papers on Instinct, on the Value of the Soul, on the Imagination, and on Immortality, are all in harmony with Locke, and bear witness to his influence. It was delightful to hear Mr. Thackeray's cordial appreciation and heartfelt praise of Addison, in his recent lectures on the wits of Queen Anne's time.

"In the form in which the spirit of sceptical argument appears in Mr. Hume's treatise, its mischievous tendency has been more than compensated by the importance of those results for which it has prepared the way. The principles which he assumes were sanctioned in common by Gassendi, by Descartes, and by Locke; and from these, in most instances, he reasons with great logical accuracy and force. Perhaps indeed it may be questioned if the errors which he adopted from his predecessors would not have kept their ground till this day, had not his sagacity displayed so clearly the consequences which they necessarily involve. It is in this sense that we must understand a compliment paid to him by the *ablest of his adversaries*," (meaning Dr. Reid, as the foot-note shows,) "when he says, 'that Mr. Hume's premises often do more than atone for his conclusions.'"

If so, these premises, we presume, could not be the errors which he adopted from his predecessors; but in truth the whole passage is an evidence of that indistinctness which is the bane of such dissertational metaphysics as those which fill Mr. Stewart's pages. What the principles alluded to were, sanctioned in common by writers whom we know to have been warmly opposed to one another on many important points; what the errors, premises, and conclusions were, about which the author says so little, because the reader is supposed to know so much, it is impossible to guess, with any confidence of being right; but it seems obvious that such remarks, with others on which some further comment will be offered, are idly designed to save the reputation of Scotch philosophy from the reproach brought on it by the most heretical and sceptical of the class, at the expense and with the sacrifice of the greatest and most honoured names of other schools. Gassendi and Locke are to be immolated to appease the manes of Hume. Accordingly Mr. Stewart, becoming bolder as he advances, goes on to say, " that we are indebted to Hume for the most powerful antidotes we possess against some of the most poisonous errors of modern philosophy. The argument stated by Hume, in his Essay on the ' Idea of Necessary Connection,' forms a more valuable accession to metaphysical science than the elaborate refutation of Spinozism by Bayle, as it lays the axe to the very root from which Spinozism springs." We are also informed that " all well-educated persons may be presumed to have acquired that general acquaintance with Mr. Hume's theory of causation," which Stewart has supposed his readers to possess ; and that in his opinion, " it will now be acknowledged by every competent judge that Mr. Hume's objections to all the pretended demonstrations produced by Mr. Hobbes, Dr. Clarke, and Mr. Locke, for the necessity of a cause to every new existence, are conclusive and unanswerable. To expose the futility of their reasonings on this subject was an important step made by Hume, who rendered an essential service to true philosophy, by thus pointing out indirectly to his successors the only solid ground on which that principle rests,—the principle, namely, 'that everything which begins to exist must have a cause.' It is to this argument of Hume's (*quære*, what argument? for none has been stated), according to Kant's own acknowledgment, that we owe the Critique of Pure Reason; and to this we are also indebted for the far more luminous refutations of scepticism by *Mr. Hume's own countrymen.*"

Thus we come round to the laudation of the Scotch triumvirate here intended,—Messrs. Reid, Beattie, and Oswald,—whose glory is but a reflection of that of Hume, their *discoveries* being a consequence of attention to his directions or his hints.

No doubt the reader has already formed an opinion of the extent to which Mr. Hume is entitled to the praise, the gratitude, and the homage which Mr. Stewart has offered to his memory. But if he ask himself what clearer conception he has gained of knowledge and probability, and of cause and effect, from the perusal of Hume's sections* on these topics, he will probably be at a loss for a reply. There is certainly one kind of philosophical relation, in addition to the four which Mr. Hume pronounces the only objects of knowledge and certainty, which it would have been desirable to take into account, that is, the relation between language and thought, between words and the objects or ideas suggested by them, and especially the relation between reasoning and definition.

Mr. Stewart, following closely in the steps of Dr.

* Book i. part iii., Treatise of Human Nature.

Reid*, greatly applauds Hume's objections to what he calls the *pretended* demonstrations by Hobbes, and Clarke, and Locke, of the maxim that every beginning of existence must have a cause of existence, and he asserts that every competent judge must admit the objections to be conclusive. It happens however that there are in Hume no distinct references to the places where the demonstrations are to be found.   Nor have Dr. Reid and Mr. Stewart taken pains to verify them, and supply the deficiency. It is possible that Hume had some particular passages of these authors in view, trusting to his memory to represent their language and reasoning with sufficient correctness for his purpose ; but if he had, it is now very difficult to trace them. Had Hume, then quite a tyro in these matters, treated the authors in question with due respect, or been earnest in the establishment of any useful truth which they had missed, he would have taken suitable pains by careful reference to induce his readers to consult their pages. I more than suspect that what Hume loosely calls their *demonstrations* are nothing more than incidental argumentative considerations, to which they attached no importance, wherever found, and by no means professed attempts to demonstrate rigidly a proposition which they were all three disposed to assume, and which they supposed their readers would willingly concede.

Thus in the first sentence of the second chapter

* See Reid's 'Intellectual Powers,' (Essay VI. c. 6.)—Hamilton's 'Reid,' p. 455.

of the 'Leviathan,' on Imagination, Hobbes assumes it as an axiom "that no thing can change ,itself;" and again, in his work on Liberty and Necessity, he says, "I conceive that nothing taketh beginning from *itself*, but from the *action* of some other immediate *agent*, without itself*." Again, he says, "It is peculiar to the nature of men to be inquisitive into the causes of the events they see, some more, some less; and secondly, upon the sight of anything that hath a beginning, to think also it had a cause, which determined the same to begin, then when it did, rather than sooner or later."

It is not probable that, at the time when Hume wrote his Treatise, he had duly read the works of Hobbes. There is so much deep thought, such keen insight into nature and human nature, in the Computatio or Logic, in the Philosophy of Body and Accident, in the controversy with Bramhall, and in his still more known treatises; there is so much discri-

---

* Molesworth's 'Hobbes,' vol. iii. p. 274. A passage near this (p. 276), intimating "that a man cannot imagine anything to begin without a cause," may be one that Hume had in his mind; but if so, he has not represented Hobbes correctly. The admirer of Hobbes, the first writer of sterling English, such as we now use it or ought to use it, however familiar with early editions, must feel greatly indebted to Sir William Molesworth for the excellent index forming the eleventh volume of the collected English works. Under the word "Cause" will be found a masterly view of almost all that has been suggested since on the subject. He defines science or philosophy to consist "in the *knowledge of the causes of all things*, so far forth as it may be attained" (Logic, vol. i. p. 68): I had not observed this when writing the sentences which the reader may remember, *supra*, p. 140.

minating remark on those difficult metaphysical topics, which Hume undertook thus early to handle,—such as cause and effect, knowledge and power, space and time, liberty and law, imagination, action, and passion,—that the philosophical Quixote, had he known them, would have paused longer, and been deterred by conscious weakness, before he ventured into the arena of dispute without any weapons taken from the armoury of the great Leviathan. Passages like the following deserved his deep attention:—" Curiosity, or love of the knowledge of causes, draws a man from consideration of the effect to seek the cause, and again the cause of that cause ; till of necessity he must come to this thought at last, that there is some cause, whereof there is no former cause, but is eternal; which is it men call God. *So that it is impossible to make any profound inquiry into natural causes, without being inclined thereby to believe there is one God eternal;* though they cannot have any idea of him (*i. e. image*, as afterwards explained) in their mind answerable to his nature."

" He that, from any effect he seeth come to pass, should reason to the next and immediate cause thereof, and from thence to the cause of that cause, and plunge himself profoundly into the pursuit of causes, shall at last come to this, that there must be, as even the heathen philosophers confessed, *one first mover, that is, a first and an eternal cause of all things*, which is that which men mean by the name of God ; and all this without thought of their fortune, the solicitude

M 2

whereof both inclines to fear, and hinders them from the search of the causes of other things; and thereby gives occasion of feigning of as many gods, as there be men that feign them."

In the fourth Book of his Essay, we find Locke thus expressing himself:—"There is no truth more evident than that something must be from eternity. I have never yet heard of any man so unreasonable, or that could suppose so manifest a contradiction, as a time wherein there was perfectly nothing,—this being of all absurdities the greatest, to imagine that pure nothing, the perfect negation and absence of all beings, should ever produce any real existence*." In other passages of the Essay, it is assumed as an axiom that nothing can change itself.

Clarke expressly calls his work a ' Demonstration.' The propositions which he undertook to demonstrate may be easily seen by recourse to his book. That which Mr. Hume mentions as his argument forms no part of them, or at least has no place of prominence and importance assigned to it. If Hume meant to represent that portion of Dr. S. Clarke's reasoning, which occurs under his first proposition, that " some-

---

* Locke's Essay, book iv. c. 10. § 8. I may add that, in Hume's Essay on the Principles of Morals, vol. ii. p. 234, there is a great misrepresentation of Hobbes and Locke. He says, " that they maintained the *selfish* system of morals." It is not true, in the sense given to it by Hume, namely, " that the most generous friendship, however sincere, is but a modification of *self-love;* and that, even unknown to ourselves, we seek *only* our own gratification while we appear the most deeply engaged in schemes for the liberty and happiness of mankind."

thing has existed from eternity," he did not trouble himself to give it correctly. It never was Clarke's argument that " an object that exists absolutely, without any cause, must be its own cause." Let us do that justice to Dr. Clarke, which the Scotchmen have refused him. The following is a portion of his argument :—" Since something now is, 'tis manifest that something always was; otherwise the things that now are must have risen out of nothing, absolutely and without cause, which is a plain contradiction in terms. For to say a thing is produced, and yet there is no cause at all of that production, is to say that something is effected, when it is effected by nothing; that is, at the same time when it is not effected at all. Whatever exists, has a cause of its existence either in the necessity of its own nature, and then it must have been of itself eternal; or in the will of some other Being, and then that other Being must, at least in the order of nature and causality, have existed before it*."

To imply that " whatever exists may have a cause of its existence *in the necessity of its own nature*," is not perhaps very happy nor intelligible, but it is not the same thing as saying that " an object absolutely without any cause, must be its own cause." It is evident that Dr. Clarke here assumes, as he appears to do throughout his work, " that a beginning of existence is an effect;" that " nothing begins to exist without a cause,"—a maxim which Hume professes

* Compare Hume's Treatise, vol. i. p. 145, with Clarke ' On the Attributes,' Prop. i. § 1.

to examine and overthrow by means of his "idea of knowledge." But what that idea is, the reader will find either very difficult to trace out, or unworthy of approbation when he does trace it.

In his section on ' Knowledge*,' Hume endeavours to make it appear that of seven philosophical relations, four only, depending solely on ideas, can be the objects of knowledge and certainty. "All certainty arises from the comparison of ideas, and from the discovery of certain relations as are unalterable, so long as the ideas continue the same. These relations are *resemblance, proportions in quantity and number, degrees of any quality*, and *contrariety;* none of which are implied in this proposition, *whatever has a beginning has also a cause of existence.* That proposition, therefore, is not intuitively certain. At least any one who would assert it to be intuitively certain must deny these to be the only infallible relations, and must find some other relation of that kind to be implied in it, which it will then be time enough to examine." Therefore, as cause and effect is either not one of these relations, or not a relation at all, it follows of course that it cannot be an object of knowledge or certainty,—a short way of disposing of the whole question.

But are these indeed the "only infallible relations"? Are they themselves infallible? The clearness and certainty of the demonstrations in propositions relating to number or quantity may be admitted. But with respect to "*degrees of any quality*," where there is no

* Treatise, vol. i. p. 126.

exact or agreed standard of comparison or measurement, it is evident the uncertainty must be greater
than the certainty. Thus in the case of sounds, colours, smells, and tastes, and all qualities of body, all
impressions from without, of which we have no perfect measures as to degree or quality, together with
that great variety of affections or states of mind, and
all the pleasures and pains accompanying them, with
their several *degrees*, comprehended under the word
feeling, of the intensity or nature of which there is no
exact standard, in point of resemblance or degree, a
relation of one state with another may certainly exist;
one state may introduce another, or necessarily accompany and imply another; these states or conditions
may be successive or simultaneous; and in some propositions or truths relating to them, the mind may be
as certain as in respect of any propositions or truths
whatever; yet the relations are not infallible—only
because the epithet infallible, if applicable to any exercises and conclusions of the human understanding,
ought to be used with the greatest modesty and caution, and is the last term suited to the mouth of a
professed sceptic. For the most part it is impossible
to reduce to measure or number the most common,
and, in point of happiness, and even life, the most
important phenomena of sensation and feeling—the
occasions of action and passion. We cannot compare,
by any exact standard, sweet with sweet, bitter with
bitter, joy with joy, sorrow with sorrow. Hence the
difficulties of mental and moral science, from the ob-

scurity and uncertainty, or indefiniteness of the terms. It is not that these sciences require a new or peculiar logic, as Mr. J. S. Mill would imply; for logic is one and the same for all science, a science *per se*—the science of inference, teaching how, in certain forms of premise, certain forms of conclusion are involved. But it is that some common logic is applied too soon and too fast, and pushed too far, or rather, that it is erroneously applied, before observation has secured good premises, or definition stripped doubtful terms of ambiguity. Thus, when Hume refers our moral sentiments to an inward taste, he abandons them as subjects of philosophical discussion and investigation. *De gustibus non disputandum.* Connoisseurs in art may acccept in poetry a Homer, and in painting a Titian or a Raffaelle, as their standard of excellence, happy if they can agree in the grounds of their appreciation. But the mathematician smiles at their logomachy, when differences or disputes become warm and personal. In the physical sciences, in the various branches of natural philosophy, in such a science as astronomy and others that might be named, that which makes the propositions relating to them clear and important, that which gives the mind a certainty in receiving them proportionably so much stronger, is the enduring nature of the phenomena to which the propositions relate,—it is the power of repeating the observations, under conditions precisely similar, and of renewing experiments—that is, of re-adjusting all the conditions on which the results or conclusions depend with exactness sufficient for proof,—it is this which makes the propositions relating to such sciences more clear and important, and the certainty which the mind feels in connection with them proportionably so much stronger, the assent proportionably so much easier, than in the case of any propositions which concern the more transitory and varying conditions of our daily moral experience,—conditions which we can never renew in precisely the same form, and upon which, when we desire to examine them closely, the lights are shifting and unsteady, both from within and from without.

But further, there is a relation, as intimated above, of which Hume has taken no notice, but which ought to be taken into account, as one of the most common and important grounds of certainty in connection with affirmations or propositions,—that is, the relation between words and thoughts, or the associated ideas. A constant experience of the uniformity of the impressions made on the senses from without, with whatever variations modified or mingled, lays the foundation for the use and application of language, that is, the employment of words, as signs or marks for these impressions, among beings who receive them together, and would communicate with one another respecting their experience of the past and their anticipation of the future. In the right use or application of these signs, whether traditionally adopted or arbitrarily invented by the persons using them, a mutual certainty consists. Nor is there any necessity

for looking further than this constant experience of
the uniformity of nature for the origin of that tendency to expect a future similar to the past, of which
every one is conscious, but of which some philosophers have made a portentous mystery, as if it were
an inexplicable law of the mind, and a fundamental
principle of belief.

Certainty is a term significant of a condition of the
mind.   It is derived from the Latin *certus,* one of the
participial forms of the verb *cerno,* and refers primarily to what the bodily eye, secondarily to what the
so-called eye of the mind, clearly sees or determines,
according to the old proverb "seeing is believing."
It may be defined, confidence in the truth of assertions, founded on confidence in the correctness of impressions.   In other words, it is founded, first, in the
trustworthiness of the senses; and secondly, on that
exercise of the mental faculties, which arises out of,
and is connected with, the use of the senses.   Of
these faculties memory is the chief, because without
memory no proposition could be framed, no comparison of objects could be made, no inference from com-
parisons or propositions could be drawn, no anticipation of a future could exist.   Relying on memory and
their faculties, the mass of mankind feel certainty in
their judgements on a thousand matters of daily experience, which come not under any of Hume's four
heads of infallible relation.   Indeed, that all the infallible relations of ideas are comprehended under these
four, and that these deserve to be called *infallible* re-

lations, is an assertion for which he has not attempted to produce any evidence; nor has any student of the philosophy of the mind followed him in an analysis which, if correct and adequate, would be capable, no doubt, of many most important applications to science, physical and moral.

And why this trifling on Hume's part, and on that of his commentators, with the great names of Hobbes, and Clarke, and Locke, and their *pretended demonstrations?* Has he overthrown the principle which these thinkers held in common, or thrown any new or strong light upon it? He pretends that he has destroyed its intuitive, no less than its demonstrative, certainty. But a very slight acquaintance with the philosophy of Aristotle, of Hobbes, of Locke, of Hartley, and Mill, and Brown, is sufficient to make it manifest that our young philosopher has given a very inadequate account of what he calls the "*only infallible relations.*" Mr. Stewart considers that, "when Hume attempts to show that the proposition in question is not intuitively certain, his argument appears to amount to nothing more than a logical quibble." The truth is, that Hume having bent his strength against the pretended demonstrations, quietly assumes, without any attempt at argument, that it is not intuitively certain. But what are intuitive or intuitional certainties? I answer, all propositions which are assented to without hesitation the moment they are heard and the terms are understood, expressing thoughts or relations of thought in harmony with all the phenomena of nature and the mind,—that is, truths conformable to invariable experience. Whether there be or be not an intuitive certainty in the proposition that " to every beginning of existence there must be a cause," every thinker will decide for himself, from an examination of his own mind, in connection with the terms. If mathematical definitions, axioms, and postulates rest ultimately upon their accordance with all the impressions of the senses, why may not an axiom, like that in question, rest ultimately upon its conformity with universal experience, or derive a part of its certainty from that source? The man who affects to doubt it, may be asked to produce an instance of a beginning without a cause, or even to imagine it. 'Ex nihilo nihil fit,' is a maxim nearly as old as the records of human thought; and he that feels he cannot destroy nor alter his own thoughts at pleasure, that he is physically and mentally subject to laws of being and an order of Nature independent of his own will, will not be easily satisfied with Mr. Hume's vague language on the relation of cause and effect, and his attempt to destroy a principle which lies at the foundation of all human art and science. When Hume's sections on the impressions of the senses and the memory, and of the inferences from the impression to the idea, are rigidly examined, they will be found, not only obscure and inconsistent, but really worthless *, as tending only to perplex and darken a subject of diffi-

* Compare Mr. Stewart's comments in the Dissertation, p. 211, on these infallible relations.

culty, rather than to arrive at principles fertile in useful application.

Mr. Stewart supposes that a truth must be weak which rests upon experience alone,—that there must be some other ground of certainty in propositions, besides harmony with fact, and agreement of ideas with one another. Hence, after Reid, he talks much of instinctive principles of belief, and fundamental laws of belief; and he implies that Hume, by revealing the weakness of all arguments relating to what has been called transcendental science, based upon experience, "has shut up for ever one of the most frequented and fatal paths which led philosophers astray," and thereby compelled them to take those better and safer paths, in which himself and his Scotch predecessors have delighted to walk.

But is Mr. Stewart consistent with himself? *What are these 'fundamental laws and instinctive principles'?* In this very critique on Hume he has supplied an answer to his own principles, in a passage well worthy of attention,—a passage which concedes everything to the most determined follower of Bacon and Hobbes and Locke and Hartley.

"The distinction alluded to by Hume between the *sensitive* and the *cogitative parts* of our nature makes a great figure in the works of Cudworth and of Kant. By the former it was avowedly borrowed from the philosophy of Plato. To the latter it is not improbable that it may have been suggested by the passage in Hume. Without disputing its justness and its importance, I may be permitted to express my doubts of the propriety of stating, so strongly as has frequently been done, the one of these parts of our nature in contrast with the other. Would it not be more philosophical, as well as more pleasing, to contemplate the beautiful harmony between them, and *the gradual steps by which the mind is trained by the intimations of the former, for the deliberate conclusions of the latter?* If, for example, our conviction of the permanence of the laws of nature be not founded on any process of reasoning (a proposition which Mr. Hume seems to have established with demonstrative evidence), but be either the result of an instinctive principle of belief, or *of the association of ideas, operating at a period when the light of reason has not yet dawned,* what can be more delightful than to find this *suggestion of our sensitive frame, verified by every step which our reason afterwards makes in the study of physical science;* and confirmed with mathematical accuracy by the never-failing accordance of the phenomena of the heavens with the previous calculations of astronomers? Does not this afford a satisfaction to the mind, similar to what it experiences when we consider the adaptation of the instinct of suction, and of the organs of respiration to the physical properties of the atmosphere? So far from encouraging scepticism, such a view of human nature seems peculiarly calculated to silence every doubt about the veracity of our faculties."

Here we have the genuine and simple truth, somewhat obscured, indeed, under a cloud of unsatisfactory phrases. *The first association of ideas is the dawn of the light of reason.* The first term rightly applied in its full and just significancy by a child, is the assurance which that child gives that the elements of reason are strong within him. Observation, memory, judgement, expectancy, are there. The apprehension of a law, and the conviction of the permanence of a law, become the highest functions of that mind, in its advanced conditions. It is certain the laws of nature —whether of matter or of mind—can be deduced only from observation of phenomena : the moment observation of fact clashes with the law, as previously received, the law is abrogated or modified. Explanations of the real or apparent exception are sought for in some still higher law, which embraces the newly-discovered order of things.

It seems perfectly evident that we can have no expectation nor imagination of the future, but what is founded on the experience of the past. For to expect that the future will be like the past, is to have had already 'a past,' which it is to resemble, and which has supplied us with conceptions and expectations. Call them, if you like, "suggestions of our sensitive frame :" it is but another phrase for the association of past with present impressions or ideas. The more you examine them, the more you will be inclined to resolve them into ideas of sensation and ideas of reflection, associated in synchronous or successive order; and when you have admitted this, you will be inclined

also to admit, that experience, which covers the whole
field of mental phenomena and development, is the
great instructor; and that there can be no stronger
evidence for any truth or principle or law, than its
agreement with invariable and constant experience,
its harmony with every known fact and repeated observation, that is, with every test to which you can
submit it.

We have now seen how difficult it is to understand
Hume's view of causation, from his obscurity and inconsistency; and especially to understand the degree
of authority which he would allow to our idea of it,
whencesoever it may be drawn. Far from conceding
to him the high merit which Stewart has assigned him,
it may be said with more justice that he impeded the
progress of metaphysical and moral science, by great
injustice to his predecessors, by his inattention to their
real sentiments, by his affectation of discoveries in
fields of research more profoundly and carefully examined before him, and especially by his passion for
literary distinction, irrespective of the truth and value
of the doctrines which he propounded.

DESCARTES AND GASSENDI ON INNATE IDEAS.

That close examination of Hume, which the reader
may be supposed now to have instituted, prepares the
way for some appreciation of the account given by Kant,
in the Prolegomena to his Metaphysics, of the manner
in which Hume's speculations affected his own. It was

Hume, he tells us, who roused him from his dogmatic slumber. But before touching upon the question how far Kant has correctly represented Hume, it will be well to open that wider field of inquiry, comprehended by the old question concerning the existence of innate ideas. Some historical investigation of this subject will enable us better to appreciate the value of the phrases now again so current, owing doubtless to the influence of the idealism of the later schools of Germany, such as *à priori* conceptions, primal instincts and intuitions, fundamental or intuitive or instinctive perceptions, notions, and principles. Until the latter part of the last century Locke was supposed by most thinkers to have exterminated the ' men of innate ideas,' of instincts, and intuitions. But the advocates of instinctive principles have re-appeared, in numbers like to those mythologic beings which sprang up from the casting of Deucalion's stones after the deluge.

It is a question of great interest in the history of modern metaphysics, and especially in weighing the merit of Locke's account of the origin of our knowledge, whether Descartes had any particular or intelligible theory of innate ideas. If he had, it is difficult to trace it. Had any such theory formed a clear and important part of his metaphysical philosophy, Mr. Hallam would surely have made some allusion to it in his account of that philosophy. Yet Mr. D. Stewart speaks of Descartes' doctrine of innate ideas "*as understood and expounded by himself*," adding these words in italics, "Because in Descartes' reasonings

N

on this question, there is no inconsiderable portion
of most important truth, debased by a large and manifest alloy of error *." Unfortunately Mr. Stewart
gives no reference to the place where this exposition
and the important truth is to be found, leaving the
reader at a loss at the moment of greatest need; nor
am I acquainted with any English work which would
supply the desired information.

In the third of Descartes' Meditations the following
passage occurs; the nearest which I have found to
the exposition in question†:—" Now with regard to
ideas, if they are regarded in themselves alone, and I
refer them not to anything else, they cannot properly
be considered false; for whether I imagine a goat or
a chimæra, it is no less true that I imagine the one
than the other. Neither is any falsehood to be feared
in the will itself, nor the affections; for however de-
praved my wishes, however much I may desire things
which exist nowhere, it is not the less true that I do
wish such things; and thenceforth there remains only
the judgments, in which I must take care that I be
not deceived. Now the chief and most frequent error
to be found in these consists in this—that I may
judge the ideas which exist *within* me, to be like or
conformable to certain things placed *without* me. For
truly, if I considered only the ideas themselves, and

---

* Stewart's Dissertation, p. 68.

† I translate it from the small quarto edition, Amsterdam, 1644, p.
19: ' Meditationes de Primâ Philosophiâ, in quibus Dei existentia et
animæ humanæ a corpore distinctio demonstrantur.'

merely certain modes of thought, and refer them to
no other thing whatsoever, they can scarcely give me
any material of error.   Now of these ideas some seem
to me innate, others adventitious, others made by myself ; for inasmuch as I understand what a thing is,
what truth is, what thought is, these I seem to have
from no other source than from my own nature.   But
that I now hear a noise, see the sun, feel the fire, these
I have judged to proceed from certain things placed
without me.   And lastly, Sirens, Hippogryffs, and
the like, are feigned by myself ; or perhaps I may
think even all to be adventitious, or all innate, or all
feigned, for I have not as yet perceived the true origin
of them."

This division of ideas into three is evidently arbitrary, and the account of those which are innate is
loose and unsatisfactory.   The classes are not distinguished by any specific difference.   To hear, see, and
feel, are no less a part of our own nature, than afterwards to think of what we have seen and felt.   Descartes himself appears afterwards little satisfied with
it.

"The opinion of Descartes upon innate ideas," says
Degerando*, "has not been well understood, nor is this
to be wondered at, for he has not well understood
himself.   On one side he repeats often that these
ideas are born with us.   He says particularly of the
idea of God, "it is born and produced with me, from
the time when I was created, in the same manner as

* Hist. Comp. des Systèmes, vol. vi. p. 185.

the idea of myself." He assures us "that the mind of the infant in the bosom of its mother has no less within itself the ideas of God, of itself, and of all those truths which are known of themselves, than adult persons have them, when they do not think of them, for it acquires them not afterwards with age"! "These ideas can have been placed in us only by God, who is their immediate cause. There is no metaphysical truth, in particular, which we cannot comprehend, if our mind is directed to consider it, and they are all "mentibus nostris congenitæ."

On the other hand, pressed by objections, Descartes admitted that these innate ideas existed only as *possibilities*. He considers them as natural, in so far as we have the faculty for producing them; he finds them not distinct from the faculty of thought*. Such admissions amount to a denial of the principle that there are ideas properly innate, since the epithet is applicable to every idea which the mind comes in process of time to entertain.

On the passage above quoted, from the third Meditation, we may remark Descartes' just observation, that "the epithets *true* and *false* are not properly applied to mere *ideas*." Thus he prepares the way for the admission that they belong more properly to propositions; although Descartes does not quite perceive this, and is by no means consistent with himself, since he makes clear and distinct perception his primary

---

* Descartes' Correspondence, edit. Cousin, vol. viii. pp. 95, 268. Also Third Meditation, edit. Renouard, p. 120.

test of truth, to which Gassendi took just exception. No doubt these epithets may be loosely applied to ideas, when it is meant that the ideas of a particular thinker on a particular subject are or are not correspondent to the qualities of the subject; are or are not in accordance with all the phenomena—and in agreement with all the perceptions and other ideas, which the same thinker will possess or entertain, when the subject of thought shall be further examined and better known. But under every such loose application, there is implied a secret reference to a proposition or conclusion of the mind not expressed; and this view of the meaning of the epithets prepares the way for easy and available definitions of truth and falsehood. This is well laid down by Hobbes in the early part of his Computatio or Logic, and in other parts of his writings, and by Locke " On true and false ideas *."

Even if we allow the application of the epithets to relations between thoughts or ideas and the objects of human contemplation, it will be found that they can be so applied with practical advantage only when such relations come to be *expressed*,—that is, when they appear in the form of propositions, and then assist in ratiocination.

That Descartes himself had no correct appreciation of the importance of the sentiment before us, I con-

---

* Essay, book ii. ch. 32. Yet Locke afterwards forgot what he had so well said, or he would have expressed himself better when he came to discuss the reality of our knowledge, and the nature of truth and universal propositions. B. iv. ch. 4, 5, 6.

clude, from what he has said in the fourth Meditation
—a most unsatisfactory one—whose subject is "the
true and the false." He begins it with speculation
on the sort of faculties with which the Deity, as a
good and powerful Being, must necessarily endow his
creatures ; and, as he advances, he connects error with
the will rather than the understanding*.

The six Meditations of Descartes are short enough
to be easily and agreeably read. But they gave rise
to disquisitions, doubts, and arguments between himself and Gassendi, to say nothing of those by Cater,
Mersenne, Hobbes, Arnauld, and divers other theologians and philosophers, six times their length, the
perusal of which is a more serious task†. Gassendi
pressed Descartes very closely ; and the Dutch printer
of the Meditations and Objections naïvely says of
Descartes that he became vehemently excited, and,
forgetful of himself, forgot reason also, to which he

---

* " D'où est-ce donc que naissent mes erreurs ? C'est, à savoir, de
cela seul, que la volonté étant beaucoup plus ample et plus étendue
que l'entendement, je ne la contiens pas dans les mêmes limites,
mais que je l'étends aussi aux choses que je n'entends pas ; aux-
quelles étant de soi indifférentes, elle s'égare fort aisément, et choisit
le faux pour le vrai, et le mal pour le bien : ce qui fait que je me
trompe et que je pèche."—Méditation 4, p. 101 : Simon's Œuvres de
Descartes.

† " Dans cette grande controverse, les objections de Hobbes pa-
raissent les moins judicieuses, et les plus confuses ; celles d'Arnauld,
les plus profondes, mais les plus réservées ; celles de Gassendi, les
plus variées, les plus développées ; celles du Père Bourdin, Jésuite,
les plus superficielles et les plus frivoles ; celles de Huet, les plus
subtiles, les plus pénétrantes."—Degérando, Hist. Comp. des Syst.
tom. vi. p. 238.

should have chiefly attended,—" Sui oblitus, rationis quoque obliviscerctur." It was in answer to Gassendi's remarks upon this portion of the Meditations that Descartes broke out into the insulting tone which has extorted even from Mr. Stewart the acknowledgment that, at least in the philosophy of the temper, the Epicurean Gassendi had greatly the advantage.

The comments of Gassendi on the passage are so instructive, not only with regard to any theory of innate ideas which Descartes may be supposed to have held, but to the whole subject which it opens, that I shall present them to the reader in an English form, —the more readily, as the question of the extent to which Locke was indebted to Gassendi for his own peculiar views, or in which Locke agreed with him or was anticipated by him, though of deep interest to the philosophical inquirer, has never been fully discussed and examined by any English metaphysical writer. Mr. Hallam justly observes, that Gassendi's works are now little known in England; and even in France they appear no longer to receive the attention due to them.

" Now the mind hath a faculty, not only of perceiving adventitious ideas, or such as it receives from things passed through the senses,—of perceiving them, I say, naked and distinct, and altogether such as it receives them; but, further, of variously compounding, dividing, contracting, amplifying, comparing them, and the like. Hence the third kind (i. e. of the three mentioned by Descartes) is not distinct from the second. For the idea of a chimera is no other than the idea of a lion's head, a goat's belly, a serpent's tail, of which the mind composes one; though they be separately and singly adventitious. So the idea of a giant, or of a man like a mountain, or of the world conceived as a whole, is no other than adventitious; the idea of a man of common size, which the mind amplifies according to pleasure, although the idea is more confused, the larger the size is conceived. So the idea of a pyramid, of a city, or any other thing never beheld, is no other than the adventitious idea of some pyramid before seen, some city, or any other thing, formed in no other way, and from thence multiplied and in some confused manner (*confusâ ratione aliquâ*) compared. As to the species which you call innate, truly there seem to be none such, and those which are called such seem also to have an adventitious origin. I have it, you say, from my nature, that I understand what a thing is (*quid sit res*). Now I suppose you are not speaking here of the power of intelligence, about which there is no doubt nor question, but rather concerning the idea of a thing. You speak not even concerning the idea of any one particular thing,—for the sun, this stone, all individuals, are things, the ideas of which you acknowledge not to be innate. You speak therefore of the idea of a thing universally considered, and as far as it is synonymous with an entity (*cum ente*), and in its utmost latitude (*tam latè quam illud patet*). But I ask how this idea can be in the mind, unless

there are at the same time so many individual things,
and their kinds, from which the mind abstracts and
forms the conception, which is peculiar to none of the
individuals, and yet is found in all. Truly, if the
idea of a thing be innate, then also will be the idea of
an animal, of a plant, of a stone, of all universals; and
there will be no need that we fatigue ourselves with
distinguishing many individuals, where, their various
differences being disregarded, we only retain that
which shall be seen to be common to all, or, what is
the same thing, the idea of the genus. You say also
that you have it from your nature, that you understand what truth is, or, as I interpret, the idea of
truth. Now, if truth be nothing else than a conformity of judgment with a fact or thing (*cum re*),
concerning which a judgment is made, truth is a certain relation, and therefore nothing distinct from the
facts and ideas so related to each other, or, what is
the same, from the very idea of the fact or thing;
since this represents both itself and the thing to which
it belongs. Wherefore the idea of truth is no other
than the idea of a thing, so far as it is conformable to the thing itself, and so far as it represents
the very thing, of what sort it is. Hence therefore, if
the idea of a thing be not innate, but adventitious,
so also the idea of truth is adventitious, not innate. And when that is understood concerning any
individual truth whatsoever, it may be understood
universally concerning truth, the notion or idea of
which (as has been already observed of the idea of a

thing) is drawn from the notions or ideas of the singulars or individuals. You say further that you have from your own nature an understanding of what thought is. But as the mind, from the idea of one city, frames the idea of another, so from the idea of one action, as of vision, of taste, it may frame the idea of another,—suppose, of thought itself. A certain analogy is indeed recognized among the knowing faculties, and one easily leads on to the knowledge of another. However, concerning the idea of thought (*cogitationis*) trouble need not be taken; but concerning the idea of the mind itself, and so of the soul, if we should grant this to be innate, there will be no disadvantage in admitting the idea of thought to be also innate. We must wait however until the fact be proved concerning the mind or soul."

There is much good philosophy in this. It opens well the whole question of the relation between complex ideas and abstract terms. On all subjects of thought, the mind advances most naturally from individuals to universals, from particulars to generals. The embarrassments of metaphysicians, the useless and unsatisfactory nature of their disputes and writings, arise from their plunging at once into abstractions, which are of little account until they come to be referred to and explained by the particulars which they comprehend, from which they are drawn, and which are always comparatively intelligible.

Descartes' response to these remarks òf Gassendi is very indifferent. He explains not his theory of innate ideas: he fences with the objections, but does not meet them. In reply to the observation that the mind has power to divide, contract, amplify, and compare, and frames its general idea out of many particulars, he merely says, " In this way you may prove that no statues were ever made by Praxiteles, since he had not from himself the marble, out of which he carved them; and that you have not made these objections, because you have composed them in words not invented by yourself, but borrowed from others." This is evidently evasive. Nay, the allusion is unfortunate for Descartes. The question related not to the existence of mental power and intentions, but to the origin of conceptions. Whence had Praxiteles his idea of the figure which he designed to execute? Yet it seems not to have occurred to Descartes nor to Gassendi, in this question, to inquire into the manner in which words first become associated with ideas in the mind of a child, and in which the power of comprehending words, as used by others, and of using them with advantage for oneself, is gradually acquired. Here, however, in this use of associated signs, lies the first great lesson in the philosophy of the mind. But surely Gassendi seems much nearer to the truth than his antagonist.

The word *innate* was from the first used vaguely, and continues to be so used; while the question that underlies it is not yet fairly disposed of, because it is seldom fairly stated. From the general prevalence, or assumed universality, of an idea or belief in the

minds of men at a mature age, or in a certain state
of culture and civilization, it was customary, even in
Cicero's time, to argue the idea to be innate, and the
belief to be well founded. " Cum enim non instituto
aliquo, aut more, aut lege sit opinio constituta, ma-
neatque ad unum omnium firma consensio : intelligi
necesse est, esse deos, quoniam *insitas eorum*, *vel po-
tius innatas cognitiones* habemus. De quo autem omnium natura consentit, id verum esse necesse est. Esse
igitur deos, confitendum est*." But the value of the
'innata cognitio' comes to nothing, or is reduced to a
vanishing quantity, when Cotta and Balbus, Velleius
and Lucilius compare their views, and endeavour to
arrive at a firm, and not an erring or vague, opinion
of the gods. If they had innate knowledge, why
should they still be inquiring and seeking ?

Among the allies of Gassendi in this great controversy, there was one who approached him in the extent of his erudition, and in the vigour and freedom
of his intellect,—Peter Daniel Huet, the Bishop of
Avranches. In the 'Censura Philosophiæ Cartesianæ'
Huet thus expresses himself † :—

" Although Descartes hath stealthily taken that
much-vexed sentiment, concerning innate ideas, from
the Platonic philosophy, yet he has interpolated somewhat, to make it appear different. Be it different, as

---

* Cicero de Naturâ Deorum, l. i. § 17.

† Translated from the Latin of the 4th edition : Paris, 1694: pp.
135, 140 :—" Falsum est, esse aliquid in intellectu, quod non fuerit
in sensu."

you please, yet with equal certainty can I show it to
be false. He has stated the genus of ideas in us to
be threefold, as I have said above; of which one is
adventitious, such as the idea of the sun, which every
man hath in himself from the visible sun; another
sort is factitious, such as that idea of the sun which
astronomers entertain by their reasonings; a third
sort however is born with us, which he calls natural,
of which sort are the ideas of God, of the mind, of
the natures which are called essences, of geometrical
formulæ, of the axioms which mathematicians use,
and of other things like to these. These natural ideas
sometimes he declares to be nothing else than the
very faculty of thinking, by which our mind hath its
power (*quá mens nostra pollet*), and which in the
schools they are wont to call the first act of thinking :
yet he continually lays it down that these ideas are
forms of thought; but that the thoughts themselves,
or, as they commonly say, the second act of thinking,
arises from the faculty of thinking. But these things
are plainly repugnant ; for if a thought arises from
the faculty of thinking, of necessity the thought differs
from the faculty of thinking, as that which is effected
differs from its cause. Again, if an idea is a form of
thought, since a form is one thing, and that of which
it is the form is another, and as the soul of a man is different from the man, so an idea is one thing, and thought
(the power of thinking it, *cogitatio*), another. Thus
Descartes recognizes three things in himself, which he
had pronounced to be one and the same ; namely, the

faculty of thinking, the thinking, and the idea. When however he discusses the idea of God, which we bear impressed upon the mind, this he maintains to be neither formed, nor possible to be formed, out of our own mind, but to be by God himself stamped and impressed in our mind, just as the idea of those axioms which are held immutable and eternal. But there is here a much greater discrepancy; for if ideas are the faculty of thinking, then the idea of God is a faculty of thinking concerning God; and the ideas of all other things, are but the faculty of thinking of those other things. But that faculty of thinking may be applied to all things whatsoever, and is one and the same faculty; as the faculty of painting, whether it be applied to paint a tree or a house, is the same faculty. Whence it is a plain conclusion, that the idea of God, and the other ideas which he calls natural and innate, differ not from the factitious nor adventitious ideas.

"But further, when Descartes writes in another place that those eternal ideas, such, namely, as geometrical axioms, are marked in our minds by God, as laws by a king in the minds of those who obey their command, he confesses a difference between ideas and the faculty of thinking. Let us however be indulgent to Descartes, and so favourably interpret his opinion, that an innate idea—such, namely, as of God—is a faculty engendered in our mind by a certain mode of thinking; so that, as often as the mind shall reflect, the idea of God will arise in the mind. But not even thus will he extricate himself; for how will the innate idea differ from the factitious or adventitious idea? For the idea of Alexander, which is factitious, may be called with equal right a faculty engendered in the mind by a certain mode of thinking, by which, as often as a man shall reflect, the idea of Alexander will arise in it. Thus Descartes vacillates in the whole of his doctrine. Moreover, when he would prove that the mind needs not the aid of the senses to form ideas, he uses this argument—that nothing reaches the mind by the aid and interposition of the senses, but certain corporeal motions, which the mind perceives to be not such as they really are in the senses; and further, that the ideas of motions and figures, and much more of pain, of colours, of sounds, and other like things, are engendered in us, and that the mind exhibits them to itself, as often as it is excited by those corporeal motions, to which ideas have no similitude; whence he infers that, since those ideas of outward objects may be innate, and not arise from external things, with greater reason may the same thing be said of common notions, or axioms, which are neither in external things, nor can have come to the mind by means of corporeal motions, or a message of the senses: for that the external things, and those motions, and the senses, are individuals, but the axioms are universals, having no affinity with the motions and the senses. Now we confess that the ideas of external things are formed by the mind, after that it has been admonished by some corporeal motion, and a message of the senses struck by outward objects (*sensuum à rebus externis impulsorum*). But we say that these corporeal motions impress a stroke (*plagam**), or mark upon the brain; which touch or stroke, the mind, very closely conjoined to it, perceiving in the brain, by this admonition as it were, conceives and forms this or that idea, though before it existed not; but by no means does it recognize it, as if it had a former existence. Nor can it moreover conceive or form any idea, unless it shall perceive a touch of it in the brain. Moreover universal ideas are taken from the singulars, since the mind, attending in many objects to the same quality, selects that from the many in which it was dispersed, gathers it into one, and thence forms its universal idea. As in Peter and John, and other individual men, perceiving that they are animals endowed with reason, but no longer regarding Peter nor John, nor any individual, it draws forth and composes into one what had been manifold, and thus forms that general and universal idea, and concludes that every man is a rational animal†."

---

* *Plaga* was the word used by Democritus, as we learn from the short but interesting fragment of Cicero, De Fato, many of the phrases of which occur in this treatise of Huet. We learn from this fragment that Democritus, Heraclitus, Empedocles, and Aristotle, were the necessarians, or fatalists of antiquity. "Aliam quandam vim motus habebunt à Democrito impulsionis, quam *plagam* ille appellat."—Cicero, De Fato, § 20.

† Censura Phil. Cartes. p. 135–140. Descartes, 3rd Medit.; and also Principles of Phil., part i. ch. 15, 16, 18; Letters, vol. ii. letter 54, vol. i. 59, 104, 99.

Hobbes also touched the subject briefly; and in his tenth objection, and Descartes' reply, we see how the controversy stood. After contending, and with reason, that our ideas of the attributes of the Deity, his infinitude and independence, involve the previous notions of things finite and dependent, Hobbes thus concludes:—" Moreover, when M. Descartes says that the idea of God is innate and resident in us, I wish much to know if the souls of those who sleep profoundly and without dream, think. If they think not, then they have no ideas—and therefore there is no idea which can be born and residing in us, for that which is innate and resident in us is always present to our thought." This argument is not very conclusive, and Descartes replies:—" None of those things which we attribute to God can come from external objects, *comme d'une cause exemplaire;* for there is nothing in the Deity like to external, that is, to corporeal things. Now it is manifest that all which we conceive to be in God unlike to the external cannot come into our thought by the entrance of these same things, but only by means of the cause of this diversity, that is to say, of God.

" And I ask here in what manner this philosopher infers the intellection of the Deity from externals. For myself I explain easily the idea which I have of it, in saying that *by the word idea I understand the form of all perception;* for who is he that conceives anything which he perceives not, and yet who has not this form or this idea of intellection? whence, ex-

o

tending it to the infinite, he forms the idea of the divine intelligence. And what I say of this perfection may be extended to all the rest.

" Now, inasmuch as I have availed myself of the idea of God which is in us, to demonstrate his existence, and as in this idea a power so immense is contained, that, if it be true that God exists, we conceive it repugnant to this truth, that anything else exists unless created by him, it follows clearly from the demonstration of his existence that all the world—that is to say, all things which exist different from God— have been created by him.

" Finally, when I say that any idea is born with us, or that it is naturally imprinted in our souls, I do not understand that it is always present to our thought, for, so understanding, there could be none such; but *I understand only that we have in ourselves the faculty of producing it*.*"

These extracts place before us with sufficient clearness the state of opinion and of the controversy concerning innate ideas before and about Locke's time. We see why Locke began his Essay with the chapter on that subject. It was necessary to clear the ground, and thus prepare a good foundation for his own account of the origin of all our knowledge. However

---

* See ' Œuvres de Descartes' by M. Jules Simon, pp. 207, 208. This volume contains the Discours sur la Méthode, Méditations, Traité des Passions, with the controversial objections and replies in a very convenient form. The reader may also consult Degérando, ' Histoire Comparée ;' and the authors of the ' Dictionnaire,' upon the articles Descartes, Gassendi, and Leibnitz.

we may regret that Locke has not given us more of historical reference to account for the course of his thoughts and investigations, his Essay owes its influence very much to the fact that he discusses the subject upon its merits, and without reference to authority; for, like Bacon, like Hobbes, like Descartes himself, he made his own, whatever he thought or considered true relating to the mind. It seems evident that Descartes was beaten from his ground; that he had no theory which he could explain and support against objections; that he had no sufficient criterion for distinguishing what was, from what was not, an innate idea; nor was there much in him to which Locke could reply, and which deserved his particular attention. If all that is innate in us be the faculty of producing ideas, then every idea, howsoever gotten, is equally entitled to that epithet.

No eulogist of Descartes has attempted to show that he had any advantage over his adversaries in this controversy. It has been said by M. Jules Simon, that "Descartes' theory of innate ideas is at bottom only the thesis common to all rationalists, namely, that all our ideas do not grow out of observation, and of the operations performed by the mind upon the data of experience, but that *there exists in us a superior faculty, by which we seize at once some ideas and principles of an authority necessary, universal, and absolute.* To this question all the great metaphysical questions attach themselves, or rather, this question decided, metaphysics are accomplished." But such statements cannot be accepted as correct. The questions at issue are changed by the introduction of new terms. The first negative has yet to be proved. The existence of some superior faculty who ever denied?

"Must I contemplate this great man (says Cousin, in his 'Eloge de Descartes'), in spite of the circumspection of his steps, wandering in his metaphysics, and creating his system of innate ideas? But this error belonged to his genius. Accustomed to profound meditations, habituated to live apart from the senses, to seek in the soul, or in the essence of the Deity, for the origin, the order, and the thread of his convictions (*connaissances*), could he suppose that the soul was entirely dependent on the senses for its ideas? Was it not *too degrading* for it to be only occupied with running over the physical world to gather thence the materials of its knowledge, like the botanist who collects his plants,—or to extract principles from sensations, like the chemist who analyses bodies? It was reserved for Locke to give us concerning ideas the true system of nature, by developing a principle known to Aristotle, and seized by Bacon, but of which Locke is not less the creator, for a principle is not created until it is demonstrated to men." The candour and the fulness of this concession in Locke's favour may be accepted and admired, but how can it be reconciled with other passages of the eloquent author?*

Mr. Stewart gives to Descartes the proud title of

* The *éloge* by Cousin, prefixed to his edition of Descartes, would be read with more pleasure by many, if the name of Bacon were

Father of the Experimental Philosophy of the Human
Mind. But we have seen what Stewart also said of
Reid, as the first who executed Bacon's plan in that
department of study. Such praises are more specious
than discriminative. Descartes is still, or rather, he
is again the idol of the French *literati*, for he was not
so in the days of Montesquieu and D'Alembert. His
independence, originality, and abstractedness,—his
effort to rear anew a temple of truth, on a foundation
of his own, designed to stand for ages as the asylum
of faith and virtue, will always have a great charm for
those who love to dwell in regions of speculation, and
on heights far above the common level. But he built
a castle in the air; he was the Phaeton of modern
philosophy: his wings melt as he rises, and we see
him at last sinking and baffled in waters too powerful
for his strength. He aspired to construct, from abstract principles, a theory of the universe and a theory
of the human mind, and he disdained to wait upon
nature as a teacher, and to receive humbly the lessons
of patient observation. Hence he paid no attention
to the first simple elements of human thought and
reasoning; he refused to look at them in the light
in which the great thinkers of his own day were disposed to view them. Hence the value of every principle and premiss which he adopted was warmly
contested by men as free from the prejudices of the

substituted for that of Descartes. If we read twenty pages of the
one and of the other consecutively, the superior richness, grasp, and
power of Bacon's intellect becomes most striking.

schools as himself, and equally anxious for light and truth; for the authority of Aristotle, or rather, of those who pretended to expound Aristotle, but substituted their own vain cobwebs in his place, was clearly gone at the end of the sixteenth century. Nor do we owe his deposition to Descartes, though he gave to Aristotelianism its most fatal blow. Even Bacon was but a bright morning star, the harbinger of the coming day. He was only the master-spirit of an age rich in great minds—minds prepared to appreciate and honour his genius, but whose lustre is not to be eclipsed in his beams. Such were the admirable Kepler, the excellent Galileo, the fertile and imaginative Campanella. Of the merits of his great contemporaries Descartes showed not a little jealousy, and the methods of Galileo in particular he vainly censured*.

On Kepler and Galileo it is not for me to enlarge. Their memory has been embalmed by worthier hands. But the name of Campanella is less known; and some notice of his worth and works may be acceptable to the reader. He entered largely and freely into metaphysical and speculative philosophy; he was among the first, not merely to discard authority, whether that of Aristotle or any other name, but to urge and support appeals to nature, observation, reason, and experience. His writings breathe an enlightened, philo-

* See a passage in Maclaurin's account of Sir I. Newton's Discoveries, ch. iii. p. 55, and the reference; Descartes' Epistolæ, part 2, Ep. 91.

sophic spirit, worthy of any age, and most remarkable
in his own, touching, as they do, wisely and beautifully on the compatibility between the acceptance of an
historical revelation, rightly interpreted, and the profoundest investigation of nature ; or as we should now
express it, between reason and faith, between natural
and revealed religion. The common English notices
of him are taken almost entirely from Brucker. They
do no justice to his vigorous and manly thought, to
the lofty poetical tone of his mind, to the manner in
which he broke loose from the chains of scholasticism,
and, emerging from the darkest cell of the cloister,
delighted to expatiate in the air, the light, the freedom of the intellectual day then advancing towards
meridian splendour. His opinion that matter is a
battle-field, on which the two great principles of heat
and cold are struggling for mastery, whose united or
balanced operation produces the beautiful phenomena
of the heavens, and the vegetation and animation of
the earth, and his disposition to believe in astrology,
or some influence of the stars on human character
and fortunes, detract little from his merits, when we
consider the state of opinion on such subjects in men
of more repute long after his time. He was among
the very first of continental thinkers to discern the
greatness of the mind of Bacon, and the rich promise
of his methods ; above all, he had the courage to stand
forth as the warm defender of Galileo, against all the
prejudices of his order and all the tyranny of Rome.
Campanella was himself a prisoner in the Inquisition

for about thirty years, and we are told that he was seven times put to the rack. His chief pieces were composed while suffering under this long oppression. They were printed at Frankfort by Tobias Adami, who received them from his hands, who supplied him with such books as Gilbert's recent treatise on magnetism, and whom he calls "nostræ philosophiæ Symmista*." They are as striking a proof of the triumph of the mind over adverse fortune, of a chivalrous and unconquerable spirit, as the annals of philosophy afford. The 'Apology for Galileo,' in particular, wherein he discusses the question, whether the method of philosophizing which Galileo celebrates, favours or opposes the Sacred Scriptures, appears to me to rank among the noblest pleas for liberty of thought,— among the sublimest, because earliest efforts for the emancipation of genius and true philosophy from the thraldom of tyrants and of bigots. Its calm, full sense, without the least extravagance, in answer to the timid prejudices and shallow sophistry of the Jesuits,—the extensive knowledge and just appreciation of classic and patristic literature displayed in it, —are a perfect marvel for its time. Thus he breaks forth :—" Galileus autem fidei fundamentis inhæret ; et de naturalibus loquitur sobriè, sicut testis observationum, non sicut opinator, uti facit Aristoteles de cerebro suo; quare propter hoc laudandus est. Infirmatio enim infidelium dogmatum, et mendaciorum gentilium, est roboratio Christianismi, non eversio

* See the De Sensu Rerum, p. 30.

theologiæ." But it is difficult to select one passage, as the key-note, from a piece so much in harmony with the sentiments which devout and philosophic Christians of every age and all churches have cherished. "That strain I heard was of a higher mood," are words forced upon the memory in the contemplation of so much wisdom, mingled with so much virtue, and both so much forgotten. Yet the imputations of atheism and insanity were hurled against him while living, and threw their dark shadow over his memory long after his decease.

The just appreciation of Bacon found in the preface, by Tobias Adami, to Campanella's chief work, the four parts of ' Real Philosophy,' published in 1623, two years before the appearance of the second part of Bacon's ' Instauratio Magna,' possesses singular interest,—the more so when contrasted with Descartes' unworthy silence, and total neglect of the great English Chancellor's works and fame. " Quod si ad finem deducetur sagacissimi philosophi Francisci Baconis de Verulamio Angliæ Cancellarii ' Instauratio Magna,' opus suscipiendum et consideratione ut et auxilio dignissimum, apparebit fortassis ad metam nos tendere unam, cum iisdem certè vestigiis rerum per sensum et experientiam indagandarum incedere profiteamur, quamvis non dubitem quin longè plura et majora per inductiones diligentiores, quibus ille insistit, investigari, multaque emendari et elucidari rectius possunt."

Those parts in Campanella's ' Real Philosophy

which treat of morals and politics, are truly remarkable for just and discriminating sentiment. In the Politics we have some anticipation of Hobbes without his extravagances, as in the statement that men are driven into communities by the stimulants of necessity, and for the purposes of the common defence. In the Morals we have a definition of virtue, perhaps as good as any that has been suggested since: " Virtus ergo regula est passionum, notionum, et affectionum animi, et operationum ad certè acquirendum verum bonum, et fugiendum verum malum." And so again, " Vitium verò est enormitas affectionum et operationum erga malum tanquam in bonum ferens. In omni nam operatione vitiosâ, est ignorantia vel inadvertentia, et odium boni et Dei interpretativè." It may be said, indeed, that the *verum bonum et malum* themselves require a definition, but the reader of Campanella would be at no serious loss. " Entia cuncta propriam beatitudinem appetunt*."

But to return to Descartes. With regard to his

* Mr. Hallam has touched, in a few paragraphs, the merits and character of Campanella, with genuine and truthful taste ; but without mentioning the 'Apology for Galileo.' In the library of Dr. Williams, in Redcross-street, there is a valuable quarto, containing the ' Prodromus Philosophiæ Instaurandæ' (Frankfort, 1617), with an admirable preface by Adami, addressed to the philosophers of Germany ; the treatise ' De Sensu Rerum et Magia' (1620) ; the 'Apologia pro Galileo' (1622) ; the ' Realis Philosophiæ Epilogisticæ Partes Quatuor,' with the ' Civitas Solis,' a kind of philosophical romance (1623). No volume affords better illustration of that renewed vigour of the human mind, which, commencing at the end of the fifteenth, was destined to shine out in all its brilliancy through the whole of the seventeenth, century.

first position, "Cogito, ergo sum," there seems little propriety in the "ergo:"—for who ever felt his own existence after that argument more strongly than before? The objections to it by his adversaries I cannot treat as merely cavils. It is not a necessary premiss for any other truth which is made to rest upon it. Every schoolboy may translate *cogito*, 'I am, or exist, thinking.' The first person of every other verb assumes, rather than proves, the existence of an active, percipient, and intelligent being. Surely the simple good sense of Locke is to be more admired, when he says, "As for our own existence, we perceive it so plainly and so certainly, that it neither needs nor is capable of any proof*." And the language of Maclaurin is not less worthy of attention. "As we are certain of our own existence, and of that of our ideas, by internal consciousness; so we are satisfied, by the same consciousness, that there are objects, powers, or causes without us, and that act upon us. For in many of our ideas, particularly those that are accompanied with pain, the mind must be passive, and receive the impressions (which are involuntary) from external causes or instruments, that depend not upon us." Maclaurin, in the admirable first chapter of his second book, on space, time, matter, and motion, also concisely touches the subject of cause and effect. "The mind is intimately conscious of its own activity in reflecting upon its ideas, in examining and arranging them, in forming such as are complex from the

* Essay, book iv. ch. 9.

more simple, in reasoning from them, and in its elections and determinations. From this, as well as from the influence of external objects upon the mind, and from the course of nature, it easily acquires the ideas of cause and effect." These sentences show us the influence of Locke's sober mental philosophy upon the tone of mind prevalent among the thoughtful and scientific about the middle of the last century. Its harmony with the Newtonian physical system of the universe is beautifully developed in Maclaurin's inestimable volume; and we remark with pleasure that the 'Principia' of Newton came forth in the same year (1687) in which Locke finished his Essay on the Understanding; both maintaining that whatever is not deduced from phenomena is to be called an hypothesis; and that hypotheses, whether physical or metaphysical, whether of occult qualities or mechanical, have no place in a just philosophy.

Again, Descartes' argument for the necessary existence of an eternal, infinite, intelligent First Cause, from the idea of such a being existing in our minds, to which there must be some outward correspondent, may give a slight satisfaction to one who has the idea already established in his mind, and who has been accustomed to rest upon it, as an indubitable and invaluable truth. But there is no evidence that it ever produced an impression on one previously inclined to disbelieve the existence of a Supreme Intelligence, whether from the difficulties involved in the conception, or the disproportion between the subject and our faculties, or the imperfection of the analogy between the human and divine works and designs. It has not been generally resorted to as a stronghold of conviction, by the firmest and most devout Theists*.

---

* Cudworth, whose 'Intellectual System' is the great treasury of learning on the history of Natural Religion, certainly was disposed to allow its full weight to every argument for the Being of a God. He considered, but he rejected, the new argument of Descartes. " It hath been asserted by a late eminent philosopher, that there is no possible certainty to be had of anything, before we be certain of the existence of a God essentially good ; because we can never otherwise free our minds from the importunity of that suspicion, which, with irresistible force, may assault them ; that ourselves might possibly be made, either by chance or fate, or by the pleasure of some evil demon, or at least of an arbitrary, omnipotent Deity, as that we should be deceived in all our most clear and evident perceptions ; and therefore in geometrical theorems themselves, and even in our common notions. But when we are once assured of the existence of such a God as is essentially good, who therefore neither will nor can deceive, then, and not before, will this suspicion utterly vanish, and ourselves become certain that our faculties of reason and understanding are not false and imposturous, but rightly made. From which hypothesis it plainly follows that all those Theists, who suppose God to be a mere arbitrary Being, whose will is not determined by any nature of good, or rule of justice, but itself is the first rule of both (they thinking this to be the highest perfection, liberty, and power), can never be reasonably certain of the truth of anything, —not so much as that two and two make four ; because, so long as they adhere to that persuasion, they can never be assured but that such an arbitrary, omnipotent Deity might designedly make them such as should be deceived in all their clearest perceptions.

" Now, though there be a plausibility of piety in this doctrine, as making the knowledge of a God essentially good so necessary a '*præcognitum*' to all other science, that there can be no certainty of truth at all without it ; yet does that very supposition, that our understanding faculties might possibly be so made as to deceive us in all our clearest perceptions (wheresoever it is admitted), render it

Even Cudworth and Clarke assign to all such demonstrations *à priori*, a negative, rather than positive
value. It is also a just observation of Mr. Stewart,
that even Descartes' argument, as he has expressed it
at the end of his third Meditation, is not entitled to

utterly impossible ever to arrive to any certainty concerning the
existence of a God essentially good; forasmuch as this cannot be
any otherwise proved than by the use of our faculties of understanding, reason, and discourse. For to say that the truth of our understanding faculties is put out of all doubt and question as soon as
ever we are assured of the existence of a God essentially good, who
therefore cannot deceive; whilst this existence of a God is itself no
otherwise proved than by our understanding faculties; that is at
once to prove the truth of God's existence from our faculties of reason and understanding, and again to prove the truth of those faculties from the existence of a God essentially good: this, I say, is
plainly to move round in a circle, and to prove nothing at all; a
gross oversight, which the forementioned philosopher seems plainly
guilty of.

"Wherefore, according to this hypothesis, we are of necessity condemned to eternal scepticism, both concerning the existence of a
God, when, after all our arguments and demonstrations for the same,
we must at length gratify the Atheists with this confession in the
conclusion, that it is nevertheless possible there may be none; and
also concerning all other things, the certainty whereof is supposed
to depend upon the certainty of the existence of such a God as cannot deceive." (Intellectual System, pp. 716, 717, 4to, edited by
Birch, 1743.) A very obscure paragraph follows this—maintaining
that, "as to the universal and abstract theorems of science, the measure and rule of truth concerning them must be native and domestic
to the mind;" "that every clear and distinct perception is an entity or truth; that the very essence of truth here is this clear per-
ceptibility or intelligibility; that in false opinions, the perception of
the understanding power itself is not false, but only obscure; that
it is not the understanding power or nature in us that erreth, but it
is we ourselves who err, when we rashly and unwarily assent to
things not clearly perceived by it." No sentences can prove more

be called *à priori*, since it is drawn from a certain phenomenon of the human mind, and professes to offer for it an adequate solution.

Again, when Descartes makes clear and distinct perception the test of truth, because every such per-

clearly than these how much Locke was wanted, to make us aware of the reality of the distinction between ideas, or the bare notions of things in the mind, and propositions relating to these ideas, for the purpose of reasoning and conviction, and of the falseness of the distinction between *ourselves* when we assent, however rashly, to error, and the *understanding nature or power* thus supposed to be always true to itself. Cudworth afterwards endeavours to make out an argument or demonstration for the existence of a God, from our idea of him, as including necessary existence in it some other ways ; and he gives us some anticipation of Dr. Clarke's *à priori* argument, with which, and with Descartes, it may be usefully compared. But he confesses that such argumentation, by reason of its subtlety, can do but little execution, nor had he any opinion of ' demonstration *à priori*,' as his preface shows.

The Rev. F. D. Maurice, in the article on Mental Philosophy, in the ' Encyclopædia Metropolitana,' intimates that the Platonists of England in the latter part of the eighteenth century, Cudworth, Henry More, John Smith, and Worthington, should rather be called Cartesians, on account of the tendency and character of their speculations. But he gives no evidence for this. The foregoing extract shows how much Cudworth was opposed to Descartes upon a main point. The sweet-tempered Henry More, in whom Platonism assumes an interesting and captivating form, though an admirer and correspondent of Descartes, was by no means disposed to put him on a level with Plato and Plotinus. In the antidote against Atheism, he declines to rest the being of a God upon an argument so frail as that of Descartes, and in his Divine Dialogues, which, though vapid perhaps for our modern taste, have yet many divine passages in them,—prelusions of the best parts of Paley's ' Natural Theology,'— speaking of Descartes' rash and frivolous attempt to explain the phenomena of nature and the universe by mechanical principles, as a design never to prove successful, Hylobares, the materialist, asks,

ception has God for its author, and God cannot be a deceiver, at the same time admitting that we are in many things the victims of error, even when we think we have clear evidence, this is either an obvious sophism, or an arbitrary principle, whose value has never been acknowledged by successors. It has not contributed to the solution of any difficulties, nor the settlement of any disputes.

Yet these are the chief principles of the 'Prima Philosophia.' Upon the whole they have passed into much the same oblivion as the physical principles of the ingenious, but not very candid nor high-minded author. Though candour compels us to acknowledge, and with gratitude, that he rendered most signal service to psychological philosophy by turning the mental vision inward upon itself, and accustoming us to watch the operations of our intellect, yet " the Cartesian philosophy, in one sense," says Mr. Hallam* excellently well, " carried in itself the seeds of its own decline. It was the Scylla of many dogs ; it taught men to think for themselves, and to think often better than Descartes had done."

"Why, where does Cartesius fail?" and he is answered by Philotheus, who certainly speaks the sentiments of More, "Nay, rather tell me, where he does not?" Smith and Worthington have left nothing behind them but some select discourses, those of the latter scarcely remembered. Norris, a name that may be associated with these, though an Oxford man of later times, in his 'Ideal World,' appears as a genuine Platonist, and censures Descartes severely (ch. vi. § 3). Descartes does not appear to have had in England any eminent disciple.

* History of Literature, vol. iv. p. 206.

The Meditations of Descartes evidently suppose a mind already in an advanced state of culture. Such a mind only can propose the doubts, entertain the ideas, and follow the reasonings, which he treats as if they were the natural and primary conditions of every thinking being. Now of such a mind, long accustomed to abstract speculations, and nurtured in the atmosphere of schools, many things are true which could not safely be predicated of the mind of an infant, of the savage, or of the uninstructed, to say nothing of idiots and the half developed. As compounds in chemistry, and in the great chemistry of nature, like air and water, have qualities wholly different from those of the elements of which they are composed, and of these elements, as they exist apart, no trace is indicated until after patient and minute analysis, so in the mind, the affections and powers habitual to the full-grown and healthily-developed intellectual and moral character, and which have become a second nature, appear to have nothing in common with the elementary sensations and feelings out of which they really arise, and which alone are discernible in the infant, when first it opens its eyes to the light, and begins to make acquaintance with the world and with itself*.

---

* I cannot quit Descartes without fortifying what has been said by the remarks of Leibnitz, who was accused of wishing to build his own reputation upon the ruins of that of M. Descartes. " Il est vrai cependant que M. Descartes a usé d'artifice, pour profiter des découvertes d'autres sans leur en vouloir paroître redevable. Il traitoit d'excellens hommes d'une manière injuste et indigne, lorsqu'ils

P

GASSENDI'S INFLUENCE UPON LOCKE.

Though the independence and originality of Descartes' speculations early attracted the sympathy of Locke, and were much preferred by him to the cloudy utterances of the Aristotelians and schoolmen still in repute and authority when Locke was a student at Oxford, it does not appear that Descartes suggested to Locke any one of the principles which 'constitute the vital parts of the Essay on the Human Understanding. Descartes and the Cartesians, if noticed at all by Locke, are noticed unfavourably*. But Gassendi, a name unnoticed in Dr. Reid's Inquiry into the Human Mind, the friend and admirer of Hobbes, came, as already intimated, much nearer to the views which Locke took of the manner in which

lui faisoient ombrage, et il avoit une ambition démesurée pour s'ériger en chef de parti. Mais cela ne diminuë point la beauté de ses pensées. Bien loin d'approuver qu'on méprise et qu'on paye d'ingratitude le vrai mérite, c'est cela que je blâme principalement en M. Descartes, et encore plus en plusieurs de ses sectateurs, dont attachement mal entendu à un seul auteur, nourrit la prévention, et les empêche de profiter des lumières de tant d'autres. J'ai coutume de dire que la Philosophie Cartésienne est comme l'antichambre de la vérité, et qu'il est difficile de pénétrer bien avant, sans avoir passé par-là : mais on se prive de la véritable connoissance du fond des choses, quand on s'y arrête."—*Leibnitii Opera, Erdmann's edition*, p. 142.

* See particularly b. iii. c. 4. § 9, 10; b. iv. c. 7. § 12, 13; and second reply to Bishop of Worcester, p. 755. The names of Gassendi and Bernier, having been mentioned by Stillingfleet, are introduced in Locke's second reply to the bishop, but without a hint of his personal acquaintance with the latter, or of any attachment to the writings of the former.

the understanding comes to be furnished with those
ideas it has, and even anticipated Locke in his great
division of the two sources of knowledge, *sensation*
and *reflection ;* at least the division follows naturally
from what Gassendi had laid down, though it be not
anywhere expressly made with the simplicity and clearness of his successor.   Gassendi was, I conceive, the
true intellectual parent of Locke; that Leibnitz was
of this opinion seems evident from the first page of
his ' Nouveaux Essais sur l'Entendement Humain ;'
but it is a question, difficult of solution, to what extent Locke was sensible of the parentage and his obligations, or when and where he studied the writings of
Gassendi, and made acquaintance with his philosophy.

Some regret may reasonably be felt at the slight-
ness of the information which can now be recovered,
respecting Locke's early studies*.   He had   read

* The life by the late Lord King adds little to what was known
of him previously in this respect.   It wants the care and completeness of a good literary and philosophical biography.   It might have
been enriched by many extracts from the correspondence of Locke
with Molyneux, Limborch, and others, first published in 1706, and
appended to Law's quarto edition, the only good one.   It even omits
some important facts, mentioned by Le Clerc, in the Life which is
the foundation of Law's, such as the times when he took his degrees
at Oxford.   The whole of Le Clerc's life of Locke should have been
given with additional notes, and especially its beautiful conclusion,
only a part of which is translated.   Yet we must be thankful for the
extracts from the journals, notes, and adversaria of Locke, never
before printed ; and accept the life as, upon the whole, an appropriate tribute from an honourable descendant of a branch of his family,
to the memory of a great and justly-revered ancestor.   The sweet
account of Locke's last hours and death was doubtless communicated

much more than can be traced, for he never makes any display of learning.   Like Bacon, like Hobbes, like Descartes, he made his own, whatever he had learnt and believed on the subjects of his special investigation.   His early residence at Oxford and in the neighbourhood, his journeys thither to consult the libraries, his occasional allusions to the best and most curious books of his day, to the pursuits of naturalists and the discoveries of travellers, and his intimacy with the most distinguished, learned, and scientific of his contemporaries, render it certain that no important source of information was overlooked by him; and it is manifest that Gassendi, after Hobbes, though perhaps in a manner forgotten by himself, had smoothed the way for the conclusions relating to the mind, which make the chief figure in the second book of the Essay.

No part of Stewart's Dissertation* is less satisfactory than that which relates to Gassendi.   He attributes to him the opinion "that there is not a single object of the understanding, which may not be ultimately analysed into sensible images, and, of consequence, that when Descartes proposed to abstract from these images in studying the mind, he (Gassendi) re-

to Le Clerc by Lady Masham, the author of the first life of Locke in the 'General Historical Dictionary,' which life may have been the foundation of the careful but not too favourable biography which we have in the 'Biographia Britannica.'   We learn this from a pleasing account of Lady Masham in a scarce book, 'Ballard's Lives of Illustrious Ladies of England.'

* See pp. 70–74.

jected the only materials out of which it is possible for our faculties to rear any superstructure." He professes to use Gassendi's own language, but without reference, in the words that "there is no real distinction between imagination and intellection." And again he asserts—"that the main scope of Gassendi's argument against Descartes is to *materialize* that class of our ideas which the Lockists as well as the Cartesians consider as the exclusive objects of the power of *reflection ;* and to show that these ideas are all ultimately resolvable into images or conceptions borrowed from things external. It is not therefore what is sound and valuable in this part of Locke's system, but the errors grafted on it in the comments of some of his followers, that can justly be said to have been borrowed from Gassendi. Nor has Gassendi the merit of originality, even in these errors; for scarcely a remark on the subject occurs in his works but what is copied from the accounts transmitted to us of the Epicurean metaphysics."

This is wholly unfounded. Mr. Stewart was unacquainted with Bernier's abridgment of Gassendi; and could not have been a diligent reader of the works in folio, or these very serious misrepresentations, which have not escaped the just animadversion of Mr. Hallam*, could not have been made.

It appears that Locke was resident in and about Amsterdam in 1680, and for some years after. The Revolution of 1688 enabled him to return with satis-

* History of Literature, vol. iv. p. 199.

faction to his country, which then, and greatly by his aid, redeemed itself from its disgrace, and escaped the greatest of calamities.   Holland was at that time in a remarkable degree the country of free thought, deep learning, and ardent literature.   At Amsterdam the 'Meditations' of Descartes and the comments of Gassendi and his allies had been published as early as 1644; and Locke was intimate with all those scholars in France and on the continent, to whom the controversy between Descartes and his antagonists was likely to be familiar.   We find from the Journal, portions of which are printed in Lord King's Life*, that when in Paris in the year 1677, Locke was very intimate with Monsieur Bernier, who must have been busy about that time with his abridgment of the 'Philosophy' of Gassendi, published at Lyons in 1678.   Although the conversations noted in the Journal turned only upon the travels in the East, by Bernier, of which sort of books Locke was particularly fond; yet it is natural to suppose that they discussed fully and freely the metaphysical questions, in which both were so deeply interested and engaged.   Before this, when at Lyons in 1676, Locke mentions an interview with a Mr. Charlton; and this was probably some relation of the Dr. Walter Charlton†, eminent in London as a physi-

* Vol. i. p. 136.

† Among the Birch MSS. relating to Locke, in the British Museum, there is a letter to one William Charleton, dated 1687. Walter Charlton was physician to Charles I., and the author of several publications.   He printed, in 1670, 'Epicurus' Morals,' collected out of his own Greek text in Diogenes Laertius, prefixing an

cian, who published 'Enquiries into Human Nature' chiefly anatomical, and an account of the 'Philosophy' of Gassendi. That Gassendi's name and works were in high esteem in England, at least among the deeper students and freest thinkers, before and about Locke's time, is evident from the manner in which he is noticed by the eminent Robert Boyle, in which Joseph Glanvil* often speaks of him, and from the publications of Walter Charlton. The plan of Locke's Essay was indeed formed as early as 1770, and a sketch of it was then made, so that it could hardly have been from Bernier's abridgment that he acquired such knowledge of Gassendi's 'Philosophy' as he may have had. But a few passages from the sixth volume of that abridgment will show how completely Locke harmonized with Gassendi, and how nearly he was

---

apology for Epicurus, as to his three capital offences: first, that he held the souls of men are mortal; secondly, that man is not obliged to worship God from hope of good or fear of evil, but rather on account of his transcendent excellency, beatitude, and immortality; thirdly, that self-homicide may be an act of heroic fortitude in cases of intolerable calamity. He also published, in 1654, a small folio, entitled "Physiologia Epicuro-Gassendo-Charltoniana; or a fabric of science natural upon the hypothesis of atoms: founded by Epicurus, repaired by Petrus Gassendus, augmented by W. Charlton." This work must be very rare, the only copy I could find being in the library of Sion College.

* See Glanvil's Essay on 'Scepticism and Certainty,' pp. 38, 39, (1676), where he praises the renowned Gassendi, as a philosopher with whom he (Glanvil) is not fit to be named, and defends him from the charge of reviving a deadly scepticism. Also Life of the Hon. R. Boyle, by Birch, p. 80, where, in a letter to Hartlib, the friend of Milton, he calls Gassendus "a great favourite."

anticipated in that great division of the two sources of our ideas, which has been generally supposed to be Locke's own.

Gassendi was for his day an excellent anatomist, physiologist, and astronomer. His analytical remarks on the senses, the organs, the brain, the nerves, and on the ideas imparted to the mind through them, and thence deposited in the memory and the imagination, are acute, profound, instructive. He passes in the fourth book to discuss the understanding or reasonable soul; and the titles of the chapters, the very first words, convict Mr. Stewart of great misapprehension.

"The first proof that the understanding is not material," says Gassendi, "is drawn from certain exertions of that faculty, which are evidently different from those of the imagination; and we expressly commence this Treatise with this remark, in order to remove a prejudice which may be held, that the understanding is not a faculty distinct from the fancy or imaginative power, and that there is no difference between them but of more or less. But I maintain that we raise ourselves by reasoning to a knowledge of that which we cannot imagine, of which we can have no image nor appearance present to the mind, whatever efforts we may make, and that thus *there is in us a species of intellection which is not imagination.*"

After adducing as examples the conclusions which, by astronomical science, we are led to form concerning the sizes and relations of the heavenly bodies, he adds, "It is true that the understanding avails itself

of the image of fancy, as of certain steps, to arrive by
reasoning at a knowledge of things, which it understands afterwards without appearances or phantasms,
but it is in order to lift itself thereby above every
material form, and to know effectively something of
which it has no phantasm; and this it is which marks
as immateriality." He finds a second reason for its
immateriality in those reflex actions, by which the
understanding knows itself and its functions: "La
seconde raison se prend des actions réflexes, par les-
quelles l'entendement se connoît soi-mesme, et ses
fonctions, et connoît spécialement qu'il connoît ou en-
tend: car cela est au-dessus de toute faculté corpo-
relle, d'autant que ce qui est corporel ne sçauroit se
mouvoir vers soi-mesme qui soit différent de lui.   Et
c'est là la cause de cet axiome, '*que rien n'agit sur
soi-mesme;*' ce qui semble quelquefois agir sur soi
n'étant jamais absolument le mesme, mais seulement
une partie qui agit sur l'autre, comme lorsque la main
frappe la cuisse, ou que l'extremité du doigt frappe le
dedans de la main; car du reste l'extremité du doigt
ne peut pas agir sur elle-mesme*." As a third reason he gives the power of forming universal notions
and of comprehending the nature of universality; "for
as it is the nature of universals to be abstract or despoiled of all material conditions and individual differences, such as greatness, figure, colour, etc., it is
certain that the understanding which considers this
abstraction is itself disengaged from matter, and of

* Vol. vi. p. 345.

a nature more eminent than anything material;" as a fourth, the consideration that if the understanding were corporeal, it would never have recognized, as it does, nor supposed, any incorporeal nature; and a fifth from the *Will*, which raises itself to honourable good, which disdains a good merely sensible and corporeal, and is above all appetites attached merely to matter.

He adds, as a sixth consideration in support of the immateriality of the mind, the disproportion and difference between the attributes or properties of matter and those of the understanding.

"Granting that matter be reduced into atoms, or if you will, into particles, small, hard, or soft as you please, however small, subtle, and fine they may be, they will never be found capable but of three properties, figure, solidity, or local movement, whence spring those other properties marked by these two verses:—

'Intervalla, viæ, convexus, pondera, plagæ,
Concursus, motus, ordo, positura, figuræ;'—

that is to say, a certain concourse, order, and arrangement, a certain disposition of movements, separations, impulses, reflexes, etc.; and the human mind will never conceive them capable of anything else.

"This being so, I ask, if we can discern any relation or proportion between these properties, and the excellence of the operations of an understanding; or if it is possible that certain small bodies, very imperfect, and which have as the appendage of their nature nothing but to be figured, round, square, pyramidal,

etc., solid, hard, and impenetrable, and to be capable
of passing from one place to another, whether these
have any relation to what we call *thought*, knowledge,
meditation, reasoning, self-reflection.   Never will you
persuade me that when we contemplate the infinite
extension of this universe, and thence see the absolute
necessity of admitting some Eternal Being, God, or
first principles, or both; when we inquire what are
the first principles of things, or what we are ourselves,
and the nature of our understanding, whether it be a
substance corporeal or incorporeal; when we remember the past, consider the present, and anticipate the
future; when by a long chain of propositions, which
we view as a whole, we thence arrive at demonstrations which have in them something of divinity; when
we converse one with another; when we dispute, reason, and reflect on our reasonings;—never, I say, will
you persuade me that in these lofty moods of mind,
these inward efforts, these profound meditations, there
is nothing within us but certain mixtures of small
bodies, and that all this takes place only by means of
shocks and counter-shocks, meetings and separations
of these same small atoms, destitute of all feeling and
all intelligence."

He concludes his first chapter with discussing the
probability of a substantial difference between the
sensitive and the reasonable soul, and the impossibility of fixing the seat, and even comprehending the
nature, of pure intellection.

In the second chapter he argues in favour of the

immortality of the human understanding, from the general consent of mankind in the belief of it, from the universality of the desire, and from the just government of God; he examines objections, and justly censures the opinion of Descartes—as a very strange foundation for a Christian verity—that *brutes do not feel, and are only machines.* In the subsequent chapters he discusses the functions, habitudes, and perfections of the understanding, in what respects it is different from the senses, how it arrives at the knowledge of *universals*, which knowledge or science is particularly the business of the intellect, and which (viz. universals) are much more easy of definition than individuals whose specific differences are not easily discerned and described.

But Gassendi was a devoted admirer of Epicurus, and Mr. Stewart condemns him for servility in his attachment to that ancient. Weakness there may be in the excessive admiration of an unworthy object; but servility, which is the being servant to another, and compliance with his will through fear or baseness, there can hardly be. Attachment to the memory or the principles of a departed worthy may be misplaced, but there can be nothing servile in what is purely disinterested and sincere. The *sty of Epicurus* is in very bad repute; but there is more affectation of delicacy than real discernment in the shock which the imagination of it gives to the nervous system. The Apostle Paul encountered at Athens certain of the Epicureans and Stoics; but we have not been favoured with means of judging to which party his sympathies leaned.   If the Stoic aimed merely at insensibility to pain as the perfection of his being, this is evidently but the perfection of a stone, hardly that of the sloth.   The nature of every man decides in favour of a state of positive pleasure.   The pleasures of Epicurus, however, were by no means sensual. His habits were simple; his life was pure; his pleasures were those of friendship, conversation, and philosophy.   He seems to have erred by placing happiness too much in indolence of body and mere tranquillity of mind.   Labour and exertion he regarded as among the worst of evils.   He dreaded the excitement so often coveted.   He did not perceive that the highest enjoyment results from the energetic pursuit of worthy objects.   Therefore he exempted the gods from interest in human affairs; and the evils of human life appeared to him a valid objection to the doctrine of a Providence, as occasioning pain to contemplate and trouble to remove them.   But the utilitarian philosopher, whether of Hartley's, Paley's, or Bentham's school, who believes happiness the end alike of the Divine government and self-government, of human laws and of private ethics, must sympathize with Epicurus, and value especially his two last principles, "that all pleasure, which either hinders a greater pleasure, or procures a greater pain, ought to be the object of our aversion; and that all pain that dispels a greater pain, or makes way for a greater pleasure, ought to be coveted."   Whoever compares the philo-

sophy, physical or moral, of Zeno and Epicurus, in
the accounts left us by Diogenes Laertius*, the chief
authority, will see reason to prefer the latter, as pos-
sessing more distinctness and more consistency, more
truth, simplicity, and exactness in terms and definitions, more of what Lucretius calls *naturæ species,*
ratioque; and will sympathize in the enthusiasm of
the poet, when he breaks out—

> " Te sequor, ô Graiæ gentis decus! inque tuis nunc
> Ficta pedum pono pressis vestigia signis.
>
> · · · · · ·
>
> Floriferis ut apes in saltibus omnia limant,
> Omnia nos itidem depascimur aurea dicta,
> Aurea, perpetuâ semper dignissima vitâ."
>
> *Lucretius,* lib. iii.

Without injustice to the proud virtues of the stoical
wise man, we may, with Gassendi, with Charlton,
and perhaps Glanvil, assign to Epicurus that superior
discernment in the elements of morals, which Bacon
and Newton certainly allotted to him in the department of physics. "The purest religion is the most
refined Epicurism," said Lavater, in those aphorisms
admired in the last century: "he who in the smallest
given time can enjoy most of what he never shall re-
pent, and what furnishes enjoyments still more unex-

---

* The edition of Diogenes Laertius, in two volumes, Amsterdam,
1692, professedly edited by Meibomius, but whose value appears
greatly owing to the Dutch printer, Henry Wetstein, is one of those
beautiful books which, like the edition of the Greek Testament,
about half a century later, by John James Wetstein, with its invaluable prolegomena, fills us with astonishment at the learning,
industry, and taste of the scholars of a former age.

hausted, still less changeable, is the most religious and the most voluptuous of men." The pious Doddridge expresses the same idea in the well-known lines—

> "Live, while you live! the Epicure may say,
> And give to pleasure e'en the longest day.
> Live, while you live! the Christian also cries,
> And give to God each moment as it flies.
> Lord, in my view let both united be,
> I live to pleasure, while I live to Thee."

The association of all duty and labour with permanent happiness, cannot be too early, nor too strongly impressed upon the mind, as the real foundation and true safeguard of virtuous habit, the principle and centre to which all morality and religion gravitate, embracing alike the law of nature and of nations, the civil law and the Divine law, the interest of the individual and of the race. We trace the incipient appreciation of this principle in the Nicomachean ethics of Aristotle, no less than in the promising investigations of Epicurus; but the full development of it is one of the great triumphs of modern mental and moral science. Humboldt has beautifully observed, that it was only after the promulgation of Christianity that a true perception of the grandeur and beauty of natural scenery, a feeling for the harmony and loveliness of nature, manifested itself in oratory and poetry, and became an element of pure devotion. To the same source of influence may doubtless be attributed that fuller development of the established connection between the Divine will and human happiness, between the security of individual and the pursuit of social good, which shines out with dazzling splendour in the Theodicy and optimism of Leibnitz, and in Hartley's rule of life.

But with Gassendi's Epicureanism, be its worth or weakness what it may, Locke had nothing to do. He has made no allusion to it, nor are we concerned with it, except in so far as without some notice our estimate of Gassendi would be incomplete. We have now seen that sensation, and the reflex acts of the mind upon itself, were principal subjects of Gassendi's attention in considering the human frame and constitution. Yet it cannot be said that he laid down the two sources of all our knowledge with anything like the distinctness of his great successor, whose simple statement has enabled us to speak with comparative precision of the world or qualities of matter, on the one hand, and of the powers and affections peculiar to the mind, upon the other. In reading Gassendi, as in the study of the ancients generally, we appreciate him better by the light of knowledge which we bring to interpret the expression. The rays of all intelligence shine brighter, whatever stars are out in our hemisphere, in proportion as the atmosphere of the observer is free from cloud, and the organ of vision itself is pure and strong.

Gassendi was the friend and warm admirer of Hobbes, and Hobbes is considered pre-eminently a sensationalist. But before I touch this line of mental genealogy, I shall revert to the true nature and intrinsic merits of Locke's first book on innate ideas.

LOCKE'S FIRST BOOK ON INNATE IDEAS DEFENDED.

Those who talk of the deep moral instincts and the "*à priori* intuitions" of our nature, in so far as by this language they imply that antecedently to observation and reflection, and independently of thought and instruction, the human mind is in possession of certain fundamental truths, axioms, principles, or feelings, whose value is to be assumed rather than weighed, which evaporate rather than become condensed and solid under any process of logical analysis, cannot admit that Locke has demonstrated the non-existence of innate ideas. Yet the demonstration is very simple. Our ideas are either simple or complex. Into these two classes they have been divided, and the division is intelligible and useful; and may be regarded as complete, till a more intelligible and useful be suggested. Now, if we have not a simple idea of sensation, not the idea of a single object of nature, nor of any quality of matter, before we have been affected from without by an object imparting such sensation; if the ideas of colours, of sounds, tastes, smells, suppose senses, and impressions on the senses, without which the ideas would not exist; if extension, motion, hardness, softness, solidity, liquidity, squareness, roundness, are terms significant of many impressions on the senses, and imply the existence of *bodies moved, extended, square, round*, etc., bodies having the qualities and imparting the ideas to which we give these names; *à fortiori*, we cannot have any innate

Q

complex idea, such as of drunkenness, theft, matri-
mony, diplomacy, war, and all the ideas of social and
moral relation, ideas of government and law, all which
Locke calls *mixed modes;* for every complex idea will
be found to imply the previous existence of many
sensations, of the relation of sensations and feelings
to each other, and to *mental states,*—that is, to percipient and sensitive natures. And what term is there
significant of a mental state or mental power, which
does not imply the previous existence of a vast sphere
of sensation, observation, and experience? In such
a sphere, memory, comparison, reflection, desire, will,
choice, imagination, anticipation, and so on, find the
occasions of their exercise,—life its school of discipline, and the intellectual faculties their soil of growth
or of decay. And although the combination of simple ideas, and the perception of their relation to one
another and to mental states, to all the wants and conditions of humanity, be the act and property of the
mind itself, no complex idea can be considered innate
which is resolvable into simple ideas admitted to come
by way of sensation from without, and to which the
previous existence of the simple ideas is essential.

There is another consideration, or another mode of
putting the argument. Is it true that all our ideas
relate either to the properties of matter, or properties
of mind? that we cannot conceive of any subject of
thought not comprised within one or other of these
two classes? that these comprise the *ego* and *non ego,*
the *moi* and *non-moi,* as some now express it, but with

less of useful distinction and preciseness? God, nature, and man, or the mind, complete, according to Bacon, the circle of the sciences. Now, of the properties of matter no one would pretend any knowledge or idea without sensation. To be the subject of sensation, to have a sensation, is the first act or condition of the percipient created mind, the first phenomenon of consciousness. But perception or percipiency cannot be conceived to exist without something perceptible existing without or independently; for even the relations of truth, a perception of the harmony or disagreement of ideas, in so far as ideas are regarded as separate entities, may be viewed as something independent of the mind perceiving those relations and that harmony. Even the percipiency of the Divine mind is not conceivable, and the terms expressive of the Divine attributes are without meaning, except as they have relation to an outward sensible universe,—that is, a universe occupied by beings whose relations to each other are totally different from those which they bear to the Creator, which relations are the subject of distinct consideration and knowledge. No power is conceivable without a sphere in which it is exercised, without things or beings acted upon; no goodness without beings to whom good is done; no wisdom without something to know or be known. Much more do the various properties and faculties of the human mind, such as memory and will, judgment, classification, and abstraction, appetite or aversion, suppose an external world to furnish sub-

Q 2

jects for memory and choice, materials for mental exercise and moral discipline, pleasures to desire, or pains to avoid.

There is yet a third consideration. Of the ideas existing in different minds, there is no possibility of ascertaining that they have any resemblance to each other, any common origin, but in one of two ways,—either by referring them to some outward object or source, marked by a common name, which, in the case of ideas of sensation, is obvious, and for which usage of common names provision is made by the uniformity of nature, and of the sensible impressions *ab extra;* or by defining the terms significant of complex ideas, that is, resolving them into the more simple elements, which definition and resolution will be found also to rest in the end upon the association of some uniform impressions *ab extra,* or upon certain feelings of pleasure or pain peculiar to the human frame, and common to beings similarly framed. This will be more clear when we come to consider what terms are, and what are not, susceptible of definition.

These are not exactly Locke's modes of attacking the existence of innate ideas; but they flow rather from the positions which he has established, and from the theory of the mind which he has developed. He contends chiefly against the supposed existence of *innate principles* and *maxims.* He maintains that they are unnecessary; that the mind arrives at them by degrees; that there is no evidence that the minds of infants and savages are furnished even with the simplest, still less with such as imply complex moral relations; that the supposition is gratuitous, and the hasty resort of indolence,—as Leibnitz would have expressed it, a "sophisme paresseuse." It was enough for him to show that every principle and every maxim implied a knowledge of objects, and a perception of the relation of objects and beings to one another, which could not exist but in a mind furnished by a world of sensation *ab extra*.

It has not been much observed, I think, that there was one English writer of the greatest eminence before Locke's time, who quite agreed in the opinion that the human mind is at first wholly unfurnished with knowledge and ideas,—a writer never suspected of any tendency to scepticism, and one of the greatest ornaments of the English church, "a man of deep thoughts," as Locke calls him, namely, the learned and judicious Hooker.

"The soul of man *being therefore at the first as a book wherein nothing is, and yet all things may be imprinted,* we are to search by what steps and degrees it riseth unto perfection of knowledge . . . . as stones, though in dignity of nature inferior unto plants, yet exceed them in firmness of strength, or durability of being; and plants, though beneath the excellency of creatures endued with sense, yet exceed them in the faculty of vegetation and of fertility; so beasts, though otherwise behind men, may notwithstanding in actions of sense and fancy go beyond them, because the endeavours of nature, when it hath an

higher perfection to seek, are in lower the more re-
miss, not esteeming thereof so much as those things
do, which have no better end proposed unto them.
The soul of man therefore being capable of more
divine perfection, hath (besides the faculties of growing unto sensible knowledge, which is common unto
us with beasts) a further ability, whereof in them
there is no show at all, the ability of reaching higher
than unto sensible things.   Till we grow to some
ripeness of years, the soul of man doth only store
itself with conceits of things of more open and inferior quality, which afterwards do serve as instruments unto that which is greater; in the meanwhile,
above the reach of meaner creatures it ascendeth not:
when once it comprehendeth anything above this, as
the differences of time, affirmations, negations, and
contradiction in speech, we then count it to have some
use of natural reason.   Whereunto, if afterwards there
might be added the right helps of true art and learning (which helps, I must confess, this age of the world,
carrying the name of a learned age, doth neither much
know, nor greatly regard), there would undoubtedly
be almost as great a difference in maturity of judgment between men therewith inured, and that which
now men are, as between men that are now, and in-
nocents, which speech, if any condemn as hyperbolical,
let them consider but this one thing: no art is at the
first finding out so perfect as industry may after make
it; yet the very first man [*he alludes to Aristotle*] that
to any purpose knew the way we speak of, and fol-

lowed it, hath alone thereby performed more very near
in all parts of natural knowledge, than sithence in any
one part the whole world besides hath done.   In the
poverty of that other new devised aid two things there
are, notwithstanding, singular.   Of marvellous quick
despatch it is, and doth show them that have it as
much almost in three days, as if it had dwelt three-
score years with them.   Again, because the curiosity
of man's wit doth many times with peril wade farther
in the search of things than were convenient, the same
is thereby restrained unto such generalities as, everywhere offering themselves, are apparent unto men of
the weakest conceit that need be ; so as, following the
rules and precepts thereof, we may find it to be an
art which teacheth the way of speedy discourse, and
restraineth the mind of man, that it may not wax
overwise.   Education and instruction are the means,
the one by use, the other by precept, to make our natural faculty of reason both the better and the sooner
able to judge rightly between truth and error, good
and evil.   But at what time a man may be said so
far forth to have attained the use of reason, as sufficeth to make him capable of those laws, whereby he
is then bound to guide his actions ; this is a great
deal more easy for common sense to discern, than for
any man by skill and learning to determine ; even as
it is not in philosophers, who best know the nature
both of *fire* and *gold*, to teach what degree of the one
will serve to purify the other, so well as the artisan
(which doth this by fire) discerneth by sense when

the fire hath that degree of heat which sufficeth for his purpose*."

What argument in favour of innate ideas, and of instinctive intellectual and moral sentiments, can outweigh these considerations? But comments, objections, difficulties, cavils, have been thrown out, and continue to be thrown out, on the opposite side. A language is still prevalent, implying that these considerations are not convincing. They are either not understood or they are purposely disregarded. Two writers of Locke's own time, one, Henry More, the Platonist, considerably earlier in the philosophical field, the other, Leibnitz, somewhat later, demand particular notice, not so much on account of the eminence of their names, or the weight of their arguments, as because little or nothing has been added by subsequent writers to their statements and views upon the subject.

In More's ' Antidote against Atheism†,' there will be found sundry considerations, designed to show that the mind of man is not *abrasa tabula*, but has actual knowledge of her own. He maintains that the mind

* Hooker's ' Ecclesiastical Polity,' book i. § 6. A portion of this passage is quoted by Locke, but for a different purpose (Essay, b. iv. c. 17. § 7). The high praise of Aristotle, the allusion to the vain verbiage of Ramus, as the *new devised aid*, and the whole character of the passage, are very remarkable. The first four books of the Eccl. Polity were printed as early as 1594.

† It was printed as early as 1653, and forms the first work in the collection of his philosophical writings, published in one volume folio, in 1712 ; see particularly the fifth and sixth chapters. More died September 1, 1687.

of man, exercised in the close observation of its own operations, cannot but discover that there is an active and actual knowledge in a man, of which outward objects are rather the reminders than the first begetters or implanters; by which he understands, not ideas flaring like so many torches before the *animadversive faculty*, but an *active sagacity*, or *quick recollection*, whereby, some small business being hinted, she runs out presently into a more clear and larger conception. He compares the condition of the soul to that of a skilful musician fallen asleep upon the grass, who, not dreaming of his musical faculty, being suddenly jogged and wakened by a friend, and desired to sing, forthwith exhibits his plentiful stores of melody and harmony. He begins with saying that the soul takes first *occasion of thinking* from external objects, and that this has imposed upon some men's judgments, they not warily enough distinguishing between *extrinsical occasions*, and adequate or principal causes of things.

In the sixth chapter he contends that the soul, on the exhibition of a circle to it, acknowledges forthwith that if it be perfect, all the lines from a point within to the perimeter must be exactly equal; and so of a triangle, that if it be the right figure, the angles must be closed in indivisible points; and because accuracy in a circle or triangle cannot be set out in any material subject, therefore the soul hath in herself a more exquisite knowledge than matter can lay open before her; that there are a multitude of relative notions or

ideas which, not being impresses of any material object, are the natural furniture of the human understanding : such are *cause and effect, whole and part,
like and unlike, equality and inequality, proportion
and analogy; these, not being sensible or physical affections of matter, are active conceptions proceeding
from the soul herself.* But he destroys the ground of
his own argument, by suggesting that if in a room of
like sides, one side be altered, and another not, the
one not altered hath the notion of dissimilitude belonging to it; and if, of two pounds of lead, the half
of one be taken, the other hath lost its notion of
equal, and acquired a new one of double the other.
He is so simple as not to perceive that the notions
are only in the mind, and that without the previous
external alteration the notions could not exist. He
goes on to say that one and the same part of matter
is capable of two contrary ideas, (meaning, of giving
occasion to contrary ideas,) adding, that " ideas are no
affections of matter, and therefore do not affect our
senses ;" and here he has no meaning, for who ever
maintained that ideas do affect the senses? and he
could hardly mean that material objects do not affect
them. He concludes that, having proved certain
single ideas to be in the mind, several complex notions are also there, such as that the whole is bigger
than the part; if you take equal from equal, the remainders are equal ; every number is either even or
odd,—which are true to the soul at the very first proposal, as any one in his wits does plainly perceive.

But the question is not as to the existence of single ideas and complex notions in the mind, but *how* they come there, and *when* they first appear.

To the student of Locke, these notions and assertions respecting the innate truths of the mind, or active conceptions proceeding from the soul herself, are scarcely worth repeating: but the advocate of innate ideas, the Platonist and Cartesian, must be allowed to have fair play, and speak for himself. With more learning than Locke, Henry More had not less the love of truth, nor less purity of design; he was looked upon by Dr. Outram as the *holiest person upon the earth*. But he wanted Locke's strong, determinate, practical sense. He had early muddled himself with Platonism: he mistook the colours of that cloud for the pure light of heaven. An enthusiastic lover of reason and philosophy in the abstract, he knew not the nature and value of its only tools, *definite terms*. He is scarcely less remarkable than Cudworth for barbarous and obsolete expressions, such as incompossibility, self-essentiated, hylopathy, idiopathy. His pages may be looked into by the curious, and are full of matter to gratify the curious; but he deserves to be remembered chiefly as a poet, whose childhood was nourished on the divine morality and fancy of Spenser's Faery Queene, and whose Platonism is most agreeable when tuned to the music of the Spenserian verse. He was one of the starry lights, gleaming through the mist, whom Locke's rise above the horizon caused to "pale their ineffectual fires."

In the expression that external objects furnish but the first *occasion* of thinking, and only stir up the soul to a sort of consciousness of the conceptions already existing within herself, More has anticipated what Leibnitz and Stewart, Cousin and others, have said in contradiction or modification of the opinion that the mind is originally without ideas, and begins to entertain them by the first impressions on the senses from without. This is a matter worthy of some consideration.

Mr. D. Stewart, in his ' Elements of the Philosophy of the Human Mind,' enlarges on the question of the origin of our knowledge, reducing it to one of fact:— " Concerning the *occasions* on which the mind is led to form those simple notions, into which our thoughts may be analysed, and which may be considered as the principles or elements of human knowledge*." Attaching great importance to Dr. Reid's inquiries concerning the history of our notions of extension and figure, and suggesting that similar inquiries may be proposed concerning the *occasions* on which we form the notions of time, of motion, of number, of causation, and an infinite variety of others, Stewart ventures to affirm, " that the mind cannot, without the grossest absurdity, be considered in the light of a receptacle, which is gradually furnished from without, nor in that of a *tabula rasa*, upon which copies or resemblances of things external are imprinted." And he goes on to say, " That those ideas, which Mr. Locke

* Stewart's Elements, p. 96, edit. 1802.

calls ideas of reflection (or, in other words, the notions which we form of the subjects of our own consciousness), are not suggested to the mind immediately by the sensations arising from the use of our organs of perception, is granted on all hands, and therefore, the amount of the doctrine now mentioned, is nothing more than this, that the *first occasions on which our various intellectual faculties are exercised,* are furnished by the impressions made on our organs of sense; and consequently, that without these impressions, it would have been impossible for us to arrive at the knowledge of our faculties. Agreeably to this explanation of the doctrine, it may undoubtedly be said with plausibility (*and I am inclined to believe with truth*) *that the occasions on which all our notions are formed, are furnished either immediately or ultimately by sense;* but if I am not much mistaken, this is not the meaning which is commonly annexed to the doctrine, either by its advocates or their opponents."

But this is a very poor way of philosophizing, first to call Mr. Locke's doctrine a gross absurdity, and then to admit everything which Mr. Locke asserts, without condescending to quote his exact expressions. The whole question turns on the value of the phrase, "furnishing the occasion." Would Mr. Locke have objected to it? You admit that a child is unfurnished with ideas of colours, tastes, smells, and so on, without an impression from without; that by an impression on the organs of sense, the ideas of sensation, properly so called, are furnished, or that the presence

of something external furnishes the occasion for the
idea.   Would the idea be there without the impression or occasion?   The follower of Locke believes
that it would not.   Is it meant that the idea is in the
mind before the occasion, or that the occasion awakens
what Henry More says was only asleep?   The follower of Locke believes such an opinion wholly unfounded.   Wordsworth, in the beautiful ode on the
intimations of Immortality, may say :—

> " Our birth is but a sleep and a forgetting :
> The soul that rises with us, our life's star,
>   Hath had elsewhere its setting,
>   And cometh from afar :
>   Not in entire forgetfulness,
>   And not in utter nakedness,
> But trailing clouds of glory do we come
>   From God, who is our home :
> Heaven lies about us in our infancy !"

And this may be delicious as poetry, where we assume
what we please, and please by assuming.   But philosophy assumes nothing, and humbly waits on nature
and on fact, " naturæ interpres et minister."   It is
hardly conceivable that an intelligent person, with the
first chapter of Locke's second book open before him,
can satisfy himself that, by substituting the word
" *occasion*" for the word " *origin*," he approaches
nearer to the philosophy of the mind; that he alters
or modifies the truth of Locke's statements; that he
throws any light whatever upon the sources of our
ideas, as comprehended by observation and experience,
and coming from sensation and reflection*.

* Whoever would inquire into the value of these terms, *occasion*

If any man could have shaken the credit of Locke's 'Essay on the Understanding,' could have modified the main conclusions which the Essay tended to establish, or thrown new and important light upon the

and *origin*, and see whether the use of the former contributes to any important modification of Locke's views, will do well to read carefully that portion of Bowen's Essays, pp. 50, 51, where, in a paper on Kant and his philosophy, he supposes "*something* (quære, what?) added by the mind to sensible impressions, originally, instinctively, and wholly unlike any quality existing in the outward thing," and also the criticism on Locke by Mr. J. D. Morell, vol. i. pp. 99–102. The latter writer says, "Where Locke found a difficulty in showing the direct dependence of any idea upon experience, he soon discovered the means of showing its indirect dependence upon it; and having done this, he incorrectly concluded that the whole of our knowledge could be derived from this one source. We owe it mainly to Kant, that this fallacy has been thoroughly probed and refuted. In the very first paragraph of his great work ('The Critique of Pure Reason') he points us to experience as the *occasion* of every possible conception, which the mind forms; but proves afterwards, most convincingly, that the true *cause* of many of our conceptions is to be found solely in the original constitution of the understanding or of the reason." And thus Locke is to be deposed, and Kant enthroned! The truth is, that Locke would have admitted not only that *many*, but that *all* "our conceptions have their cause in the original constitution of the understanding or of the reason." But to say that conceptions have their cause in the original constitution of the mind, is nothing to the purpose in determining the real nature of a particular part of that constitution. My impression is, that Kant never condescended to quote correctly a single statement of Locke, and the whole is of a piece with Cousin's unpardonable misrepresentations, when, in the second lesson of his 'Cours d'Histoire de la Philosophie Morale' (1839, pp. 82, 83), he makes Locke say that "sensation is the source of *all* our ideas," and asks, "Is the mind, before experience, void of every *faculty*, of all intellectual *virtualité?*"—as if Locke denied this, as if he had not asserted an original capacity for knowing whatever could be known,

subjects which it discussed, that man was Leibnitz.
The extent of his attainments, the freedom and boldness of his speculations, the penetration, the ardour,
the activity, the comprehensiveness of his intellect, his
untiring labour, his love of truth and knowledge, all
these eminent qualities (dashed a little by too much
self-confidence, too great ambition of distinction, originality, and display) enabled him to follow Locke's
course with every possible advantage. As a sharp-
shooter in ambush, watching from a height the course
of a regiment marching in the valley below, may pick
out every distinguished foe, or every weak straggler,
for fatal aim, so Leibnitz, when in his 'Nouveaux
Essais' he criticizes the 'Essay on the Understanding,' chapter by chapter, paragraph by paragraph, may
be supposed to allow no defective argument, no weak
point, no hasty assertion, to escape him. Not that he
criticized Locke in any hostile spirit; on the contrary,
he does ample justice to the intellectual, as he deeply
felt the great moral qualities of the English philoso-

---

as if he had not dwelt at length on various natural faculties; nay
more, "I deny not," he says emphatically, "that there are *natural
tendencies* imprinted on the minds of men, and that from the very
first instances of sense and perception, there are some things that
are grateful, and others unwelcome to them; some things that they
incline to, and others that they fly; but this makes nothing for innate characters on the mind, which are to be principles of knowledge,
regulating our practice."—Essay, b. i. c. iii. § 3. The reviewer of
Cousin's 'Histoire,' in the 'Edinburgh Review,' some years ago, observed this and his unjust and perverse attempt to identify Locke
with the school of Condillac, and such writers as Helvetius, Saint-
Lambert, and Volney.

pher. But he admitted nothing without the principle of "*sufficient reason*," and he unfortunately preferred his own reason before another man's, as he did in the case of the great Newton, if he could find or make a plausible excuse for doing so.

Leibnitz published, as early as 1696, some reflections upon Locke's Essay, now to be found in the editions of Locke. They were early put into Locke's hands by his Dutch correspondents, one of whom thus wrote to Locke:—"They say a thousand good things of this mathematician. He threatened long ago great and excellent things, without producing anything but some detached demonstrations. I think, nevertheless, that he does not understand you, and I doubt whether he understands himself." "This sort of fiddling" (says Locke to Molyneux*, in reference to this paper of reflections) "makes me think that he is not that very great man as has been talked of him;" to which Molyneux replies, "He is either very unhappy in expressing, or I am very dull in apprehending his thoughts."

Upon a careful perusal, it will be seen that these early reflections of Leibnitz are not very consistent with his subsequent remarks in the more lengthened criticism of the 'Nouveaux Essais,' which latter work probably Locke did not live to peruse, for they were not published till 1703, when Locke had received many warnings that his departure was at hand. In

* See Locke's Correspondence with Molyneux, Law's quarto edition, vol. iv. pp. 354–358.

the reflections, Leibnitz thinks there is something solid in Plato's doctrine of *reminiscences*. In the ' Nouveaux Essais' he has an ingenious argument to show that this doctrine affects not the question of innate ideas. He contends that not only our ideas, but even our sentiments, spring from our own proper depths, and so in the Essays he talks much of the depth of the soul, comparing it to an inward spring, as if anything in Locke was inconsistent with this, be its depth and capacity, or its inward active life, what it may. When he says, " that ideas, true or real, are those of which we are assured the execution is possible, others are doubtful, or (in case of the proof of impossibility) chimerical ;—now the possibility of some ideas is proved as much *à priori* by the demonstrations, wherein we avail ourselves of the possibility of other ideas more simple, as *à posteriori* by experiences, for that which exists must be possible ; but primitive ideas are those whose possibility is indemonstrable, and which are in fact nothing but the attributes of God ;"—surely M. Le Clerc, Molyneux, and Locke, were justified in considering him unintelligible to others, whether he understood himself or not.

Leibnitz, in the ' Nouveaux Essais,' adopted a mode of criticism not favourable to distinctness, namely, that of a dialogue, in which Philalethes, a disciple, acts as the representative of Locke ; and Theophilus appears as a modified, or improved Cartesian, and speaks the sentiments of Leibnitz. Philalethes appears rather to a disadvantage ; he is not quick in seizing the weak points of his antagonist; he does not quote very carefully Locke's exact words; he omits some of the most telling and powerful of Locke's observations. Theophilus speaks with freedom and confidence, and pours out a torrent of remark, which sweeps before it the straws of objection, and even blocks of difficulty, a torrent turbid and impetuous, often throwing up beautiful foam, but more wild and astonishing than useful and clear. There are nevertheless in the latter part of the 'Nouveaux Essais,' many very pleasing and just observations and illustrations, particularly when touching the subject of language, which the lover of metaphysical reading, with Locke open before him, will thoroughly enjoy.

Great obscurity pervades the doctrine of Leibnitz concerning innate ideas. It is almost impossible to condense it,—to represent in a few words what his theory on this subject is, and even to make out the one proposition, or the several propositions which he undertook to establish, and in which he conceived himself successful. We have no translation of Leibnitz's chief metaphysical works in English, and no tolerable representation of his course of thought and argument in the 'Nouveaux Essais.' The accompanying short but candid representation of his comments on the first book of Locke may therefore be welcome to the reader.

Theophilus, who speaks for Leibnitz, sets out with stating that he aspires to new views, to go further than any one had yet gone into the depths of metaphysical truth. He professes to unite Plato with Democritus, Aristotle with Descartes, the schoolmen with the moderns, theology and morality with reason. He finds an intelligible explanation of the union of body and soul, of the true principles of things in the unity of the substances, and in their harmony pre-established by the primitive substance. Besides a new analysis of things, which was to explain every-thing, he comprehended better than any one else the analysis of notions, or ideas and truths : he under-stood better than any one, the nature of a " true, clear, distinct, adequate idea; of primitive truths and true axioms ; of the distinction between necessary truths, and truths of fact ; between the reasonings of men and the deductions of brutes, which are a shadow of them." His system would render more admirable the sovereign source of creation and its beauties. He had at one time an inclination for the side of the Spi-nozists, who leave only infinite power to the Deity, who, recognizing neither perfections nor wisdom in a supreme intelligence, and despising the search for final causes, derive everything from a brute necessity. But new lights had cured him, and he had since taken the name of Theophilus—the lover of God.

"I have long been," says Theophilus, " for the in-nate idea of God with Descartes, and consequently, for other innate ideas, which come not from the senses. *I go further, and think that all our thoughts and actions come from our soul, from its own depth, without being given by the senses.*

" But granting for the present that the external senses are the cause of part of our thoughts, I shall inquire how we may say that there are ideas and principles which do not come from the senses, which we find in ourselves without forming them, though the *senses give us occasion to perceive them*. Your author [Locke], with laudable zeal against the idleness of taking things for granted which ought to be proved, has not sufficiently distinguished the origin of necessary truths, whose source is in the understanding, and those of fact, which we draw from sensible experiences, and even from the confused perceptions which are in us. The disposition which we have to recognize the idea of God is in human nature; a readiness to receive the doctrine comes from the nature of the soul. General consent is an index, though not a demonstration, of an innate principle : the decisive proof is, that their certainty comes only from what is in us ; though they be not known, yet they may be innate, inasmuch as we recognize them when they are first heard. We have an infinity of convictions which we perceive only when we have need of them.

" *Philalethes*. Can we say that all propositions which are reasonable, and which the mind may come to regard as such, are already imprinted on the soul ?

" *Theophilus*. Truly ; in respect of pure ideas, which I oppose to the phantasms of the senses, and of necessary truths, truths of reason, which I oppose to truths of fact. In this sense we may say that *all arithmetic and all geometry are innate*, and are in a manner virtually in us. All truths which we can derive from innate primitive convictions, may be called innate, because the mind can draw them from its own depth, though it be not easy.

" *Ph.* Are there then truths graven in the soul, which it never has known, and never shall know?

" *Th.* I see no absurdity in this; for some things superior to any we can now know, may develope themselves in another state. It is certain that the senses suffice not to show the necessity of certain truths, and that the mind has a disposition to draw them, as well active as passive, from its own depths; that the senses are necessary to give occasion and excite attention to them, and to carry the mind to some rather than to others. The able persons who are of a different opinion, appear not to have sufficiently meditated on the difference between necessary or eternal truths, and truths of experience, as all our discussion shows. The original proof of necessary truths comes from the understanding alone, other truths come from experience and observation; our mind is capable of knowing the one from the other, but is the source only of the first, and whatever number of particular experiences one may have of a universal truth, one can never be sure of the universality by induction, without knowing the necessity by reason.

" *Ph.* But all who reflect will find that the consent which the mind gives, without difficulty, to certain truths, depends on the faculty of the human mind.

" *Th.* It is the relation of the mind to such truths

which renders the exercise of the faculty easy and natural, and which makes us call them innate. It is not a naked faculty, which consists in the possibility of understanding them; it is a disposition, an aptitude, a pre-formation, which determines our soul, and causes them to be drawn from it.

"Intellectual ideas, which are the source of necessary truths, come not from the senses. It is true that the express knowledge of truths is posterior (in nature or time) to the express knowledge of ideas, as the nature of truths depends on the nature of ideas, before we form expressly one and the other, and the truths or ideas, which come from the senses, depend on the senses at least in part. But the ideas which come from the senses are confused in some degree, and the truths which depend on them are so also; whilst the ideas of intellect and the truths which depend on them are distinct. The latter have not their origin from the senses, though it may be that we should never know them without the senses.

" *Ph.* If any one can find a proposition, the ideas of which are innate, he cannot do me a greater favour than to name it.

" *Th.* I should name the propositions of arithmetic and geometry, which are all of this nature ; and in matters of necessary truth, one may find others.

" *Ph.* Can we say then that the most difficult and profound of sciences are innate ?

" *Th.* The actual knowledge of them is not so ; but the virtual knowledge may be called so, as the figure

traced by the veins of marble is in the marble before
it is discovered by working.

"*Ph.* It is difficult to conceive that a truth is in the
mind, if the mind has never thought of such truth.

"*Th.* That is to say, it is difficult to conceive there
are veins in marble before we discover them. The
objection approaches too near to a *petitio principii*.
All who admit innate truths without founding them
upon Platonic reminiscence, admit such as have never
yet been thought of. In other respects this reasoning proves too much. For if truths are thoughts,
we must be deprived of truths, not only on which one
has not thought, but of which we are not actually
thinking. And if truths are not thoughts, but *habitudes and aptitudes, natural or acquired*, nothing hinders there being some in us, of which we have never
yet thought,—no, nor ever will think."

The last sentiment is extraordinary. There appears
to be nothing, in the subsequent criticisms by Leibnitz
on the second and third chapters of Locke, touching
innate principles, which adds to the clearness or to the
force of the above. He speaks of "maxims known
by instinct, and of innate principles, which are not *a
part of natural light*,—of innate truths, known in two
fashions, *by light and by instinct*. Thus," he says,
"we are carried to acts of humanity by instinct, because they are pleasing; by reason, when they are
proved to be just." Here every sentence introduces
new terms of doubtful value; he lays down new propositions which have nothing to do with the question

at issue; and he brings in analogies which, like the veins of marble, mislead rather than illustrate.

The weightiest passage in Leibnitz, much applauded and often quoted by his admirers, occurs in his remarks on Locke's second book.

" *Th.* They will oppose to me this axiom received among philosophers, ' that there is nothing in the soul which comes not from the senses.' But we must except the soul itself and its affections. Nihil est in intellectu, quod non fuerit in sensu; excipe—*nisi ipse intellectus.* Moreover the soul includes being, substance, unity, identity, cause, perception, reasoning, and a quantity of other notions which the senses cannot give. This agrees sufficiently with your author of the Essay, who seeks a good part of our ideas in the reflection of the mind upon its own nature.

" *Ph.* I hope then you will grant to this able author, that all ideas come from sensation or reflection; that is, from observations made on objects external and sensible, or upon the internal operations of our soul.

" *Th.* To avoid a contest which has already detained us too long, I profess that when you say that ideas come to us from one or other of these causes, I understand it of the actual perception of them, for I think I have shown, *that they are in us, before they are perceived,* in so far as they have anything distinct."

Leibnitz is not so much read, nor are his principles so familiar to English thinkers as to render this translation of select passages from his ' Nouveaux Essais' unnecessary. Few will go along with him, no one has undertaken to support him, in the sentiments and assertions which have been given. They scarcely bear examination; being in fact scarcely intelligible. On the one hand, they seem to concede to Locke everything which he lays down; on the other, they contend for so much as, if received, must overthrow Locke's system and make his statements comparatively worthless. But let us hear Locke himself:—" To say a notion is imprinted on the mind, and yet at the same time to say that the mind is ignorant of it, and never yet took notice of it, is to make this impression nothing. No proposition can be said to be in the mind which it never yet knew, which it was never yet conscious of."—" If the capacity of knowing be the natural impression contended for, all the truths a man ever comes to know, will, by this account, be every one of them innate; and this great point will amount to no more, than only a very improper way of speaking, which, whilst it pretends to assert the contrary, says nothing different from those who deny innate principles."—" That certainly can never be thought innate, which we have need of reason to discover, unless, as I have said, we will have *all* the certain truths that reason ever teaches us, to be innate."* Now this is precisely what Leibnitz did contend for. Why, then, did he not quote these expressions of Locke, and defend the propriety of his way of speaking? It seems a monstrous extravagance to assert that the truths of Newton's Principia, and of every other profound work,

* Locke's Essay, b. 1, c. ii., §§ 5, 9.

however remote from common studies and apprehension—such as the Institutes of Justinian, or the principles of his own Theodicæa—are innate in all human minds, because a few have known them; or because (what is more doubtful) all may be capable of knowing them. The discussion turns upon the word *innate,* whether it refer to the capacity of forming notions and ideas, which Locke asserts as distinctly as possible, or the actual conscious existence of notions and ideas, previous to sensible impression, or to reflection, which Locke denies, and Leibnitz too.

With regard to the celebrated exception taken by Leibnitz to the old maxim—" that there is nothing in the intellect which hath not been first in the senses, *nisi ipse intellectus*"—it is of no value; because the intellectus cannot be in the intellectus; both the intellectus and sensus being taken for granted in the maxim, the value of which depends upon what is meant by intellectus and sensus. If by the intellect be understood all those intellections, those conclusions of the reasoning power from phenomena, those complex ideas and notions, clusters of sensible impressions and mental states associated together under one term, and united in propositions, of which, as Gassendi says, there neither is nor can be any sensible image or impression, the disciple of Locke and Hartley does not maintain the maxim. But if it be meant merely that to all such intellections a sensible impression, or a feeling of some kind, derived from the sensitive frame, is a necessary groundwork,—that there is a

root or seed, so to speak, of the most refined intellectual results in sensation; that sensations are the primary elements on which "the soul and its affections"
begin to operate; that what we first remember, name,
and compare, are these sensations and feelings or
clusters of sensible impressions, without which we
should not know we have a soul; if by sensus be
meant the perceptive power, the recipient of impressions *ab extra*, without which there never was any
intellectual power in man, in this sense the disciple of
Locke and Hartley and Mill might hold the maxim
to be true, nor is it clear that the disciple of Leibnitz
and Stewart would deny it. For when we talk of
the depths of the soul, be they as profound as we
please, let its original activity be as great, and its innate faculties and capacities and affections be as numerous as we please, this makes nothing against the
justness of that analytical view of the mind of which
Locke and Hartley and Mill are the great teachers;
nor does it modify or shake in the least the importance of that law of association, and the truth of the
related doctrines which Hartley first comprehended in
entirety, and of which Leibnitz had scarcely a glimmering perception.

This topic might be pursued; but it is a waste of
reasoning to confute authors who confute themselves.
There is a very short mode of putting to the test the
soundness of the instinctive or innate principle philosophy. It rests too much upon a fallacious metaphorical language, in a manner self-destructive; a

language indebted for its force to those very phenomena of the senses, which it affects at the same time
to despise. Thus it makes much of the inward depth,
and capacity, the activity and fulness of the soul*.
But the very difficult question, whether the most comprehensive and refined intellectual conclusions—whether the results of the reflective powers in their most
perfect and beautiful developments—whether the most
refined affections and habits of theopathy, sympathy,
and the moral sense, are traceable or not to a common
sensational root, so to speak, as Hartley was disposed
to believe, is not to be decided by the language of
metaphor, imagination, and enthusiasm. It is a question of nature and fact; a question of that nice and
difficult introspection, which nothing hinders more
effectually than the dust of words.

Now, the examination of the philosophy and natural
history of language contains within itself the confutation of the philosophy of instinctive principles or innate ideas. For, putting aside the question whether
words are the arbitrary signs of ideas, or themselves
the result of a law of nature, deep and subtle, when
we inquire what words are, and what are not, capable
of definition, we find that all such words as are significant of simple ideas of uniform impressions on the
senses,—such as of colours, taste, sounds, and smells,
whose meaning depends on the uniformity of the sen-

* Compare the account of Condillac in the 'Dictionnaire des
Sciences Philosophiques,' where his philosophy is said to have been
buried in the tomb of De Stutt de Tracy.

sible impressions, are incapable of definition. Such also are words significant of states of inward feeling, —*e. g.* pain and pleasure, joy, sorrow, hope and fear, and many others, comprehending classes of emotional states, when considered without reference to any of the particulars that give them force. But words significant of a cluster of sensible impressions, marking a property or union of properties common to a number of individuals; words significant of complex ideas, or collections of simple ideas, passing under one name, these are susceptible of definition; and the definition is useful when he to whom the explanation or definition is given, has in him all the simple ideas for a collection of which the name defined is made to stand*. Thus every definition is made ultimately to rest upon the uniformity of sensible impressions, or of simple emotional states. Hence there can be no reasoning upon ideas existing in different minds, but what is based upon a uniformity of impressions *ab extra*, or a similarity of emotions and passions *ab intra;* the language appropriate to the latter being obscure, unscientific, and incapable of application to reasoning, in proportion to the difficulty of referring it to a common external object, as an admitted common measure or test of reality and truth. The assent to the postulates and axioms of geometry depends on the rapid associa-

---

* See the fourth chapter of Locke's second book, with which Locke's logic may be said to begin. Compare also an admirable passage on words susceptible of definition, in Bernier's abridgment of Gassendi, liv. iv. c. v.; also Trendelenberg's Elements of Aristotelian Logic, § 59, on definition.

tion of uniform sensible impressions with the meaning of the terms. Such are the following :—" The whole is greater than a part ;" " If equals be taken from equals, the remainders are equal." To argue that the ideas of totality and divisibility, of equality and inequality, are innate in the mind from the readiness of the assent to these axioms, is the same thing as to say that a child has got all the ideas of number, before it has learnt to count its fingers, and all the ideas of morality before it has seen a mother's frown, or been forbidden to snatch an ornament and play with the fire. It is much the same as to suppose that all the laws of nature are known *à priori ;* that examples in grammar are made to fit rules, instead of rules being merely the exponents of phenomena; that theory precedes observation ; that the human mind is not the subject but the source of law. It is to arrogate an original divinity for the mind, and by that arrogance to rob it of its real strength. It is to refuse to acquire Divine science by the study of nature and history, and the patient reception of Divine instruction. As we derive our ideas of number from the existence of things capable of being numbered, so we derive our ideas of geometrical figures from the existence in nature of forms and figures corresponding to their definitions.

Leibnitz, like many others before and after him, speaks of instinct as if it were a term applicable to the intellectual and moral developments of man. But the term instinct is always best regarded as merely a term of ignorance. It is significant of that propensity peculiar to some insects and animals, such as the bee, the ant, the beaver, and the bird, whereby they build their habitations and provide for their future, in a manner for the most part undeviating, without instruction, observation, or experience, and for which we can account in no other way, than by ascribing it to the force of nature. The bees of the present day build their cells, and collect their honey, precisely like the bees in Virgil's Georgics,—the last bees are as the first. There is nothing in man analogous to this. The human child can do nothing, knows nothing, without guidance, without instruction. Even the use of articulate sounds for the expression of thoughts and emotions, the distinguishing characteristic of man, is an acquisition slowly made, and so various in quality and degree as to remove it from the category of instincts. Though we may say, in common parlance, that the infant sucks the breast, and begins to use its senses and its hands by instinct, and we may talk of instinctive powers, passions, and emotions, because of a prevalence of such powers and passions approaching to universality, it is only justifiable in common parlance, intimating our willing ignorance of the ultimate character and laws of all such functions and tendencies, beyond the fact of their existence, and our indisposition to inquire further*.

* Compare a passage on the terms Instinctive and Instinct, in Austin's Jurisprudence, p. 96. Mr. James Mill, in his Analysis of the Phenomena of the Human Mind, takes a similar view. See also Law's preface to King on the Origin of Evil.

Tendencies, capacities, appetites, powers, which may be called instinctive, are not denied by the disciple of Locke and Hartley. He may term those rare gifts and endowments, which distinguish some persons so remarkably from the common herd, *natural* and *inward*, when he chooses not to seek further for their origin, and comprehends them in that NATURE, which stands for everything that has been, is, or shall be. But whether we raise our thoughts to contemplate the genius of Homer, of Plato and Aristotle, of Shakespeare, of Bacon and Newton, or turn them downwards to the lowest and humblest forms of humanity, scarce raised above the brutes, no doubt some approach to an explanation of the diversity of character, to a correct theory of the phenomena of life and mind, may be found in the peculiar aptitude resulting from original physical conformation, acted upon by favourable external conditions, for that precise development of intellectual power and moral tendency, which marks and makes the individual, both in what he has in common with the race and what is singular. Every child is born with a frame like that of other children, but with modifications and peculiarities inherited from the parents. It brings into the world a constitutional tendency to associate some classes of sensations and ideas rather than others. One sense being from the first more acute than others, the pleasures and pains, the tastes and predilections, differ from the first in kind and in degree; one child is constitutionally phlegmatic,—another irritable. Now, the original

s

perceptive power and the associative tendency taken together form the primary elements of our intellectual and moral life. Hence the justification of the sentiment, "Poeta nascitur, non fit;" and what is true of the poet is true of the musician, the painter, the sculptor, the orator, the statesman, the philanthropist. The acuteness of the sense, and the predisposition to retain some impressions, to neglect and discard others, gives early bias to the imagination, the trains of which soon become habitual; these mix themselves in ways and degrees imperceptible with the moral sense, and with the social, sympathetic, and theopathetic affections, as Hartley calls them, as these again are subsequently developed. According as external conditions operate upon the original basis, the native tendency is favoured or counteracted. Thus the analogy is complete between the development of vegetable and of intellectual life. For as from every seed and its germ of vegetation springs the appropriate leaf and flower and fruit, so from every sensitive frame, with its predisposition to associate and retain certain classes of sensation, and ideas of sensation, there is developed, in infinite variety, a certain definite form of intellectual power and moral grace on the one hand, or what we esteem deformity and weakness and depravity on the other. Were it conceded that men are born naturally equal, according to the opinion of those who, like Helvetius, attribute everything to education, nothing to endowment of nature,—an inequality, a marked and essential difference of power and tendency in children becomes palpable to the accurate observer after a few months of existence. When Wordsworth says that—

> " Men from men
> Differ in constitution of their minds
> By mystery *not to be explained*,"

, the sentiment may be modified by this recognition of some of the broad facts of nature, and some of the known laws of the mind. With these facts and laws, the genius of a Pope, " who lisped in numbers, for the numbers came," and of a Newton, who is said to have anticipated or known by intuition the demonstrations of Euclid without perusing them, are sufficiently in harmony. One child, habituated from the first dawn of intelligence to accurate observation and just expression, speaks truthfully, describes faithfully, and reasons consecutively ; habituated only to good arguments, it rejects bad ones, with a facility or faculty that may be called natural and instinctive. But it is in reality as much acquired as the skill of a rope-dancer, or the endurance of a fetish, there being a foundation for both in nature and nature's pliancy. Another child never reasons but in the fashion of Dame Quickly or the late Mr. Southey. When terror and falsehood have been the primary elements of education, when thieves and outlaws have been the guardians and tutors of youth, all the subsequent exercises of reason and habit will resolve themselves into predatory cunning and skilful self-defence.

Upon the principle of Leibnitz and his followers—

that everything in man is innate and instinctive—the vilest passions, the wildest delusions, the most extravagant errors, no less than the sublimest forms of intellectual and moral greatness, shelter themselves equally under the authority of nature; and nothing remains but the temporary will and caprice of the individual, to determine what shall be chosen as valuable, and what rejected as worthless or hurtful among the opinions and predilections of mankind. The advocates of intuitions forget that they wield a two-edged sword, a weapon easily turned against themselves, and as powerful for him who denies as for him who asserts what they are pleased to assume as instinctive truth. The doubts of Bayle, the caustic satire of Voltaire, the pantheism of Spinoza, are at least as natural, and may plead the authority of instinct quite as well, as the pre-established harmony and monadology of Leibnitz; and surely the wild excesses of the Munster Anabaptists, or the Family of Love, and the heathen superstitions of the poor priest-ridden papists, present forms of faith and practice far more congenial to the natural dispositions and innate faculties of the multitude, than the mild and practical religion of a Fénelon and an Oberlin, or the philosophic faith of a Newcome and a Paley, of a Priestley and a Channing. Surely no man, who has paid due attention to the melancholy history of human superstition, and watched the reluctance with which mankind associate the idea of duty with happiness, of virtue with benevolence, can attach value to instincts and intuitions as a guide and authority in religion.

Gibbon has touched with a master's hand the character of Leibnitz, not only in various passages of his beautiful essay on the Study of Literature, but chiefly in the paper on the Antiquities of the House of Brunswick. " The genius and studies of Leibnitz have ranked his name with the first philosophic names of his age and country : but his reputation, perhaps, would be more pure and permanent if he had not ambitiously grasped the whole circle of human science. As a theologian he successively contended with the sceptics, who believe too little, and with papists, who believe too much, and with the heretics, who believe otherwise than is inculcated by the Lutheran confession of Augsburg. Yet the philosopher betrayed his love of union and toleration : his faith in revelation was accused, while he proved the Trinity by the principles of logic ; and in the defence of the attributes and providence of the Deity, he was suspected of a secret correspondence with his adversary Bayle. The metaphysician expatiated in the fields of air : his pre-established harmony of the soul and body might have provoked the jealousy of Plato ; and his optimism, the best of all possible worlds, seems an idea too vast for a mortal mind."

The portrait is completed with these true touches. " He designed more than he could execute : his imagination was too easily satisfied with a bold and rapid glance on the subject which he was impatient to leave ; and Leibnitz may be compared to those heroes whose empire has been lost in the ambition of universal conquest."

The great work of Leibnitz is the 'Theodicæa.' There he puts forth all his strength, and appears to the best advantage. In all the array of learning and of literature, he sallies forth as a champion, confident of victory, to contend against every subtlety of scepticism. When Bayle opens his batteries, and levels his syllogisms against the citadel of faith, Leibnitz feels that he has built ramparts, within which he can lie entrenched and secure; and the keep may be acknowledged to be invulnerable, although the "pre-established harmony" and the principle of "the sufficient reason," with other distinctions without a difference, may be surrendered as outworks incapable of defence. To the lover of metaphysical studies nothing can be more delightful than this work of Leibnitz. He has lightened the heaviest, and adorned the gravest subject, with the riches of forgotten literature, and every variety of pleasing observation, —"égayer une matière, dont le sérieux peut rebuter." He seems more than Gassendi to deserve the character of "the most philosophic among literati, the most literary among philosophers." How has it happened that the chief production of so great a name should have produced on the whole so little effect on English philosophy and English thought? We have translations of Bayle, of Helvetius, of Montesquieu; why not of the 'Theodicæa' of Leibnitz? Was the subject too difficult for the many, or the treatment too little satisfactory for the few? The familiarity of the French language to the student and the scholar cannot account for the preference given by translators and publishers to far inferior works. Perhaps, like the learned 'Histoire du Manichéisme,' by Beausobre*, which Lardner long ago wished translated, and to which Gibbon confessed his obligations, the work was too free and too good, too remote from the common paths to suit the purposes of trade. Yet many considerations suggest themselves to explain, in some degree, the slight impression produced by this work of Leibnitz: 1, the difficulty of the subject, and the little attention given to the higher metaphysics;

---

* I may here be allowed to correct a very serious mistake made by Mr. J. D. Morell, in the 'Historical View of the Speculative Philosophy of Europe, during the Nineteenth Century,' relative to Beausobre. Speaking of the confusion attendant on the progress of the Leibnitzian-Wolfian system in Germany, he says (vol. i. p. 196), in the midst of it, "Scepticism, as might be expected, also made its appearance, and the celebrated divine M. de Beausobre, *whom we may regard as its best representative*, wrote an ingenious work, in which he advocated an almost undisguised Pyrrhonism, and made the Wolfian philosophy an especial object of his attack and ridicule." This is grievously erroneous. The learned divine was no sceptic, and deserved far other notice at the hands of Mr. Morell. It were to be wished that at least that portion of his valuable work on Manicheeism had been translated which is entitled, "A discourse, showing that the apocryphal and fabulous books, very far from casting suspicion upon the certainty of the miraculous facts contained in the Gospels, and by consequence the certainty of the Christian religion, concur to confirm them." Beausobre died in 1738. A good biographical notice is prefixed to the second volume of the 'Histoire du Manichéisme.' The sceptic and sensualist was one Lewis Beausobre, privy-counsellor of Frederic the Great, who published 'Le Pyrrhonisme du Sage,' 1754, and 'Les Songes d'Epicure,' 1756, and who died in 1783, and had no known connection even with the family of the divine.

2, the strict Lutheranism, or modified Calvinism, in the interpretation of Scripture, which pervades the work, rendering it from the first distasteful to the Arminian predilections of the English school of liberal theology, an interpretation now considered quite un-philosophical; 3, its pure necessarianism, equally ob-noxious to the orthodox, who, like Calvin, have always dreaded the attempt to harmonize the decrees of God with the deductions of reason, and to level to human comprehension the Divine works and ways; 4, the the-ories and distinctions with which the work abounds, such as that of the harmony between the soul and body, without any mutual dependence or connection, such as the distinction between an absolute and a hypothetical or metaphysical necessity, between the freedom of the will *from any constraining power*, and its subjection to *the law of the greatest apparent good*, together with the non-existence of any liberty or equilibrium of indifference, any proper self-moving power; theories and distinctions peculiar to Leibnitz, more subtle than satisfactory; 5, the jealousy and in-justice which Leibnitz had manifested towards New-ton, and his opposition to the Newtonian philosophy. This alienated the minds of many of the philosophic English from him. On the whole he does not shine in the controversy with Dr. Samuel Clarke*. But

* There is an amusing evidence of this, and of Dr. Johnson's readiness and reading, in a characteristic conversation between the lexicographer and the Rev. Hector M'Lean, pastor of Col and Tyryi, recorded in Boswell's ' Tour to the Hebrides.' "Mr. M'Lean said he had a confutation of Bayle, by Leibnitz. *Johnson:* ' A confuta-

what controversy, even between greatest men, has settled disputed points in metaphysical philosophy? The 'Theodicæa' itself probably would have been more valued, had it been more an independent work, and less a work of criticism and of reply to Bayle.

The 'Theodicæa,' after an excellent preface, proceeds with a discourse on the conformity of reason with faith. Here the author pursues a beaten path, which Locke and others had well cleared before him. Unhappy the man whose faith and reason are at war; who cherishes a faith which he dares not bring to the light of day; which is a mere relic of traditional and ignorant reverence, valued only when secreted from inspection, worthless for the uses of life; a flame trembling at every breath of opinion, and expiring in the first process of examination and analysis, just as a light goes out, or an insect dies when plunged into a phial of hydrogen or azote.

The discourse is followed by essays in three parts, on the goodness of God, the liberty of man, and the

tion of Bayle, Sir! what part of Bayle do you mean? The greatest part of his writings are not confutable: it is historical and critical.' —Mr. M'Lean said, 'The irreligious part;' and proceeded to talk of Leibnitz's controversy with Clarke, calling Leibnitz a great man.' *Johnson:* 'Why, Sir, Leibnitz persisted in affirming that Newton called space 'sensorium numinis,' notwithstanding he was corrected, and desired to observe that Newton's words were 'quasi (he should have said *tanquam*) sensorium numinis.' No, Sir; Leibnitz was as paltry a fellow as I know. Out of respect to Queen Caroline, who patronized him, Clarke treated him too well.'" This conversation took place in October, 1773, and, with what follows relative to Dr. Clarke, is worthy of note.

origin of evil.   The first part treats the subject chiefly on its merits ; the second and third dwell at length on the difficulties and doubts of Bayle.   As there can be no nutriment more wholesome for the heart, no medicine to " minister to a mind diseased" more efficacious than the sentiments of Leibnitz on the goodness of the Deity, I shall give in the Appendix an analytical view of his first essay on that topic.   They present a happy contrast to those gloomy and cheerless views of the prevalence of evil and misery in the world, which are usually taken by sceptics and unbelievers.   Who has not observed that the extremes of a harsh theology and of total unbelief meet upon the common ground of the excessive wickedness of man, and of the miseries and hopelessness of life ?

Leibnitz had paid great attention to all that in English literature and philosophy related to that most difficult question, " the origin of evil."   Nothing connected with the subject seems to have escaped him. He was familiar with the controversy between Bishop Bramhall and Hobbes.   He criticized with justice and acuteness the essay by Archbishop King, written originally in Latin, while a taste for Latin yet lingered as the proper language of philosophy,—the essay afterwards translated with learned notes by Dr. Edmund Law.   He perceived the great defect of that essay. It is the failure, in the fifth and last chapter, of applying to moral evil the same simple principle which had been established in relation to physical evil, namely, that only so much evil is admitted as

could not be avoided, but with the sacrifice of greater
preponderant good; that therefore benevolence itself
required the existence of the evil, inasmuch as benevolence could not be satisfied with less than the
greatest possible amount of good. This is the principle which runs through the 'Theodicæa,' as its key-
note. It is a principle as intelligible as tenable; no
less capable of useful practical application to all the
speculative difficulties of the understanding, than con-
solatory in all the pains and sorrows of human life;
the only principle that can harmonize faith and reason,
which is the axis of religion, natural and revealed, and
the acceptance of which is alone needed to give to the
optimism of Leibnitz an easy and sure triumph over
the virtual atheism of Spinoza. Yes! " there is some
soul of goodness in things evil, would men but carefully distil it out ;" and the great poet of human nature
may have felt, when giving utterance to that sentiment, that he was then assigning to mankind the
office which raised them nearest to the Deity, and
giving them the key to unlock all the mysteries of
Providence.

> " From seeming evil still educing good,
>   And better thence again, and better still,
>   In infinite progression*."

Touching the essay on the origin of evil, and the

* Thomson's Hymn, at the close of the ' Seasons,' from which,
as well as from many passages of Pope and Akenside, it may be inferred that the philosophy of Locke and the optimism of Leibnitz
had taken stronger hold of the affections, and more deeply tinged
the imaginations of the thinking men of the last century than we
are now accustomed to suppose.

subject, it would be injustice to pass over the excellent observations of the Rev. Latham Wainewright, in his Appendix (p. 177) to a vindication of Dr. Paley's ' Theory of Morals,'—a vindication whose merit is far above its fame. " With respect to this celebrated work of Archbishop King, the reasoning contained in the first four chapters on the evil of defect, and on natural evil, is, I think, rational and satisfactory, as far as it extends, considering the obscurity in which the disquisition is involved; but when he comes to treat of the origin of moral evil, he seems to be totally unable to contend with the difficulty of his subject. The hypothesis by which he attempts to reconcile the different solutions of the long-debated questions respecting liberty and necessity, is as curious as it is unfounded; namely, that the will possesses the power of rendering things agreeable which were before indifferent, merely by its own agency. . . . The notes of Bishop Law to the first part of this treatise contain many valuable, and some very profound remarks; but as soon as he undertakes the defence of his author's singular hypothesis, his efforts are as little successful in producing conviction as those of the latter. Both the comment and the text have equally failed."

Mr. Wainewright is perfectly right. He would probably have referred to the paper by Leibnitz on the work of Archbishop King, had he been aware that the same observation had occurred to the German critic; nor need I scruple to add, that these defects of a book, repeatedly perused, had become palpable to myself, before I had made acquaintance either with Leibnitz or Wainewright*.

There is another work on the origin of evil, that by Dr. John Clarke, a brother of Dr. Samuel Clarke, and an expositor of Newton's philosophy, who treated

---

* Mr. Dugald Stewart's notice of this work of King and of Law's translation, in the Preliminary Dissertation, affords a striking instance of his inaccuracy. "The name of Law (he says, p. 170) was first known to the public by an excellent translation, accompanied by many learned and some very judicious notes, of Archbishop King's work on the origin of evil; a work of which the great object was *to combat the optimism of Leibnitz*, and the Manicheism imputed to Bayle." It were charitable to suppose that the translation alone is here alluded to. King's original Latin work ' De Origine Mali,' appeared in 1702. It was impossible it should combat an optimism which did not come forth to the world till about twelve years after Leibnitz published his 'Theodicæa' in 1710, and his object was precisely the same with that of King, whose defects he thought to remedy. That object was far nobler, and more important than Stewart represents it. It is not to be degraded into a merely personal dispute. It was, as the translator of King states it, to enable us clearly to " comprehend how the present state of things is the very best in all respects, and worthy of a most wise, powerful, and beneficent Author : and why, taking the whole system of beings together, and every class in its order, none could possibly have been made more perfect or placed in a better." It was, in short, to furnish an ample vindication of Divine Providence, in the production, preservation, and government of the universe. It may be doubted whether Stewart ever had a copy of King's ' De Origine Mali' in the original before him ; and certainly he was not acquainted with the animadversions of Leibnitz upon it ; and I must add that he appears incapable of treating the subject of it and the argument without mingling in his comments offensive personalities, coarse and unjust invectives. Why else does he charge Law with *affecting* that profound veneration for Locke, the sincerity of which is proved by every line of his writings, and by the care and dignity with which he edited Locke's works ? Why else does he speak of the *coarse caricatures,*

the subject in the Boyle Lectures*. It is unsatisfactory from the same defect, though not to the same degree. It is a somewhat laboured and dull reply to the sceptical difficulties of Bayle, who felt the existence of evil under the government of one supremely perfect Being, incomprehensible and inexplicable, and of whom Hume was in this respect the immediate follower. Dr. Clarke, endeavouring to show the harmony of the physical universe, builds upon the principles of the great Newton, whose philosophy he expounded in a distinct work. He had only to apply, in the second volume, to moral evil the principle which he lays down with success in the first in respect to physical evil, and to bring out that principle more distinctly, and with more force, thrusting the argument home, as in the following passage :—"The whole therefore is reduced to this; either that there must be no created beings at all, or they must be liable to some evils. Let the supposition be what it will, it amounts to the same. All that is reasonably to be expected, or agreeable to the notions we have of wisdom is, that there should be variety in the works of creation; that every part should be as perfect as it can be in its place; that they should all be sub-

by Hartley and Priestley[1], of Locke's refined remarks on the Association of Ideas, when he must have known, if he knew anything, that such caricature was as far from their thought as it was alien from their feelings, no less inconsistent with the earnest spirit of their philosophy, than with their unfeigned reverence for the master?

* These were published in two volumes, 8vo, in 1720.

[1] See the Notes NN to the Dissertation, p. 269.

servient to one another, and promote the *good of the whole.*" Again ; " It is agreeable to the notions we have of wisdom in general, and to what we know of creation from observation and fact, to think that every the most minute part of the universe is governed by a certain law, which tends to the good of the whole, and that every evil or irregularity is the natural result of this under particular circumstances, and is of small moment, compared with the general good, and consequently no reasonable objection*."

In such views as these, all inquiries into the origin of evil, and all attempts to reconcile the vices of mankind, pain, diseases, poverty, and death, with the existence and government of a God supremely good, must at last terminate ; they are the only refuge from aching scepticism ; and where men like Boyle, Newton, and Leibnitz, and Hartley, and Lindsey, and Priestley, have rested, weaker heads may well be content to find repose.

In such a view Soame Jenyns also rested, in his 'Free Inquiry into the Nature and Origin of Evil.' His speculations on the unavoidableness of moral, political, and religious evils, in such a world as this, are not only bold and ingenious, but they are often satisfactory and well founded. He thought himself original in the opinion, that " God would never have permitted the existence of natural evil, but from the impossibility of preventing it without the loss of su-

* Dr. John Clarke's ' Enquiry into the Cause and Origin of Evil,' vol. i. pp. 217–219.

perior good; and on the same principle the admission of moral evil is equally consistent with the Divine goodness; and who is he so knowing in the whole stupendous system of nature as to assert, that the wickedness of some beings may not, by means unconceivable to us, be beneficial to innumerable unknown orders of others? or that the punishment of some may not contribute to the felicity of numbers infinitely superior?" To this purpose the learned Hugenius says, with great sagacity, "Præterea credibile est, ipsa illa animi vitia magnæ hominum parti, non sine summo concilio, data esse: cum enim Dei providentiâ talis sit Tellus, ejusque incolæ, quales cernimus, absurdum enim foret existimare omnia hæc alia facta esse, quam ille voluerit, sciveritque futura*."

* See the collected edition of Soame Jenyns' works, vol. iii. p. 102; and Hugenius, Cosmotheoros, lib. i. p. 34, there quoted. On this work of Jenyns, Dr. Samuel Johnson fell, armed with his gigantic club, in a review which has been called "one of the finest specimens of criticism in the language." The critic dealt some heavy and successful blows against its weaker parts. He turned into admirable pleasantry the notion that men's calamities may be the sport and pastime of a superior order of beings. But the book is better than the review, and after all in better spirit, more thoughtful and suggestive. It supplied the reviewer with some of his best sentiments, such as those on the nature and criterion of virtue (both Johnson and Jenyns being what we now call utilitarian), and on death as the infallible cure for all other evils. Johnson's temper and views of life were at first harsh and gloomy. His early experiences were very bitter. The evils of the world were serious evils with him. He remembered his own struggles with poverty and wretchedness, and seems to have considered his escape exceptional, and the common condition of mankind hopeless and miserable. If he could admit for a moment that out of some evils a higher good

When views like these have been entertained by so many thoughtful religious men, it is idle to say with Gibbon, that they are "too vast for a mortal mind." There is nothing in them particularly difficult. If we may speak of the "problem of creation being solved under some restricting conditions," these conditions may best be found in the unavoidable limitations of finite created beings in their sphere of action and perception. All evil, natural or moral, resolves itself ultimately into the pain felt by sentient beings. This is the "nodus, vindice dignus." The only question of moment is, is that pain subservient to a superior good? would the happiness of creation have been less, upon the whole, without it? would the abolition of the particular pain have involved the abolition of we know not what superior amount of good? There is no difficulty in supposing and maintaining with Leibnitz the affirmative.

Nor is there any necessity for the supposition to which Leibnitz and Jenyns give too much countenance, that the sufferings of some moral agents may be accounted for, on the principle that these sufferings are more conducive to the happiness of other beings

and superior happiness might spring, he had not power to grasp it and apply it as a general principle, and use it as the key to unlock all the secret chambers, the lamp to irradiate all the darkest recesses of Providence. Johnson must be ranked among those who, whether sceptics or christians, consider the existence of evil under the government of an infinitely wise and benevolent Deity inexplicable, and all attempts to solve the difficulty unsuccessful, if not presumptuous.

T

than ultimately to their own. There is no necessity for supposing that any beings exist, whose existence is not on the whole a blessing to themselves; whose non-existence, taking in the whole of their time, be it longer or shorter, would not be so much detracted from the happiness of the universe. The scriptural Christian remembers with pleasure that the word applied to punishment, and to the retributions of a future state, in the New Testament, signifies "*corrective discipline**," and intimates the subjugation of evil, if not a final issue in virtue and happiness. The destruction of sin, the triumph of life over death, the working of all things together for good, is a favourite doctrine of the Apostle Paul. And Origen was not the worse Christian, nor the worse philosopher, for believing in what is now called "universal restoration," that all would be ultimately holy and happy. Leibnitz, therefore, who contended so warmly for the preponderance of good in this life, and who maintained that every sane man at its close would wish to go through a similar course, should not have burdened his defence of the goodness of God with the gratuitous supposition that the preponderance of good might be less in a future state; that some might then and there be left in a position justly to curse their being and its author, without motive to gratitude or obedience, cradled in horrors, and condemned to pangs

---

* See the admirable observations of Jortin, ' Remarks on Ecclesiastical History,' vol. i. pp. 220–223 ; and ' Lindsey's Conversations on the Divine Government,' a charming volume.

unending and unmitigated. For if the tendency of things in this life on the whole is good, and not a single law of nature and of life, not a single sense, limb, part, or faculty of organized being can be adduced, which is not conducive more to the conservation, the enjoyment, the perfection of its possessor and his existence, than the contrary, then *à fortiori* in a future life, only conceived and hoped for as a consummation of the present, the tendency to good will be more rapid, the happiness unsullied and complete.

"To reconcile the existence of evil with the wisdom and goodness of God," says Mr. Austin, "is a task which surpasses the powers of our narrow and feeble understandings. This is a deep which our reason is too short to fathom. From the decided predominance of good which is observable in the order of the world, and from the manifold marks of wisdom which the order of the world exhibits, we may draw the cheering inference that its Author is good and wise. Why the world which he has made is not already perfect, or why a benevolent Deity tolerates the existence of evil, or what (if I may so express myself) are the obstacles in the way of his benevolence, are clearly questions which it were impossible to solve, and which it were idle to agitate, although they admitted a solution. It is enough for us to know that the Deity is perfectly good; and that since he is perfectly good, he wills the happiness of his creatures. *This* is a truth of the greatest *practical* moment. For the cast of the affections, which we attribute to the Deity, determines, for the most part, the cast of our moral sentiments*."

Sentiments on such a subject, adopted after so much careful reflection, and expressed with so just a regard to the best feelings of our nature, especially when taken in connection with those preceding them, it would be presumptuous to expect to modify. Still it is possible for the mind, in its highest meditative moods, to view all evils, physical and moral, only as shadows that heighten the beauty and warm the colour of the picture and the landscape, like discords that give richness to harmony, like acids that give pungency to sweets; and why can we not apply a principle of reason and analogy, manifest in small things, to the greater and more serious? If eclipses were unavoidable in the natural universe, the plan and motion of the heavenly bodies being what they are, then the terror and superstition of mankind on observing the phenomena were equally unavoidable, mankind being what they are. It is evident that the intellectual powers, the social affections, the moral graces, the earnest sympathies of our nature, all these, which constitute the charm of cultivated and vigorous life, are developed by the struggle with difficulty, with danger, and with death. Thus what we call evil, in its darkest as well as lightest forms, is the school of human virtue, and the great element of superior and lasting happiness.

He who reads often, and considers deeply, the de-

* Province of Jurisprudence determined, p. 93.

monstration of Hartley (Proposition 103), that " *God is infinitely benevolent*," may find all his difficulties respecting the moral government of the universe gradually disappear. In Hartley's own language he will be convinced that, "since this world is a system of benevolence, and consequently its Author the object of unbounded love and adoration, benevolence and piety are the only true guides in our inquiries into it, the only keys which will unlock the mysteries of nature, and clues which lead through her labyrinths. Of this, all branches of natural history and natural philosophy afford abundant instances; and the same thing may be said of civil history, when illustrated and cleared by the Scriptures, so as to open to view the successive dispensations of God to mankind; but it has been more particularly taken notice of in the frame of the human body, and in the symptoms and tendencies of distempers. In all these matters let the inquirer take it for granted previously that everything is right, and the best that it can be ' cæteris manentibus;' *i. e.*, let him, with a pious confidence, seek for benevolent purposes, and he will be always directed to the right road; and after a due continuance in it, attain to some new and valuable truth; whereas every other principle and motive to examination, being foreign to the great plan upon which the universe is constructed, must lead to endless mazes, errors, and perplexities*." This is the only philosophy worthy

---

* Hartley's Observations on Man, Prop. 155. "The pursuit of the pleasures of imagination ought to be regulated by the precepts of benevolence, piety, and the moral sense."

of the Christian!   Of late it has gone much out of
fashion.   Such philosophy gave a tone to thought and
imagination in the earlier part of the last century; it
found its way into poetry, and is not faintly echoed
in a certain optimism, an earnest, hopeful faith and
devotion glowing in the beautiful pages of Pope and
Thompson and Akenside.   It has tinged the spirit of
Wordsworth, in that portion of the ' Excursion,' called
" Despondency corrected;" and in his earlier and
better days, it was the philosophy of Samuel Taylor
Coleridge, when he gave to his son the name of
Hartley, when he wrote the best parts of the ' Friend,'
when he sought the sympathy and encouragement of
earnest and independent men, and before his habits
became morbid and debased, and his mind therefore
preyed upon itself.

The question, whether the laws of creation and animated being are designedly beneficent, expressions of
the will of an active, intelligent, and infinitely benevolent Being, transcends in interest and importance
every other which can be placed before the human
mind for answer and solution.   To that question all
inquiries respecting the laws of mind as well as matter evidently lead up.   No one has treated it in a
more interesting manner than Leibnitz.   It alone is
worthy the name of transcendental philosophy.   An
answer in the affirmative lies at the base of all philosophical belief in an historical revelation, and in the
line of evidence lies the point of contact between a
sound mental philosophy and an elevating religious
faith.

The optimism of Leibnitz has been compared with that of Plato*; but there can be no legitimate comparison. The optimism of Leibnitz is clear, and his opinion is firm, founded on the existence and government of one infinitely good Creator. It is more than doubtful whether Plato had any distinct and steady conception of such a Being, so as to reason from it as a first principle. We may find passages in the Timæus, the Republic, the Phædo, which taken by themselves, and interpreted by the light of our modern knowledge and convictions, may satisfy a philosophical and devout theist. French and English translators have often given to Plato as much as possible the air and language of a Christian philosopher. In selections, like that of Dacier, the study of Platonism may be easy and agreeable. But those who endeavour to interpret Plato by himself will not presume upon superior penetration to Cicero's, when in the De Naturâ Deorum† he breaks forth,—"Jam de Platonis inconstantiâ longum est dicere; qui in Timæo, partem hujus mundi nominari neget posse: in Legum autem libris, quid sit omnino Deus, anquiri oportere non censeat. Quod vero sine corpore ullo Deum vult esse, ut Græci dicant ασωματον, id quale esse possit, intelligi non potest. Careat enim sensu, necesse est, careat etiam prudentiâ, careat voluptate; quæ omnia una cum deorum notione comprehendimus. Idem et in Timæo dicit, et in legibus, et mundum Deum esse, et cœlum, et astra, et animos, et eos quos majorum

* Stewart's Dissertation, pp. 126, 127.   † Lib. i. §. 12.

institutis accepimus : quæ et per se sunt falsa per-
spicuè, et inter sese vehementer repugnantia*."

Leibnitz, it has been said, belonged to that noble
family of thinkers which numbers among its chiefs
Pythagoras, Plato, and Descartes, who, " seeing in the
human mind something more than the passive subject
of sensation, an empty possibility, a product of physical organization, would ascribe to reason a divine
origin, and an authority superior to that of sensible
experience, and would subject facts to principles,
things to ideas. He sprang historically from Descartes, and was the immediate adversary of Gassendi
and of Locke.†"

But names and epithets must not deceive us, nor
be too readily accepted. The leading principles of

* "Now of the inconsistency of Plato it were long to speak. He
in the Timæus says that the Deity cannot be called a part of this
world ; but in the books of Laws, he considers that the question
what the Deity is in all respects ought not to be entertained. When
he would have the Deity without any body, how that can be, it is
impossible to understand ; for if he be destitute of perception, he
must be also destitute of foresight, destitute of enjoyment ; all
which we comprehend in the notion of the Gods. The same philosopher says, both in the Timæus and in the books of Laws, now that
the world is God, now the heaven, and the stars and the earth and
souls, and those whom we have been taught to receive as such by
the institutions of our ancestors. These things are manifestly false
in themselves, and intensely repugnant to one another."

† See the article *Leibnitz* in the ' Dictionnaire des Sciences Philosophiques.' Those who wish for a short view of the philosophy of
Leibnitz, will find it best in the paper entitled Monadologie, printed
in 1714, containing a *résumé* of his Theodicæa, and of all his philosophy.

the 'Theodicæa' are separable from the peculiar theories of Leibnitz, from his spiritual monads, his pre-established harmony, his sufficient reason; and perhaps it might be shown that Leibnitz, in whatever he possessed of useful knowledge of the mind, owed more to Bacon, to Gassendi, and to Locke, than to Descartes.

All who have paid attention to the history of philosophy, recognize at once two tendencies of thought, which, like streams rising among the distant hills, have continued strikingly distinct, though often approaching and sometimes mingling their waters; sometimes, after long windings, lost in distance and obscurity, re-appearing, sparkling with light and extending in beauty. These streams are the Platonic and the Aristotelian. The one gathers its strength from native and inward resources : its waters well up, as it is expressed, from the deep fountains of the soul. The other is enriched by the perpetual accession of many small but separate rills, that pour their contributions into the common receptacle of waters. The Platonist, imaginative, poetical, impatient of the restraints of logical deduction, seizing the broad facts and first phenomena of our so-called moral consciousness, without analysis, repudiating definition, relies on strong impressions, stirring words, and popular predilections. The Aristotelian, taking his lessons and laws from repeated observation, and justifying his conclusions by actual experiment, by the faithful interpretation of phenomena, endeavours to make his mind a mirror of the universe.   Cautious, exact, consistent, definite, he is not like the spider spinning cobwebs from his own bowels, to use Bacon's admirable simile, but like the bee gathering treasure from the sweets of nature, and storing them up for lasting uses and future happiness.   Perhaps the later continental metaphysicians, from Descartes through Leibnitz and Kant downwards, have allied themselves to the school of Plato, imitating his manner, and coveting his distinction.   But on the continent, as in political movements everything has been lost by the attempt to reconstruct society on abstract principles, and bring new and untried theories suddenly into action ; by the neglect and contempt of ancient and existing institutions, instead of the endeavour to adapt them to altered circumstances, and thus to introduce changes at once possible and safe, which time might show to be amendments ; in short, as there has been a perpetual change of masters, without increased security of law and wider scope for social action ; so in literature and philosophy, the passion for originality, the desire of every man to found a school and shine apart with unborrowed light, rather than to form part of a bright galaxy adding to the general illumination ; the disdain of known truths, received principles, plain language, and syllogistic reasoning,—these have been unhappily the obstacles to progress and to truth. More especially they have been so in those departments of thought, such as morals, jurisprudence, psychology, and theology, wherein it is so much easier by new, uncouth, or obsolete expressions, to play with the bubbles of reputation and raise the stare of wonder, than by the discovery of new facts, or by the better arrangement and classification of admitted and positive phenomena, to illustrate old principles or establish new.

I know not whether we have in English literature a work of criticism of equal dimensions so just, so instructive, so beautiful, as that of René Rapin, 'La Comparaison de Plato et d'Aristote.' It is noticed by I. D'Israeli in the Curiosities of Literature, in a short paper on the same subject. A similar comparison has been instituted and pursued with power and discrimination by Degerando in his 'Histoire comparée des Systèmes.' After holding the balance very evenly, and doing full justice to the fine taste and beautiful spirit of Plato, Rapin gives the palm of real worth to Aristotle, and adds his strength to the opinion of our learned Selden, no inferior judge, "that there never breathed that person to whom the world is more beholden than to Aristotle*."

Happily the English mind has been and is essentially Aristotelian, practical rather than sentimental, using imagination to adorn, not to pervert truth,—to polish, not to conceal facts. To the greatest names that can be mentioned of the Platonic family, it opposes names of superior weight, those of Bacon, Hobbes,

---

* Selden's Table-talk, edit. 1716, p. 124; a manual of wisdom in matters of Church and State. Rapin sums up his judgement in the words, " Plato frequently only thinks to express himself well; Aristotle only thinks to think justly."

Newton, Boyle, Locke, Hartley, Paley, Bentham, and many others, eminent disciples and coadjutors, men whose method of philosophizing has been fundamentally the same; whose great aim it ever was to be consistent with nature, and consistent with themselves; who believed the Divine will and human duty and human happiness ultimately to coalesce. This may be more fully developed when we come to trace briefly the genealogy of English metaphysics. Meantime there are welcome signs of a better era in the foreign schools. Trendelenberg, in the admirable preface to his 'Elementa Logices Aristoteleæ,' turns in the right direction. He observes that nothing now seems firm or settled in philosophy; that such is the inconstancy and variety in the use of philosophical terms, that often a merely perplexing and learned loquacity puts on the specious ornaments of philosophy; that he who seeks the elements of logic must be commanded to return to the refinement and simplicity of Aristotle. And Barthélemy St. Hilaire, in the preface to his valuable translation of the Logic of Aristotle into French, has demonstrated how widely the modern German writers of eminence, Hegel, Fichte, and Schelling, have departed from the path of useful philosophy, by neglecting the chart and guidance of Aristotle, and mingling, like Hegel, under the title of logic, in one mass of confusion, metaphysics, the entire body of philosophy, the intelligence of man in all its developments, nay the very history of humanity itself[*].

* See Logique d'Aristote, par J. Barthélemy St. Hilaire: preface, p. 149. Paris, 1844.

REFLECTIONS ON KANT.

The name of St. Hilaire brings us to the inquiry whether there be anything in the philosophy of Kant enabling us to solve questions left difficult and dark by his predecessors. St. Hilaire*, surely a competent judge, has asserted that in Kant's judgement respecting the categories of Aristotle, there are almost as many errors as thoughts; that he mistook altogether the design and spirit of Aristotle's logic; that while Aristotle was seeking the most general signification of all words in their relation to things, the design of Kant was wholly different; that while Aristotle was building his logic upon observation and experience, as he built his natural history, his meteorology, and his politics, Kant was seeking for pure conceptions of the understanding and necessary forms of thought. Though Aristotle has never spoken of what Kant calls conceptions, Kant would judge Aristotle as if Aristotle were merely one of his own disciples, but a faithless or stupid disciple. If St. Hilaire is right, the offence is great. There can be no progress in philosophy, when the paths smoothed by preceding labourers are not only deserted, but their very direction and character misrepresented, for the sake of acquiring a false distinction by the pretence of new discoveries and superior methods of procedure.

Kant as a thinker appears to have purposely isolated himself from mankind. He was not only self-ba-

* Preface, p. 80.

nished from the commonwealth of literature by the use of a language peculiar to himself, but there is ground for thinking that he loved much more to dogmatize among people who could not correct him, on subjects which they either had not studied or could not comprehend, than to find out what had been already wisely established, and to render more intelligible and easy what was before difficult and obscure. It has been observed by Rémusat, a favourable critic, that the student should bring to his pages a very amiable spirit, and be willing to interpret him in the manner most favourable to truth and to himself. But an author, whether he write to instruct or to please, should tax the patience of his readers as little as possible. If he cannot attract their sympathies by the graces of composition, he should not repel them by harshness and barbarisms, for which there can be no excuse in necessity. Sciolists and novices in metaphysical speculation, who are ever ready to mistake obscurity for depth, may continue to look into the dark waters for what they will never find. But to German transcendentalism the disciple of Aristotle and Bacon applies the proverb, " He who blows into the dust will be sure to fill his own eyes."

The injustice which Kant has done to Aristotle is accordant with the treatment of his more immediate predecessors. By the absence of careful reference to their pages, he conceals his own misconceptions or misrepresentations, and secures an air of novelty for statements and views which, so far as they are intelligible, are by no means original or peculiar. Thus in the preface to his ' Prolegomena zur Metaphysik' he gives an account of the influence of Hume's speculations upon his own*. But could any one understand what Hume's views and speculations were from Kant's account? We have seen how obscure and inconsistent Hume's language and statements are; yet it is necessary to know them accurately, in order to understand how far comments upon them are just. How vain is the reply to assertions which, perhaps, were never made; and, on language originally vague and inconsistent, how idle are comments still more mysterious!

" Since the Essays of Locke and Leibnitz, or rather since the origin of metaphysics, so far as their history reaches, no circumstance has occurred which could be more decisive of the fate of this science, than the attack which David Hume made upon it. He brought no light to this part of cognition, but he struck a spark, by which, had it met with susceptible tinder, a light steadily increasing might have been obtained. Hume set out from a single but important notion in metaphysics, namely, the connection of cause and effect, and with this the consequent conceptions of power and action; and he requires of Reason to answer him, what right she has to think that something may be so laid down, that if it be settled or granted

---

* There appears to have been an early translation of Hume's Essays into German, in four volumes, from which, in his notes, Kant quotes a passage.

(*gesetzt*) something else must also of necessity be granted; for this the notion of cause implies. He proved incontrovertibly that it is impossible for reason to conceive of such a connection *à priori* and from notions; for this involves necessity. But we cannot discover why, because something is, something else must necessarily be; and how the notion of such a connection *à priori* can be introduced. Hence he inferred that reason entirely deceives herself with this idea, and takes it falsely for her own child, when it is nothing but a bastard of the imagination, which, impregnated by experience, has brought certain conceptions under the law of association, and substitutes a subjective necessity thence arising, that is custom, for an objective insight. Hence he concluded that reason has not a power of thinking of connections of this sort, of themselves universally, for her conceptions would be in that case mere fictions; and all her cognitions pretending to subsist *à priori* would be mere falsely stamped common experiences, which is as much as to say that there are no metaphysics, and can be none*."

After some observations on the effect of Hume's conclusion in setting the good heads of his time to work to solve the problem, and on his being misunderstood by them all, the transcendental philosopher

---

* I have seen several translations of this passage (Kant's Sämmtliche Werke, vol. iii. pp. 5, 6), but it is difficult to give a satisfactory one; part of it is given from the Latin version of Born, in Stewart's Dissertation, p. 193, quoted from Willich.

goes on: "The question is not whether the conception of causation is right, useful, and relatively to the
whole cognition of nature indispensable, for of this
Hume never harboured a doubt; but whether it is
thought of *à priori* by reason, and in this manner
has internal truth independent of all experience, and
consequently more extensive utility, which is not limited to objects of experience merely; on this subject
Hume wanted information, and, as he himself tells us,
always kept his mind open to instruction, if any one
would vouchsafe to bestow it upon him."

"I freely confess that it was this very hint of David
Hume which first roused me from my dogmatic slumber, and gave to my investigations in the field of contemplative philosophy a totally different direction. I
was far from acceding to his conclusions, which I considered to arise only from this, that he did not contemplate the whole question, but only a part of it,
which could lead to nothing, unless the whole were
taken into account. When we proceed from a well
founded, though not thoroughly digested thought,
suggested by another, we may certainly hope, by continued investigation, to advance further than the acute
man could do to whom we are indebted for the first
spark of the light. I first inquired, therefore, whether
the doubt of Hume could be regarded as a general
one. I soon perceived that the conception of the connection of causes and effects is by no means the only
one by which the understanding thinks of the connections of things *à priori* (or as Born has it, *ex*

anticipatione), but rather that the whole of metaphysics depends on these (conceptions?).   I endeavoured to ascertain their number, and when this succeeded with me beyond expectation, I advanced to the deduction of those conceptions, which I was now persuaded were not derived from experience, as Hume feared, but *arise from the pure understanding.*   This deduction, which seemed impossible to my acute predecessor, and which no one besides him had conceived, although every one confidently used such conceptions, without caring on what their objective validity depended,— this deduction, I say, was the most difficult which could be undertaken for the behoof of metaphysics; and what made the matter worse, metaphysics, as far as the science already existed, could render me no assistance, since the very possibility of metaphysics depended on that deduction.   When, therefore, I had succeeded in solving the question of Hume, not merely in the particular instance, but in respect of the whole faculty of the pure reason, I could then take sure steps, though slow ones, so as at length to determine fully and on universal principles, the whole extent of the pure reason, both as to its boundaries and materials.   This metaphysics required, to erect a system on a plan determinate and secure."

On this passage Mr. Stewart has given some useful and instructive observations, showing the injustice of Kant to his predecessors, and the absence of that originality to which he lays claim.   But it is open to much graver objections.

After that careful examination of Mr. Hume's language and reasoning, which the reader may be supposed to have made, he is prepared for an estimate of the value of the foregoing representation. And it may be asked, would Hume have recognized his own meaning or thought in the dress which Kant has given to it? Would he have assented to the correctness of such an account of his problem, doubt, scruple, or whatever other name be given to his theory of the origin and his opinion of the value of our 'idea of necessary connection'—'our notion of *cause* and *power?*' Would he have understood it?

There is no clear statement, in the midst of what professes to be an historical account, of Hume's real argument and position. There is nothing in Hume about 'subjective necessity' or 'objective validity'— nothing about a conception of a connection of things *à priori*. Such language, borrowed from the schoolmen, would probably have been as distasteful and unintelligible to him as to subsequent thinkers. Nobody would conceive, from anything which Kant has said, that Hume contended, rightly or wrongly, that " this idea of a necessary connection amongst events arises from a number of similar instances which occur of the constant conjunction of these events." There is nothing in Kant to help us in ascertaining whether it do or do not arise from this source. The absence of distinct reference to Hume's actual language, and even to the particular Essay in question, is destructive to exact inquiry. Hume's question was not—

" whether the conception of cause is thought of *à priori* by reason, and in this manner has internal truth independent of all experience?" He would either not have understood this language, or he would have said it was idle, since in his own opinion he had proved, at any rate he had laid it down as a first principle, that *every idea arises from an impression,* —and therefore there could be in the human mind no idea or conception *à priori,* if by *à priori* be meant conceptions antecedent to all impressions *ab extra,* or to all experiences. The proposition just mentioned was the real foundation or starting-point of Hume's metaphysics. It pervades his metaphysical and sceptical Essays. That proposition, with its various applications, forms the subject of Brown's minute and careful criticism in his 'Essay on Cause and Effect,' where Hume's inconsistencies are pointed out. Yet it is one which Kant has never touched; and he did not perceive that the man who, like Hume, deduced all ideas from impressions, and yet comprehended under impressions all our inward passions, emotions, and desires,—that is, the most complex states of feeling, the rank growth of an indefinite experience,—had done nothing to clear but much to perplex the question of the origin of our ideas, of the security of our knowledge, and of the compass of the human understanding.

The language and the principles of the Kantian or critical philosophy can never come into general use in England, being remote from the tastes, the habits, and the practical aims of the English scholar, gentleman, statesman, or man of business. Nevertheless a certain number of writers and readers will continue to trouble themselves with the transcendental school of philosophy, flattering themselves that their notions on the highest subjects will transcend thereby the notions of ordinary men. The name of Coleridge, who did what could be done to introduce into the speech and thought of Englishmen the distinction between the *understanding* and the *reason**, between the spe-

---

* See Coleridge's ' Friend,' 5th Interposed Essay, vol. i. edit. 1818; the article on Coleridge's Plagiarisms, in ' Blackwood's Magazine' for March, 1840; and the note in Sir W. Hamilton's ' Dissertation on the History of Association,' appended to his edition of Reid, p. 800.

"L'entendement est la faculté des règles, la raison la faculté des principes; à l'une, les règles de l'expérience; à l'autre, les principes des règles." So C. Rémusat in the ' Essay on Kant,' vol. i. p. 405. Unfortunately for such distinction, the words understanding and reason have got a meaning and force in the English language inconsistent with it, of which meaning it is impossible to deprive them. I have read attentively the long note in Hamilton, p. 806, and the short one in Thomson, on the words *subject* and *object, subjective* and *objective,* and have often considered their worth without finding any. The meaning is for the most part arbitrary; that is, such as may be assumed and conceded for the moment without being in harmony with received use or any substantial advantage. They are commonly interchangeable, every subject being the object, and every object the subject, of thought, consideration, and reasoning. " *The subject,*" says Mr. Thomson, " *is the mind that thinks.*" " *The subject of knowledge is exclusively the* ego *or conscious mind,*" says Sir W. Hamilton. The objection is that such a meaning is wholly contrary to the received use, and to the etymology of the term. The subject of a discourse is always that particular matter or range of idea which subjects—that is, lies under (*sub-*

culative and the practical reason, and to make the terms subject and object, æsthetic and dialectic, available for common use, may long continue to exert some influence, notwithstanding the proof that he copied largely from the Germans without acknowledging his obligations, trusting to their statements and references without attempting to verify them, and thus affecting a knowledge of the schoolmen, which might easily appear considerable amid the total ignorance of other men. It may long continue to be thought and said, especially by younger men, whose time and powers will be wasted in the pursuit of shadows, or of sounds less real and instructive even than shadows, that there is a depth and truth, a fundamental science, in the ' Critique of Pure Reason,' which would resolve all doubts and difficulties could we but reach it. It will be said that no one can judge of Kant's philoso-

jicio)—the thinking power; like the insect or the drop for the microscope, not the magnifying or visual power itself. We speak of the subject under consideration, and the object of our attention : the first has reference to the course and flow of our thoughts, the second to the use and impression of the senses—such as a sound, a light, etc. But the meaning is by no means constant. As to the compounds, *subject-object*, and *object-object*, they are self-destructive. The attempted explanations of such compounds, so absolute, and so relative, are worse than useless ;—would they were amusing ! They only support Hobbes in the opinion that there is nothing so absurd but it may be found in the books of philosophers.

The terms subjective and objective are not infrequent in Cudworth and Norris, and writers of their day. Probably they were gradually dropped by subsequent metaphysical writers, by Locke and his successors, because they wanted other, and found better, terms to express all that they wished to say.

phy who has not mastered his peculiar style. Obscurity will be in the master an argument for depth, and in the disciples, who cannot, however, be interpreters, an argument for penetration. But what is implied by this? Are there phenomena of nature and of the mind capable of being discerned in Germany and expressed in German, which cannot be expressed in English, though with less conciseness and felicity? Are the definitions of terms, fitted for reasoning in German, incapable of being rendered fit by any transmission into English? There is no doubt a wide difference between the mental habitudes and characteristics of the German metaphysicians and the English, but the difference may be lessened by a willingness to approach each other; and the only mode of doing this is by a scrupulous adherence to the common ground of fact well ascertained, carefully sifted, and faithfully mirrored in language not to be mistaken. Do we see in Kant or his translators any evidence of this philosophic spirit and philosophic power? Was it not far less his ambition to arrive at truths where others had arrived before him, to rest on facts where others could rest with him, than to strike into new paths, to found a new school of inquiry and philosophy, in which he alone was to be leader and master? With this view, was it not much easier to use terms in a manner regardless of their customary use than to observe facts, overlooked before, but whose value must be recognized the moment attention is directed to them? Hence Aristotle,

Bacon, Hobbes, and Locke were held comparatively light in his esteem, notwithstanding what he has said occasionally in their praise. It was not to be supposed that they had any adequate insight into the nature either of matter or of mind. As Euclid and Euler are to be of no moment until the question is answered, "how are pure mathematics possible?" so Locke and Hartley are not to be allowed to contain any valuable observations on the laws and powers of the human mind until they have answered a question peculiar to the transcendental philosopher, according to whom "all metaphysicians were to be suspended from their occupation until they had answered the question, 'Wie sind synthetische Erkenntnisse *à priori* möglich?'" ("How are synthetical cognitions *à priori* possible?")—a question ridiculous by reason of the absence of meaning in the terms. For it may be asked, first, do they exist?—possible in reference to whose or what capacity?—what is a cognition *à priori?*—and next, what a synthetical cognition *à priori?*

Not only are the words analytical and synthetical continually applied by Kant to judgements or propositions which are neither one nor the other, but the words *à priori* and *à posteriori* are also applied by him to propositions, to facts, and conceptions, sometimes admissible, at others doubtful, as if such words were significant of qualities by which these conceptions and propositions could be satisfactorily distinguished from each other, and classified accordingly.

It is now high time to consider and to determine how far Kant's obscurity, as the acknowledged fountain of a stream whose waters are colouring and obscuring the progress of English metaphysical science, arises merely from this perversion of terms, from the use of terms apparently logical, learned, and classical in an illogical, unlearned, and barbarous manner. Almost every page of Kant's ' Critique,' whether you read it in German, Latin, or English, will furnish ample material to guide in the decision of this question; and that, not merely where he undertakes to correct Aristotle, as in respect of the categories, predicaments, or post-predicaments, but where he darkens by attempted explanation the common or fundamental conceptions of the human mind, whether innate or acquired. If we examine first Kant's metaphysical explanation, and next his transcendental exposition of the conceptions of space and time, we find the following assertions:—1. *Space is no empirical conception derived from external experiences.* And this for the one reason repeated in various forms, a reason which is in fact but a repetition of the assertion,—namely that external experience itself is first only possible by the representation of space already existing in the mind, and lying at the foundation of experiences ; 2. *Space is a necessary representation à priori* which lies at the foundation of all *external intuitions;* 3. It is no discursive or universal conception of the relationship of things in general, but ' *a pure intuition*'; 4. Space is represented as *an infinite given quantity.*

Then, after being told that we must think each conception as a representation contained in an endless
multitude of different possible representations, he
concludes, *consequently* the original representation of
space is *intuition à priori*, and not *conception**.

These assertions are followed by conclusions from
the above conceptions, which are—1. "Space represents no property at all of things in themselves ; 2.
Space is nothing else but *the form of all phenomena
of the external senses*,—*i.e.*, the subjective condition
of sensibility, under which alone external intuition
(äussere Anschauung) is possible to us." We might
here ask how far the sensations of smell, of sound, of
taste, which are among the phenomena of our senses,
would give any notion or conception of space without
the help of sight and touch, and how far space can be
rightly called their *form ;* but passing this, and passing also an attempted distinction between *sensible intuition* and *pure intuition*, we come to the conclusion
" that the *empiric reality of space is to be maintained*
(in respect to all possible external experience), although we acknowledge the *transcendental ideality of
the same ;* that is, *that it is nothing*, so soon as we
omit the condition of the possibility of experience, and

---

* This is from the translation of the 'Critique,' published by Pickering, in 1838. I admit it does not fairly represent the German, an
edition of which, by Karl Rosenkrantz, of Leipzig, 1838, is before
me ; but no possible translation makes any important difference.

On Kant's *contorted* and *abusive* use of terms, the reader must
consult Sir W. Hamilton's ' Dissertation on the Philosophy of Common Sense,' edit. of Reid, pp. 762–768, 769.

assume it (space) as something which lies at the foundation of things in themselves."

Then follows a metaphysical explanation and transcendental exposition of Time : which also is, 1. *No empirical conception ;* 2. It is *a necessary representation*, lying at the foundation of all intuitions, given *à priori ;* 3. Upon this necessity, *à priori*, is grounded the possibility of apodictical principles, or axioms, as to time in general. 4. Time is no discursive or general conception, but a *pure form of sensible intuition. Different times* are only *parts of the very same time.*

That these statements have in them nothing particularly novel, any one may see who looks into the writings of Cudworth and Price, referred to by Mr. Stewart, or into the amusing disquisitions of Soame Jenyns, who, in the fourth, on the nature of time, says, " It is only the mode in which some created beings are ordained to exist, but in itself has really no existence at all ;" or into the early work of Law, on ' Space, Time, Immensity, and Eternity,' or Watts' ' Philosophical Essays.' But be they new or old, they are indefensible. They are assertions which cannot be accepted as just. They have no foundation in reason, being unsupported alike by reflection on what passes within and observation of things without. They all proceed upon the false assumption, which is the vital principle of the Kantian philosophy, that there are representations (a very bad word) or conceptions given subjectively, and existing *à priori* in the mind, which are necessary to the admission of

objective realities. This is wholly incapable of proof.
It is contrary to the known manner in which our
knowledge of objects and of their qualities, and their
relation to each other, is attained. When Kant lays
down the axioms,—that different times are not contemporaneous, but in succession, and that different
spaces are not in succession, but contemporaneous,
—it may be asked how any one comes to assent to
these axioms but by having observed some things to
exist together in space, and some events to follow
each other in succession. And be the assertions respecting space and time, true or false, valuable or
worthless, no light is thrown upon the origin of our
ideas and the certainty of our knowledge, nothing is
proved with respect to the powers, operations, and
habitudes of the human mind.

To appreciate the value of all this language about
space and time, it is necessary to consider the speculations and sentiments of preceding thinkers ; to
compare their definitions ; and to ask ourselves whether these definitions and assertions render our ideas
clearer, or serve any purpose in reasoning for the support of further conclusions. It may be further asked,
whether similar accounts may be given with equal
propriety of all other abstract terms or complex ideas,
such as truth, virtue, beauty, glory, life, the soul, the
will ; whether these are pure intuitions existing *à
priori* in the mind ?   We may ask whether the same
account may or may not be given of our notions of
the elements, air, fire, water, moisture, heat, and so

on, and all things whatsoever, whose objective reality may perhaps be conceded, but whose philosophical definitions will depend on their subjective character; that is, on the mode in which the mind conceives them, and reasons upon them.

How much more satisfactory is the account of space and time, of body and motion, given by Maclaurin, in his account of Sir I. Newton's discoveries!

"Space is extended without limits, immovable, uniform and similar in all its parts, and void of all resistance. It consists indeed of parts which may be distinguished into other parts, less and less, without end, but cannot be separated from each other, and have their situation and distances changed."

"Body is extended in space, moveable, bounded by figure, solid and impenetrable, resisting by its inertia, divisible into parts, less and less without end, that may be separated from each other, and have their situation or distances changed in any manner."

"From the succession of our own ideas, and from the successive variations of external objects in the course of nature, we easily acquire the ideas of duration and time, and of their measures. We conceive time, or absolute time, to flow uniformly in an unchangeable course, which alone serves to measure with exactness the change of all other things."

He goes on with an account of motion, real or absolute, relative and apparent.

The worth of these definitions or accounts consists, not merely in their subserviency to subsequent reasoning and conclusion, not merely in their consistency with all other phenomena and noumena—with all that is objective and subjective, if we must use those terms, but in their applicability to our notions of particular spaces and particular times, as well as to the abstract notions, if such there be. Unfortunately, with the abstract notions alone the transcendentalist deems it proper to concern himself; and, by attempting to account for the abstract notions, and define the terms, without any regard to particulars, he soon reasons them away to nothing, and all his language is destitute of practical value and application. Such mental philosophers, like botanists and physiologists who build arbitrary systems without attention to nature, are soon encumbered with their own rubbish. The worth of Maclaurin's account is evident, by its applicability to all spaces and all times, to all the phenomena of the heavens and the earth, to seasons and their change, to the largest and longest conceivable as well as to the smallest and shortest, to the revelations of the telescope and the microscope, to astronomical spaces and geological eras and epochs, the experience of a life and the history of a nation and of the world. It is consistent with any and every measure of them; time being measured by motion, and space by body. Far different is it with the language of the transcendentalist. It is utterly incapable of satisfactory application to particulars. Our notion of the space occupied by a particular body,—our notions, for example, of the space of a

room, a house, a garden, a field, an estate, a kingdom, a globe, a planetary system,—may be called
pure intuitions, or representations *à priori* lying at
the foundation of things, if any one chooses so to
call them.   But he who maintains that our notions
of such particular spaces, and of the relative proportions of bodies in them, do not come from sensible
observation, and are not dependent upon observation
ab extra, appears not to be worth an argument.
Now if our notions of any and all the parts of space
—that is to say, of all given or actual spaces, are
altogether dependent upon sensible observation, and
do not and cannot exist without it, with what propriety can you maintain that we have in our mind a
notion of space in the abstract, existing previous to
all observation as a pure or *à priori* intuition ?   The
very existence of one and the same abstract notion
in different minds may be questioned, and the term
space is only valuable-when employed in some positive relation to existing bodies.

So with regard to time and times.   If we have not
in our minds *à priori* the ideas of a minute, an hour,
a day, month, year, or any measured period, if our
ideas of these parts of time are entirely dependent
upon the succession of impressions, and of observed
changes and motions, by means of which we make
these divisions, and understand one another's language in reference to them,—if no one of these ideas
would exist without the uniformity of the sensible
impressions to which they refer, upon what grounds

can it be maintained that every man, that every child
has a notion of time in the abstract, existing as a
pure intuition, previous to all experience? It is
contrary to all we observe of the progress and development of the intellect. You may call time a necessary representation, which lies at the foundation of
all intuitions; "eine nothwendige Vorstellung*, die
allen Anschauungen zum Grunde liegt." But the
language is without meaning, or fallaciously, unscien-
tifically metaphorical. Time is no representation of
anything. A representation cannot lie at the foundation of anything. Intuitions, in the sense of the
transcendentalist, whether internal or external,—for
he does not scruple to speak of both kinds,—do not
exist. Every proposition may be called an intuitive
truth to which assent is given the moment it is heard,
the terms being understood; and because it requires
no reasoning, nor new observation to support it.
Does the readiness of the assent and the perception
of the truth depend on the conformity of the proposition to universal experience, or on ideas for which
no experience has been necessary?

Far more to the purpose, in point of thought and
reasoning, than all the indefinite verbiage of the
transcendentalist,—far more consistent with all the
phenomena of observation and the uses of science,
with the Newtonian philosophy of the universe, and
the Hartleian theory of association, are the ingenious

* On the vague generality of the word *Vorstellung*, see Sir W.
Hamilton, whom nothing escapes, in his edit. of Reid, p. 805.

remarks of a forgotten and now almost unknown English writer, to which it is a pleasure to turn, and in which the thoughtful reader may find some little satisfaction. " 1. As space in the total is illimitate and immense, so is time in its totality non-principiate and interminable. 2. As every moment of time is the same in all places, so is every canton or part of place the same in all time. 3. As place, whether any or no body be allocated therein, doth still persist the same immovably and invariably so doth unconcerned time flow on eternally in the same calm and equal tenour, whether any or no thing hath duration therein, whether anything be moved or remain quiet. 4. As place is incapable of expansion, discontinuity, etc., by any cause whatever, so is time incapable of acceleration, retardation, or suspension, it moving on no less when the sun was suspended in the days of Joshua than at any time before or since. 5. As God was pleased out of the infinite space to elect a certain determinate region for the situation, so hath He, out of infinite time, elected a determinate part for the duration of the world. 6. And therefore, as everything, in respect of its *here* and *there*, enjoys a proportionate part of the mundane space, so likewise doth it, according to its *now* and *then* of existence, enjoy a proportionate part of mundane duration. 7. As in relation to place we say *everywhere* and *somewhere*, so in relation to time we say always and sometimes: and as it is competent to the creature to be only somewhere in respect of place, and sometime in respect of time, so it is the prerogative of the Creator to be everywhere as to place, and for ever as to time; and therefore those two illustrious attributes, immensity and eternity, are proper only to God. 8. As place hath dimension permanent, whereby it responds to the longitude, latitude, and profundity of body, so hath time dimension successive, to which the motion of bodies may be adequated; hence comes it that as by the longitude of any standing measure (*e.g.* an ell) we commensurate the longitude of place, so by the flux of an horologe do we commensurate the flux of time. . . . .

"From this parallelism it is difficult not to conclude that time is infinitely older than motion, and consequently independent upon it, as also that time is only indicated by motion, as the mensuration by the mensura *."

Good sense like this is consistent with any and all other propositions which we may lay down, not only

---

* Abbreviated from the 'Physiologia Epicuro-Gassendo-Charltoniana.' See *supra*, p. 215. Hobbes defines Space " *the phantasm of a thing existing without the mind simply*," and Time, *a phantasm of motion*. See his 'Philosophy of Place and Time,' Molesworth's edit. vol. i. pp. 94–96. All that the logician requires is that the subsequent reasoning be consistent with the definition; and perhaps this definition will be found as useful, and the subsequent reasoning as much to the purpose, as anything in Kant. Apply the language of the latter to the philosophy of Galileo and Kepler,— as it is developed in their own works, or in the 'Lives of Eminent Men,' published by the Society for the Diffusion of Useful Knowledge, a precious and admirable volume,—and its worthlessness becomes transparent.

concerning time and space, but concerning the bodies that fill the one, and the events that follow in the other. The doctrines and the principles of the æsthetic transcendentalist, whether they be *à priori* judgements or the contrary, are inconsistent alike with our common language, and with all the perceptions and notions to which that language is adapted.

In the tolerably intelligible and certainly conscientious account of the philosophy of Kant, which we find in the essays of Rémusat, the proposition that there are in the mind cognitions or conceptions given *a priori* antecedent to experience, is the gate of entrance to the whole field of his speculations. It is continually repeated, continually implied; whoever declines assent to it is stopped at the threshold.

"Experience gives," according to Kant, "not a rigorous universality, but a generality springing from induction. But there are judgements rigorously universal: such are mathematical propositions. Reason employs such judgements, and takes them for *points d'appui*. Could experience exist if there were not rules which give it form and value? The conditions by which a judgement is good or bad, are apparently ' *à priori* ' in the mind. Mathematics are built upon *ideas à priori**."

Is not this mere assumption, not only unsupported by evidence, but refuted by the consideration that no two persons reason together save by the help of agreed signs significant of ideas common to both, forming a

* Abbreviated from Rémusat.

part of their common conscious experience, of which universality, or absence of exception, is an ingredient? while not a single term employed in these assertions can be of value except as associated with the same or a like idea, whencesoever gotten.

When it is asserted that mathematical ideas,—that is, the ideas of figure, number, quantity, or magnitudes, of lines, angles, circles, proportion, and so on,—that the propositions or judgements relating to them—whether in arithmetic, algebra, or geometry— exist in the mind à *priori*, antecedent to experience and observation, the assertion seems nothing better than a bold defiance of nature and fact. In mathematical reasoning, no axiom is more constantly employed than this—'things which are equal to the same are equal to one another.' Are the ideas of equality and inequality in the mind of a child before things have been observed, measured, or weighed? He must be obstinately determined to support a theory who has the hardihood to assert it.

Among the many writers who have undertaken to give an account of Kant's philosophy, scarcely any attempt it by a close adherence to his own language. It may be therefore always a question whether the account is correct and ought to be accepted. But whether we read the original, or study it in a transmuted and diluted form, the most important inquiry is, what new facts we obtain, before unknown or disregarded, and to what new principles and laws of the mind we are conducted by a more able or judicious classification of phenomena previously known and admitted. The account given under the article Kant in the ' Dictionnaire des Sciences Philosophiques' is highly favourable, and evidently written by a warm admirer. Let us take an important passage.

" The *à priori* principles, *which serve to constitute the knowledge of nature*, or, as Kant says, to render experience possible, that is to say, the principles of speculative or theoretic reason, are without doubt necessary principles ; but what right have we to affirm that this necessity is not purely relative to the constitution of our mind ? How can we pretend that they are anything but the conditions imposed by this very constitution on the possibility of experience ? But if, on the other side, we conceive anything which escapes these conditions, on what foundation are we to determine its nature and to affirm its reality, at least when we do not address ourselves to morals,— that is to say, when we do not pass from the speculative to the practical reason ? So far there will be for us only pure conceptions, possible, without doubt, and perhaps even necessary for the attainment of speculative knowledge, but whose objective reality will remain hypothetical. But ask the practical reason,— that is to say, examine the principles *à priori*, which it imposes on the will : these principles are necessary not only for our will; they are absolutely necessary, for they are imposed equally on the will of every rational being whomsoever ; consequently they have an objective value, which it is impossible to doubt.

Behold then, established by the practical reason, an objective truth, absolutely independent of experience —the truth of the moral law. However, all which is necessarily bound to this truth, everything which is a condition or consequence of it, must be admitted by this very thing. Now, such are precisely the liberty of the will, the life of the soul after death, the Divine Providence. The first is the very condition of the moral law ; the other two are consequences of it. Thus the practical reason, in laying down the moral law as an absolute truth, secures at the same time the objective reality of that of which the speculative reason can affirm only the possibility. The moral law is therefore, according to Kant, the sole foundation on which we can rest, in order to determine or affirm anything beyond experience ; and, since this foundation is the only one, every determination and affirmation of this kind has value only in so far as it rests upon, and finds its limits in, this very condition. It is thus that Kant opposes to the scepticism to which the critic of speculative reason has conducted him, a moral dogmatism, which has for its foundation the indestructible authority of the moral law, and for its corollaries the fact entirely certain of liberty— which fact is the very condition of the operation of this law, and belief in the immortality of the soul, and in Divine Providence, without which the moral destination of man could not be accomplished. Such is the solution to which Kant arrives upon that great question, which he has made the principal object of his Critick. " Metaphysical scepticism and moral dogmatism—behold, in a word, on this point the twofold result of the Critick of Kant*!"

And are we in these days to accept this as the philosophy of the mind? Is this a satisfactory account of the grounds and certainty of human knowledge, of the powers and operations of the human understanding, of the pure reason? In these assertions, unsupported by argument or evidence,—in a a mass of terms thus used without regard to propriety or definition,—in a scepticism thus dogmatical, united with a dogmatism thus sceptical, are we to find repose? By reason thus suicidal, its two arms, the speculative and practical, fighting against each other, are the most difficult of philosophical questions to be supposed at rest? Assume, if you will, as postulates and axioms necessary for all philosophy, the liberty of the will, the existence of a moral law, the immortality of the soul, and a Divine Providence; but do not pretend that by virtue of these assumptions you rightfully claim to be monarch of metaphysical science, or that you have thrown any light upon the manner in which the mind comes to be furnished with its ideas, upon the laws of thought, upon the extent and limits of human knowledge, the power or weakness of the human understanding. He who turns over the pages of Hobbes, and Locke, and Hartley, and believes they contain

* Translated from the French; 'Dictionnaire des Sciences,' vol. iii. pp. 404, 405.

some valuable sense and truth, explanatory of the nature of the mind, can only smile with astonishment at the high pretensions, the mysterious jargon of the transcendentalist, and call to mind the youth and the philosopher so admirably described in the ' Rasselas ' of Johnson; when the pupil, after listening for some time to a discourse on what it is ' to live according to Nature,' feeling that he should understand the master less as he heard him longer, "bowed and was silent; and the philosopher, supposing him satisfied, rose up, and departed with the air of a man who cooperated with the great and unchangeable system of things."

ON THE TERMS A PRIORI AND A POSTERIORI.

The terms *à priori* and *à posteriori* are now continually used as epithets descriptive of qualities, real or imaginary, by which certain ideas and principles, certain conceptions, judgements, and intuitions, are supposed to be distinguished from other ideas and principles. Of this, the foregoing pages supply many instances. What is the distinction? Is it intelligible? Is it useful?

" *Principles à priori* bear the name," says the translator of Kant*, " not merely on this account, that they contain in themselves the foundation of other judgements, but because they are not them-

---

* ' Kant's Critic of Pure Reason,' p. 142 ; Pickering's edit. 1838. The translation may not be good ; but could any translation be given not open to insuperable objections ?

selves grounded upon higher and more general cognitions. Still this property does not exempt them always from a proof. For although such (*quære, proof*) could not be carried further objectively, but rather lies at the foundation of all cognition of its object, this still does not prevent a proof from being possible to be procured from *the subjective sources of the possibility of the cognition of an object in general;* nay, even that *it* is necessary, since the proposition otherwise would bring upon itself the greatest suspicion of a mere subreptitious assertion."

Allowing this to be English,—allowing for some obvious changes of the terms from a *principle*, which is a statement used in proof, to a proposition, which is commonly a statement to be proved, are we any nearer to a comprehension of the judgements not grounded upon higher and more general cognitions, and therefore called *à priori*, by summoning to our aid, in proof of their possibility, " the subjective sources of the possibility of a cognition of an object in general"? Of these subjective sources we confess a perfect ignorance, and feel ourselves in rayless darkness. The perusal of such a passage is like entrance into a damp, dark cavern, in which we have nothing to guide, instruct, or amuse us, but the echoes of our own noises.

A passage from a thoughtful English writer, which relates to the historical and illustrates the modern use of the terms now under consideration, will show the importance of attending closely to their meaning.

" Pure logic," (says Mr. Thomson, in his ' Outline of the Necessary Laws of Thought') " *treats only of those laws and conditions to which objects of sense are subjected in the mind;* and hence it is called an *à priori* science. It unfolds the laws of the *intellectus ipse*, and gives no account of the impressions of the senses. This view of logic it is hoped will meet with general assent." The hope appears a desperate and forlorn one. What is there in the logic of Aristotle, in Whately, De Morgan, or the Mills, about the *laws and conditions to which objects of sense are subjected in the mind?* and how can you treat of these without any account of the impressions of the senses? He adds : " Before leaving the subject, it must be noted that the term *à priori* has undergone important changes of meaning. In Aristotle's philosophy the general truth is 'naturally' prior (πρότερον τῇ φύσει) to the particular, and the cause to the effect. But since *we* know the particular before the universal, and the effect before we seek the cause, the particular and the effect are each prior in respect to us (πρότερον πρὸς ἡμᾶς). (Anal. Post. 1. ii. ; Top. 6. iv. ; Metaphys. 5. (Δ) xi. p. 1018, edit. Berol.) Following this, the schoolmen call the argument which proceeds from cause to effect *à priori* demonstration. But with Hume ('Sceptical Doubts') *à priori* has the sense given in the text, which *Kant has fixed** in the lan-

---

* On Kant's use of the terms *à priori* and *à posteriori,* and twisting of other received logical terms into new significations, I commend to the reader's earnest attention the remarks of Sir William

guage of philosophy ; and we purposely abstain from touching the great question of metaphysics—how much of our knowledge is from the mind itself, and how much from experience. The conflicting opinions upon this matter will never be reconciled ; and perhaps the best service which philosophy could receive, would be rendered by marking out the region which must be mutually ceded by the opposite schools."

On this passage I remark, that Aristotle's meaning is clear enough, and worthy of himself. He frequently intimates that nature proceeds upon a general law or principle, of which individual things or phenomena present to us the examples, and that in nature the order or law exists before the individual thing or phenomenon, which is but a consequence of that order or law ; in other words, the general cause precedes every individual effect. There is a foundation for this position in philosophical thought and scientific observation. Thus it is the law of gravitation which sooner or later brings every ripe and ungathered apple to the ground. Thus it is the law of vegetation, or the continued action of the same causal power, which produces the blossom and fruit, season after season, upon every tree. Thus the laws of planetary motion determine the place in the heavens of every wandering star at every given moment. But Aristotle also de-

Hamilton, in his 'Dissertation on the Philosophy of Common Sense,' p. 762 *et seq.*, which contains a vast amount of useful historical matter, but with many assertions over which the thoughtful reader will pause with hesitation.

cides, at least by implication, that for man there can be no *à priori* knowledge of nature or its laws, no *à priori* judgement or principle, because he must observe individual things before he can generalize; he can only deduce nature's order or laws from the phenomena; and he can know nothing of effects or causes prior to observation—that is, to experience.

There is an admirable passage on the value of the word 'prior,' or the πρότερον, in the Categories of Aristotle, of which the following translation may be proposed*. " One thing is said to be prior to another in four respects : first and chiefest, in respect of time, in reference to which one thing is said to be older and more ancient than another ; by its time being longer, it is called older and more ancient. Secondly, one thing is before another when there is no reciprocal correspondence in the order or consequence of their existence, as, for instance, one is prior to two, because of two things existing, it follows immediately that one exists ; but from the existence of one it is not necessary that there are two ; so that there is no correspondence between the existence of one thing and the existence of any more. Hence it appears that whatsoever is prior is such that its existence is not consequent upon the existence of any other thing† (or,

---

* I translate from Bekker's ' Aristotle' (4to. Berol., 1831. p. 14). Those who have attempted to turn Aristotle into exact and elegant English know its difficulty.

† 'Αφ' οὗ μὴ ἀντιστρέφει ἡ τοῦ εἶναι ἀκολούθησις ; the Latin, " A quo non reciprocatur existendi consecutio ;" the French of St. Hilaire, " Quand il n'en sort pas réciproquement l'existence d'un autre."

when it springs not necessarily from the existence
of another thing).   Thirdly, priority applies to any
order whatsoever, as in respect of sciences and discourses.   In demonstrative sciences the prior and the
posterior exist according to a certain order; thus the
elements precede in order the demonstrations of geometry, and in grammar the letters (or elements, στοι-
χεῖα) precede the syllables.   In discourses, in like manner, the exordium precedes the narration.   Besides
what has been mentioned, whatever is better and more
honourable seems by nature to hold the first rank.
Thus many are wont to call those first in rank among
themselves (priores), whom they love and honour most.
However, this is the least common of the modes of
using the term.   Such, for the most part, as have been
mentioned are the modes of speaking of priority.   But
in addition to those mentioned, there may appear to
be another mode of priority.   Thus, in things which
involve reciprocally their existence, that which is in
any manner the cause of existence to another thing,
may reasonably be called prior by nature.   Manifestly there are some such things.   That man exists,
is involved, with reference to the consequences of that
existence, in every true discourse concerning him.
For if man exists, the proposition is true in which
we say that man exists, and reciprocally—if the proposition be true in which we assert that man exists,
man does exist.   But though the true proposition is
by no means the cause of the existence of the man,
yet the existence of the man appears to be in some

manner the cause of the existence of the true proposition; for, according as a thing does or does not exist, the proposition is true or false. Thus in five modes one thing may be said to be prior to another."

Thus much for Aristotle's use of the term πρότερον; and well he knew the importance of using terms consistently and with meaning. We may judge from this what he would have understood by an argument *à priori*. Some priority in respect of time, of place, of rank, or authority, would always have been regarded by him. Whether the schoolmen were led by Aristotle's language and logic to their use of the term *à priori*, as an epithet for certain kinds of argument, it may not be easy to ascertain. But it is evident that, according to his use of the term, there can be no *à priori* argument for the existence of a Deity; for if we mean by the Deity the *First* Cause, to him there there can be nothing prior in time, or place, or authority.

It is said that Hume began that new use of the term *à priori*, which afterwards became fixed by Kant. Now Hume, as we have shown, and as any one who examines his Treatise and Essays may soon convince himself, was a very loose writer, and his example in the use of terms was a bad one; for he wrote merely for the sake of literary distinction and advancement. The desire for truth, and of human improvement and happiness, had a very small share of influence upon him. But it is not clear that Hume meant by 'reasons *à priori*' (a frequent expression with him), anything but what was then commonly meant, namely arguments from a cause known or assumed to the effect, and he was certainly not the first who used the expression loosely and in a doubtful sense.   Leibnitz furnishes many instances of such use.   For instance, in the preface to the 'New Essays' he says, " Il y a encore un autre point de conséquence, où je suis obligé de m'éloigner non seulement des sentimens de notre auteur, mais aussi de ceux de la plupart des modernes : c'est que je crois, avec la plupart des anciens, que tous les génies, toutes les âmes, toutes les substances simples créées, sont toujours à un corps, et qu'il n'y a jamais des âmes qui en soient entièrement séparées.   J'en ai *des raisons à priori**."

The expression 'reasons *à priori*,' thus used by Leibnitz and Hume, may easily be supposed to signify arguments from a known cause or an assumed premiss, in favour of a certain effect or conclusion. But whatever their meaning, it cannot justify the application of the term ' *à priori* ' to a conception, an intuition, a judgement, analytic and synthetic, in order thereby to give peculiar and intrinsic authority to some proposition which may be very doubtful and disputable.   Let it not be supposed that, by the use of that or any other term, it is proved that there are conceptions, judgements, or principles, which do not come to the mind through the senses, and do not rest ultimately upon phenomena *ab extra*, which may

* Compare also a passage of Leibnitz, quoted *supra*, p. 242.

be assumed as belonging to the mind *per se*, and independently of sensible experience, except as hypotheses for the purpose of an argument.

Upon what Mr. Thomson* calls *the great question of*

---

* Thomson's ' Outline of the Necessary Laws of Thought' is an instructive and thoughtful volume. But is it not unfavourably influenced by modern transcendentalism? Why is logic called '*a science of the laws of thought*'? Are there not many such laws, of which logic takes no account?—such as the law, that sensations and the ideas of sensation recur in the order in which they were originally associated or experienced, as in the repetition of prayers and of familiar passages of poetry, and in counting. It is easy to count and repeat forwards; not so backwards. It is a law of thought that men can only reason with the signs to which they have been accustomed; that minds can only communicate with minds by help of signs previously known and agreed upon. But the study of languages and grammar, and of Roman and Arabic numerals, and of the meaning of algebraic symbols, forms no essential part of logic. It is a law of thought, that men's habits and occupations determine the nature of their knowledge and their mental character. In vain do you apply to the breaker of stones, the hedger and ditcher, for an opinion on the respective merits of Bacon and Aristotle. Again, drunkenness and disease impair the faculties and take away the voluntary and the reasoning powers. But the subjection of thought to the laws of habit and the physical conditions of the brain forms no proper part of logic.

The only laws of thought with which Mr. Thomson's book is really concerned are those that relate to reasoning, proof, argument, or demonstration; and logic is in fact with him, as with Aristotle and De Morgan, nothing more than " the science of inference," but at the same time nothing less.

Mr. J. S. Mill is inclined to define logic " as the science which treats of the operations of the human understanding *in the pursuit of truth*." The last words must not be forgotten; but he adds, " The sole object of logic is the guidance of one's own thoughts:" and again, " It takes cognizance of our intellectual operations only as they conduce to our own knowledge." (Mill's Introduction,

metaphysics,—" how much of our knowledge is from the mind itself, how much from experience?"—on which it is said, "conflicting opinions will never be reconciled," the preceding remarks, under the head of Locke and Leibnitz, on innate ideas, were designed to bear; and, if just, they may help to settle it. But at the risk of some repetition, as it is called *the great metaphysical question of the day,* the subject may with advantage be touched again, the light upon it being somewhat varied. The following propositions seem tenable; and the appeal being to facts, and the facts not very far from us,—either the phenomena of ob-servation or of consciousness,—if there were a dis-position among metaphysical inquirers to understand each other, and to attend to the real nature of the mind and the meaning of their terms, the decision of such a question should not be very difficult.

1. A question which opposes experience to the mind as a distinct source and fountain of knowledge, either in reference to quality or copiousness of sup-ply, seems not a very wise one, since one cannot exist without the other; for when we talk of experience, we mean the experience of the mind, or that which could not exist without it; and when we talk of the mind and our knowledge, we never mean to exclude,

'Definition and Province of Logic,' pp. 4 and 5.) Now the object of logic, as an art, used to be to *prove* or *convince;* the object of rhetoric, to persuade or induce ; and the word συλλογίζω meant, I collect and infer, or, as I have sometimes thought it might be, I think or reckon with another,—to count together,—*computatio,* as Hobbes calls it.

Y

but, on the contrary, to include, whatsoever is conformable to and within the range of our experience, at least when we lay down true propositions concerning it. But perhaps the question is only intended to put in another form an inquiry into the value of Locke's two sources of knowledge, sensation and reflection; and it means, how many of our ideas have their origin in the one source, how many in the other? and how many true propositions the wisest are in possession of, relating to each? But even with that meaning, the question is not a very wise one, because we are without means of measurement; while nothing that Locke has taught is controverted, and no light upon his philosophy is thrown, by any opinion respecting the quantity of knowledge traceable to sources with which he did not concern himself. By a man's mind is commonly meant either the actual amount of his knowledge, howsoever obtained, or the instrument and faculties by which he acquires knowledge of any sort or degree.

"There are of *knowledge* two kinds," says Hobbes*, with that clearness and strength which satisfy and gratify; "whereof one is *knowledge of fact*, the other, knowledge of the consequence of one affirmation to another. The former is nothing else than sense and memory, and is *absolute knowledge*, as when we see a fact doing or remember it done; and this is the knowledge required in a witness. The latter is called science, and is continual; as when we know that *if*

---

* 'Leviathan,' ch. ix.: Of the several subjects of knowledge.

*the figure shown be a circle, then any straight line
through the centre shall divide it into two equal parts;*
and this is the knowledge required in a philosopher,
that is to say, of him that pretends to reasoning.".

This last kind of knowledge seems much the same
with what Locke calls demonstrative, and includes
his relation of ideas, or perception of agreement and
disagreement of ideas, with one another. But whether this be true or not, the above distinction is as
good as it is simple, and is in harmony with all we
know and all we think, whether of inductive or de-
ductive science.

2. *Whatever we know of the mind itself is from
the mind.* Its powers and qualities are known by
their exercise; and the powers may be confessed innate, although no idea, especially in the form of a proposition, can be called so. Thus we know from reflection alone, taught by experience, what is meant by
the will, the memory, the judgement, a sensation, a
thought, and by all other terms significant of emotions and passions, and all our internal states. Generally speaking, these terms do not require, and perhaps they scarcely admit of, definition. Yet the philosopher may try, and often with success, to analyse
the more complex states of mind and feeling into
the more simple and elementary. Thus the will may
be defined, that state of desire, accompanied by consciousness of power, which immediately precedes
muscular action. Every one is conscious of the difference between an accidental and an intentional

movement, between a pain endured and a pain inflicted, between a pleasure unexpected and a pleasure sought and procured. Motives and intentions, immediate or remote, mingle with and modify, if they do not constitute, the will, which is sometimes significant of the single and simple desire preceding a particular act, sometimes significant of a more complex —a less definite and distinct—condition of the mind, accompanying a series of acts, and extending its influence over a longer time. Care must be taken that a different definition, or idea of it, be not assumed or implied in the same argument.

Let us take an account or definition of memory. "Memory," says Ergates, in the 'Physiological Inquiries*,' "memory is a recurrence of sensations which existed formerly, produced by the operation of some internal changes, after the causes by which the first sensations were excited have ceased to exist." In such a definition or account of memory, is there not at once too much and too little? To sensation should be added, at least, "ideas of sensation" and of reflection, and former mental states—results of previous thought. From it should be taken away all allusion to theory about the manner in which the recurrence of sensation is produced. An inquiry into the internal changes which may precede memory is not necessary to understand the term. The assumption that some, though unknown, internal changes, whe-

---

* A small volume just published, and understood to be by Sir Benjamin C. Brodie.

ther of the brain or not, do precede and produce it, ought not to be mixed up with a definition of memory itself. The word memory has not commonly, nor ought it to have philosophically, any reference to such changes, whether they exist or not. But, be the definition of the terms significant of mental states right or wrong, it is required by good reasoners that the subsequent reasoning be consistent with the definition,—that is, with itself.

Now, as there are many sensational states,—many shades, for example, of whiteness and blueness, and of other colours, and many kinds of sweet and bitter, many tastes and many sounds which cannot be described or defined, and which cannot be conceived by those who are not able to make acquaintance with them through the eyes, ears, and palate,—so there are many states of desire and aversion, of joy and sorrow, which cannot be described in words, and are wholly incommunicable; and the best terms, which we can employ as significant of such states, can only be intelligible to those who interpret them by help of a similar or analogous past experience.

3. *All mental and emotional states are phenomena of consciousness; but the word consciousness covers, or includes, all that we reflect upon, all that we experience.* Is there any mental power or state that does not imply a sensational experience? In order that a sensation be remembered, that its recurrence be dreaded or desired, it must have been first experienced. Before an act can be willed, the results of

a muscular act being anticipated, there must have been experience of similar results from similar muscular action. The sucking of a child is at first automatic, and may be called instinctive; in process of time it becomes voluntary. The arts of talking and walking are acquired by effort and degree. At first each step and each word require the will; soon they become automatic, or secondarily automatic. And thus the study of the voluntary and the mechanical conditions of our mental and physical frame, under the guidance of the Hartleian theory of Association, becomes a most important and most interesting part of the science of human nature. The memory of pleasure originates the desire to renew it,—of pain, the desire to avoid it. Memory and desire are elements in the formation of the will. Whoever marks the growth of thought, and its expression, in a child, observes that, after the first dawn of intelligence, in the notice of objects, accompanied with smiles or tears—a language not confined to the human race, —it soon begins to mark, with a term significant, some outward object, such as mother, nurse, flower, tree, dog, cat, and so on, each term being associated with a cluster of sensible impressions. When the child has been accustomed to recall the sensations which have occurred together in past time, and to anticipate their recurrence in the future, and to mark the cluster of sensations by a term or sign, then the term, whenever used in the absence of the object or objects, calls up, in Hartleian language, the miniatures of the sensations. By degrees the child learns to interpret and apply a variety of terms significant of inward or emotional states, of desire and aversion, of hope and fear, pain and pleasure, memory and forgetfulness. It begins to explain its physical conditions, mental or metaphysical, objective and subjective; and it speaks of being hungry and thirsty, envious or complacent, knowing or ignorant.

4. These facts being heeded, the existence of any *à priori* or intuitive knowledge,—in the sense of knowledge altogether independent of or antecedent to experience,—can never be admitted. Every finite created mind emerges, so to speak, out of a state of nothingness, darkness, ignorance. It has nothing but what is given it. It knows nothing but what it learns. In the sense of a recipient of impressions, every mind may at first be compared to a *tabula rasa*, to which Aristotle justly compares the soul or thinking power; and even if there may belong to the tabula, metaphorically speaking, a colour of its own, which gives to the impressions a tint peculiar to the individual, of that tint no opinion can be formed prior to experience. In most cases, it is certain that the mind acquires all its valuable and communicable knowledge by slow degrees; though the degrees in facility or power of acquisition be infinitely varied. Of self-knowledge, sometimes called the most valuable knowledge, the knowledge of the inward propensities and powers which affect our conduct and

happiness as individuals, there can be none, till, as
the divinest of poets expresses it,—

> " Till old experience do attain
> To something of prophetic strain."

5. If there be truths, or axioms, entitled to be
called *à priori*, such truths and axioms cannot con-
tradict our experience, but must be conformable and
in harmony with it. If not derived from experience,
they must be supported by it. The terms in which
such *à priori* judgements are expressed must be in
harmony with all our natural and acquired associations, when they embody propositions which have the
firm, unhesitating, and unqualified assent of the understanding. And further, in order that a foundation be laid for the use of language, mutually intelligible, in order that two or more persons may reason
and syllogize together, the phenomena of sensation
and thought must be common to all who use the language ; and the terms so used must be the received,
authorized, and standard coin of the realm of the republic of letters ; not the spurious and unrecognized
issue of some private speculator or joint-stock company, whose promise to pay in the full value of sterling sense will perhaps never be honoured. It is the
utter ignorance or perverse rejection of the Hartleian
theory of Association, which raises so many difficulties in the path of inquirers, who will not accept its
aid to remove them*.

---

* On the received use of the terms " argument or reasoning *à
priori* and *à posteriori*," some accounts are given and some exam-

These remarks on the great metaphysical question of the day may place it in a light new to some readers, and help to its decision.

It cannot be necessary to enlarge further on the common and formerly received meaning of arguments *à priori* and *à posteriori*. But, as Bernier's Abridgment of Gassendi on the Understanding is less readily met with than some of the other works to which a note refers the reader, the following remarks of that writer on the subject seem to be worth attention, especially in connection with what has been said above respecting Aristotle.

" The understanding always commences with known individual things. Thence it happens that when we say, with Aristotle, that singulars are truly more known and more manifest in respect to us (*quoad nos*), but that universals are more known and manifest as to nature (*manifestiora naturâ*), it is certainly very difficult to understand well what he would say ; for all the notion and evidence which we can have of universals depends on the notion and evidence of the individuals.

" No doubt we prove many things of such and

ples may be found in Law's Preface to the translation of King on ' The Origin of Evil,' p. ix.; in Watts' Logic; in the learned dissertation of Waterland upon ' The Argument *à priori* for proving the Existence of a First Cause,' before referred to; and in Dr. John Clarke, on the Origin of Evil. Our own modern logicians, Whately, De Morgan, and Mill, do not make such kinds of argument the subject of their particular attention, nor admit any distinction as an important part of logic.

such individuals by general axioms, which are consequently more known and more manifest, but we have first drawn these axioms from individuals,—that is, by an induction which we have made of many individuals; insomuch that all the clearness and credence which these axioms have in our esteem, they owe it to preceding singulars, which have so much the more right to have this clearness and credence attached to them when the formal axiom is present, —'propter quod unumquodque est tale, et illud magis est tale.'

" Hence it happens that we have ordinarily more consideration for the demonstration called *propter quid*, or *à priori*, than for that which we call *quia*, or *à posteriori;* because the former proceeds from universals to particulars—from causes to effects, while the latter proceeds in a manner wholly contrary. We must nevertheless see whether we have a right to do this; since no demonstration *à priori* can have credence, or be received, without supposing the demonstration *à posteriori*, by which it must be proved. For how is it, for example, that, having to prove that *man feels*, from this proposition, Every animal feels; —how, I say, will you establish the truth of this position, should some one hesitate to grant it, except by making induction of the individual animals, of whom there is not one that does not feel*?"

* Translated from the French of Bernier's Abridgment of Gassendi, 'De l'Entendement,' vol. vi. pp. 349–441.

OUTLINE OF THE PROGRESS OF
ENGLISH PHILOSOPHY.

Bacon.—English philosophy, mental and moral no less than physical, properly begins with the great name of Bacon. In writers of an earlier date, such as Anselm and Bradwardine*, some anticipations of the most profound metaphysical speculations of a later day may be found. They discussed the nature and freedom of the will, the arguments for a Providence, the dependence of man on the laws of nature. But they can scarcely be said to have entered upon the study of the mind as a distinct subject for scientific observation, even had they written in English. Not so Bacon. His comprehensive mind failed not to observe how necessary it is, with a view to the advancement of learning, to know the nature and power of the instrument with which man acquires knowledge, the mind, according to Aristotle, being the ' form of forms†.'

---

* Thomas Wright published in 1604 a work on the ' Passions of the Mind,' of considerable interest. Huarte's ' Triall of Wits,' translated out of Spanish into Italian, and Englished out of the Italian in 1596, is also a book full of curious metaphysic thought. But they are fitter for the antiquary and minute inquirer than for one who would take a rapid but just view of the progress of mental philosophy since the revival of letters. Anselm in some measure anticipated Descartes. Bradwardine, whose works, ' De Causâ Dei,' etc., were edited by Sir H. Savile in 1618, was the first English Necessarian. The reader may consult Chalmers' Biographical Dictionary, and Priestley's Works, vol. iii. p. 456.

† On the meaning of the word *form*, see a very good note in Thomson's ' Outline,' pp. 27–31.

The Essays of Bacon, first published in 1597, under the title 'Counsells Civil and Moral,' are a treasury of observations on what has since been called 'private ethics.' In the 'Advancement of Learning,' first printed in 1605,—in all that relates to the reason and the four kinds of demonstration, to invention, to suggestion and the art of memory, to the false appearances imposed upon us by the general nature of the mind, by every man's individual nature, by custom, and by words,—we have a rich collection of pregnant hints, if not anticipating much that Hobbes, and Locke, and Hartley afterwards taught, following the Baconian method, yet laying deep the foundation for their work, and in harmony with all that has since been discovered and enforced by the physicians and metaphysicians of most exact and patient observation*.

We should not now define metaphysics to consist " in the inquiry of formal and final causes," as Bacon

* The passage on the connection of the mind and body—their mutual influence and dependence, suggests the thought that Leibnitz had not studied Bacon carefully enough to profit by him as he might have done. See 'Advancement of Learning,' Bacon's Works, 4to edit. 1778, pp. 64-70. The letter and discourse to Sir Henry Savile, touching helps for the intellectual powers, appears to be a fragment unfinished, but eminently worthy of the great author. It was first published in Stephens' collection, but unfortunately appears without date as to the time of its composition. The modern editors of English classics and philosophers, such as Bacon and Hobbes, would do well to mention the copies and editions which they have used for their reprints, and to mark the time when the several works were composed. When the works are not printed in the order in which they were originally published, nor accompanied by any dates of original publication, nor by any biography

does*; although this is perhaps what Kant would make it, interpreting him charitably, when he speaks of transcendental metaphysics, because he makes no distinct reference to Bacon or Bacon's meaning. Metaphysic is become a humbler study. It is now generally confined to an analysis of the faculties of the mind. It deals with the study of the extent and limits, the power and weakness of the human understanding in the search after truth; and with the study of the propensities to action, of pleasures and pains, with a view to the regulation of the desires and passions. But Bacon suggested the path. "The knowledge which respecteth the faculties of the mind of man," says Bacon†, "is of two kinds; the one respecting his understanding and reason, and the other his will, appetite, and affection; whereof the former produceth position or decree, the latter action or execution." "Human philosophy hath two parts, rational and moral."

Of the first part of the 'Advancement of Learning,' Bacon sweetly says, "This writing seemeth to me not much better than that noise or sound which musicians make while they are tuning their instruments, which is nothing pleasant to hear, but yet is a cause why the music is sweeter afterwards. So have I been

from which the dates can be gathered, the study of the author's mind, and of the course and changes of his thoughts and occupations, is involved in difficulties, which such information would help to remove.

    * Works, 4to, vol. i. p. 57.   † *Ib.* vol. i. pp. 72, 73,

content to tune the instruments of the Muses, that they may play that have better hands."

The first part was but a prelude to the second; the 'Instauratio Magna, or Novum Organum for the Interpretation of Nature,' published and dedicated to King James in 1620. With its noble and immortal aphorisms, it may be compared to a splendid overture, prophetic of choicest melodies soon to delight the ear, and breathe into the soul a spirit of power and hope far above its ordinary moods.

The axioms and aphorisms which Bacon lays down, as essential to the profitable pursuit of the knowledge of material and external nature, are also applicable to the study of the mind. The same tendency to hasty generalizations from partial and imperfect observation is to be guarded against. The same constant recurrence to observation of facts and *instances* is to be observed. The same emancipation from the slavery of words is to be achieved. The laws of thought, like those of matter, must be studied in and deduced from phenomena; and the phenomena can only be known by observation, first of what passes in ourselves, and next by the signs of the processes to which other minds are subject. Thus in the philosophy of the mind, no less than in the philosophy of matter, experience and induction, in Bacon's sense of these terms, constitute by far the best, if not the only demonstration. " Sed demonstratio longè optima est experientia; modo hæreat in ipso experimento" (Aphorism lxx.). The principles of Bacon were appreciated and acted upon by Hobbes and Gassendi, by Locke and Newton, by Boyle and Hartley, all of whom entered into his spirit and followed in his path; while Descartes showed not a little jealousy of the great master, and employed his imagination in constructing *à priori* systems; and even Leibnitz was not a little unwilling to be guided by one, in whose light his own grew dim or was eclipsed*.

" If the moral philosophers, that have spent such an infinite quantity of debate touching good and the highest good, had cast their eye abroad upon nature, and beheld the appetite that is in all things to receive and to give; the one motion affecting preservation and the other multiplication; which appetites are most evidently seen in living creatures, in the pleasure of nourishment and generation; and in man do make the aptest and most natural division of all his desires, being either of *sense of pleasure*, or *sense of power;* and in the universal frame of the world are figured, the one in the beams of heaven which issue forth, and the other in the lap of the earth which takes in : and again, if they had observed the motion of congruity or situation of the parts in respect of the

---

* How altered is the state of opinion in England since Warburton, among his memoranda, wrote :—" Descartes and Leibnitz were both great geniuses. I pity the first, for he was a visionary : I despise the other, for he was a cheat"! See selection of papers of Warburton, edited by Rev. Francis Kilvert, 1841, p. 332. It is said of Mr. Jackson, that he once heard Sir Isaac Newton pleasantly tell Dr. Clarke that he had broken Leibnitz's heart with his reply. See Whiston's Hist. Memoirs of Dr. Clarke, p. 132.

whole, evident in so many particulars : and lastly, if they had considered the motion familiar in attraction of things, to approach to that which is higher in the same kind : when by these observations, so easy and concurring in natural philosophy, they should have found out this quaternion of good, in enjoying or fruition, effecting or operation, consenting or proportion, and approach or assumption, they would have saved and abridged much of their long and wandering discourses of pleasure, virtue, duty, and religion. So likewise, in this same logic and rhetoric, or acts of argument and grace of speech, if the great masters of them would but have gone a form lower, and looked but into the observations of *grammar concerning the kinds of words*, their derivations, deflexions, and syntax, specially enriching the same with the helps of several languages, with their differing proprieties of words, phrases, and tropes, they might have found out more and better footsteps of common reason, help of disputation, and advantages of cavillation than many of these which they have propounded." (' Valerius Terminus, of the Interpretation of Nature,' Bacon's Works, 4to, vol. i. p. 380.)

Upon this suggestion of Bacon, Hobbes and Locke appear to have acted, however unconsciously. The sense of pleasure and the sense of power were, in the estimation of Hobbes, the great if not sole movers of mankind—the real and rightful governors of the political and moral world. The later and larger portions of Locke's Essay turn on the kinds and the value of words; not indeed on their derivation, but their definition, that is, their fitness for the purpose of exact reasoning and true science. In Horne Tooke's estimation, it was more a work on grammar than on the mind. It might be a very profitable task so to systematize the works of Bacon and of Hobbes, as to mark exactly the points of agreement in what they teach concerning human nature, and concerning the advancement not only of learning, but with it all the interests of mankind.

Of all the writers who have put their thoughts on record for the delight and improvement of mankind, Bacon seems most to deserve the praise that he never sleeps. I speak of his philosophical works. Open where you will, his pages teem with observations and expressions worthy of everlasting remembrance; rich with a knowledge of fact, a purpose of good, and a felicity of illustration, that mixture of fruit and flower which constitute the highest feast of reason, a banquet for the mind wholesome and delicious. He may not be always faithful to his own principles. He may sometimes be rash in concluding, and mistake a complex for a simple phenomenon. He may not be always just to his predecessors, and Aristotle certainly deserved from him a better title than that of sophist[*].

[*] "The 'Organon' of Aristotle and the 'Organum' of Bacon stand in relation, but the relation of contrariety : the one considers the laws under which the subject thinks; the other, the laws under which the object is to be known. To compare them together is therefore to compare together qualities of different species. Each proposes a different end; both in different ways are useful; and both ought to

But no philosopher has equalled him in the utterance of great thoughts in a style proportionately great; and his works are indeed as an awaking, a trumpet-note, "both of the wants in man's present condition, and the nature of the supplies to be wished." His errors as a man are unwillingly remembered in connection with so much intellectual greatness. No man has so largely overpaid the evil which he inflicted on the living generation, by the greatness and splendour of his bequests to posterity.

Hobbes.—It must have been between the years 1612 and 1620, in which last year the second part of the 'Novum Organum Scientiarum' was published, that Hobbes assisted Bacon in turning his writings into Latin, Hobbes being then in repute for the excellence of his Latin style. We are indebted primarily

be assiduously studied." So Sir W. Hamilton, note, p. 712, to Reid's 'Brief Account of Aristotle's Logic.' This is said loosely, with more apparent, than adequate truth. Aristotle's doctrine of the syllogism, or view of the laws of inference, is here chiefly regarded. But he never mistook this doctrine for a complete view of the laws of the mind, nor advanced it for more than it was worth. His 'Ethics,' and 'Rhetoric,' and 'Natural History,' and paper on 'The Soul,' are Baconian, so to speak, in method and spirit. Of Bacon it certainly is not true, that in attention to "the laws under which the object is known,"—a sentence which does not express happily either the aim or character of his 'Instauratio Magna,'—he overlooked the laws affecting the mind itself; or, as he expresses it, "the doctrine of the soul and of its faculties." The real relation of Bacon to Aristotle is not a subject for hasty decision. Something is said of it, and with his lively force, in Macaulay's article on Bacon, though more of Bacon's relation to Seneca and to Plato. The depreciation of syllogism and induction drew forth the defence of both by Mr. De Morgan, in his 'Formal Logic.'

for our knowledge of this intercourse between the philosophers of Malmesbury and of Gorhambury to that singular being, John Aubrey, the antiquary, himself a friend of Hobbes—a pupil of the same tutor[*]. Aubrey's account runs thus: "The Lord Chancellor Bacon loved to converse with him. He assisted his lordship in translating several of his essays into Latin; one I well remember is that of the 'Greatness of Cities:' the rest I have forgott. His lordship was a very contemplative person, and was wont to contemplate in his delicious walkes at Gorhambury; and dictate to Mr. Bushell, or some other of his gentlemen, that attended with ink and paper, ready to sett down presently his thoughts. His lordship would often say that he better liked Mr. Hobbes taking his thoughts than any of the others, because he understood what he wrote; which the others not understanding, my lord would many times have a hard task to make sense of what they writt[†]."

It has been considered remarkable that Locke has nowhere expressed any obligations to Hobbes, nor spoken respectfully of his intellect and writings; but it is still more remarkable that Hobbes has never alluded to this intimacy with Bacon, nor uttered a word of grateful admiration. We do not know that Locke ever saw Hobbes, though they were forty years

[*] Aubrey communicated to Antony à Wood the particulars inserted in the 'Athenæ Oxonienses;' and from Aubrey, Blackbourn got the information inserted in the 'Vitæ Hobbeanæ Auctarium.'

[†] See 'Letters written by eminent Persons, and Lives of eminent Men, by John Aubrey, Esq.' (1813, vol. ii. p. 602. Edited by Bliss.)

contemporaries, and there is reason for thinking that
Locke never paid that attention to the works of Hobbes
which they deserved at his hands. In the case of
Bacon and Hobbes there was, it appears, intimate
personal intercourse. Hobbes was twenty-eight years
the younger; yet the sense of generous appreciation
appears, by the above testimony, only on the side of
Bacon*. It is possible that Hobbes remembered with
pain Bacon's moral defects; for he had none of Bacon's passion for wealth, splendour, and power. It was
about the time of this intimacy with Bacon, or soon
after, that Hobbes began to be deeply impressed with
the nullity of the logic and metaphysics of the schools,
and to perceive the importance of attending to the
mathematical modes of reasoning in connection with
the study of morals and politics†. Yet perhaps we
cannot attribute much influence to the authority and
guidance of Bacon in the formation of Hobbes's intellect. Both were born great; that is, endowed with

* Bacon's name occurs once in the English works of Hobbes, vol.
vii. p. 112, and once in the Latin works, vol. iv. p. 316; but only
in connection with experiments relating to water and its motion.
Bacon died in 1626. It was not till about twenty years after
that Hobbes first appeared as an author in the book, ‘De Cive’;
although he had printed his translation of Thucydides as early
as 1628.

† It seems scarcely credible that he was forty years old before he
looked on geometry, when his attention was accidentally attracted
to Euclid's Elements, which lay open before him in a gentleman's
library. That book now forms a part of every boy's education; yet,
such is Aubrey's account. What could have been the course of education at Oxford when Hobbes was at Magdalen Hall, whither he
went, as a good scholar, in 1603?

a pre-disposition to thought, with an inherent energy of mind, which would have forced their way to distinction, through all impediments, independent of slight adventitious aids; like that ivy which, by its power of native growth, whether it cling to the mouldering wall or the decaying tree, overtops and at length upholds that from which it originally derived support. Nature and history were for both the great instructors. To both the past and the present opened their treasures. Both were earnest to extend and to secure the empire of man over nature and himself.

In addition to this intercourse with Bacon, Hobbes enjoyed the society, and even intimacy, of most of the great thinkers of his day; but of no one more remarkable than the great Galileo, whom he is said to have attended daily when at Pisa in Italy, where he was with his patron from the year 1634 to 1637. They are reputed to have been alike in temperament and manners, and united in friendship the more closely because both had been tormented by the censures of the ecclesiastics. Something of resemblance is discernible in their portraits; in the square and expansive brow, in the deep-sunk and piercing eye, in the firm and expressive mouth.

A difficulty in the study of Hobbes's philosophy and writings arises from the circumstance that the same thoughts and principles are repeated so often, in different forms, in what appear to be at first so many different works. Not only have we his philosophy in an English and Latin form, but in the 'Treatise con-

cerning Human Nature,' in the ' De Corpore Politico,
or the Elements of Law, moral and politic,'—both of
which were extracted from him by friends, and published in 1650,—and again in the ' Philosophical Rudiments concerning Government and Society,' printed
in 1651, we have only an extended view of the little
treatise ' De Cive,' first printed for private circulation
in 1642; while the matter of all appears in the most
mature form in the ' Leviathan,' wherein his system of
religious, political, and moral principles is complete,
and digested with great care and pains*.

The independence and originality, the earnestness
and depth of Hobbes' thoughts, together with his clear,
nervous, masterly style, cannot fail to attract the admiration of every generous and high-minded reader.
Such a reader perceives at once that he has in him
" such things as challenge the greatest attention;"
and he has only to read the epistle dedicatory to the
Earl of Devonshire, and the preface to the reader, prefixed to the ' Philosophical Rudiments ' in 1651, to
conceive for the author high esteem, " as a man who
thought no expense of time and industry too great for
the scrutiny of truth;" and who sought for it in the
most difficult matters, in moral and civil prudence,
" matters most necessary to the completion of that
happiness which is consistent with human life."

Public opinion has its effective *Index Expurgatorius*.
No body of men exercises a more powerful influence
over public opinion in England than the clergy; but

* See Life of Hobbes, prefixed to the folio of 1771, p. xv.

no works are more fatal to this influence, none more
hostile to spiritual pretensions and ecclesiastical do-
mination, than those of Hobbes. Hence no writer of
equal merit has been so much neglected, none is so
entirely out of fashion; yet no writer is more fitted
to form the strong, the independent, self-relying mind;
to remove from fact and nature the veil of words, to
make us understand both what we think and why we
think it. He regarded the clergy as factious towards
the state, tyrannous and grasping towards the people.
Their conduct in his day gave much reason for so regarding them. Religion was then, as often before
and since, if not the chief source of civil discord, at
least a great element in the excitement and the strife.
There can be no more effectual preservative against
the tendency to mistake submission to a priest and a
credulous superstition for the spirit of religion, and
against the tendency to confound the Church of Christ
with a body of domineering ecclesiastics, than that
part of the ' Leviathan' entitled ' Of the Kingdom of
Darkness.' The comparison of the Papacy with the
kingdom of the fairies, and the short account of the
whole synthesis and construction of the Pontifical
power, is a delicious morsel of history and satire.

It is not, however, the clergy only who appear to
disadvantage in the ' Leviathan,' but human nature
itself. Men are there represented as in constant danger from one another, the objects of a just suspicion
and mistrust; herding together solely for mutual protection, and kept together by the necessary ties of a

selfish interest; using each other's weaknesses for self-glorification,—envy and malice being large ingredients in the compound of good manners and social order. If any metaphysician deserve the title of sensationalist, it may be Hobbes. Significant of an opinion of fact, it is no title of reproach. All our conceptions, according to him, proceed from the sense or action of things upon the brain. If any moralist deserve to be called selfish, it is Hobbes, who says that by love is understood the joy man taketh in any present good; and who speaks of the affection which men bestow on strangers, as "either contract, whereby they seek to purchase friendship; or fear, which maketh them to purchase *peace*." (Human Nature, ch. ix.) With him, might is the foundation of right, and goodness is constancy in attention to self. Obedience to law must be enforced by power; and moral obligation* arises from fear of evil and necessity of submission.

Yet, whatever his defects, the metaphysician will delight in the depth and truth of his observations on the intellect, the imagination, and the passions; the logician will peruse and re-peruse his excellent remarks on definition and demonstration, and the nature and value of first principles; and the philosophical Christian will weigh with candour and attention his estimate of the relation of the Church to the State, of Scripture to the civil law, and learn to test in silent

---

* "There can be no obligation without an obliger," says Seldon, in his 'Table Talk,' a book which indicates, if not the influence of his friend Hobbes, a general harmony of opinion.

meditation the amount and value of his faith, and the
real but secret nature of his hopes and fears.

It is not easy to give a short, and at the same
time just, account of the moral and political principles of Hobbes.   In 1637, Hobbes returned from
Italy with the Earl of Devonshire into England.   The
troubles in Scotland growing high, and popular discontent spreading southwards, threatening the entire
subversion of the peace of the island, he bent his
thoughts to politics, and composed something against
the pestilential opinions which began generally to prevail.   It was this that engaged him to commit to paper certain observations, out of which he first composed
his book 'De Cive,' and which grew up afterwards
into that system called the 'Leviathan.'   "The true
scope of his discourse was no more than this," says the
author of the Life prefixed to the folio of 1751, "that
security can be only enjoyed where there is peace;
that peace cannot be maintained without dominion;
that dominion cannot be supported without arms; that.
arms will prove but a weak defence, if not put into
one hand; and, even then, that they will scarcely restrain such as shall be prompted to discord by the fear
of an evil greater than death itself, which is the case
in religious disputes."   This account of the scope of
the 'Leviathan' is just.   The most doubtful proposition is, "that arms will prove but a weak defence, if
not put into one hand."   The comparative safety of
the mass of the people under a despotism, and under
a mixed form of government, is a subject which Hobbes

has discussed, but on which the materials for forming
a just judgement have much increased since his time;
and we must be sensible, that there had been no such
experience before his days, as there has been since, of
the peace and prosperity of mankind under a constitutional monarchy and in a free republic.

Enough has been made of the peculiarity, and, as
some think, the absurdity, of certain of his definitions;
such as, that " laughter proceedeth from a sudden conception of some ability in him that laugheth;" " glory
is the passion which proceedeth from the imagination
or conception of our own power above the power of
him that contendeth with us*." But he is not without
sentiments which imply a delicate and refined appreciation of true goodness of heart and the true graces
of life and happiness; thus he says, " that much laughter at the defects of others is a sign of pusillanimity.
For of great minds, one of the proper works is to help
and free others from scorn, and compare themselves
only with the most able." As with other philosophical writers, perhaps it is less by the chief propositions which he seeks to establish, than by the profound truth of incidental and subordinate passages,
that the excellence of Hobbes is to be appreciated.
So with the greater poets,—it is less the subject and
construction of their poem, than the beauty of favourite passages, that wins admiration, and leaves an
indelible impression on the memory and the heart.

If we judge of Hobbes by the dedication to his

* See chap. ix., ' Treatise on Human Nature.'

patron and the preface to the reader, attached to the
' Philosophical Rudiments concerning Government and
Society,' we shall give him credit for pure motives, and
form an opinion highly favourable of his temper and
intent.   He saw his country boiling hot with questions concerning the rights of dominion and the obedience due from subjects, the true forerunners of an
approaching war.   He hoped to persuade his readers
rather " to brook with patience some inconveniences
under government (because human affairs cannot possibly be without some), than self-opinionatedly to disturb the quiet of the public; that, weighing the justice
of things, not by the persuasion and advice of private men, but by the laws of the realm, they would
not suffer ambitious men to wade through streams
of blood to their own power; that they would esteem
it better to enjoy themselves in the present state, than,
by waging war, endeavour to procure a reformation
for other men in another age, themselves in the meanwhile either killed or consumed with rage."   He first
sets it down for a principle, " by experience known to
all men, that the dispositions of men are naturally
such, that except they be restrained through fear of
some coercive power, every man will distrust and
dread each other; and as by natural right he may,
so by necessity he will, be forced to make use of the
strength he hath toward the preservation of himself."
" Though mankind be not wicked by nature, nor all
nor the larger part wicked, yet, because we cannot
distinguish the wicked from the righteous, there is a

necessity of suspecting, heeding, anticipating, subjugating, self-defending, ever incident to the most honest and fairest conditioned." Building on this foundation, he demonstrates first, that the state of men, without civil society, properly called the state of nature, is nothing else but a mere war of all against all; and in that war, all men have equal right to all things: next, that all men, as soon as they understand this hateful condition, have a natural desire to be freed from this misery. But this cannot be done, except by compact they all quit that right they have to all things. He then declares what the nature of compact is; by what the right of one might be transferred into another to make their compacts valid; also, what rights and to whom they must be granted, for the establishing of of peace; meaning, what those *dictates of reason* are, which may be properly termed *the laws of nature.* These he discusses under the title *Liberty.*

Under the title *Dominion* he shows what civil government is, and the supreme power in it, and what the divers kinds are; he discusses their several conveniences and inconveniences; he unfolds what those things are which destroy it, and what his or their duty who rule in chief.

Under the title *Religion* he endeavours to demonstrate, by strong reason, that the powers exercised by rulers over their subjects, and the obedience due from subjects unto their princes, are not contrary to religion, nor to the Christian religion. Finally, he requests his readers, " if they meet with some things which have more of sharpness, and less of certainty, than they ought to have,—since they are not so much spoken for the maintenance of parties as the establishment of peace, and by one whose just grief for the present calamities of his country may justly be allowed some liberty,—to deign to receive them with an equal mind."

In the tone of this address to his readers, there is much to win respect; nor can there be a doubt of Hobbes's earnest desire for truth and peace, and of his profound and anxious thought on the most difficult and important questions in moral and political philosophy. But his opinion of human nature, of its inherent and unconquerable selfishness and folly, oozes out when he exhorts his readers to consult their ease and enjoyment, rather than seek to procure a reformation for other men in another age; while all that he says, under the head of Liberty, indicates his belief, not only in the original, but the continued and lasting predominance of the selfish passions, of suspicious and hostile feelings.

The defects of Hobbes seem to lie rather in what he omits than in what he asserts. Thus he frequently alludes to the infinitude, the eternity, the omnipotence of the Deity. He expatiates not on his wisdom and his goodness. He admits, for piety's sake, the propriety of giving to the Divine Being every title indicative of our desire and willingness to honour him; but he urges no reasons for that honour, and is evidently a stranger to the fervours of devotion. He con-

tends that sovereign power is the source and foundation of law, and that punishment or fear of evil alone
enforces obedience.   He rarely, if ever, intimates that
the power, whether divine or human, originally benevolent, is exercised for good; and although this in-
dubitably follows from what he himself lays down, it
enters not into his philosophy to consider how the
motives to obedience may be strengthened by a perception of the ultimate harmony between self-love and
social, the human and divine.   He argues at length,
from passages of Scripture, that obedience to the civil
sovereign, being Christian, is a part of the duty of a
Christian; but he drops no word of encouragement
for any Christian believers to seek the improvement of
the civil law, by an infusion of the peace-preserving and
benevolent spirit of the Gospel.   It may be true, that
the natural state of man is, very often and very much,
a state of warfare.   The history of nations commonly
accounted civilized, testifies the amount and constancy
of the struggles in which mankind engage for aggran-
disement or preservation.   How bloody are the early
annals of all civilized countries !   What treachery, ra-
pine, and murder make up the history of the Middle
Ages !   Until times comparatively recent, how foul
and savage have been the domestic feuds of Scotland !   What frightful suffering has the mad ambition
of France repeatedly spread over Europe !*   What

---

* See a description of the horrors of the wars of Francis I. and
Charles V. in Sismondi's 'Histoire des Français,' vol. xii. p. 74, and
' Essay on the painful moral of History,' by the Rev. George Walker.

horrors afflicted the Netherlands under the government of Alva! How long, how melancholy, are the records of persecution for opinion's sake! What a fiend in the shape of man, and under the name of Christian, was the Inquisitor! It may be true that a selfish interest is the secret spring of a vast majority of human actions; for every individual has the care of his individual life, which is made up of bodily functions and of mental trains. It may be true that men enter into society for mutual safety, and convey to a supreme power, or common master, something of original freedom, called natural right, to secure a greater good, under the name of social right. But when Hobbes labours to support the paradox, that man is not born fit for society*, and that he is made so only by education, he is merely fighting against himself. For if, according to himself, faith and compacts are necessary to civil societies, he should have shown, not merely that children and fools are incapable of appreciating their defects and wants, but that men, as rational beings, are unfitted to form compacts and to observe faith. He should have shown that men are, by nature, more disposed to roam the desert and the prairie, as solitary beasts of prey, than to be united in bands of friendly alliance and joyful communion. He omits to observe that man, in his wildest state, exhibits the influence and appreciates the happiness of the domestic and social relations; that if by the necessity of nature he is driven into

* See the note, vol. ii. p. 2, Molesworth's ' Hobbes.'

society, he is soon bound to it by the strongest ties
of habit, and by the immediate and constant perception of advantage; that the conjugal, parental, and
filial affections are early developed; and that the desire for self-preservation is stimulated, and the motives for personal security are strengthened, by whatsoever makes life itself more happy as well as more
secure.   But the impossibility of being happy in oneself without seeing others also happy; the pleasure,
genuine, though rare, of contributing to human enjoyment and improvement; the natural strength and
rapid development of the social affections, their purity
and their force; the power of self-sacrifice for the
sake of country and mankind, whose interests are identified with the pursuit and dissemination of truth and
liberty;—these are considerations which rarely, if ever,
enter into the speculations of Hobbes.   He did not
view nature from the golden side.   He dwelt more on
that which was to be feared or despised in man, than
to be loved and honoured.   Though he lived among
the first men of his time, he formed no ardent friend-
ships.   He knew not, from his own experience, the
influence of any refining domestic ties, and earnest
social affections.   To enjoy the ease which was his
utmost moral ambition, he was content with finding
shelter and protection in the house of a powerful patron; and, from his chamber of security and seclu-
sion, he looked out upon the world, only to observe
and register the struggles and animosities of nation
against nation, sect against sect, neighbour against

neighbour; and while he employed his reason in spe-
culating on the causes of social discord and the securities of peace, he examined the nature of the human
passions and the strength of the human understanding, with the value of common language and the notions in repute, to discover and expose the dangerous
and evil tendencies of the one, and the weakness and
absurdity of the other.

Yet, though Hobbes looks habitually on the darkest
side of human nature, no writer is more suggestive.
With unsparing hand he strips off the disguises and
lays bare the pretences by which men who relinquish
no interest, who forego no pleasure, which submission to
power and compliance with custom can secure them,
would persuade themselves and others that they are
the most religious, most patriotic, and most benevolent of beings; but at the same time he compels the
candid and disinterested reader to turn a searching
eye upon the condition of the inner man, and to examine in what respects his purposes and conduct are
conformable to that rule of life which the understanding approves, and the conscience acknowledges as
binding. Upon that great question raised by Hobbes,
namely, in what cases the private conscience or opinion should be obeyed when it dictates a course contrary to that which public authority—in the shape
of law, civil and ecclesiastical—may determine to enforce, he may throw no valuable light; but when
touching on the impotence of human laws and institutions, among men who dread a greater evil than any

which their fellows can inflict, or hope a greater good than any they can give, he makes us comprehend the serious nature of the position taken when we assume superiority to the leaders of society around us in our knowledge of truth and human good,—and identify, perhaps too readily and confidently, the dictates of our own reason with the laws of nature and of God.

No great writer can be judged by a selection of peculiar, and perhaps highly exceptionable, passages. From this rule Hobbes is the last to be exempt.   A good body of important rules for social conduct, and of hints for the improvement of life and society, may be gathered from his pages, by one who searches them in the love of truth and goodness.   He is commonly quoted as if he had said and taught that " might is right;" and it is true that, in what he calls a state of nature,—a state in which human law restrains not, and reason has reached no sense of a divine law,—the power of a man to get and to keep constitute his right; but, in such a condition of things, moral terms are no more applicable to men than to the beasts of the forest.   It is more just to Hobbes to represent him as maintaining that " might makes right;" a truth which no one can consistently dispute who judges law to emanate from power, and rights to be possessions or liberties or faculties secured to an agent by laws human or divine.   The divine power must be the first and original source of all rights enjoyed by beings created and subordinate, whether in relation to other beings they be subject or sovereign, governors or governed. The will or law of God is to all mankind the ultimate rule of right. It would have helped Hobbes, in some portions of his argument, had he adverted to the derivation of the terms '*right*' and '*just*,' a derivation which furnishes the clue to their only valuable meaning. The right and the just are clearly *that which is ordered*, first, by the law of God—the supreme will; or, secondly, the law of the land—the civil or supreme earthly power; or, thirdly, the law of society or public opinion, imperfectly declared; or lastly, the law of conscience—that opinion of good which determines every man in his private course. When these laws or commands point to one and the same course of action, coalesce in their decision, and that course is practically followed, then we may say that all is right*. Those who talk of the rights of man as well as of the laws of nature are seldom aware how much their meaning is disguised in metaphor, and how often they conceal the most anarchical and dangerous fallacies under the specious gloss of liberty and truth.

In reading Hobbes, it must ever be remembered that he is writing against anarchy and those who fa-

---

* The article on "Rights" in the ' Encyclopædia Britannica' is worth attention. It divides them into natural and adventitious, alienable and inalienable, perfect and imperfect. On the first it takes the view of Hobbes; on the last it shows the difficulty of drawing the lines of moral right with distinctness and precision. See also Bentham's papers " on anarchical fallacies and on principles tending to anarchy,"—full of a just political philosophy, and deserving careful study. Vol. ii. and iii. of Bowring's edition of Bentham.

voured it, or the principles which led to it. His mind
was sorely impressed with the frightful evils of civil
contest, which in his view were more dreadful than
those of despotism; and without attempting to overthrow, appearing rather to support, the authority of
the Scriptures, he wished to guard against the danger
of that private interpretation of them which encouraged rebellion against the civil sovereign. The Co-
venanter, wielding the sword in one hand and the
Bible in the other, and gloating over the texts of the
Old Testament to inflame his wrath against his mis-
believing neighbours, as the enemies of Israel and of
Jehovah, was in his opinion a most unhappy model of
the man and of the Christian. In the attempt to de-
pict the incompatibility of such a character with civil
order and improvement, he could hardly avoid sentiments offensive to those who, upon different principles
or pretences, were disposed to exercise a tyranny op-
pressive and injurious, and to claim exclusive privileges which must foster in the rest of the community
a natural and well-founded jealousy.

One of the most obnoxious sentiments of Hobbes
was that the Deity was a spirit corporeal,—meaning
'a substance that has magnitude.' Incorporeal substances—pure spirit without body, were words to him
without meaning, incomprehensible. In a remarkable
passage, he maintains " that the universe,—that is, the
whole mass of things that are,—is corporeal; that it
hath dimensions, namely length, breadth, and depth;
and because the universe is all, that which is no part

of it is *nothing*, and consequently *nowhere*. Nor does it follow from hence that spirits are nothing, for they have dimensions, and are therefore really bodies, though that name be given in common speech to such bodies only as are visible, or palpable, that is, have some degree of opacity. But for spirits, they call them incorporeal; which is a name of more honour, and may therefore with more piety be attributed to God himself; in whom we consider, not what attribute expresseth best his nature, which is incomprehensible, but what best expresseth our desire to honour him*."

This opinion, of what he calls the corporeity of the Deity, was connected by Hobbes with a theory of the origin and cause of motion. There is no such thing, he asserts, as an *incorporeal movement*†; and by motion Hobbes endeavoured to explain everything, as far as explanation is possible to man, namely, sensation and perception, and all the affections and qualities of the mind, as well as all the changes and appearances of matter; and from it he deduced the necessity of human actions.

From these opinions it was inferred that Hobbes was an atheist at heart, and that his philosophy was atheistic; and among those who so considered it Dr. Samuel Clarke ranks first and highest. Dr. Clarke devotes to Hobbes a great portion of the latter part of his demonstration of the Being and Attributes

---

* Works: Leviathan, vol. iii. p. 672.

† Works, vol. i. p. 430.

of God.   He uses towards Hobbes no language
of virulence, but endeavours to play him off against
himself, nor altogether without success.   But Dr.
Clarke has mixed up two questions wholly distinct:
the existence of an intelligent first cause, having a
power of beginning motion, who has endued created
beings with perception and motion; and the question
of the freedom of the human will.   He has not adduced from Hobbes any passage in which he denies the
first proposition; and a careful reader easily discerns
a wide difference between the language and sentiments of Hobbes and those of Spinoza.   The omni-
science, omnipotence, eternity, and goodness of the
Deity, Hobbes has never questioned, nor is there anything in his works inconsistent with belief in them.
He has avoided the use of the word matter, and preferred that of body, which he considered to be involved in that of substance.   His philosophy of body,
or natural philosophy, and the attempt to account for
the origin of motion, must not be confounded with
his religious philosophy, if such it may be called.   The
last is best seen in the final chapters of the ' Philosophical Rudiments of Government and Society;' and
the rational Christian will find nothing to disapprove
in his language concerning the Deity.

" But that we may understand what manner of worship of God natural reason doth assign us, let us begin from his attributes.   Where, first, it is manifest
that existence is to be allowed him; for there can be
no will to honour him who, we think, hath no being.

Next, those philosophers who said that God was the world, or the world's soul, that is say, a part of it, spake unworthily of God; for they attribute nothing to him, but wholly deny his being.   For by the word God we understand the *world's cause;* but in saying that the *world* is God, they say *that it hath no cause,* that is as much as there is no God.   In like manner, they who maintain the world not to be created, but eternal, because there can be no cause of an eternal thing, in denying *the world to have a cause,* they deny also that *there is a God.*   They also have a wretched apprehension of God, who, imputing idleness to him, do take from him the government of the world and of mankind.   For say, they should acknowledge him omnipotent: yet if he mind not these inferior things, that same threadbare sentence will take place with them: 'quod supra nos, nihil ad nos:' what is above us doth not concern us.   And seeing there is nothing for which they should either love or fear him, truly he will be to them as though he were not at all. Moreover, in attributes which signify greatness or power, those which signify some finite or limited thing are not signs at all of an honouring mind.   For we honour not God worthily, if we ascribe less power or greatness to him than possibly we can.   But every finite thing is less than we can, for most easily we may always attribute more to a finite thing.   No shape therefore must be assigned to God, for all *shape* is *finite;* nor must he be said to be conceived or comprehended by imagination, or any other faculty

of our soul ; for whatsoever we conceive is *finite.*" . .
He concludes :—" He therefore who would not ascribe
any other titles to God than what reason commands,
must use such as are either negative, as infinite, eternal, incomprehensible, etc.; or superlative, as most
good, most great, most powerful, etc.; or indefinite,
as good, just, strong, creator, king, and the like; in
such sense as not to describe what he is (which were
to circumscribe him within the narrow limits of our
phantasy); but to confess his own admiration and
obedience, which is the property of humility and of
a mind yielding all the honour it possibly can do.
For reason dictates one name alone which doth signify
the nature of God, that is *existent,* or simply *that he
is :* and one in *order* to, and in relation to us, namely
God, under which is contained both *King,* and *Lord,*
and *Father.*"

" The charge of *Atheism,*" says Dr. Priestley*, " has
been so much hackneyed in religious controversy, as to

* See the Introduction to 'A Free Discussion of the Doctrines of
Materialism and Philosophical Necessity, in a correspondence between Dr. Price and Dr. Priestly.' (Priestley's Works, vol. iv. p. 12.)
He adds in a note, " Whatever views of Divine revelation were entertained by this philosopher, he has not always been fairly controverted;" and he afterwards points out the partial and unfair manner in which Lord Clarendon and even Leland treated him. " I am
rather surprised," says Dr. Priestley, in another part of his works
(vol. iii. p. 457), " that Mr. Locke, who seems to have been so much
indebted to Mr. Hobbes for the clear view which he has given us of
several principles of human nature, should have availed himself so
little of what he might have learned from him on this subject" (viz.
of the doctrine of necessity). " I cannot find, what I would gladly
discover, that Mr. Locke acknowledged his precursor either in the

have passed almost into ridicule.   It was the common
charge against the primitive Christians, and has hardly
ever failed to be urged, on one pretence or other,
against every man who has dissented from the generally received faith.   But perhaps no character has
suffered more generally, and at the same time more
undeservedly, on this account, than that of Mr. Hobbes,
who, notwithstanding his heterodoxy in politics, appears to me, as far as I can judge from such of his
writings as have fallen in my way, to have been no
atheist, but a sincere Christian, and a conscientious,
good man."   The passage is worthy of Dr. Priestley's
discriminative, candid, and fearless mind ; worthy of
one anxious and careful to judge for himself, without
any bias of prejudice or interest, and for truth's sake
alone.   No doubt it is very difficult to determine what
degree of importance Hobbes attached to the light and
truths of Scripture, what hopes and fears from their
promises or threatenings he entertained in his secret
heart.   He strains not a few passages to a purpose
evidently beside and beyond that of the writer or

Essay or his Defences. In his 'Second Reply to the Bishop of Worcester' he seems to shun the acquaintance ; for, referring to some
statement of his opponent, he says, ' I am not so well read in Hobbes
or Spinoza, as to be able to say what were their opinions in this
matter.'   He presently after alludes to them as 'those justly decried names.' "

I have already intimated, p. 340 *supra*, that Locke was not well
read in Hobbes, and that his agreement with Hobbes in some principles was owing to the influences of Gassendi.   A wide difference
in political views may account for some of that aversion which Locke
expresses.

speaker, as when he argues for an unlimited obedience
to civil rulers, from the direction of Christ to his hearers to obey the instructions of those who sit in Moses'
seat.　He calls fear of power invisible, feigned by the
mind or *imagined from tales publicly allowed, religion;
not allowed, superstition.*　It may be asked, is such a
notion of religion compatible with any serious faith in
the government of a good Providence? and what room
or provision does it leave for gratitude and hope? He
calls the scriptural writers " an innocent kind of men,
without much knowledge of the world."　It is language so different from that commonly used by all
who wish to be understood as reverencing the Bible,
and deriving from it their light of duty and comfort
in sorrow—their rule of life and their hope in death,
that it needs a very large allowance for all the peculiarities of the human mind to believe him sincere, or
using other than the *argumentum ad hominem*, in the
attempt to support, by the Scriptures, his own views
of the natural moral laws, and of the duty of obedience in all things to the civil power.　Could he
have believed, it may be asked, in a power of rationally and philosophically interpreting the Scriptures
by the help of learning and the learned, when he
contended that the right and power of interpretation
rested with the State?　The answer may be, that
he thought the disadvantages of allowing the right of
a private interpretation greater than that of refusing
it; that the learned must submit their judgement, as
he himself professed to do, to the supreme power;

and he does less than the Papist, who places his ecclesiastical superiors above the State, and no more
than the statesman, who enjoins what shall be taught
as the doctrine of Scripture, who determines what men
shall be teachers in the Church, on what conditions
they shall hold livings and enjoy benefices, who decides
what assemblies of Christians and what ceremonies
shall be lawful. His principle of the subordination of
the clergy to the state was nothing more than the
Erastianism* upheld by some of the most noted of
the clerical order and others in England long before
and after his day, among whom may be placed Hooker
and Parker, Whitgift and Lightfoot, Selden and Whit-
lock. In the present day there seem not to be two
opinions among thinking men, who are not biassed by
their order, on the necessity of submission to the civil

* The book of Erastus, an eminent German physician, the full
title of which is " Explicatio gravissimæ quæstionis utrum Excom-
municatio, quatenus religionem intelligentes et amplexantes, a Sacra-
mentorum usu, propter admissum facinus arcet, mandato nitatur
divino, an excogitata sit ab hominibus," was published in 1589, six
years after his death, according to his dying request. It is significant of the times that both the place of publication and name of the
editor and publisher were concealed, Pesclavii being put for Londini,
and Sultaceterum for Castelvetrum. The book is probably scarce,
little known, and less read ; but full of just criticism, solid learning,
and wise thought. In seventy-five theses he examines the nature of excommunication, so far as it is determined by the Scriptures ; he shows
that excommunication, as practised in the Roman Catholic church
and by the clergy, was a usurpation contrary to the spirit of Christianity ; and that all power of punishing for offences, and of excluding from privileges, religious as well as civil, ought to reside in the
magistrate alone. There is a copy of the work, with valuable MS.
notes, in the library of Dr. Williams' foundation in Redcross-street.

The necessary or useful relations of the church to the state, and

power on the part of those who are discharging a duty
which the state prescribes, or enjoying privileges which
the state secures. Those who have controverted Hobbes
have rarely treated him with fairness. What can be
more in accordance with the abject views of human nature, which Hobbes is charged with, than the intimation to Sir C. Cavendish by Clarendon, as recorded by
himself: "For such a book, by the constitution of any
government now established in Europe, whether monarchical or democratical, the author must be punished
in the highest degree, and with the most severe penalties"? Tenison, who published the ' Creed of Hobbes
examined,' in 1670, makes it the business of his little
book " to expose this *insolent and pernicious* writer;
to show unto his countrymen that weakness of head
and venom of mouth which is in the philosopher, who
hath rather seduced and poisoned their imaginations
than conquered their reason." He alleges twelve articles as those of Hobbes's ' Creed,' selecting the most
obnoxious opinions or statements, but not always

of the clergy to the church, are subjects that must occupy more and
more the attention of statesmen and philosophical inquirers. The
history of opinion on the subject is full of interest. Erastus had
among his predecessors Occam, so called from the village of that name
in Surrey, who, in the fourteenth century, opposed the tyranny of the
papal over the civil power, in a book ' De Potestate Ecclesiastica et
Sæculari.' Of this, or a part of it, entitled " A Dialogue between a
Knight and a Clerke, concerning the power spiritual and temporal,"
a most interesting account may be found in Oldys' ' Librarian,' p. 5.
Erastus has been followed by Archbishop Wake in his ' Authority of
Christian Princes over their Ecclesiastical Synods asserted,' in 1697.
Many supported Wake in the controversy on the rights and powers
of the English Convocation. Hoadly, and more recently Whately,
take similar views in their sermons on the Kingdom of Christ.

adhering to Hobbes's own language; rather giving inferences from some of his expressions and arguments without regard to the qualifying considerations and practical ends with which in Hobbes's mind they were connected.   Both Clarendon and Tenison were very unjust to the philosopher of Malmesbury, by charging him with design to support the usurpation of Cromwell; but from the fact that his book 'De Cive' got abroad as early as 1642, which contained the elements of his philosophy of man and of government, as well as from his own credible assurances, it is clear that the evils of civil war and of popular discontent had early led his thoughts to consider the true bonds of civil society, the conditions of civil liberty, and the compatibility of the exercise and utterance of private judgement with social union and the public interest.

Among the most candid, liberal, and philosophical of the antagonists of Hobbes, the amiable Richard Cumberland, afterwards Bishop of Peterborough, deserves honourable mention.   The 'Disquisitio Philosophica de Legibus Naturæ,' in which he professes to refute the elements of the moral and political philosophy of Hobbes, came forth in 1672, about seven years before the death of Hobbes, then an octogenarian, and probably little disposed to pay attention to his new and youthful critic.   Mr. Hallam has judiciously devoted to Cumberland a good portion of his literary labour, and given a very fair view of his merits and defects.   In his attempts to unfold the principle

that we are carried by the laws of nature to the practice of virtue, which consists in the pursuit of the
common good, some anticipation may be traced of the
Hartleian theory concerning the development of the
social affections, and the ultimate coalescence of universal philanthropy with refined self-interest.   But
even Cumberland does not do justice to Hobbes's intentions.   The tone of his book is pleasing ; but his
style is diffuse and his terms very indefinite.   Of this
fault we are perhaps less aware when we read it in the
Latin than in translation.   Probably Hobbes would
not have disputed the main principle which Cumberland sought to establish, namely, " that the pursuit,
according to our ability, of the common good, con-
duces to the good of each of its parts, in which our
own felicity, as that of one part, is contained."   But
of the common good our knowledge is comparatively
imperfect. Our power to promote it is confined within
limits infinitely small. We promote it most when we
serve the interests and discharge the duties which are
our peculiar province—that is, when we care for those
individuals specially dependent on our care*.

Hobbes is remarkable for his anticipation of many
of the doctrines subsequently adopted and expounded

* Compare Cumberland, 1, § 16.   A translation of Cumberland's
'Disquisitio' was published in 1727, in 4to, by the Rev. John Max-
well, accompanied by dissertations on the laws of nature. In this work
the thread of the verbosity is so much finer than the staple of the
argument, that it may have suggested to Johnson that delicious bit
of satire upon the philosopher who explained what it is to live according to nature, already alluded to as occurring in the ' Rasselas.'

by the profoundest investigators of the mind. He attributes the beginnings of all the thoughts of man, to that which we call sense; "for there is no conception in a man's mind, which hath not, at first totally, or by parts, been begotten upon the organs of sense; the rest are derived from that original." In attributing the beginning of sensation to motion, he may be considered to have made some approaches to the theory of vibrations which Sir Isaac Newton suggested, and which Hartley afterwards adopted and developed. Even Locke leaned to the opinion, if we judge from some passages in the 8th chapter of his second book, where he speaks of " all sensation being produced in us only by different degrees and modes of motion in our animal spirits, variously agitated by external objects," and of " bodies producing ideas in us manifestly by impulse, the only way which we can conceive bodies to operate in."

Hobbes has been also represented as understanding fully the principle of Association, when, under the head of imagination, he teaches that " not every thought to every thought succeeds indifferently;" " that the train of the thoughts or of mental discourse is of two sorts, —the first unguarded, without design, and inconstant; the second more constant, as being regulated by some desire and design*." This however seems no more

* See Dr. Whewell on Hobbes, in his recent volume on the History of Moral Philosophy, Lecture II.; and Sir W. Hamilton on 'The History of Mental Association,' in his edition of Reid, pp. 892, 893. "The cause of the coherence or consequence of one conception to another is their first coherence or consequence at that time, that they are produced by sense; as, for example, from St. An-

than Aristotle taught before him in connection with
the phenomena of memory, and with the efforts of the
mind to recall what was formerly observed or known
but cannot be immediately remembered, on which Sir
W. Hamilton has founded the opinion that Aristotle
was the first teacher of the doctrine of Mental Association. But notwithstanding some explanation of the
phenomena of memory, and of terms significant of the
passions, in a manner accordant with the law of asso-

drew the mind runneth to St. Peter, because their names are read
together; from St. Peter to a stone, from the same cause; from stone
to *foundation*, because we see them together."—Treatise on Human
Nature, ch. iv.

" The train of thoughts, or mental discourse, is of two sorts. The
first is unguided, without design, and inconstant; wherein there is
no passionate thought, to govern and direct those that follow to itself, as the end and scope of some desire or other passion; in which
case the thoughts are said to wander, and seem impertinent one to
another, as in a dream. Such are commonly the thoughts of men
that are not only without company, but without care of anything;
though even then their thoughts are as busy as at other times, but
without harmony; as the sound which a lute out of tune would
yield to any man, or, in tune, to one that could not play. And yet
in this wild ranging of the mind a man may oft perceive the way of
it, and the dependence of one thought upon another. For in a discourse of our present civil war, what could seem more impertinent
than to ask (as one did) what was the value of a Roman penny? Yet
the coherence to me was manifest enough. For the thought of the
war introduced the thought of the delivering up of the King to his
enemies; the thought of that, brought in the thought of the delivering up of Christ; and that again the thought of the thirty pence
which was the price of that treason; and thence easily followed that
malicious question; and all this in a moment of time, for thought
is quick."—Leviathan, ch. iii., Of the Consequence or Train of Imagination.

ciation, that either Aristotle or Hobbes understood that law, or had any perception of its importance in explaining the phenomena of the mind and reasoning, in forming the character and affections, as afterwards expounded in the works of Hartley, Brown, and Mill, were an assertion not to be received without a much more exact comparison than has yet been instituted or given to the world.

There were other points clearly intimated by Hobbes on which Locke laid no little stress, such as that truth always involves a reference, tacit or express, to propositions; that government is founded on a compact, virtual or express; that the doctrine of the Messiahship of Christ is the simple and single fundamental article of the Christian faith as developed in the Scriptures;—principles on which Locke dwelt at length in his Treatises on Government, his letters on Toleration, and his admirable work on the ' Reasonableness of Christianity according to the Scriptures.'

I have been the longer upon Hobbes, from a conviction that he deserves to occupy a far higher place in the estimation of English readers, even of the most liberal school, than is usually allowed him. Yet none but the disinterested lovers of truth and goodness, warped by no sinister bias of interest or ambition, agitated by no passion for place and pelf, degraded by no dependence on the opinion of a greater or lesser public, yet earnest in pursuit of human good, should trouble themselves with his pages, which, like a medicine bitter but wholesome, purge the mind from prejudices of selfishness and vanity, and clear the understanding to appreciate the sources of its weakness and its strength. Comparing him with Montaigne, Rochefoucauld, and La Bruyère, Hallam, an upright and not usually a severe judge, says that "a cold and heartless indifference to right distils from his pages." I should rather say, there is in him a sort of contemptuous and bitter satisfaction in exposing the selfishness, falsehood, and cruelty of mankind, the shallowness of much that passed for philosophy, the predominance of the animal and hostile passions, and especially the pretences of men desirous of power and reputation, concealing their real ends; and all this without any corresponding 'regard to the unnoticed virtues of our common humanity and the kindly offices of daily domestic life to balance the impression. This gives an air of cynicism and misanthropy to his philosophy, more apparent than real. It is not without good effect in counteracting that weak and amiable sentimentalism, which delights to view mankind as merely the creatures of innocence and misfortune; which sometimes indulges a morbid tenderness for crime and criminals; and forgets that the chief part of human suffering arises from the oppression of the few, the supineness of the many, the avarice, the self-indulgence, the negligence, and vice of all*.

* I cannot forbear reprinting the admirable remarks on Hobbes by Mr. Austin in his ' Province of Jurisprudence Determined.' The note is long, but the book is now scarce and out of print, and the matter is of supreme importance. " By his modern censors, French, German,

In reading Hobbes, we cannot but observe with pleasure how vast is the improvement in the state of

and even English, Hobbes's main design, in his various treatises on politics, is grossly and thoroughly mistaken. With a marvellous igno-rance of the writings which they impudently presume to condemn, they style him ' the apologist of *tyranny ;*' meaning by that rant, that his main design is the defence of monarchical government. Now, though he prefers monarchical to popular or oligarchical government, it is certain that his main design is the establishment of these pro-positions :—1. That sovereign power, *whether it reside in one, or in many or a few*, cannot be limited by positive law ; 2. That a present or established government, *be it a government of one, or a govern-ment of many or a few*, cannot be disobeyed by its subjects consist-ently with the common weal, or consistently with the law of God as known through utility or the Scriptures. That his principal pur-pose is not the defence of monarchy, is sufficiently evinced by the following passages from his ' Leviathan :—" The prosperity of a peo-ple ruled by an aristocratical or democratical assembly, cometh not from aristocracy or democracy, but from the obedience and concord of the subjects : nor do the people flourish in a monarchy because they are ruled by one man, but because they obey him. Take away, in a state of any kind, the obedience, and consequently the concord of the people, and they shall not only not flourish, but in short time be dissolved. And they that go about by disobedience to doe no more than reforme the commonwealth, shall find they doe thereby destroy it.' ' In monarchy one man is supreme ; and all other men who have power in the state, have it by his commission, and during his pleasure. In aristocracy or democracy there is one supreme assembly ; which supreme assembly hath the same un-limited power that in monarchy belongeth to the monarch. And which is the best of these three kinds of government, is not to be disputed there where any of them is already established.' So many similar passages occur in the same treatise, and also in his treatise ' De Cive,' that they who confidently style him the ' apologist of tyranny or monarchy,' must have taken their notion of his purpose from mere hearsay. A dip here or there into either of the decried books would have led them to withhold their sentence. To those who have really read, although in a cursory manner, these, the most

society since his time.   He evidently could not conceive that condition of constitutional liberty which,

lucid and easy of profound and elaborate compositions, the current
conception of their object and tendency is utterly laughable.

" The capital errors in Hobbes's political treatises are the following :—1. He inculcates too absolutely the religious obligation of
obedience to present or established government. He makes not the
requisite allowance for the anomalous and excepted cases wherein
disobedience is counselled by that very principle of utility which
indicates the duty of submission.   Writing in a season of civil discord, or writing in apprehension of its approach, he naturally fixed
his attention on the glaring mischiefs of resistance, and scarcely
adverted to the mischiefs which obedience occasionally engenders..
And although his integrity was not less remarkable than the gigantic
strength of his understanding, we may presume that his extreme
timidity somewhat corrupted his judgement, and inclined him to
insist unduly upon the evils of rebellion and strife. 2. Instead of
directly deriving the existence of political government from a perception by the bulk of the governed of its great and obvious expediency, he ascribes the origin of sovereignty, and of independent
political society, to a fictitious agreement or covenant. He ima-
gines that the future subjects covenant with one another, or that
the future subjects covenant with the future sovereign, to obey
without reserve every command of the latter ; and of this imaginary covenant, immediately preceding the formation of the political
government and community, the religious duty of the subjects to
render unlimited submission, and the divine right of the sovereign
to exact and receive such submission, are, according to Hobbes,
necessary and permanent consequences. He supposes, indeed, that
the subjects are induced to make that agreement, by their perception of the expediency of government, and by their desire to escape
from anarchy.   But, placing his system immediately on that interposed figment, instead of resting it directly on the ultimate basis of
utility, he often arrives at his conclusions in a sophistical and quib-
bling manner, though his conclusions are commonly such as the
principle of utility will warrant. The religious duty of the subjects
to render unlimited obedience, and the divine right of the sovereign
to exact and receive such obedience, cannot, indeed, be reckoned

since the Revolution of 1688, the British dominions
have enjoyed, and in which so many of the citizens of

amongst those of Hobbes's conclusions which that principle will
justify. In truth, the duty and the right cannot be inferred logically even from his own fiction. For, according to his own fiction,
the subjects were induced to promise obedience, by their perception
of the utility of government; and, since their inducement to the
promise was that perception of utility, they hardly promised to
obey in those anomalous cases wherein the evils of anarchy are surpassed by the evils of submission. And though they promised to
obey even in those cases, they are not religiously obliged to render
unlimited obedience; for, as the principle of general utility is the
index to religious obligations, no religious obligation can possibly
arise from a promise whose tendency is generally pernicious. Besides, though the subject founders of the political community were
religiously obliged by their mischievous promise, a religious obligation would hardly be imposed upon their followers, by virtue of a
mischievous agreement to which their followers were strangers.
The last objection however is not exclusively applicable to Hobbes's
peculiar fiction. That, or a like objection, may be urged against all
the romances which derive the existence of government from a fan-
cied original contract. Whether we suppose, with Hobbes, that the
subjects were the only promisers, or we suppose, with others, that
the sovereign also covenanted; whether we suppose, with Hobbes,
that they promised unlimited obedience, or we suppose, with others,
that their promise contained reservations; we can hardly suppose
that the contract of the founders, unless it be presently useful,
imposes religious obligations on the present members of the community.

"If these two capital errors be kept in mind by the reader,
Hobbes's extremely celebrated, but extremely neglected, treatises
may be read to great advantage. I know of no other writer (ex-
cepting our great contemporary Jeremy Bentham) who has uttered
so many truths, at once new and important, concerning the necessary structure of supreme political government, and the larger of
the necessary distinctions implied by positive law. And he is sig-
nally gifted with the talent, peculiar to writers of genius, of inciting
the mind of the student to active and original thought.

this great country, of every grade, unite to consider
and to pursue the public good; in which there has
been unexampled security for person and for property; ample liberty of discussion and of the press,
without danger to the public peace; while, aided by

" The authors of the antipathy with which he is commonly regarded, were the papistical clergy of the Roman Catholic Church,
the high-church clergy of the Church of England, and the Presbyterian clergy of the true-blue complexion. In matters ecclesiastical
(a phrase of uncertain meaning, and therefore of measureless compass), independence of secular authority was more or less affected
by churchmen of each of those factions. In other words, they held
that their own church was co-ordinate with the secular government; or that the secular government was not of itself supreme,
but rather partook in the supreme powers with one or more of the
clerical order. Hobbes's unfailing loyalty to the present temporal
sovereign, was alarmed and offended by this anarchical pretension;
and he repelled it with a weight of reason, and an aptness and pungency of expression, which the aspiring and vindictive priests did
bitterly feel and resent. Accordingly, they assailed him with the
poisoned weapons which are ministered by malignity and cowardice.
All of them twitted him (agreeably to their wont) with flat atheism;
whilst some of them affected to style him an apologist of tyranny or
misrule, and to rank him with the perverse writers (Macchiavelli,
for example) who really have applauded tyranny maintained by ability and courage. By these calumnies, those conspiring and potent
factions blackened the reputation of their common enemy. And so
deep and enduring is the impression which they made upon the
public mind, that ' Hobbes the atheist,' or ' Hobbes the apologist
of tyranny,' is still regarded with pious or with republican horror,
by all but the extremely few who have ventured to examine his
writings.

" Of positive atheism; of mere scepticism concerning the existence of the Deity; or of, what is more impious and mischievous
than either, a religion imputing to the Deity human infirmities and
vices;—there is not, I believe, in any of his writings, the shadow of
a shade."

the fostering influence of commerce and literature, of art and science, there has been an increasing adaptation of institutions to the welfare and improvement of every sect and class; and the problem of the greatest degree of individual freedom, compatible with the general good and the speedy, upright, and effective administration of law, approaches solution.

Locke.—Amid the abundance of critical remarks on Locke, which have dropped from metaphysical writers since his time, and which show that no book in the English language has commanded more attention and exerted greater influence than the ' Essay on the Human Understanding,' there exists no criticism of marked importance and authority in which the contents of the Essay are fully and carefully examined, and its true merits are determined.   Among the critics, a high place, as we have seen, must be assigned to Leibnitz; less on account of the success with which he has controverted Locke's views, than of his great name and learning, and of the pains with which he went over every part of the Essay.   Yet the ' Nouveaux Essais' of Leibnitz have had few readers in England, partly because the path of inquiry pursued in it is remote from common studies, still more perhaps because the clearness and simplicity were wanting in him, for which Locke on the whole is remarkable, notwithstanding the occasional clouds allowed, through inadvertence, to gather and settle over his path.   After what has already been said of Leibnitz, it will be enough to repeat that none of the leading principles of Locke are

overthrown by him ; and in many important respects
there is a complete agreement, e. g. that of the harmony between faith and reason. The most successful
and valuable criticisms are those in which his great
stores of philological learning are brought forth in support of Locke's hints on *words* and *language ;* and in
which he defends Aristotle and syllogism from Locke's
inconsiderate disparagement*.

The subject of the first book of Locke's ' Essays,'
Innate Principles, has been somewhat fully discussed, not to say disposed of, in the foregoing pages.
Those who contend that Locke has not established
his negative generally show that they have paid little
attention to his arguments, that they do not understand the question, that they have not carefully weighed,
as they do not quote correctly, his language. They
confound the presence and existence of some determinate ideas at an advanced period of life with the capacity for forming and entertaining them. They confound

---

* See particularly the ' Nouveaux Essais,' on the Reason, book iv.
ch. 17. It may be doubted whether Locke had read Aristotle in the
original, or studied the Analytics, Ethics, and Rhetoric as they came
from the author. In his estimate of the nature and value of syllogism he appears to have considered only the abuses of it among
the schoolmen, whose influence still reigned in the Universities
when Locke was a student, not yet overthrown by Bacon, nor the labours of Ramus and Wilson, and Bishop Sanderson. What particular instances of abuse of syllogism among the schoolmen had given
Locke his evident disgust it is not easy to decide. A short and very
just view of the place which logic and the syllogism ought to hold
in our esteem, is given in the closing pages of Thomson's ' Outline
of the Laws of Thought.'

the uniform or probable development of certain fundamental conceptions or notions,—such, for instance, as those of space, time, number, and causality,—inseparable from all intellectual functions and processes, and necessary to all reasoning, with their presence in the mind of an infant or an embryo. They assume that the ideas which they choose to call innate, and which they arbitrarily fix upon without any definite principle of selection or any attempt at enumeration, are not complex; that they are not capable of being traced to ulterior sources,—that is, to more simple ideas of sensation or reflection. They assume, not only that they exist in all rational minds capable of being defined or sufficiently clear for reasoning, but that they are wholly independent of impressions from without. They also imagine that an idea or a principle is of less value or of less authority in proportion as it is deducible from any other latent root or fact or law of the mind, as if then destitute of the stamp of nature and but an arbitrary construction of the human will. But the question turns upon what is the law of nature and of the mind? That any idea or principle should be imagined of less value when shown to grow necessarily out of our constitution, and to be the legitimate result of the exercise of the senses and thoughts thence arising, seems to be an absurdity too great to be entertained by any man who is capable of estimating the difference between a child, a Hottentot, a wild Indian, and a Bacon or Newton, a Galileo or Humboldt; between the vacancy of ignorance on the one hand, and a mind enriched with all the sources of information, and all the stimulants and aids to reflection, which belong to man in the most highly refined and civilized condition. Declaimers, addressing an audience disposed to agree with them, may appeal with safety to the deep indestructible principles of our nature, and talk of the instinctive emotions welling up from the fountains of the heart, and of the primary innate convictions stamped upon the mind; but the moment a doubtful proposition is enunciated, or a phrase that jars upon the ear of reason is breathed, the force of the appeal is gone, and the hearer inwardly ejaculates, "What will this babbler say?" He multiplies words without knowledge! Every word which the rhetorician utters is merely an illustration of the nature and power of the law of association, governing the intellects and emotions of his hearers. One simple paragraph of Locke decides the question. "If we will attentively consider new-born children, we shall have little reason to think that they bring many ideas into the world with them. For bating, perhaps, some faint ideas of hunger and thirst and warmth, and some pains which they may have felt in the womb, there is not the least appearance of any settled ideas in them; especially of ideas answering the terms which make up those universal propositions that are esteemed innate principles. One may perceive how, by degrees, afterwards ideas come into their minds; and that they get no more, nor no other, than what experience and the observation of things, that come in their way, furnish them with:

which might be enough to satisfy us, that they are not original characters stamped upon the mind*."

The difficulties of Locke's 'Essay,' and the objections raised against it, have arisen chiefly out of the contents of the second book, in which he unfolds his view of the original sources of all our ideas. "These two, I say, viz. external material things, as the objects of sensation; and the operation of our own minds within, as the objects of reflection, are to me the only originals from whence all our ideas take their beginnings." " The understanding seems to me not to have the least glimmering of any ideas which it doth not receive from one of these two.   External objects furnish the mind with the ideas of sensible qualities, which are all those different perceptions they produce in us; and the mind furnishes the understanding with ideas of its own operations."

A beautiful passage follows on the state of a child at his first coming into the world, and on the late period in which the operations of the mind are made the distinct and separate objects of contemplation.

In the existence, influence, and importance of sensations and ideas of sensation, all philosophers seem agreed.   The use of language depends, it is evident, upon the reality and uniformity of the impressions of the senses, and on the presence of similar ideas and feelings in thinking minds connected with them.   Were there not marks or signs commonly agreed upon, significant of such impressions and of the associated ideas

* Essay, book i. ch. 4, § 2.

and feelings, there could be no mutual converse. Nevertheless two great questions have arisen, and are yet in abeyance, touching Locke's account of the sources of our ideas, and affecting chiefly the second of the two, which he calls *reflection*. First, whether it be really a distinct source, and not ultimately resolvable into sensation. So thought Condillac, who called ideas of reflection" transformed sensations,"—a phrase which met with no acceptance, and is not a happy one to express the mental phenomena. So thought Hartley, who says, " It appears to me that all the most complex ideas arise from sensation, and that reflection is not a distinct source, as Locke makes it." So thought also Peter Browne, Bishop of Cork, who contends " that that maxim of the logicians, *nihil est in intellectu, quod non fuit prius in sensu*, is to be taken for a sure and fundamental truth ; the true meaning of which is, that the ideas of sense are the first foundation on which we raise our whole superstructure of knowledge, and that all the discoveries we can make in things *temporal* and *spiritual*, together with the most *refined* and *abstracted* notions of them in the mind of man, take their rise originally from *sensation*." It is remarkable that this Bishop of Cork considered the dangerous and sceptical influence of Locke, who was no favourite with him, to arise out of his having made reflection a distinct source of ideas*.

* Those who do not consult Condillac's ' Traité des Sensations,' a book well worthy of attention, will find him not unfairly represented in Brown's thirty-third ' Lecture on the Philosophy of the Mind.'

A second question is—admitting the reality and value of Locke's two sources, whether the enumeration is complete, and there be not ideas of the highest importance referable to some other source. So thought Dr. Price, who says, " It is hard to determine exactly what Locke meant by sensation and reflection ;" " that it will be impossible to derive some of the most important of our ideas from them." He adds, towards the close of his section on the origin of our ideas in general :—" After the mind, *from whatever possible causes*, has been furnished with *ideas of any objects*, they become themselves *objects of our intellective faculty*, from whence arises a new *set of ideas*, which are the *perceptions of this faculty.*" He speaks also of " ideas arising from intuitions of the natures of things." The logician may ask, what is this new intellective faculty? How does it differ from Locke's reflective power? and what is the determinate characteristic of this set of ideas, to constitute the class ? of what one thing or object of nature have we an intuition prior to observation and reflection? And if we have not an idea of the simplest object of external nature prior to observation, what valuable ideas can we have of the operations and principles of the human mind and morals, intangible and evanescent as the phenomena of imagination and emotion are, without reflection—the element of self-knowledge ?

See also ' Hartley on Man'; ' Eighty-eighth Proposition on Logic'; and Browne's ' Procedure, Extent, and Limits of the Human Understanding, 1729 ' (a book to which Stewart has drawn attention), part 3, chapter 1, *et seq.* Compare also Locke, b. ii. c. 12. § 8.

Dr. Reid, whom Price admired, gives us about twelve instinctive principles of nature or elements of knowledge in his inquiry into the mind*. It is clear that Locke has failed to satisfy a large number of eminent writers on the mind†.

The student must give his deepest attention to these questions, turning the mind inward on itself, aided by whatever light other investigators may have thrown upon its darkest recesses; but always carefully distinguishing the statements of Locke himself from those of any other writer, whether of his own school or a school the most opposed to his.

---

* See Priestley's enumeration, in his Examination of Reid.

† In the course of some admirable observations on Locke by the Rev. John J. Tayler, in his 'Retrospect of the Religious Life of England' (p. 348), the following passage occurs : " He (Locke) looked for the ultimate source of knowledge and ground of certainty, not in abstractions, which he treated as gratuitous figments of the mind, but in facts of a twofold order which admitted of no dispute,—the impressions of sense and the suggestions of consciousness ; the mind, as he argued, coming into the world a mere *tabula rasa*, and deriving the ideas which furnish the materials of its knowledge exclusively from this twofold experience. It may be questioned whether this view, called forth by a strong feeling of error in the opposite direction, *embraces the entire subject of the mind*, and does not rather *confine itself to one side of it ; whether it allows enough to the influence*, not indeed of innate ideas, but *of inherent tendencies,*—some common to the race, some peculiar to individuals, and giving birth to all the varieties of genius and character—*which control the associations and determine the conclusions of the mind, independent of all external influence, and so yield a higher kind of certainty on some subjects, than is attainable by logical deduction from the simple facts of experience.*" On this passage I remark—1st. That the phrase " suggestions of consciousness" does not express happily Locke's second source of ideas—namely, " reflection on the operations of our

Having laid down these two sources of our ideas, Locke proceeds to consider them as simple and complex ;—the former simple ones coming both from sensation and reflection, " the materials of all our knowledge, neither invented, nor framed, nor to be destroyed ; the latter, *made at pleasure*,"—" the mind having the power to repeat, compare, and unite the simple ideas even to an almost infinite variety." (Book ii. ch. 2, p. 2). But this power of the mind to make complex ideas for itself requires qualification. What we can do is to put together arbitrarily a cluster of

own minds;" but this is of minor importance. 2nd. That Locke's view of the sources of our knowledge allows quite as much to " inherent tendencies," whatever these may be, as any other view or system : it is not incompatible with any truth concerning these tendencies. It has never yet been shown, and it ought not to be taken for granted, that there are associations and conclusions on any subjects " independent of all external influences," and not flowing from " inward experiences," in Locke's sense of the terms. By an inherent tendency we may understand a tendency or predisposition, arising out of the physical frame and constitution, to remember (associate) some ideas rather than others. No philosophical observer doubts the existence of such a tendency. Locke expressly asserts it ; and his view of the mind is quite compatible with any amount of strength in it. 3rd. There is no higher certainty attainable on any subject of human thought than that which arises from the evidence of the senses, or which consists of rational conclusions—the agreement of ideas and propositions with that evidence. If we do not know and rely upon our own sensations, thoughts, and feelings, we can know nothing else. No " higher certainty" is conceivable than that felt in conclusions fairly deduced from, or necessarily involved in, premises received as true. On this all mathematical and moral evidence and reasoning,—that is, all truth,—ultimately rests. It is the spring of induction and deduction. It includes instances and principles, phenomena and laws.

simple ideas, and to give to that cluster a name; as centaur, hippogriff; and we call the cluster of ideas, attached to the name, a complex idea. To what extent, however, this power of the mind over its simple or complex ideas reaches, and how far the nature of the complex ideas is adequately explained by Locke, are matters for consideration arising out of the subsequent chapters. Among the simple ideas of sensation, Locke gives a whole chapter to solidity, selected somewhat arbitrarily for discussion: solidity, he says, distinguishes the extension of body from the extension of space; and he passes on to consider other simple ideas both of sensation and reflection. In these chapters, the 7th and 8th, he has laid himself open to the just animadversion of successive critics, such as Stillingfleet, Berkeley, and Dugald Stewart. His distinction between the primary and secondary qualities of matter, a distinction made by preceding writers and perhaps prevalent in his day, is now universally given up; nor can many of his sentiments and statements be successfully defended by his warmest admirers. One apologetic sentence of Locke's requires to be often borne in mind by the candid reader. *Powers* in outward objects to produce ideas in us, he says, " I call *qualities;* and as they are *sensations or perceptions* in our understandings, I call them ideas: which ideas, if I speak of sometimes *as in the things themselves,* I would be understood to mean those qualities in the objects which produce them in us." In the course of his ' Essay ' he is often regardless of this distinction, and confounds qualities of outward objects with ideas of them in our minds.

Regardless of a just order, when we might expect him to proceed with the discussion of ideas he interposes three chapters,—9th, 10th, and 11th,—on the faculties of the mind. These chapters deserve careful perusal from the student; but his view of the faculties of the mind cannot be regarded as complete, nor his discussion of them as very satisfactory*. A sweet modesty graces their close, conciliating the reader. "I pretend not to teach," he says, "but to inquire; and therefore cannot but confess here again, that external and internal sensation are the only passages that I can find of knowledge to the understanding. These alone, as far as I can discover, are the windows by which light is let into this dark room." "These are my *guesses* concerning the means whereby the understanding comes to have and retain simple ideas."

What are the faculties of the human mind? After all that has been written on this branch of philosophy, we are yet so much in the dark, that few even of the most thoughtful agree in their enumeration and description.

When Bacon, in his 'Advancement of Learning,' speaks of the faculties of the soul, he had evidently formed no distinct view of the nature and number of

---

* It is significant of the slight importance which Locke attached to these chapters, that he passes them over without comment in the abstract of the Essay given to Le Clerc, published in French in the ' Bibliothèque Choisie,' and printed in Lord King's Life of Locke.

these faculties, though he abounds with excellent ob-servations on the memory and its improvement, on the imagination and its pleasures, on the reason and its uses. In his general distribution of human knowledge, he tells us, that history addresses itself to the memory, poetry to the imagination, philosophy to the reason. He divides the soul into two, parts, the understanding or reason, and the will or appetite; but when he treats of the understanding or reason, which terms he uses synonymously, he turns from an analysis of it to speak of the arts of invention, of judging, of remembering, and of demonstrating.

When Hobbes treats of the virtues commonly called intellectual*, he contents himself with speaking of such abilities as men commonly admire and desire in themselves; of a wit natural and acquired, quick or slow; of good judgment, discretion and prudence, and power. In his work on human nature he begins with the sense, and proceeds to the imagination, remembrance, and discourse.

Hartley, after treating of the ideas generated from sensations and their association, proceeds to consider the application of his theory to the understanding, affection, memory, and imagination; and in the accuracy and fulness of his observations of fact, in the charm of a condensed thought and simplicity of style, he far excels all other metaphysical writers.

Reid, in his 'Essays on the Intellectual Powers,' begins with the powers we have by means of our ex-

* Leviathan, ch. viii.

ternal senses, under which he treats of sensation, perception, and its objects; and he then treats of memory, conception, abstraction, judgment, and reasoning.
Dugald Stewart, in his 'Elements of the Philosophy
of the Mind,' discusses attention, conception, abstraction, the influence of association, memory, and the
imagination. It is evident from his pages how little
philosophers agree in the use of these terms, how
often they are used interchangeably, and how many
different terms are significant of the same phenomena
and processes of thought. James Mill, in his 'Analysis of the Mind,' following very much the order of
Hartley, treats first of sensation, then of ideas and the
association of ideas, next of naming. He discusses
well the use and value of the terms *consciousness* and
conception ; he observes that Mr. Stewart did not
understand the real distinction between conception
and imagination; he believes the last to consist in
trains of ideas ; and he proceeds to treat of classification, abstraction, memory, belief, ratiocination, and
evidence.

Thus, with some agreement, there is great diversity
among philosophers in their enumeration and analysis
of the faculties of the mind, soul, reason, or understanding, which terms, for the purposes of analysis, are
used synonymously. Hence much of the difficulty
and perplexity in the character and condition of mental science. A reference to the pages of Brown and
Abercrombie would strengthen this evidence, and a
collection of the definitions would be very curious.

Adam Smith founds his theory of moral sentiments upon sympathy, which he makes a distinct principle of our nature and of the mind, without seeking to determine how much all sympathy is dependent on memory, imagination, and the judgment. Some writers, following Kant, make the pure reason a faculty distinct from the understanding; and others speak of an æsthetic faculty, to which they assign the province of taste. Common language implies that whatever increase of power may be gained by culture or habit to the original capabilities of our nature, such increase of power may be considered new faculties. Thus we talk of a faculty for languages, for music, for drawing. Faculty seems here *facilitas*—from *facio*—a power of accomplishing. Now, since the memory, the imagination, and the reason, whatever its functions, are concerned in everything which we attempt and accomplish, these may be considered *primary faculties*.

To return to Locke. *Perception* he treats of as the first faculty, *Retention* the next, *Discerning* he calls another faculty; and, among other operations, he speaks of comparing, compounding, naming, and abstracting. It is evident that "*perception*," as the first step and degree towards knowledge, and the inlet of all the materials of it, is with Locke sometimes equivalent to sensation, sometimes to reflection [*].

---

[*] Locke's Essay, b. ii. ch. 9, § 15. Comp. b. ii. ch. 1 and 6. Locke often uses the word perception in the sense of a sensation; at other times in the sense of the recognition of an idea as an idea of sensation or of reflection. Thus he says (b. ii. ch. 8, § 1), "Whatsoever is so constituted by nature as to be able, by 'affecting our

Perception, like consciousness, is therefore a word of little value in the analysis of the mind; for to have a sensation or idea, and to perceive that we have it, or to be conscious we have it, is all one. When treating of perception as a faculty of the mind exercised about its ideas and the inlet of all knowledge, he had forgotten his frequent use of the word in previous chapters, particularly in the first of the second book on the original of all our ideas, where he says, "To ask at what time a man has first any ideas, is to ask when he begins to perceive : *having ideas*, and *perception*, being the *same thing.*"

After all that has been written on perception and theories of perception, it will never have other than a general and vague signification, being equivalent, as Locke suggests, to *thinking in general.* Thus we speak of a man of quick or of dull perceptions, having reference to the speed with which he arrives at just conclusions from the incidental phenomena of the senses, whether as to their causes or consequences. Its etymology may be some guide to its best meaning; perception, from *percipio*, being an idea caught (*per*) by means of some sensation. Thus we hear words, and perceive their meaning. We see a smile or frown, and perceive the thought or feeling which

senses, to cause any *perception in the mind*,' doth hereby produce in the understanding a simple idea." Is there any difference in such a passage between an *affection* of the *senses*, a *perception* in the *mind*, and an idea in the understanding? Are they not different phrases for one and the same phenomenon? Compare ch. i. § 3 and 4.

occasions it. We perceive the conclusion at which an argument or speech is tending, before it is announced; we perceive, that is, we anticipate the result in which a train of events will issue, or to follow the employment of certain means and agencies, before it comes about. But this use of the words *perceive* and *perception,* however common, will not be acceptable to all philosophers; for Sir William Hamilton expressly says[*], we perceive nothing but what is actually present to an organ of sense[†]; and "that we reach a distant reality, not by sense, *not by percep-*

---

[*] See a note to his edition of Reid, p. 247.

[†] Among the dissertations, historical, critical, and supplementary, appended by Sir W. Hamilton to his edition of Reid, is one,—Note C, "On the various theories of *external* perception,"—in which he considers that he has accomplished his primary end, which was to display, to discriminate, and to lay down a nomenclature of the various theories of perception, actual and possible. But in describing or attempting to ascertain the doctrine of preceding metaphysicians, especially that of Reid and Stewart, he introduces a number of new terms which help us to understand neither the philosophers nor the mind. He speaks of two kinds of consciousness—one a conception, the other a perception (p. 820); of two or four kinds of perception— one presentative, the other representative; one mediate, the other immediate (822); he talks of egoistical and non-egoistical idealism, presentationists and representationists. That we may appreciate the value of these terms, he refers us chiefly to his own notes and papers. Among them is the remarkable one (p. 806) on the terms *object* and *objective, subject* and *subjective.*

The learned reader will consider whether his knowledge of the mind be improved, and any useful distinctions arrived at, in these papers of Sir W. Hamilton. The less learned may be advised to compare with them the chapters of Hobbes (Leviathan, ch. vii. and viii.), on the *Ends of Discourse* and the *Virtues commonly called intellectual, and the contrary Defects.*

tion, but by inference." This limitation of perception to mere sensation is quite inconsistent with the old and received use of the term, of which we have many examples in the common version of the Scriptures ; a very good standard of legitimate English.   An admirable instance is given by Johnson, under the word *perceive*: Mark ii. 8, " Jesus *perceived* in his spirit, that they so reasoned within themselves." We have another in 1 Sam. iii. 8, " And Eli *perceived* [that is, he drew the conclusion] that the Lord had called Samuel."

Of memory Locke treats under the term *retention*. Of all the faculties of the mind, commonly so called, the memory seems the most clear and determinate in its character and functions.   Its importance is universally recognized.   Its influence dawns with the first smile of intelligence in infancy, and in mature life it is in constant exercise, essential to all intellectual functions and processes; an ingredient in all the moral affections, dispositions, and habits. Without memory, though present sensations should make a present impression, there could be neither reason, nor hope, nor desire.   The mind would be only like a mirror, that passively reflects the transient image, or an instrument that produces sounds unconsciously.   A memory, full, exact, and ready, is the chief element of all intellectual power.   Most of Bacon's hints on the culture of the intellectual power, in the fragment to Saville, turn upon helps for the memory.

The eleventh chapter Locke entitles " Of discerning

and other Operations of the Mind." He calls the "power
of discerning and distinguishing between the several
ideas we may take notice of in our minds, a faculty;"
and adds: " If in having our ideas in the memory ready
at hand consists quickness of parts; in this, of having them unconfused, and being able nicely to distinguish one thing from another where there is but the
least difference, consists in a great measure the exactness of *judgment* and clearness of *reason* which is to
be observed in one man above another." But when
we discern that a colour is not a sound, that a smell
is not a taste, is this owing to a peculiar faculty? Has
not Locke here made a faculty for himself, or ascribed
to a peculiar faculty a common phenomenon of the
mind, inseparable from sensation, perception, and memory, and from every process of thought and reasoning? In the same chapter Locke speaks of comparing,
compounding, and abstracting ideas as other operations, intimating a design to treat of them more fully
afterwards. He was attacked by Berkeley*, not without reason, for what he says of general signs and universal ideas; and while we trace in the observations
on the faculties of brutes as compared with men, on
the characteristics of wit and judgment, much that
indicates acute thought, the careful reader discerns a
want of clearness and mastery of the subject. He
considers the faculty of abstracting or making *general
ideas* as peculiar to man, and that which puts a per-

. * Comp. Berkeley's ' Principles of Knowledge,' p. 9, and Locke,
b. iii. ch. 3, and on General Terms.

fect distinction betwixt man and brutes. But though brutes do not use general signs, it does not at all follow that they have not the power of abstracting. In denying them this power, it seems to me that Locke is much too positive. Thus, a dog abstracts his master from his dress, and mankind from other animals. Animals certainly remember, imagine, or dream, and infer or conclude. These elements of reason they possess; and could they tell us all their ideas, they would probably surprise us by the amount of their power in forming, cherishing, and associating ideas, in anticipating consequences, and in feeling attachments.

The exact student will turn with interest to those chapters of the fourth book (the fourteenth and seventeenth), in which Locke treats of the *judgment* and the *reason* as distinct faculties. He will observe that in the former he says:—" The mind has *two faculties* conversant about truth and falsehood; first, knowledge, whereby it certainly perceives and is undoubtedly satisfied of the agreement or disagreement of any ideas. Secondly, judgment, which is the putting ideas together, or separating them, when their certain agreement or disagreement is not perceived, but *presumed*, which is, as the name imports, taken to be so before it certainly appears. If it so unites or separates them as in reality things are, it is right judgment." Reason Locke describes variously, as " that faculty whereby man is supposed to be distinguished from beasts;" " as necessary and assisting to all our other faculties, and indeed containing two of them, viz. *sagacity* and *illation*—or inference —which finds out the means or intermediate ideas, and rightly applies them to discover certainty in demonstrations, and probability in opinion." In reason he considers there are four degrees—first, the discovering of truths; second, the methodical disposition of them; third, the perceiving their connection; and fourth, making a right conclusion.

In the chapter on Reason, he discusses, as before observed, the use of syllogism, which upon the whole he considers but as " the art of fencing with the little knowledge we have, without making any additions." Even were it only this, a mere art of fencing, it might be useful exercise and practice—the *gymnastics* of the mind. But it is remarkable that Locke did not perceive that mathematical demonstrations, instead of being without syllogisms, are strictly syllogistic, and that true syllogism, Aristotle's legitimate logic, is neither more nor less than that exercise of the reasoning power, that art of adjusting terms, collecting intermediate ideas, and discovering connections and dependencies, on the importance of which he is himself dwelling through the whole of the last two books of his Essay. If all reasoning, whatever the subject, can be reduced to syllogistic form, as the profoundest reasoners seem to admit, it is manifestly no mean part of knowledge to be able to distinguish a perfect from an imperfect syllogism, and to know what sorts of conclusion are legitimate under certain sorts of premiss.

Such knowledge would seem to have a much closer connection with all the business of human life, and all the exercises of the understanding, than that of many branches of physical science, which are far more re- mote from any immediate purpose of utility; such as the characteristics, subdivisions, classes, and proper- ties of mosses and ferns, of seaweeds and shells. But no part of knowledge, no path of curiosity, is to be despised. It is no more an argument against formal logic that a country gentlewoman naturally connects the ideas of wind, clouds, rain, wetting, taking cold, relapse, and danger of death, and easily understands that she must not go abroad in bad weather after a fever, than it is an argument against grammar that the same gentlewoman speaks and writes correctly without having studied the rules, or in her own mind distinguishing and remembering the names of the parts of speech.

The account which Locke has given of the faculties of the mind, his attempt at an analysis of the reason, cannot be regarded as distinct and successful. When writing of the judgment and reason in the fourth book, he had probably forgotten what he had said of per- ception, retention, and the discerning faculty in the second; and no small part of the obscurity of the Essay arises from this want of distinctness in the ar- rangement and treatment of his matter concerning the faculties commonly called intellectual. To ordi- nary readers this must be a source of obscurity and confusion next in its influence to the cloud that lowers under the word 'idea,' and the related words, simple and complex, *mixed modes, relations, substances,* and *essences.* In an essay on the human understanding we should now expect a more distinct account of these faculties, and their peculiar or distinctive functions, and indeed we have it in Hartley and in James Mill. That Hume, in his 'Treatise on the Understanding,' and Kant, in his 'Critic of the pure Reason,' have supplied any deficiency in Locke or corrected any error in him, I have failed to discover.

Upon the imagination, as a distinct faculty, Locke has not touched; and the omission has been made a heavy charge against him*   He speaks indeed of "pictures and visions of the fancy," and could not be unaware of the nature and importance of a faculty which he has himself not seldom beautifully exercised. A chapter upon it would have been most welcome from his hand, and made a valuable addition to his work. Its omission may be due to the consideration that the imagination is subservient for the most part to pleasure and amusement, while Locke was concerned with the pursuit of truth, and with the exercises of the understanding in relation to the reality and extent of human knowledge. He appears to have considered it more dangerous than useful,

---

* See particularly Sedgwick's ' Discourse on the Studies of the University of Cambridge,' pp. 49, 50, edit. 1834. The Professor makes ' *the omission*' of what he calls ' *the faculties of moral judgment,*' another great fault of Locke.

more a friend to error and superstition than to truth and philosophy. But even in this view, its influence over the mind and reasoning powers deserved his more considerate attention, while the imagination is not without importance in the discovery and development of strictly scientific truth. It is an element in what we call invention, not merely as exercised in works of imagination commonly so called, poems and tales, the novel and the drama, pictures, statues, and music, but in all the arts and ends of life, in tracing the connection between causes and effects, means and ends, and in all that contributes to conviction and persuasion,—that is, logic and rhetoric. When analysed, perhaps it will be found to consist in the voluntary combination of the ideas of sensation and reflection, simple or complex, in an order different from that in which they were originally impressed, whether for purposes of pleasure or utility. By it we renew past enjoyments and anticipate new, and thus we are enabled to adorn, enjoy, and enrich the present. Its existence and power among the faculties of the mind furnishes one of the best illustrations of the wisdom and benevolence of the Author of our frame, since it is to the capacities of the mind what perfume and colour and form are to external nature, whence come the charms of variety and beauty in the vegetable and animal kingdoms. It is to the mind what the breath of summer is to the strings of the Æolian harp, or the light of day to the bosom of the still and all-reflecting lake. The sense of beauty springs from the ima-

gination.   Affection and love accompany her path.
The poet, the painter, the sculptor, the musician, follow in her train, and do her selectest homage.   Even
the logician and philosopher confess her "awful
charms."   Religion sanctions and hallows her influence.

Upon the whole, the simple division of the primary
faculties adopted by Bacon* seems as good as any that
has been suggested since ;—1, memory; 2, imagination ; 3, the reason.   The memory recalls and cherishes
the impression of the past in the order synchronous
and successive.   Imagination combines and deals with
them for the purpose and gratification of the present.
Reason examines the necessary connection, agreement
or disagreement of ideas, of causes and effects, and
especially recognizes the relation of all events and all
being to law, and this may be considered its highest
function.   Of reason it may be said that it marks
objects, and their conceived relations to one another,
with appropriate names ; that it arranges and classi-
fies ; it distinguishes, separates, and combines ; it

* In a passage in the 'Novum Organum' (lib. 1, § 127), in which
Bacon expressly considers his logic of induction applicable to the
study of mental and moral affections and states, as well as to inani-
mate nature, he speaks particularly : " De motibus mentalibus *memo-
riæ, compositionis et divisionis, judicii, et reliquorum.*" The distinction attempted by some moderns between the reason and the understanding, as faculties with separate and distinguishable functions,
seems to me arbitrary, unintelligible, no less inconsistent with the
usage of the past than incapable of useful application to the future.
A really useful analysis of the "pure reason" must be something
very different from Kant's 'Critic.'

counts and concludes; it forms propositions and traces connections and consequences. Thus its two great functions may be considered to be induction and deduction, of which geometry and the mathematics furnish the most simple, easy, and perfect examples. Its province is the attainment of knowledge and the establishment of truth. But I do not presume to attempt an exact philosophical analysis of the functions included in what we term exclusively and *par excellence* the Reason. There is beautiful simplicity and force in the Baconian statement and division, that memory makes the historian; imagination the poet and the artist; reason the philosopher. Each of these faculties is accompanied in every moment of exercise by perception and consciousness, while sensation may be regarded as the root and trunk of which these are the flower and fruit.

Having disposed however summarily of the faculties, Locke proceeds to the discussion of "*complex ideas*," his chapter on which is by no means a happy one. He speaks of such ideas as being compounded and decompounded, and reduced under three heads: 1st, modes, which also he divides into simple and complex, apologizing for the use of the term; 2nd, substances; 3rd, relations. He then enters upon a discussion of the simple modes of space, duration, and number; of infinity; of other simple modes, meaning the sensations of sound, taste, colour, and the ideas of such sensations.

On modes of thinking, modes of pleasure and pain,

he gives a very instructive and useful chapter, worthy of great attention; the long chapters on Power, and on Identity and Diversity are interposed; he then touches more fully on what he calls mixed modes, complex ideas of substances and of relations; and finishes with the chapters on ideas, as they are obscure and confused, real and fantastical, adequate and inadequate, true and false.

Having touched before on the origin, nature, and metaphysical difficulty of the ideas of space and time, I shall not dwell at length on Locke's account, nor examine closely his definitions, but repeat an observation implied on the former occasion. It is this:—Whether we have, or have not, determinate ideas of space and time, whether they are complex, simple, or abstract; whether we can or cannot give satisfactory and available definitions of the terms significant of the ideas, both the ideas and terms are then clearest and most useful when considered as altogether relative,—space as related to bodies, and time as related to the succession of impressions. Take other words, such as magnitude or size, height and depth. The abstract ideas are obscure. The terms are clearest when relative to objects compared and measured, and to the conceived position of an observer; that is, to the present or remembered impressions of sense.

Careful examination of Locke's second book will furnish the student with a variety of observations, acute, profound, instructive; but he will detect not a little obscurity and inconsistency, arising from phrases ill guarded, and corroborating the account of the manner in which the Essay was composed, namely, by snatches and at distant intervals; the matter being put together before the whole subject and the dependence of the several parts had been well considered, and the arrangement fully determined. The use of the terms *simple* and *mixed modes*, which seems in a great measure peculiar to Locke, is now almost obsolete, and a source of difficulty to the ordinary reader of the Essay, without any corresponding advantage.

It would make a volume, if all the exceptionable and infelicitous passages in the chapters on Ideas were marked and duly commented upon. But the logical reader will see without difficulty Locke's defects. He will see that when he wrote these chapters he had not wholly disengaged himself from the jargon of the schoolmen or later metaphysicians about modes and accidents, substances and essences. He will see that he often confounds ideas with the objects which give occasion to them; that he speaks of the mind as compounding and decompounding ideas, when it is only embarrassed by words without distinct ideas annexed. It will be seen that the vast importance and influence of language, and the necessity of taking into account its rationale and philosophy, had not dawned upon Locke's mind when he wrote this part of the Essay; that he became more and more deeply alive to it as he advanced towards the conclusion; and that if Locke had from the first entertained the views which he sub-

2 D

sequently unfolded, as to what words are and what are
not susceptible of definition, much of what he has
written on ideas, obscure and confused, adequate and
inadequate, true and false, would have been omitted,
more would have been modified, and all would have
been improved.   In proportion· as Locke himself
went over what he had written, he found that he
had much to alter and to add.   In a very interesting letter to Dr. Sloane, dated December 2, 1699,
he says: "I took the liberty to send you, just before I left town, the last edition of my Essay.   There
are two new chapters in it: one of the Association
of Ideas, another of Enthusiasm.   These two I expect you should read and give me your opinion upon,
though I have made other large additions*." With respect to the chapter on *Power* in particular, we see
the difficulties in which Locke felt himself involved,
and the little satisfaction which it gave, partly by the
correspondence with Limborch, which occupied Locke
within a few months of his decease, partly by the ad-

---

* This is said of the fourth edition, printed in 1698. The chapter
on Identity and Diversity was added at the instance of Molyneux
to the third edition, which contained also, in the epistle to the reader,
a characteristic vindication of his view of "moral relations," in reply to the animadversions of Mr. Lowde, who published in 1692 a
discourse concerning ' The Nature of Man.' See the letters between
Molyneux and Locke, Law's edit., vol. iv. p. 292, and the note by
Law, vol. i. p. 209. Compare a remarkable passage referring to the
Chapter on Power, in the preface to Law's edition.

The letter to Dr. Sloane is now among the MSS. of the British
Museum. It is printed in Forster's Original Letters of Locke, Sidney, and Shaftesbury (1830).

ditions and alterations made in the third and subsequent editions, to which he thus beautifully alludes:
" The ideas of will, volition, liberty, and necessity, in this chapter of *Power*, came naturally in my way.   In a former edition of this treatise I gave an account of my thoughts concerning them, according to the light I then had; and now, as a lover of truth, and not a worshiper of my own doctrines, I own some change of my own opinion, which I think I have discovered ground for.   In what I first writ, I with an unbiassed indifferency followed truth whither I thought she led me.   But neither being so vain as to fancy infallibility, nor so disingenuous as to dissemble my mistakes for fear of blemishing my reputation, I have, with the same desire for truth only, not been ashamed to publish what a severer inquiry has suggested.   It is not impossible but that some may think my former notions right, and some (as I have already found) these latter, and some neither.   I shall not at all wonder at this variety in men's opinions : impartial deductions of reason being so rare, and exact ones in abstract notions not so very easy, especially if of any length.   And therefore I should think myself not a little beholden to any one who would, upon these or any other grounds, fairly clear this subject of liberty from any difficulties that may yet remain." (Book ii. ch. 21, § 72.)

We learn from the correspondence with Molyneux that some parts of the third book of the Essay concerning words, though the thoughts were easy and clear enough, yet cost Locke more pains to express than all the rest; and we see him again struggling with difficulties in a net of his own making, when touching on real and nominal essences, names of mixed modes and of substances. At length he breaks into light as he advances to consider the imperfection and abuse of words, and the remedies for these imperfections and abuses, with which he concludes this book. " I must confess then, that when I first began this discourse of the understanding, and a good while after, I had not the least thought that any consideration of words was at all necessary to it. But when, having passed over the original and composition of our ideas, I began to examine the extent and certainty of our knowledge, I found that it had so near a connection with words, that, unless their force and manner of signification were first well observed, there could be very little said clearly and pertinently concerning knowledge; which, being conversant about truth, had constantly to do with propositions. And though it terminated in things, yet it was so much for the most part by the intervention of words, that they seemed scarce separable from our general knowledge."

" I am apt to imagine that were the imperfections of language, as the instrument of knowledge, more thoroughly weighed, a great many of the controversies that make such a noise in the world, would of themselves cease; and the way to knowledge, and perhaps peace too, lie a great deal opener than it does*."

* The above is quoted by Tooke, ' Epea Pteroenta,' vol. i. pp. 31, 32, Taylor's edition. Locke's Essay, b. iii. ch. 9, 10, 11. While

Two exquisite sections* follow, on the difficulties arising from words in discourses of religion, law, and morality, "matters of the highest concernment." And to these, as well as to the practical treatise on the Conduct of the Understanding, which is their corollary, the observation of the excellent Hallam will apply :—" I cannot think any parent or instructor justified in .neglecting to put them in the hands of a boy when the reasoning faculties become developed. It will give him a sober and serious, not flippant or self-conceited, independency of thinking ; and, while it teaches how to distrust ourselves and to watch those prejudices which necessarily grow up from one cause or another, will inspire a reasonable confidence in what he has well considered, by taking off a little of that

engaged in this Work, I have looked with pleasure into the copy of Locke's Essay formerly belonging to John Horne Tooke, with his MS. notes in pencil, now happily deposited in the British Museum. The notes are such as the reader of the ' Epea Pteroenta' would expect.   He observes the superiority in the tone and spirit of Locke's preface and dedication to anything to be found in Harris, the author of the Hermes.   He marks with strong disapprobation—' No! no! no !'—the many chapters and passages relating to complex, adequate and inadequate, false and obscure, ideas ; intimating that all the difficulties and obscurities arise not from ideas, which are well enough, but from mistakes in words, incorrect language, and bad grammar. He grasps with eagerness at every passage intimating Locke's attention to philology and early dictionaries.

The late Sydney Smith, in his amusing, and in many respects excellent, Lectures on Moral Philosophy, joins J. H. Tooke with Hume, as one of the authors who disparage Locke : but surely this is a mistake.

* Book iii. ch. 9, § 22, 23.

deference to authority which is the more to be regretted in its excess, that, like its cousin-german, party spirit, it is frequently united to loyalty of heart and the generous enthusiasm of youth."

The attention which Locke gives to ideas, and his frequent introduction of that word, when his meaning would be clearer had he attended more to *things* or propositions, has darkened more particularly his discussion of the applicability of demonstrative reasoning to morality, a subject to which he has reverted again and again, and with which he has mixed up a considerable number of sentiments that cannot be accepted*. Before examining his views on this topic with the care which it demands, it is worth while to observe that Locke's division of knowledge into three kinds, intuitive, demonstrative, and sensitive, is open to objection. The division is not good, because the two first seem to rest upon and to include the last, and it may be questioned whether Locke has assigned to each kind a mark sufficiently distinct. His account of knowledge seems in itself unsatisfactory ;—he represents it as consisting *alone* in " the perception of the connection and agreement or disagreement and repugnancy of any of our ideas." This notion is very often repeated, and

---

* The portions of the Essay in which this subject is touched are, b. iii. ch. 11, § 16–18 ; b. iv. ch. 2 and 3, § 18–20 ; ch. 4, § 6–10 ; ch. 12, § 6 to the end. These passages the student should carefully compare and endeavour to analyse. All that Locke says elsewhere on truth, certainty, general and trifling propositions, on maxims, ideas, their origin, their combination, their archetypes, will be modified by the result of such analysis.

it is one on which he lays great stress. Surely he is much nearer to the truth and to the account which would in general be given, when he intimates, as in several other places, that our knowledge consists in having ideas conformable to the real qualities of things, and that words are valuable only as they lead us to the " *thoughts of things.*" When, therefore, he speaks (b. iv. ch. 2, § 1) of a " kind of truths which the mind perceives at the first sight of the ideas together—*by bare intuition*"—without the intervention of any other idea, and " of this kind of knowledge as the clearest and most certain that human frailty is capable of "!— and when he adds, " Thus the mind perceives that white is not black, that a circle is not a triangle, that three are more than two, and equal to one and two ;" it is apparent that what we know is merely that one object or idea is not another ; that we have different names for different objects or impressions, sensations, or ideas ; and that we are not to call one by the name which it has been agreed shall be the name of another. This knowledge, if worthy to be called such, is after all more a knowledge of names, and of agreed signs for ideas, than of the agreement or repugnancy of ideas among themselves ; about which, as will be shown, there is much difficulty.

Another notion, which I humbly think is a very serious error on Locke's part, runs very much through the latter part of the Essay. It is the more necessary to point out this error distinctly, because it has not been dwelt upon, if observed, by former critics. Nay, it has been assumed that Locke is correct, and his opinion has been adopted and enforced by some of his thoughtful successors*. The notion is this:—that the complex or abstract ideas, the essences of mixed modes, are made by the understanding, "very arbitrarily," "independent from any original patterns in nature†." "There is nothing more evident, than that for the most part, in the framing these ideas, the mind searches not its patterns in nature, nor refers the ideas it makes to the real existence of things; but puts such together as may best serve its own purposes, without tying itself to a precise imitation of anything that really exists." This Locke afterwards modifies a little by the statement that such ideas "are not indeed jumbled together at random, but SUITED TO AN END." "Though they be combinations that are loose enough, and have as little union in themselves as several other to which the mind never gives a connection that combines them into one idea; yet they are always made for the convenience of communication, which is the chief end of language." He contends, nevertheless, that "for the originals of mixed modes, and for the meaning of terms significant of such modes, we need look no further than the mind itself, where their original patterns and essences are; and hence "that the real and nominal essence in mixed modes are the same." He asks,

* See a passage in Law's preface, page ix, and compare the dissertation by Gay, prefixed to Law's translation of King, ' De Origine Mali.'

† See b. iii. ch. 5, § 5, 6, 7.

" whether children learn not the names of mixed modes before they have their ideas ?   What one of a thousand ever frames the abstract idea of glory or ambition before he has heard the names of them ?   In simple ideas and substances, I grant, it is otherwise, which being such ideas as have a real existence and union in nature, the ideas or names are got one before the other as it happens*."

This whole argument he considers " new and a little out of the way."   It is on the ground of the supposed similarity of the complex ideas of morality to the ideas concerned in mathematical reasoning, " in this respect, that *they are alike framed by the mind without any real archetypes*, that he founds his opinion of the possible application of demonstrative reasoning to morality as well as to the mathematics†."

* Book iii. ch. 5, § 15.

† Comp. b. iii. ch. 11, § 15.   Morality—being such combinations of ideas—*not having standing patterns existing*—their names may be defined. *Men may exactly know the ideas that go to each composition, and so use their words in a certain and undoubted signification; perfectly declaring what they stand for.*   And therefore the negligence or perverseness of mankind cannot be excused, if their discourses in morality be not *much more clear than those in natural philosophy*, since they are about *ideas in the mind*, which are none of them false and disproportionate, they *having no external beings for the archetypes* which they are referred to, and must correspond with.

Supposing the last sentiment well founded, it seems to me that it should have led Locke to an opposite conclusion.   For is it not the want of a standing pattern existing, which renders the name indistinct, and the attainment of an acceptable definition difficult, if not impossible ?

Comp. also, § 18 ; " Another reason that makes the defining of mixed modes so necessary, especially of moral words, is what I men-

Now Locke has repeatedly observed, that our complex ideas are collections of simple ideas, and that abstract names are only valuable as they stand always for the same collections. The conveniency of language consists, he justly says, in the tying of similar collections by one term together. But if the most complex ideas are collections of simple ideas; if they may at last be analysed into simple ideas, of which they are composed; and if the simple ideas, whether of sensation or of reflection, come from existing things; (*e.g.* simple ideas of sensation from objects, beings, or substances whose qualities affect the senses, and simple ideas of reflection from conditions or states of the mind, and inward feelings known by *consciousness*, which is here but another word for reflection, and which states and feelings are capable of being marked and recognized by words), it follows that the terms significant of the complex ideas have just as much reference to real existences as the terms significant of the simple ideas which enter into the complexity, and

tioned a little before, namely, that it is the only way whereby the signification of the most of them can be known with certainty. For the ideas they stand for being for the most part such, whose component parts nowhere exist together, but scattered and mingled with others, it is the mind alone that collects them, and gives them the union of one idea; and it is only by words, enumerating the several simple ideas which the mind has united, that we can make known to others what their names stand for; the assistance of the senses in this case not helping us by the proposal of sensible objects, to show the ideas which our names of this kind stand for, as it does often in the names of sensible simple ideas, and also to some degree in those of substances."

no more. Take Locke's favourite instance. What a
great mixture of independent ideas are contained in
that complex one of a *procession*, a *triumph!*—ideas of
persons, habits, tapers, orders, motions, sounds, cha-
riots, horses, elephants, banners, the fasces, laurels,
captives, conquerors. Surely Locke is wrong in supposing that such a complex idea or cluster of mul-
titudinous impressions, synchronous and successive, is
more arbitrary—that is, less dependent on real outward existences and phenomena—than the idea of any
one of the substances, gold, wood, cloth, tallow, iron;
or any one of the sensations, of colours, sounds, motions, without which there could be neither procession,
nor idea of it, nor term significant.

"When we speak," says Locke*, " of justice and
gratitude, we frame to ourselves no imagination of
any thing existing which we could conceive; but our
thoughts terminate in the abstract ideas of those virtues, and look not further, as they do when we speak
of a horse or iron, *whose specific ideas* we consider not
as barely in the mind, but as in things themselves,
which afford the original patterns of those ideas."
I apprehend this is wholly fallacious; and if Locke
had not elsewhere made the certainty and reality of
knowledge to consist in the conformity of ideas to the
real qualities of objects—if he had not strenuously
maintained its reality on that ground, the charge of
scepticism might have been brought with more sem-
blance of plausibility against him, as maintaining that

* Book iii. ch. 5, § 12.

moral ideas were wholly arbitrary, and that the terms significant of them had no clear, positive, and traceable relation to existing beings.   It is true that ideas, whencesoever derived, exist nowhere but in the mind; but the ideas themselves and terms significant are of value solely by their relation to the actual phenomena of nature, and the real and positive conditions of human feeling and human beings.   In reasoning upon moral relations, such as justice and gratitude, our thoughts no more terminate in the abstract ideas than in the case of the horse or iron.   The actual relations of moral beings to one another are the subject of thought and question.   The terms are of value, and attempts to settle that value are of importance, solely on account of their reference to existing beings.   The archetypes or patterns of moral ideas, to use Locke's words, are the pleasures and pains of existing moral beings.   Because they are so, it is necessary to seek, and desirable to determine, of what combinations of simple ideas the complex ones are made up ; for upon this depends the significancy of the terms.   Yet sentimental moralists, confident in their knowledge of the Deity's revelations, and giving to their private notions the reverenced name of conscience, which they do not admit to be perverted or ill-informed in their own case, despise inquiry into the sources and securities of human happiness, and stigmatize the calculation of pleasures and pains as a cold utilitarian selfishness. This is the ignorant and fashionable sentimentalism of the day. It may be itself the cloak of a selfish and malignant

spirit; a shelter for every species of fraud, vice, falsehood, injustice, and oppression. Of the worth of such
a theory, Philip the Second of Spain presents a nota-
ble illustration. He thought he should be wanting in
his duty to God, to the Church, and the State, if he
did not exterminate heretics with fire and sword. But
whence had he obtained his notions of the Deity, of
the Church, and of the State? Of what sort were his
moral instincts and innate ideas, and in what mould
cast? He brought them from Spanish nurses and the
school of the Jesuits. And when the plea of conscience
is set up for a practice adverse to the happiness of
mankind, and for an opinion that sanctions such practice, and which appears to another utterly erroneous
and mischievous, of what value is the plea? what test
does it furnish of truth or virtue?

Among the many admirable observations which
Mr. Hallam has made on Locke, there are some relating to Locke's error about the want of correspondence between the *mathematical conceptions* and the
real existence of geometrical figures, which deserve
repetition here, no less on account of their intrinsic
worth, than of their connection with inquiries into
the nature of demonstrative reasoning and the certainty of our moral knowledge. After quoting several passages from Locke, and among them the following, " All the discourses of the mathematicians
about the squaring of a circle, conic sections, or any
other part of mathematics, concern not the existence
of any of those figures; but their demonstrations,

which, depending on their ideas, are the same whether there be any square or circle in the world or no;" Mr. Hallam observes, " A geometrical figure is a portion of space contained in boundaries determined by given relations. It exists in the infinite round about us, as the statue exists in the block. No one can doubt, if he turns his mind to the subject, that every point in space is equidistant in all directions from certain other points. Draw a line through all these, and you have the circumference of a circle; but the circle itself and its circumference exist before the latter is delineated. The orbit of a planet is not a regular geometrical figure, because certain forces disturb it. But this disturbance means only a deviation from a line which exists really in space, and which the planet would actually describe, if there were nothing in the universe but itself and the centre of attraction. The expression therefore of Locke, ' whether there be any square or circle existing in the world or no,' is highly inaccurate, the latter alternative being an absurdity. All possible figures, and that in ' number numberless,' exist everywhere; nor can we evade the perplexities into which the geometry of infinites throws our imagination, by considering them as mere beings of reason, the creatures of the geometer, which I believe some are half-disposed to do, nor by substituting the vague and unphilosophical notion of indefinitude for a positive objective infinity*."

* Hallam's Literature of Europe, vol. iv. pp. 280 *et seq*. The reader will do well to consult the instructive paragraph which follows this

This error of Locke's, of a supposed want of conformity in real existences to the mathematical ideas of figure and number, is the more remarkable on account of his frequent allusions to the strength and clearness of mathematical reasonings, derived from the diagrams and the sensible impressions. " Wrong names," he observes, with great truth, " in moral discourses, breed usually more disorder, because they are not so easily rectified as in mathematics, where the figure once drawn and seen makes the name useless and of no force. For what need of a sign, when the thing

in Mr. Hallam's Literature, and mark attentively the whole of his criticism on Locke.

Locke's Essay, b. iv. ch. 4, § 8. " That which is requisite to make our knowledge *certain*, is the clearness of our ideas ; and that which is required to make it real, is that they answer their archetypes. Nor let it be wondered that I place the certainty of our knowledge in our ideas, with so little care and regard (as it may seem) to the real existence of things, since most of those discourses, which take up the thoughts, and engage the disputes of those who pretend to make it their business to inquire after truth and certainty, will, I presume, upon examination, be found to be general propositions and notions, *in which existence is not at all concerned.*" Then, following Mr. Hallam's quotation : " In the same manner the truth and certainty of moral discourses abstracts from the lives of men, and the existence of those virtues in the world, whereof they treat. Nor is Tully's Offices less true, because there is nobody in the world that exactly practises his rules, and lives up to that pattern of a virtuous man which he has given us, and which existed nowhere when he writ, but in *idea*. If it be true in speculation, *i. e.* in idea, that murther deserves death, it will also be true of any action that exists conformable to that idea of murther. As for other actions, the truth of that proposition concerns them not. And thus it is of all other species of things which have no other essences but those ideas which are in the minds of men."

signified is present, and in view? But in moral names that cannot be so easily and shortly done, because of the many decompositions that go to the making up the complex ideas of those modes. But yet, for all this, miscalling of any of those ideas, contrary to the usual signification of the words of that language, hinders not, but that we may have certain and demonstrative knowledge of their several agreements and disagreements, if we will carefully, as in mathematics, keep to the same precise ideas, and trace them in their several relations one to another, without being led away by their names. If we but separate the idea under consideration from the sign that stands for it, our knowledge goes equally on in the discovery of real truth and certainty, whatever sounds we make use of *." It is remarkable that Locke did not perceive, when writing such a passage, that if our ideas want conformity to the reality of nature,—if our moral ideas do not conform to the positive relations of moral beings, we cannot properly be said to have moral knowledge at all.   Our notions, without such conformity, are merely dreams.   A madman may reason consecutively and demonstratively upon his own erroneous conceptions; but he is mad nevertheless, and the madness consists in the want of conformity between his ideas and the reality of things.   The man who believed he was made of glass, was right in concluding that he must not knock himself against a wall.   His first idea was the great delusion.   False assumptions are pro-

* Essay, b. iv. ch. 4, § 9.

bably a far more frequent source of error than incon-sequential reasoning.

Thus it appears that Locke, in seeking to determine the nature of demonstration, has dwelt too much on the agreement and disagreement of ideas, and ideas alone. If he were right in this, of course it would lead us to consider whether there be any, and what may be the specific difference between the ideas of figure, number, and magnitude, and the ideas of morality ; and no doubt there is a simplicity and uniformity in the ideas, or it were better to say, the subject-matter of geometrical reasoning and of arithmetical and alge-braic calculation, not belonging to the subject-matter of moral reasoning*. There is, as Locke perceived, far greater complexity in the latter. It is further evi-dent that Locke had not a clear view of the nature of demonstration. To demonstrate is to show that a proposition not granted to be true is true by virtue of some premiss previously admitted or assumed as a criterion of truth, or by virtue of some other truth previously demonstrated. Such is Mr. De Morgan's

---

* Hence, perhaps, something of mechanical character in all the branches of mathematics, exclusively pursued. Notwithstanding the intensity of application, the closeness and continuity of attention required for them, to which comparatively few are equal, but which are in themselves most valuable and enviable qualities of the intel-lect, yet, *when exclusively pursued*, they may give a character of nar-rowness and poverty to the understanding. The furniture of the mind, supplied by figures and numbers only, may have far less con-nection with all the wants and uses of life than that stored up by the diligent and philosophical student of history and nature, of lite-rature and art.

just account of it; and it deserves to be well laid up
in the mind.   If we examine Locke's favourite example,—the demonstration that the three angles of a
triangle are equal to two right angles,—the ideas of
any given angles in a given figure remain distinct, and
probably no young geometer ever thinks about the
agreement or disagreement of the ideas, but he refers
the angles in question to a common measure which all
angles have; he considers their equality to all the possible angles on the same side of a straight line; and
he admits the proposition because he has admitted
this common measure or test; and he perceives that
the reasoning will apply to every example.

This simplicity and uniformity in the subject-matter
of mathematical reasoning, and comparative complexity
in the subject-matter of moral science, has not been
sufficiently regarded by those who have sought to distinguish between contingent and demonstrative reasoning, as if the contingency were in the reasoning, not in
the matter.   The relations of figure and numbers, angles and lines, magnitudes and motions, to one another,
which are the subjects of mathematical investigation,
and on which the axioms and definitions turn, remain
the same through all time and to all observers.   The
figure of the earth, and all figure and all number, that is,
everything with which the geometrical and arithmetical
reasoner is concerned, are the same now as in the days
of Euclid and Archimedes.   But the phenomena with
which moral propositions and historical statements are
concerned, are comparatively evanescent.   It is impos-

sible to fix and recall them, to renew them in precisely the same conditions. The actors in the tragedy of the death of Cæsar, their actual thoughts and passions, are no more. A brief record, the words of an historian, alone remain to excite our imagination and form opinion. Still it is only in proportion as mankind are subject, from age to age, to similar thoughts and passions, that is, in proportion as their physical and mental frame presents some uniform characteristics, that we can arrive at general propositions in morality, the truth and value of which must ever rest, like those of mathematics, upon the facts,—upon certain ever-recurring, if not permanent phenomena, determinate and admitted. But general propositions consist of words or signs; and the sole question is, how far the words or signs are free from ambiguity.

Now Locke decides that the names of simple ideas, and those only, are incapable of being defined. This he illustrates at some length, and on it we have already made some observations. But the names significant of complex states, we are told, may be defined*. If then the complex ideas or states are made up of a collection of simple ideas, it follows that we can only define by enumerating the several simples that enter into the collection; that is to say, in the examination of complex

* Hartley, Prop. 80, divides words into four classes. 1. Such as have ideas only. 2. Such as have both ideas and definitions. 3. Such as have definitions only. 4. Such as have neither ideas nor definitions. I demur to the last class, and to his reason for making such a class. How can *particles vary the sense* of a sentence, if they *signify nothing* of themselves?

2 E 2

states of mind, and in the definition of the terms significant, we must find out and enumerate the more simple
and elementary. Now the subject-matter of morality
being the actions, habits, and dispositions of moral
agents, their motives and consequences, their causes
and effects, supposing every action to have an object,
and that object or motive to be the attainment or communication of a pleasure, the avoidance or infliction
of a pain, to some sentient being,—it follows that a
study of human pleasures and pains must form the
chief part of the study of morality. Morality thus becomes neither more nor less than the study of human
happiness and of the rules or means for promoting and
securing it; and until this is clearly seen and admitted
by professed moralists, no progress can be made in the
scientific treatment of their subject. In this view the
classification made by Hartley in the first instance, and
by Bentham afterwards, of pleasures and pains, form
by far the most important contributions to ethical
science in modern times.

In the chapter on the improvement of our knowledge—the 12th of the 4th book—Locke returns to
the proposition that "*morality is capable of demonstration,*" and he talks "of the habitudes and relations
of the ideas, which are *the real essences* that ethics
are conversant about." But, after all, he gets no further than this one rule,—"to get and fix in our minds
clear, distinct, and complete ideas, as far as they are
to be had, and annex to them proper and constant
names." Now distinct ideas are gotten from careful

observation of nature; that is, in morality, of the actions and passions of men; and our chief concern
must be the *propriety and constancy of the names.* In
the chapter on wrong assent or error, in one short
sentence Locke puts in a strong and just light the
connection between men's notions of truth and morality and their practical behaviour: " as the foundation
of error will lie in wrong measures of probability, so
the foundation of vice will lie in wrong measures of
good." If this be true, and perhaps on close examination of fact it will be found to be a pregnant truth,
the object of the scientific moralist is evidently to find
out for himself and point out to others, the right measures of good.

Where are these measures to be had? Is this only
an improved form of the old inquiry after the *summum
bonum?* It is but an endeavour to determine the rule
of life. Now the common practice of mankind affords
some rule or measure; their opinions or principles,
in so far as we can gather them, a better rule; the
opinions of the select few, of the choicest thinkers or
most careful observers, a still higher rule; and the rule
of life thus formed may be supposed to harmonize
with what is called the divine rule, as deduced from
nature and Scripture. Thus the devout theist, the
philosophical Christian, the patriot citizen, the lover
of mankind, will be least at a loss to determine what
is the rule of life and duty. For the most part, whatever difficulties or differences there may be in the
theory of morals, there is an agreement in practical re-

sults; and the voice of mankind, by express laws, by books, by converse, and by daily examples, agrees in pronouncing some actions and their class right and virtuous, others as determinately wrong and vicious.

Yet such is the complexity of the matter entering into the settlement of moral truth, and such the obscurity and ambiguity of the terms, that when the most candid give a close attention to the subject, they find themselves embarrassed to a degree which, without such attention, they could not have anticipated. When, for example, we peruse a chapter in Blackstone's Commentaries touching on public or private wrongs; when we seek to determine the difference between justifiable and felonious homicide, between killing by culpable neglect of proper precaution against accident and killing with intent to take away life, without lawful plea of self-defence, with malice aforethought; and when further we attend a court of law and bring logic and philosophy to bear upon the evidence there given and the language there employed by witnesses, by the counsel, and by the judge, we learn the difficulty of appreciating, by agreed measures, the complex matters concerned in moral and social right, and of determining the application of the rules to particular cases. We shall be often deeply affected by a sense of the difficulty and obscurity attending first upon inquiry into the facts, and next, upon clothing in suitable language the impressions of facts, which go to the settlement of moral truth. The intent of the law-makers, the application of that intent to the case in hand, the

guilt of the respective agents in their present infraction
of the law, the amount of evil accruing from that infraction, and the means of preventing the like evil in
time to come,—all appear involved in hopeless obscurity; and a rare combination of integrity and experience is required for a safe conclusion. Yet such is the
perverseness of mankind, that even those, from whom
better things might be expected, systematically discou-
rage a serious attention to the difficulties and obscurities of moral and political science; and they who
descend with the lamp of patient thought into the
darkest caverns of prejudice and error, who take most
pains to shed a ray of light upon the path of safety
and of progress, are commonly vilified as the advocates of sensualism and selfishness.

As the last chapters, on the imperfection and abuse
of words, and the remedies thereof, constitute the
most valuable portion of the third book, so the later
chapters of the fourth book of the Essay, on the existence of a Deity, the improvement of knowledge, the
nature and degrees of assent and error, on faith and
reason, and the division of the sciences, deserve the
deepest attention.   No writings in the English language breathe a purer and loftier spirit, or tend more
powerfully to form the candid, philosophical, religious
mind.   It is not only that high ethical character to
which Mr. Hallam does full justice, that freedom from
the spirit of party and absence of partiality even to
his own opinions, apart from the evidence which facts
and reasonings furnish, but what is more, because so

rare in the philosopher, a constant remembrance of the relation between the human finite intellect and the infinite unknown ; that modest sense of human ignorance and error, combined with an anxiety to turn to good account whatever can be known with any approach to certainty ; and above all, that disposition to find the final cause of everything in the wisdom and benevolence of the Creator ; these are the moral graces that shed their halo round the memory of the illustrious Locke, and make his Essay on the Understanding at the same time a work well fitted to purify and enlarge the heart. Should any taste for genuine English thought and literature survive the present race of thinkers, should it again be reckoned among the needful accomplishments of an English gentleman to know well the greatest and best authors of his country, the estimation of Locke will rise once more to its just height, and the candid youth of universities and halls will be taught to pronounce with veneration the name of the most philosophical of Christians, the most Christian of philosophers.

A review of the writings and philosophy of Locke would be unpardonably defective without some careful reverential notice of the works, whose merit has been thrown too deeply into the shade by the peculiar interest of the Essay. The sixteen years, which Locke spent chiefly at the seat of the Mashams at Oates, from the time of the Revolution in 1688 to his death in 1704, give us a most agreeable picture of the life of a patriot and philosopher. The Essay on the Understanding had been prepared for the press and was finished in Holland about the end of 1687*; the papers on Toleration also had been published in Latin before Locke returned from Holland, and the Thoughts on Education had been communicated to Edward Clarke, of Chipley, in letters, before 1690.   Still the larger part of the four goodly quartos which now make up Law's edition, were written during those years of comparative retirement, —the fruit of his mature and patient thought, the produce of an industrious hand, guided by a benevolent, religious mind. Thanks to the smoky atmosphere of London, and to the asthmatic pains and troubles which drove him to the fields of Essex ! To these we owe in part, under Providence, the noblest vindications of civil and religious liberty, some of the worthiest tributes to the reasonableness and value of the Christian's faith, which adorn the literature and history of England. They compelled the philosopher's withdrawal from engagements, honourable and important, which the greatest and best of his country pressed upon his acceptance ; and this retirement gave him " leisure for immortal occupations."

No foreign critic can be expected to do full justice to the merits and character of Locke. He is the type of the English mind, and " its large, sound, roundabout sense." His spirit was eminently practical. He had in view, in all his writings, a direct practical result. He never for a moment forgot the subserviency of

* The original copy is said to exist, dated 1671. See Lord King's Life, vol. i. p. 10.

truth to virtue, of virtue to happiness. To the last he studied no less for his own improvement than for that of his country and mankind; and he had the happiness of laying deep the foundation of England's future greatness, in two most important constitutional measures, the one touching its material prosperity, the other its religious and moral progress, in which, to his immortal honour, his influence over the sovereign and the government was exerted with the best effect. The Act of Toleration was among the earliest fruits of that revolution which placed William and Mary on the throne, and was passed in the first session of 1689. " There is a tradition," says Lord King*, " that the

* See King's Life, vol. i. p. 327. In a careful Life, more distinct information on such a point, and extracts from Locke's correspondence, would have been given. The following translation of the portions of Locke's letters relating to the subject may be acceptable to the reader. But the whole correspondence will be found translated by J. T. Rutt, Esq., in the Monthly Repository for 1818, vol. xiii., with good historical notes.

" In Parliament measures are already commenced in favour of toleration under a double title—namely Comprehension and Indulgence. The first proposes that the benefits of the Church are to be extended, so that by the removal of part of the ceremonies it may comprehend more persons. The other aims at the toleration of those, who will not or cannot unite themselves to the English Church on the offered conditions. How lax or strict these conditions will be, I scarcely yet know; but this I feel, that the episcopal clergy do not much favour these and other matters, which are now agitated; whether to their own or the republic's advantage, let them see. Farewell.—Your most affectionate   J. L."

This is dated, " London, March 12, 1689." A second letter is dated, " London, 6th June, 1689."

" I do not doubt that you have heard before this that toleration is now at length established by law among us. Not perhaps with that

terms of the Toleration Act were negotiated by Locke himself: and the fact is in some degree confirmed by an expression in one of his letters to Limborch." The subject had long employed Locke's thoughts. The letter to Limborch, written while he was in conceal-ment in Holland, in 1685, was translated into English in 1689 by a nephew of Andrew Marvell's—a Rev. Mr. Popple, and defended against one Proast in two later publications in 1690.

The considerations on the state of the coinage—concerning raising the value of the money and lower-ing the interest, were printed in 1691, and some fur-ther considerations in 1695. They were addressed to

latitude which you and the like of you, without ambition or dread of Christian truth, might wish. But it is something to go thus far. With these beginnings I hope the foundations of liberty and peace are laid, on which the Church of Christ may be once for all esta-blished. None are prohibited from worship of their own, nor ex-posed to punishments, except it be the Romanists, provided only they will take the oath of fidelity, and renounce transubstantiation and certain dogmas of the Romish church. But the Quakers are ex-cused from the oath; nor upon them would that confession of faith, which you will see in the Act, have been obtruded by a bad example, if some of them had not offered that confession, an imprudence which many among them, and those the more earnest, greatly de-plore. I thank you for the copies of the tract concerning tolerance and peace which you have sent me : the bound I have received; the unbound have not yet come to hand. I understand that some Eng-lishman is already employed in translating the little book concerning toleration. That principle, so favourable to peace and probity, I wish everywhere to prevail. I rejoice that you have written the history of the Inquisition, and hope it will soon come forth, a work useful and expected. I have sent to Le Clerc the Act passed in favour of tolera-tion, from whom you will learn how far this liberty is extended."

the great Lord Somers, and show Locke's mastery
over the principles of what has since been called "political economy," as well as the pure patriotism and
high moral feeling which animated all his proceedings.
He cleared the subject of trade and commerce and the
uses of money from mystery. His wisdom happily
was recognized.   His advice, that there should be no
alteration of the standard, nor any attempt to raise the
denomination, was followed.   The consequence was
that disturbances in many parts of the country were
quieted.   The clipped and bad coin in circulation was
called in, and the great recoinage of 1695 restored
the current money of the country to the full legal
standard; and England was saved from one cause of
those convulsions which have afflicted her nearest
neighbours.

Besides these labours in connection with the religious liberty of his country and the security of its commerce, Locke had been employed in examining the
rational foundations of human society and the philosophy of government.   In 1689 he gave to the world
the fruit of his meditations, in two treatises on the
subject; in the first, overthrowing the false principles
of Sir Robert Filmer and his followers, whose works
even Locke's antagonism and Algernon Sydney's elaborate papers on government before him have scarcely
saved from oblivion; the second, treating of the true
original, extent, and end of civil government.   Of
the excellent fifth chapter, in this second treatise,
Mr. Hallam justly says, " it would be sufficient, if all

Locke's other writings had perished, to leave him a
high name in philosophy." The same may be said
of its later chapters on prerogative, conquest, usurpation, tyranny, and the dissolution of governments.
The treatise was written, it has been supposed, to
justify the Revolution of 1688, which placed William
the Third on the throne, but it has nothing of a party
character. It is the result of those profound and anxious thoughts on the philosophy and ends of government, called forth in times of political disturbance and
change; and it remains one of the few very important
works which our literature has to boast on that difficult subject, deserving the special study of the educated Englishman*. "The importance of labour in
the production of wealth," says James Mill†, "was
very clearly perceived both by Hobbes and Locke;"

* Of the works on the philosophy of government, the most important in English literature seem to be, after Bacon and Hobbes, the
following. Dr. John Taylor's ' Elements of Civil Law,' 3rd edit. 1755 ;
Beccaria's ' Treatise on Crimes and Punishments,' translated in 1766;
Priestley's ' Essays and Lectures ;' Bentham's ' Fragment on Government,' a critique on Blackstone's Preface, and his ' Treatise of
Morals and Legislation ;' Paley's ' Political Philosophy ;' James
Mill's Article ' On Government' in the Encyclopædia Britannica,
7th edit. ; Austin's ' Province of Jurisprudence determined.' Besides
these we have a slight treatise by Mackintosh ' On the Law of Nature and Nations,' and an ' Essay' by Sir W. Temple. We have
also translations of Grotius, Puffendorf, and Montesquieu, and numerous works on the English Government and Constitution, besides
the works on political economy. But the greatest and best writers
may be considered to have built upon Locke's principles and sprung
from his school.

† Article on ' Political Economy,' Encyclopædia Britannica, vol.
xviii. p. 273. Locke's Treatise on Government, ch. v. § 40–43.

but after quoting the sections* in which Locke shows
" that if we rightly consider things as they come to
our use, and cast up the several expenses about them,
what in them is purely owing to nature and what to
labour, we shall find that in most of them ninety-nine
hundredths are wholly to be put on the account of labour ;" and again, " 'tis labour which puts the greatest
part of value upon land, *without which it would scarcely
be worth anything ;*" he adds, " *this is a very remarkable passage. It contains a far more distinct and comprehensive statement of the fundamental doctrine, that
labour is the constituent principle of value than is to be
found in any other writer previous to Smith, or than is
to be found even in the Wealth of Nations!*" Labour,
Locke teaches, in the beginning gave a right of property,—in the maintenance of which right all society
is interested, and for which chiefly it is constituted,
right and conveniency going together. He appears
to have a great advantage over Hobbes in the view
that, not merely mutual fear, which if alone prevailing
must drive every individual into solitude, but obligations of necessity, convenience, and inclination, which
God put him under, drove man into society, fitting
him also with understanding and language to enjoy it.
Locke also maintains much more distinctly and im-
pressively than Hobbes the responsibilities and duties
of the governing, as well as of the governed, in a civil
society. " Absolute arbitrary power, or governing
without settled standing laws, can neither of them con-

* Locke, ch. v. § 40, 41, 42, 43.

sist with the ends of society and government, which men would not quit the freedom of the state of nature for, and tie themselves up under, were it not to preserve their lives, liberties, and fortunes, *and by stated rules of right and property to secure their peace and quiet.* It cannot be supposed that they should intend, had they a power so to do, to give to any one or more an absolute arbitrary power over their persons and estates, and put a force into the magistrate's hand to execute his unlimited will arbitrarily upon them. This were to put themselves into a worse condition than the state of nature, wherein they had a liberty to defend their right against the injuries of others, and were upon equal terms of force to maintain it, whether invaded by a single man, or many in combination."

Adam Smith, in his great work, ' The Wealth of Nations,' has not treated his subject historically ; but in his early chapters on the origin of the use of money, and the settlement by law of its relative value in exchange, he might have adverted with advantage to Locke's clear views upon this subject, and to his great influence in saving England from those evils which in other countries have arisen from the pernicious interference of governments with the standard of value. The study of Locke would probably have saved him from some other errors into which he seems to have fallen, as to the relative productiveness of labour, and its uniformly equal value. The absence of any reference to these papers of Locke on the part of Adam Smith is one indication, among many others, of the neglect or

the partiality with which English literature and philosophy have too commonly been treated in Scotland.
The chief difficulty in Locke arises from his supposing
the existence of a known law of nature, distinct enough
to be recognized, directing men in their conduct to
each other antecedently to their entering into civil society; by which law he seems to understand something more than a principle of self-preservation,—a
perception of the advantage to be derived from some
restraint of individual liberty and submission to a
common rule.   When he makes individual assent the
foundation of obligation to civil obedience, the reader
must carefully note the many modes in which he supposes that assent to be tacitly given; and how it is
implied in any the least enjoyment of a privilege or
right conferred by an existing community; such as "a
lodging only for a week; or whether it be barely travelling on the highway; and in effect it reaches as far
as the very being of any one within the territories of
that government*."

Paley, in his chapter on the duty of submission to
civil government, discusses briefly, but dismisses summarily, the notion of its being founded on compact,
though supported by the venerable name of Locke.
He asserts that "no such compact was ever made in
reality, no such original convention of the people was
ever holden, or in any country could be holden, antecedent to the existence of civil government in that
country."   But surely it is true that in all govern-

* Locke on Government, b. ii. ch. 8, § 119.

ments, called constitutional, the actual laws have been matters of express compact between the parties governing and the parties to be governed, as in the case of our own Magna Charta, and the earlier statutes of the Witenagemote ; and in the earliest forms of government supposable, the parental or patriarchal, there is an implied compact of obedience on the one hand, for care, provision, and protection on the other.

Whatever views may be taken of the origin of civil government, and of the forms deemed most fit to attain its ends, certainly no philosopher would think any government defensible in so far as it was proved or believed to be hostile to human happiness, or would deny that form to be the best which could be shown to secure the greatest amount of human good.   The maxim at the end of the Roman law, quoted by Bacon in his Essay on Judicature, " salus populi suprema lex," must be the maxim of every philosophical legislator*."

In the treatise on government Locke makes great use of the matter of the tenth section of the first book

* A controversy of considerable interest and importance arose out of these papers on government in the latter half of the last century, between Tucker, Dean of Gloucester, who attacked and misrepresented, and Dr. Joseph Towers, who ably and successfully vindicated, Locke's principles. The political and other tracts of Towers, collected in three volumes in 1796, now scarce in their collected form, are an able and valuable vindication of civil and religious liberty, of philosophical and enlightened religion. Dr. Towers, the assistant of Dr. Kippis in the ' Biographia Britannica,' was one of the first to perceive and correct the offences of Hume against the principles of both.

of Hooker's Ecclesiastical Polity, where Hooker enters upon the origin of government, and founds all upon consent. Hooker did not live to finish his great work. The subject seems to have been too difficult for him. The later books, though probably not altered from the MSS., are evidently not as he would have published them, had he lived to send them forth*. Upon the whole, Hooker must be considered as resolving the Church as a power into the State, and his work was equally exceptionable to Episcopalians and Presbyterians, that is, to all who had high notions of ecclesiastical independence and supremacy.   Fuller, in

---

* Can the Church have a polity, in a strict sense, that is, be a society, wherein the majority enforce their will and opinion by temporal penalties?   Can it be anything but a society, like that of the first Christians, voluntarily meeting to cultivate together, with forms changeable at pleasure, the feelings of devotion, benevolence, and hope?   " Our citizenship" (πολίτευμα), says Paul, " is in heaven." Philippians iii. 20.   " The kings of the Gentiles exercise lordship over them ; but it shall not be so among you," said the Saviour, " for whoso is greatest among you, let him be your servant."   " The weapons of our warfare are not carnal, but spiritual."   A number of passages will occur to the thoughtful reader.   An important criticism of Hooker and his connection with Locke occurs in Hallam's Constitutional History of England, vol. i. pp. 292–302.   See also a note at the end of the Rev. J. J. Tayler's Retrospect of the Religious Life of England.   Mr. Hallam says, " that whatever may be the imperfections of the Ecclesiastical Polity, they are far more than compensated by its eloquence and reasonings ;" but with the highest admiration of the piety and general spirit of Hooker, and the grandeur of his march as to style of composition, I cannot feel that he mastered his subject, or that his reasoning is satisfactory.   His important terms, especially in the later books, are by no means cleared from ambiguity, and his sense is overpowered by his literature and learning.

his notice of Hooker, among the worthies of Devon, puts in his quaint way the difficulties felt by his readers. "Hereupon it is that they (*i. e.* people who read his book with a prejudice, that as Jephtha vowed to sacrifice the first living thing which met him, these are resolved to quarrel with the first word which occurreth therein) take exception at the very title thereof, 'Ecclesiastical Politie,' as if unequally yoked,— Church with some mixture of *citiness ;* that the discipline, *jure divino*, may bow to human inventions. But be it reported to the judicious, whether, when all is done, *a reserve must not be left for prudential supplies in Church government.*" The judicious will not undertake to explain very confidently the meaning of these last words.

Before these admirable treatises on civil society, or what concerns the happiness of a community, were written, Locke had turned his attention to the subject of education, and the formation of individual improvement and character. Nowhere does his admirable temper and philosophy shine more brightly than in those thoughts dedicated to his friend Edward Clarke, of Chipley. "He has uttered more good sense on the subject," says Hallam[*], "than will be found in any preceding writer." "Much has been written, and often well, since the days of Locke; but he is the chief source from which it has been ultimately derived. The patient attention to every circumstance—a peculiar characteristic of the genius of Locke—is in none of his

[*] Literature of Europe, vol. iv. ch. 4.

works better displayed.   His rules for the health of
children, though sometimes trivial, since the subject
has been more regarded; his excellent advice as to
checking effeminacy and timorousness; his observations on their curiosity, presumption, idleness, on their
plays and recreations, bespeak an intense, though
calm, love of truth and goodness ; a quality which few
have possessed more fully, or known so well how to
exert, as this admirable author."

It is pleasing to compare Locke's treatise with Milton's on the same subject.   Both were called forth at
the instigation of eminent friends.   Milton dedicates
his to Master Samuel Hartlib, an active promoter of
all that was good in his day, one of whom all that we
can now learn is eminently favourable; Locke his to
Edward Clarke, of Chipley, and speaks with interest
of some children and parents, now unknown, whom
he had specially in view.   Both display the characteristics, the peculiar mental habitudes and tastes, of the
authors.   While Milton's is a brief plan, and upon the
whole a very impracticable one, of an academy or gym-
nasium for an assemblage of youth educated together,
Locke is more full on the special influences to be exerted by parents or tutors on the individual.   Milton
seems to have least hesitation in prescribing a wide
range of intellectual tasks—particularly when enumerating the classical authors, whom he supposes his
pupils competent to master. He talks of " heroic poems
and Attic tragedies, of stateliest and most regal argument," and of " recreating and composing the travailed

spirits with the solemn and divine harmonies of music
heard or learned." Locke speaks of gardening and
carpentering as diversions not unsuited for a gentleman. In gardening he delighted and excelled. In the
soft air of lawns and flowers his difficulty of breath-
ing was relieved. He tells us, " it is very seldom
seen that any one discovers mines of gold or silver in
Parnassus; that it is a pleasant, but a barren soil."
This is in connection with the practice of exercising
boys much in making Latin verses, now far less in
fashion than formerly. " Of music," he says, " that
it wastes time and engages in odd company, and is
seldom much commended and esteemed among men
of parts and business. But," he adds,—and here
Milton and all good men are at one with him,—
" the great business of all is virtue and wisdom—a
mastery over the inclinations, and submitting appetite to reason. Under whose care soever a child is
put, during the tender and flexible years of his life,
this is certain, it should be one who thinks Latin and
language the least part of education ; one who, knowing how much virtue and a well-tempered soul is to
be preferred to any sort of learning or language,
makes it his chief business to form the mind of his
scholars, and give that a right disposition, which if
once got, though all the rest should be neglected, would
in due time produce all the rest; and which, if it be
not got and settled, so as to keep out ill and vicious
habits, languages, sciences, and all the other accom-

plishments of education, will be to no purpose but to make the worse and more dangerous man*."

In the year 1697 Locke was engaged in controversy with Stillingfleet, the Bishop of Worcester, on the merits of certain portions of the Essay on the Understanding, which the Bishop thought open to objection. These portions had supplied John Toland with some of the weapons with which, in his work entitled 'Christianity not Mysterious,' he was considered to wound the Christian religion in its vital or tenderest parts. A very unfavourable estimate of the Bishop's share in the controversy is given by Law, in his Life of Locke. But Mr. Hallam considers that the Bishop does not make so poor a figure as is commonly supposed. The patience and care with which Locke examines his statements and pursues him through every turn are almost unique in controversy, and Locke's prolixity indicates not only the man of leisure, but the invalid. While he treats the Bishop with formal deference, he is sore and indignant at being mixed up with writers in whose conclusions and arguments he was in no way concerned, with Hobbes and Spinoza, no less than Toland. If the Bishop had any advantage over Locke, it was in connection with those notions about ideas, as a ground of certainty, wherein, as we have intimated and as the controversy with Stillingfleet further shows, Locke is often at fault. Toland's work, though it gave great offence at the time, appears now but a very mild defence of the sim-

* Locke on Education, § 177.

plicity and intelligibleness of the Christian scheme, since we have become accustomed to the extravagances of German rationalism, under cover of which a man holds himself entitled to the name of Christian because he obeys the high impulses and instincts of his own spiritual nature, even when he finds himself impelled to deny the existence of an historical Christ, and even of a personal Deity*.

To the generality of readers probably the most interesting portion of Locke's letters to Stillingfleet will be the conclusion of his second letter, where he discusses the supposed connection between the immateriality and natural immortality of the human soul, and the opinions of the ancients on this point, and enlarges on the value of the Christian religion, in bringing life and immortality to light. Locke here shows himself familiar enough with Cicero, Plato, and Aristotle. He indicates also the relative importance which will be attached to an historical revelation, according as the natural arguments for a future state rise or fall in estimation. Some, with Leibnitz, we

---

* See an instructive letter of Niebuhr to a friend, relative to Cousin's cloudy utterances, the echoes of Hegel, in the Life of Niebuhr, translated by Miss Winkworth; and Andrews Norton on the ' Latest Form of Infidelity.'

Toland was from the first a troublesome adventurer, and seems to have ended with being an atheist of Spinoza's school. But he had much curious learning, and was perhaps persecuted into atheism, when, if he had been let alone, he would have struggled out of that whirlpool of scepticism, and reached some *terra firma* of philosophy on which the seeds of social virtue and religion may be sown with promise and ripen for harvest.

find still disposed to contend "that it must be infinitely more advantageous to religion and morality to demonstrate that the soul is naturally immortal, than to rest the belief in a future state upon the promise of God;" others again, with more support in the language of the New Testament, will maintain with Locke, that though the light of nature gave some obscure glimmering, some uncertain hopes of a future state, yet human reason could attain to no certainty about it, but that it was " Jesus Christ alone who had brought life and immortality to light through the Gospel."

We derive from what may be called, though perhaps not deservedly, Locke's *minor* works, much valuable light on the course of his reading and studies. In these he acknowledges his obligations to Descartes for freeing him from the trammels of the schoolmen, and teaching him to think for himself, not for any accurate knowledge of the human mind and constitution. We see that he had studied Bacon and Gassendi, and that high estimation of Hooker, to which we have already alluded, whom he calls the *arch-philosopher.* The opinion expressed above, that he was not well read in Hobbes, is confirmed by a passage towards the close of his second vindication of the Reasonableness of Christianity, in reply to Dr. Edwards, wherein Locke says that he did not know that " certain words, equivalent to his proposition that Jesus is the Christ, were in the Leviathan, or anything like them*."

* Law's edition of Locke, vol. iii. p. 270.

In 1695 Locke published his Reasonableness of Christianity, according to the Scriptures, at first anonymously, but it was soon known to be his. This work may be considered the earliest philosophical defence of Revealed Religion in the English language, a defence of Christianity in the sense in which the Arminian or latitudinarian divines of the Church of England and the learned English Presbyterian dissenters of a later day have understood it. After showing, by copious extracts from the New Testament, that the one simple doctrine which lies at the foundation of the Christian faith is that Jesus is the Christ, he vindicates its importance by a summary of the related principles and of the advantages accruing from their establishment and diffusion. First, it made the " one invisible and true God" known to the world, and that with such evidence and energy that polytheism and idolatry have nowhere been able to withstand it ; 2, it gave that " clear knowledge of their duty which was wanting to mankind ;" 3, it brought in a plain, spiritual, suitable worship of the Deity, teaching every one to look after his own heart, and to know that it was that alone which God had regard to and accepted ; 4, it brought the greatest encouragement to a virtuous and pious life by its doctrine of a future state—before our Saviour's time not wholly hid, yet not clearly known—upon which foundation, and upon which alone, morality stands firm and may defy all competition ; 5, and besides all this, it gives the promise of divine assistance, God's spirit, to help us to do what and how we should.

Whatever deficiencies there may be supposed to be in Locke's view of revealed religion, the philosophical and devout religionist of every school will read with candour and delight, the admirable observations with which he has accompanied and enforced it, and the more he reads and ponders them, the more highly will he esteem their truth and beauty.

Fabricius*, in his Syllabus of the writers who have written on the truth of the Christian religion, enumerates as of the English school before Locke, Stillingfleet, Baxter, Whitby, Henry More, Jeremy Taylor, Samuel Parker, Burnet, and Halliwell. Some translations of Grotius had appeared, which Fabricius does not mention, and a few other works not unworthy of attention to the minute inquirer. In the writers whom he does mention, many profound and valuable remarks in vindication and illustration of the religion of the Old and New Testament Scriptures may be found. But they are all more darkly tinged with what the scholar and philosopher of our day would be apt to consider error and superstition than Locke. The writer who seems to come nearest to him in the excellency of his matter and thought on this great subject is the learned, eloquent, and philosophical Dr. Isaac Barrow, whose sermons on the Christian religion were edited by Tillotson in 1683. Barrow was an eminent Arminian divine; and his sermons on God the Father Almighty, on Jesus as the true Messiah, and particularly one on

---

* J. A. Fabricii Delectus argumentorum et syllabus Scriptorum qui veritatem R. Cæ asseruerunt. 4to.

the excellency of the Christian religion, while full of noble thoughts on reason and duty and natural religion, are for the most part in beautiful harmony with Locke's conceptions, although expressions occasionally drop from him which Locke would not have used.

Locke's high social position and reputation contributed to draw to his work on Christianity the greatest attention, independently of its intrinsic merits. It was natural that it should be attacked in some quarters, as warmly defended and applauded in others. He was soon charged with Socinianism, in those days and still a very odious epithet, very few having read a line of the works of Socinus, Crellius, Schlichtingius, and the other learned Fratres Poloni. Among the violent opponents of Locke, one Dr. John Edwards was foremost, a bitter and prolific polemical writer, who in his Thoughts concerning the Causes of Atheism, 1695, a Discourse on Truth and Error, and Socinianism Unmasked, emptied the vials of his wrath upon Locke's metaphysics and religion, and scrupled not to apply to him the epithets *false, perfidious, shuffling*, among many others characteristic of the writer and his age*.

Locke soon published a first and second vindica-

---

* This John Edwards was the son of Dr. Thomas Edwards, a famous Presbyterian writer, and enemy to the Independents, the author of the 'Gangræna.' He inherited the bitterness of a father, who considered toleration the last and strongest hold of Satan. He was but one of a number of Edwardses, who were zealous against heresy and Socinianism. Two gloried in the name of Jonathan Edwards, one of Wrexham in North Wales, and a second of New Jersey in America, author of the celebrated treatise against free-will.

tion of his work in reply. Far from treating his opponent with the severity which some have charged
upon him, he exhibits a patience and condescension, of
which only his anxiety for truth and goodness could
be the spring.   Locke met with an able and warm
supporter in a rector of Steeple, in Dorsetshire, the
Rev. Samuel Bolde, whose tracts in vindication of the
Essay on the Human Understanding and of the work
on the Reasonableness of Christianity, in reply to
Edwards and Broughton and Norris, were collected in
1706. Mr. Locke was also complimented by a writer
who dedicates to him one of the Unitarian tracts, in
4to, entitled 'The Exceptions of Mr. Edwards, in his
Causes of Atheism against the Reasonableness of Christianity as delivered in the Scriptures, examined, etc.,'
1695.   "Some ingenious persons have judged this
piece to be by Locke himself, and if," says his editor,* "they are right in their conjecture, *as I have no
doubt they are*, the address to himself that is prefixed
to it must have been made on purpose to conceal the
true author, as a more attentive perusal of the whole
tract will convince any one†."

* Bishop Law's Preface, pp. vi. vii.

† The conclusion is much in Locke's style and temper, but that the
dedication to himself should be Locke's own—though it be a modest
composition, savours perhaps too much of artifice for that upright
and conscientious philosopher. These double-columned prints, as
Edwards styles them, published during the last decennium of the seventeenth century, under the patronage of Firmin and his associates,
display quite as much learning and acuteness on the subject of "primitive Christianity" as will be found in any subsequent productions
in English theological literature, and they kept public attention quite

Thus the controversies produced by Mr. Locke's writings were warm and active, and no doubt they contributed powerfully to that silent change in men's views and tempers, and that greater exactness in their reasonings on philosophy and religion, that sobriety of thought and mutual toleration, which began to prevail at the beginning of the eighteenth century.

The four last years of his life were employed by Locke in the calm and diligent study of the Scriptures; and particularly of the writings of St. Paul. Of this we have the pleasing and valuable fruits in the Paraphrase and Notes upon the Epistles to the Romans, the Galatians, and the Corinthians, but more especially in the admirable preface, which appears to be the earliest work in English on the philosophical criticism of the Scriptures, a short piece, which no man who would study for himself the important records of revealed religion can be excused for neglecting to peruse. " In his paraphrase and notes upon the Epistles of St. Paul," says Bishop Law, " how fully does our author obviate the erroneous doctrines (that of absolute reprobation in particular) which had been falsely charged upon the Apostle ! And to Mr. Locke's honour it should be remembered, that *he was the first of our commentators*

as much alive to it. Then Sherlock and Wallis shook the Universities with their differences, and the learned author of the treatise ' De Uno Deo Patre,' Crellius, was in frequent conference with Archbishop Tillotson, and sometimes an inmate of his house.

An anonymous work on Mr. Locke's religion was printed in 1700, which has been attributed to Atterbury. It is not without learning and some acquaintance with the metaphysics of his day.

who showed what it was to comment upon the Apostolic writings; by taking the whole of an epistle together, and striking off every signification of every term foreign to the main scope of it; by keeping this point constantly in view, and carefully observing each return to it after any digression; by tracing out a strict, though somewhat less visible, connection in that very consistent writer, St. Paul, touching the propriety and pertinence of whose writings to their several subjects and occasions he appears to have formed the most just conception; and thereby confessedly led the way to some of our best modern interpreters."

The works of Lord Barrington, of the learned Peirce of Exeter, of the not less learned Dr. George Benson, and particularly that of Dr. John Taylor on the Epistle to the Romans, bear testimony to the salutary influence of Locke on rational theology and the interpretation of Scripture. Lord Barrington wrote much in vindication of dissent and of civil and religious liberty. Strong testimony to the influence of Locke in the formation of his opinions is borne by his son Shute Barrington, the Bishop of Durham*. The 'Miscellanea Sacra' were published in 1725. In the same year, James Peirce, of Exeter, dedicated to the nephew of Locke, Sir Peter King (who was in that year created Lord Chancellor, with the title of Baron of Ockham), his Paraphrase and Notes on the Epistles to the Colossians, Philippians, and Hebrews, after the manner

* See the Life prefixed to the edition edited by the Rev. George Townsend, p. xx.

of Mr. Locke. This was followed by Dr. Benson's
work on the remaining Epistles, to Philemon, to the
Thessalonians, to Timothy, and Titus, in 1734; and
by Benson's history of the first planting the Christian
religion in 1735. An edition of Dr. Taylor's work on
the Romans came forth in 1745. Its invaluable key
to the Apostolic writings was wisely placed by Bishop
Watson, in his excellent collection of theological tracts,
in company with some of the works of Locke, Barrington, and Hartley. But one learned dissenting divine,
the celebrated Dr. Isaac Watts,—who made great,
though not always wise, use of Locke's philosophical
writings in his Logic, and his little work on the Improvement of the Mind, much praised by Dr. Johnson,—represents Locke in heaven as repenting of
this work on Paul; and the poetical divine concludes
some verses on this subject by making the philosopher exclaim,

> "Eternal darkness veil the lines
>   Of that unhappy book,
> Where glimmering reason with false lustre shines,
>   Where the mortal pen mistook
>   What the celestial meant!"

These lines however were written in Watts's earlier
days. He lived to nearly the middle of the eighteenth century, dying in 1748; and in his age would
probably have looked back with the greatest satisfaction to the lines, full of praise and admiration, addressed to John Shute, afterwards Lord Barrington,
'On Locke's dangerous Sickness some time after

he had retired to study the Scriptures,' dated June,
1704.

> And must the man of wondrous mind
> (Now his rich thoughts are just refined)
>   Forsake our longing eyes?
> Reason at length submits to wear
> The wings of Faith; and lo, they rear
> Her chariot high, and nobly bear
>   Her prophet to the skies.

We have now seen that in the philosophy of the
mind, of government, of education, and of the connection between natural and revealed religion, Locke
stands far above all his predecessors after the revival
of letters; and further, that he prepared the way for
whatever additions have been made since his day to
our knowledge of the human mind, of the principles
of moral and political philosophy, and to the rational
criticism of the Scriptures. We have shown what are
his real merits, and his chief defects; and this is essential, not only to the just appreciation of the admirable
philosopher himself, but, what is of more importance, to
an estimate of the present condition of the science of
mind and morals, and to any well-founded expectations
of the progress of mankind in self-knowledge, which is
the instrument of self-government and improvement,
and in the virtues and habits which are the best security for social happiness. He therefore is scarcely
worthy of the name of Englishman,—he can have no
proper sense of the value of the literature and institutions of his country, who does not assign to Locke a
place in the first rank among the instructors and be-

nefactors of his species. There Barry has placed him, conspicuous among his great compeers, in that admirable but little estimated production of England's art—the large picture of Elysium, which adorns the room of the Society of Arts in the Adelphi, a picture which renders heaven inviting by the noble society which it assembles, and which awakens the rapture of confidence and hope in connection with the assurance of the poet—

> " Yet there the soul shall enter which hath earned
> That privilege by virtue*."

We now come to the important question, what has been done since Locke's time, and by whom, to advance our knowledge of the laws of thought?

Hartley.—In the later editions of Locke's Essay appeared a chapter on Association, a term not originating with Locke, but significant with him of a certain number of facts,—such as the connection of ideas with sensations, which he thought particularly worthy of attention in the study of the mind. He applied it to explain some of the remarkable peculiarities in the temper and habits of individuals; and that in this light only or chiefly he viewed the law of association is evident from the posthumous work on the Conduct of the Understanding, where he enlarges somewhat upon it. Thus in the Essay he dwells on what is odd and extravagant in the opinions of men; on a sort of madness to which the minds of some are subject from wrong connections of ideas; on darkness bringing with it the

* Wordsworth's Laodamia.

2 G

ideas of goblins and sprites; on custom " settling habits
of thinking in the understanding, as well as of determining in the will, and of motions in the body; all
which seems to be but trains of motion in the animal
spirits, which once set agoing, continue in the same
steps they have been used to." He intimates however
that some of our ideas have a *natural correspondence
and connection* one with another; that it is the office
and excellency of our reason to trace these; and that
those who have children, or the charge of their education, should diligently watch and carefully prevent the
undue connection of ideas in the minds of young people. " Though I have (he observes, § 41 of the Conduct of the Understanding), in the second book of my
Essay concerning human understanding, treated of the
association of ideas, yet having done it there historically, giving a view of the understanding in this as
well as its several other ways of operating, rather than
designing there to inquire into the remedies that ought
to be applied to it, it will under this latter consideration afford other matter of thought to those who have
a mind to instruct themselves thoroughly in the right
way of conducting their understandings; and that the
rather, because this, if I mistake not, is as frequent a
cause of mistake and error in us, as perhaps anything
else that can be named; and is a disease of the mind
as hard to be cured as any, it being a very hard thing
to convince any one that things are not so, and naturally so, as they constantly appear to him."

It had been well had Locke pursued the inquiry

into the natural and rational connections and correspondence of ideas.   He however caught but a dim
view of the influence of custom in forming the mind
and character towards the close of his meditations.

It was reserved for the great and good Dr. Hartley
to follow up the inquiry, and to demonstrate the entire
dependence of the phenomena of language, and consequently of reasoning, upon the principle of association, and to show the immense influence of that principle upon all the affections and habits, the emotions
and passions, of our active and moral nature, of which
the love of money and the desire of reputation and
glory afford the most obvious instances and proofs.
Among those who affect a knowledge of the philosophy
of mind, hardly one can be found who disowns altogether the vast importance of this principle of association ; but very few recognize the full extent of it ; still
fewer are disposed to do justice to Hartley in developing the theory.   The injustice of the Scotch school
to his merits, the bitterness of Stewart in connection
with his memory and name, are unaccountable. Even
the English school of metaphysics, so far as it is represented by some of the modern utilitarians, if Mill's
analysis of the human mind may be considered a
standard, has cast only dark shadows over the remains
of the sweet-tempered philosopher whose religious
faith and anticipations that school would hold in
scorn.

The dissertation by Gay, of Sidney College, Cambridge, of whose studies and life unfortunately little

can now be recovered*, appended to Law's translation
of King ' On the Origin of Evil,' further suggested
the possibility of accounting for almost all the com-
plicated phenomena of the human mind, its powers
and dispositions, by the principle of association. In
that dissertation Mr. Gay had observed, that " our
approbation of morality and all affections whatsoever
are finally resolvable into reason pointing out *private
happiness,* and are conversant only about things ap-
prehended to be means tending to this end; and that
whenever this end is not perceived, they are to be accounted for from the *association of ideas,* and may
properly enough be called habits." It was in opposition to Francis Hutcheson's theory of a moral sense,
who published his Inquiry into the original of our
Ideas of Beauty and Virtue in 1726, that Gay sent
forth his dissertation. But his observations amount
to little more than conjectures†.

The following are among the important propositions which Hartley has demonstrated :—1, that sensations leave traces of themselves in the mind, such as
are called simple ideas of sensation; 2, that it is the
tendency of simple ideas to run into complex ones by
means of association; 3, that voluntary and semivoluntary motions are deducible from association, the

---

* "Our Bishop (*i. e.* Law) always spoke of this gentleman in terms
of the greatest respect. In the Bible, and in the writings of Mr.
Locke, no man, he used to say, was so well versed. Law calls him
' honest Mr. Gay.' "—Nichols' Literary Anecdotes, vol. ii. pp. 66, 535.

† See the second of the valuable Introductory Essays prefixed to
Priestley's Abridgment of Hartley, 1775, p. xxii.

voluntary being sometimes converted by association into automatic, the automatic into voluntary ; 4, that compound or mental pleasures and pains arise from simple bodily ones by means of words, symbols, and associated circumstances ; 5, that the arts of logic and rational grammar depend entirely on association ; 6, and that our passions and affections can be no more than aggregates of simple ideas united by association. The bearing of these important truths upon all mental and even physical science, upon the principles of religion and morality, upon education and the whole discipline of life, must strike the minds of the thoughtful and inquisitive at once ; but their importance can be fully appreciated only by the diligent study of Dr. Hartley himself, who has pursued his theory with a patience and caution, an exactness and consistency, unequalled by any other metaphysical writer. He has examined, in a manner worthy of the subject and a great philosopher, the agreement of the phenomena of sensation generally, that is to say, of taste, sight, smell, hearing, and touch, of muscular motion, intoxication, disease, sleep, dreams, and other conditions of our bodily frame, with his doctrine of vibrations and of the generation and association of ideas. By these he has explained, in a rational and clear manner, the formation of the passions and affections in all their complexness, as we find them in actual and social life. He has divided our intellectual affections, that is, our intellectual pleasures and pains, into six classes ; namely, those of imagination, ambition, self-interest, sympathy, theopathy, and the moral sense. All these classes have their minor subdivisions. They all presuppose the existence and continuance of pleasures and pains of mere sensation, from which all take their rise. Although the classification may not be considered quite satisfactory, nor the order in which he has handled them the most natural, no approach had been made before Hartley's time to a more convenient or philosophical division and classification of the phenomena. It assigns a place for every important principle or truth which concerns our individual and social improvement and happiness.

The only other moralist who has attempted a scientific and practical catalogue, an exact, careful, and useful division of our pleasures and pains, is Bentham. According to Bentham, the several simple pleasures of which human nature is susceptible are these:—1, the pleasures of sense; 2, of wealth; 3, of skill; 4, of amity; 5, of a good name; 6, of power; 7, of piety; 8, of benevolence; 9, of malevolence; 10, of memory; 11, of imagination; 12, of expectation; 13, those dependent on association; 14, of relief.

Bentham's remarks on morals must be judged of in connection with his purpose. He had in view chiefly the principles of legislation and the objects and duties of the legislator. He therefore touches but incidentally on the formation of a rule of life, or the maxims which should govern private behaviour, and which he calls private ethics. These rules or maxims he considers dependent upon those particular conditions of

age, sex, health, social connections and relations, property, etc., which are so variable as almost to baffle
classification and enumeration. Hence, while he contends that pleasures are valuable in proportion to their
duration, their intensity, their security, their fecun-
dity, and their purity, he leaves his reader without
means of judging how far, in his opinion or in truth,
the pleasures of amity, of benevolence, of the moral
sense, and of religion, admitting the last to coincide
with those of utility and of enlightened benevolence,
are more durable, more pure, more fertile than the
simple pleasures of the senses. Nor is his account
and division of the several pleasures very satisfactory.
From his catalogue we might strike out, with advantage, the pleasures of malevolence. For malevolence
can only arise from the recollection of past, or the anticipation of future suffering; and if we are ever malevolent, if we really wish evil to another sentient being,
it must be on the ground of some associated good—
of a remedy for an evil past—or, since the past is
irrevocable, the prevention of a like evil in time to
come. On a close examination of his classes it will
be found that they run much into each other in the
manner which Hartley has beautifully shown. Thus
Bentham speaks of the pleasures of novelty excited by
the appearance of new ideas, which he calls, at one
time, pleasures of the imagination; but he tells us at
another, they may be excited by the appearance of sensible objects. And we may have novelty in odours,
tastes, shades of colour, and forms of beauty, which

are pleasures of the senses. He speaks of the pleasures of imagination produced by association. But
all the pleasures of wealth, of piety, of memory, imagination, and expectation resolve themselves into cases
of association, which cannot therefore be made a distinct class. He also identifies the pleasures of amity
with those of honour and the moral sense; and the
connection no doubt is very close. But if the moral
sense be a compound of our opinions respecting the
value or lawfulness of pleasures and the guide to their
enjoyment, its pleasures resolve themselves into self-ap-
proval or amity. They must spring from a consciousness of acting ourselves, or from observing others to
act, in conformity with our rule.

In this respect Hartley has a great advantage. He
not only leads the individual to aspire, but points the
way, and builds the steps by which he may ascend.
He proves that the pleasures of the senses, the most
innocent and allowable, are subordinate to the development, and become enhanced by the pursuit, of the
pleasures of sympathy, of imagination, of the intellect,
and of the moral sense; that the pleasures of sensation, imagination, of the intellect, of ambition, require
to be regulated by a regard to the moral sense; and
that the moral sense itself is purified and perfected by
theopathy, that is, by the precepts of piety or the love
of God. " For the perpetual exertion of a pleasing
affection towards a Being infinite in power, knowledge,
and goodness, who is also our friend and father, cannot but enhance all our joys and alleviate all our sor-

rows; the sense of his presence and protection will restrain all actions that are excessive, irregular, or hurtful; support and encourage us in all such as are of a contrary nature; and infuse such peace and tranquillity of mind, as will enable us to see clearly and act uniformly. The perfection, therefore, of every part of our natures must depend upon the love of God, and the constant comfortable sense of his presence.

" With respect to benevolence, or the love of our neighbour, it may be observed, that this can never be free from partiality and selfishness, till we take our station in the divine nature, and view everything from thence, and in the relation which it bears to God."

Now if there be any ground for believing in the existence of an intelligent Creator and governor of the universe, infinite in power, and willing the happiness of his creatures, these views of duty and rational self-interest are demonstrably just. But they are alien from the views and speculations of the political utilitarian school, who, if they do not expressly renounce and systematically argue down the sublime pleasures of the religious sense or sanction, evidently treat them as purely visionary, irrational, and impossible. Perhaps they habitually conceive of religion in the light of a dangerous, pernicious, and malignant fanaticism and superstition.

I conceive that Bentham, in whatever he has of valuable truth, and he has much,—for who can read his sixth chapter, on the circumstances influencing sensibility, without being wiser and better?—in his analysis of motives and his classification of pleasures and pains was far more indebted to Hartley and his school, perhaps than he was aware of, certainly than he has acknowledged. He refers indeed to Priestley's edition of Hartley for a very satisfactory account, upon the principle of association, of the phenomena and influence of habit. But Hartley's rule of life was not included in Priestley's edition, and to the complete work I have not found an allusion in Bentham. He acknowledges that he took his favourite principle of the greatest happiness of the greatest number from Priestley's Essay on Government, in 1768, or from Beccaria, whom he calls "an angel of light." He seems not to have been aware that he was perfectly anticipated in his view of the sanctions of morality by Gay, in the dissertation often alluded to*.

* It is remarkable that Dr. Whewell, in his recent History of Moral Philosophy, has not even mentioned the name of Hartley, though he has devoted many lectures to Bentham's morals and legislation. Dr. Whewell gives two reasons why we cannot make *the truth*, "that actions are right and virtuous in proportion as they promote the happiness of mankind," the basis of morality; first, "we cannot calculate *all* the consequences of any action; second, happiness is derived from moral elements, and therefore we cannot properly derive morality from happiness." I submit, in reply, first, that we calculate, as much as we can; that it is by such calculation only we arrive at or justify general rules; that in the most important steps of life, and where we have no rules, or very imperfect rules, as in the use of superfluous wealth, in the choice of a profession—of a dwelling—of companions or society, of relaxations, we always act upon such calculation of consequences as is within our power. He that is habitually reckless of consequences is in danger of being habitually immoral or a vicious fool. Secondly, what is meant by moral elements? Dr. Whewell uses morality in a double

The merits of Hartley, his most important views and propositions, with the facts and arguments adduced in support of them, have been systematically ignored by most of those who even in England have treated of the same subjects after him, and ventured criticisms on his system.   Of this I shall adduce striking instances, while I show the true relation in which some of the more eminent later metaphysicians, such as James Mill, Brown, Adam Smith, Alison, Paley, and Tucker, stand to Hartley.

Thus James Mill prefaces the chapter on the Association of Ideas, in his Analysis of the Mind, with a quotation from Brown's Lectures ; yet he took from

sense,—at one time as an epithet for the actions or *mores* of men; at another, for a system of rules to be applied to those actions. His argument appears to be, that because happiness is derived from human actions—therefore the consideration of that happiness can furnish us with no rules, can be no sufficient criterion of the worth of some acts, the worthlessness of others. The inference should be precisely the contrary. In another sentence he takes the term virtue in two or more senses : at one time it seems the name of an act in itself; at another, for a rule of action, or the conformity of that act to a rule ; and at another, for a portion of the happiness resulting from an act, " *one of the things determining happiness.*"

Dr. Whewell appears not to have read the answers given by Mr. Austin, in his ' Province of Jurisprudence,' to the old and oft-repeated objections to the principle of utility and the difficulties attending it. And he applies to such a system as Rutherforth's the epithets low and lax and poor.   Are there fewer difficulties attending any other system ? To whose system will he give the names of high and strict and rich ? From whose system will he hope to derive a greater number of acts beneficial to mankind, or more strength and fervour of benevolent effort and disposition ? The philosopher and Christian will welcome the system, be it whose it may.

Hartley its chief matter*. From Hartley came the important distinction of the two cases of association, the *synchronous* and the *successive*. From Hartley came the principle that the causes of strength in association are two—the vividness of the associated feelings, and the frequency of the association ; and that simple ideas run into complex ones by means of association. He has mentioned Dr. Hartley, at the close of his chapter, as calling the union of two complex ideas into one by the name of a duplex idea; but I have not found the word duplex in Hartley. What Hartley lays down in the fourth corollary of his twelfth proposition is, that " as simple ideas run into complex ones by association, so complex ideas run into decomplex ones by the same; but here the varieties of the associations, which increase with the complexity, hinder particular ones from being so close and permanent between the complex parts of decomplex ideas, as between the simple parts of complex parts of complex ones : to which it is analogous in languages, that the letters of words adhere closer together than the words of sentences, both in writing and speaking." Mr. Mill's subsequent chapters on naming, on classification, memory, belief, and ratiocination are all founded on Hartleian principles, and coloured with Hartleian language; but without any acknowledgment of obligation to that great author, whose chapters on words and the ideas associated with them, may be justly considered the basis of all accurate metaphysical study.

* Compare Hartley's Tenth Propos. with Mill's Analysis, p. 53.

Dr. Brown, himself one of the best investigators of the mind among the Scotch, devoted many of his Lectures to the phenomena of what he calls simple and relative suggestion; " of these two *orders of feelings,* and these alone," he says, " consists the whole varied tissue of our trains of thought*." The author whom he seems to consider as worthy of most attention for his classification of the associate feelings is Mr. Hume, to whom the philosophers of his own country are accustomed to refer.   But Hume knew comparatively nothing of the nature and importance of the law of association.   In a criticism on Dr. Hartley (43rd Lecture), Brown acknowledges that there is considerable acuteness displayed in his work, that it contains some successful analyses of complex feelings, and that it has been of service in promoting a spirit of inquiry. He asserts however that the advantage has been inconsiderable compared with the great evil which has flowed from it, by leading the inquirer to acquiesce in remote analogies and to adopt explanations and arrangements of the phenomena of mind, not as they agree with the actual phenomena, but as they chance to agree with some supposed phenomena of our material part.   Of this evil he has adduced no instance. He has not condescended to quote with care a single sentence of Hartley, nor adduced an example of such a misled inquirer.   He has chosen to represent the hypothesis of vibrations as merely Hartley's; but the

* Dr. Brown's ' Lectures on the Philosophy of the Mind,' from 34th to 52nd.

truth is, that the suggestion, as it emanated from Sir
Isaac Newton, had produced on the students of human
nature, before Hartley's time, a far deeper impression
than any but minute and careful inquirers into the
history of metaphysical speculations would suppose.
I gather this from a remarkable passage in Dr. John
Clarke's work on the Origin of Evil, and incidental observations in other authors*.

* " The seat of sensation is in the brain. In order therefore to
perception, it is necessary that the particular motions excited by
external objects should be conveyed thither ; which make different
impressions, or raise different ideas in the mind, as they are propagated by a different medium or through different senses. Thus, to
produce vision it is necessary that the object be capable of reflecting rays of light, and that those rays also should be capable of being
reflected ; that they may be thrown upon the eye ; and the same may
be said of refraction likewise, that they may meet to form the image
at the bottom of the eye. Hence it is that the eye is composed of
different humours, having different degrees of the power proportioned
to the distance. It is also necessary that the rays of light should be
very small, that they may freely pass through those humours : yet
that they should be of different bigness and shape, to excite different
sorts of colours by their *vibrations*. After this manner the images
of external objects are conveyed to the bottom of the eye, from
whence they are carried along through the optic nerve to the sensorium, and are there taken notice of by the mind ; in order to effect
which it is necessary also that these vibrations should be continued
along those nerves, which are therefore compounded of solid, uniform, and transparent *capillaments* containing a medium proper for
that purpose. In the same manner are sounds likewise excited by
the different vibrations of the air, in the same proportion as those of
light, and carried to the sensorium by the auditory nerves. These
are all subject to particular laws, the least alteration or disturbance
of which immediately creates a proportionable disorder or confusion."—Dr. John Clarke's Enquiry into the Origin of Evil, vol. i.
pp. 250–252. 1722.

Had Brown taken his view of the doctrine of Association from Hartley's statements, he would not have said that the term was limited to those states of mind which are exclusively denominated " *ideas ;* " and " that this has deprived us of the aid which we might have received from it in the analysis of many of the most complex phenomena;" nor would he have proposed to drop the term association, to make way for that of suggestion.   Dr. Hartley had shown at large before him that every sensation possible to the human frame may by association enter into our more complex emotions, and " that the influence of the associating principle extends not to ideas only, but to every species of affection of which the human mind is susceptible."

Dr. Brown, like a racer bolting from the course, instead of bending his efforts steadily towards the goal, breaks away into the regions of poetry and rhetoric, and dazzles us with the splendours of Virgil, and Cicero, and Seneca, and Akenside, when his reader is anxious to consult the simple phenomena of his own mind, or to listen reverently to the oracles of nature and of truth.

Thus the question, "what are the general circumstances which regulate the succession of our ideas? what the primary and secondary laws of simple and relative suggestion ?"—a question propounded in the 34th—is not answered till we come to the 37th Lecture of his volume.   The remarks on these laws, however just, are perfectly familiar to the Hartleian.   Though he has not told us very distinctly what the primary laws of suggestion, founded on the mere relations of objects or feelings to each other, are, he gives the name of secondary laws to those operations which account for the variety in the effects of the former. The occasional suggestions that flow from the primary are various, according as the original feelings have been, 1st, of longer or shorter continuance; 2, more or less lively; 3, of more or less frequent occurrence; 4, more or less recent; 5, more or less pure from the occasional and varying mixture of other feelings; 6, according to differences of original constitution; 7, according to differences of temporary emotion; 8, according to changes produced in the state of the body; 9, according to general tendencies produced by prior habits. In the 45th Lecture, following Hartley, without acknowledgment, he arranges the phenomena of relative suggestion under the two orders of coexistence and succession.

He proposes to drop the term *association* to make way for that of *suggestion;* but the suggestion has not been adopted because the terms had been already appropriated to their respective meanings. Association expresses the primary fact. Before one object, sensation, or idea can suggest another, they must have been previously experienced in company; that is, there must be a previous association binding them together in order of time or place. It is remarkable that Brown has not dwelt on the phenomena of language, on the suggestion of ideas by words, to illustrate the importance of the law of association. Yet he has made great use of the principle throughout his volume, in explaining every important faculty—whether conception, memory, imagination, or reasoning;—and every natural or acquired emotion, immediate, prospective, or retrospective;—and every complex notion, such as those which we form of matter and resistance. He has made use of it when contending, in opposition to Dr. Reid, who calls perception " a *peculiar mental faculty*," that " perception, in its relation to our original sensations of touch, as much as in relation to the immediate feelings which we derive from smell, taste, sight, and hearing, is only one of the many operations of the suggesting or associating principle." He tells us that " of the influence of association on the moral character of man, the whole history of our race, when we compare the vices and virtues of ages and nations with each other, is but one continued though varied display." He illustrates its influence at great length and with great beauty of sentiment and language in " the moral inspiration of parental love," in the force and direction given to the passion of ambition. He might have found a familiar instance of its power in the passion for money, and its intensity in the habits of the miser. While going over all this ground he has not adverted to the investigations of the great Hartley, whose principles he was indeed confirming, but whose facts in illustration of the principle are more numerous and more impressive, and whose deductions and methods are more simple, more logical, more convincing. Is there

2 H

anything in Brown equal in value to this single corollary of Hartley*? "It is of the utmost consequence to morality and religion, that the affections
and passions should be analysed into their simple
compounding parts by reversing the steps of the associations which concur to form them. For thus we
may learn how to cherish and improve good ones,
check and root out such as are mischievous and immoral, and how to suit our manner of life, in some
tolerable measure, to our moral and religious wants.
And as this holds in respect of persons of all ages, so
it is particularly true and worthy of consideration in
respect of children and youth. The world is indeed
sufficiently stocked with general precepts for this purpose, grounded on experience; and whosoever will
follow these faithfully may expect general good success. However, the doctrine of association, when
traced up to the first rudiments of understanding and
affection, unfolds such a scene as cannot fail both to
instruct and alarm all such as have any degree of interested concern for themselves or of a benevolent one
for others. It ought to be added, that the doctrine of
association explains also the rise and progress of those
voluntary and semivoluntary powers which we exert
over our ideas, affections, and bodily motions (as I
shall show hereafter), and by so doing this teaches us
how to regulate and improve these powers." Hartley
afterwards shows in a most instructive and philosophical manner, by the power of using the hand and

* Compare Brown, Lecture 25, and Hartley, Props. xi. and xxi.

the legs gradually acquired by children, of producing
intelligent sounds, of speaking and writing, and by a
variety of other instances, that the voluntary and semivoluntary motions are deducible from association, and
"that it will be found upon a careful and impartial inquiry that the motions which occur every day in common life, and which follow the idea called the will
immediately or mediately, do this (*i.e.* do occur and
do follow) in proportion to the number and degree of
strength in the associations." This is true, and one of
the most important and suggestive truths connected
with the structure and laws of the mind. It furnishes the real clue to the explanation of character and
habit. It suggests the proper methods for self-disci-
pline and improvement, and for the discipline and improvement of others. Every object in life confirms its
truth. The rod of the schoolmaster, the sceptre of the
sovereign, the ermine of the judge and the lawn of the
priest, the cradle of the infant and the grave of the
philosopher, the dungeon and the church, the charge
to the jury and the sermon of the preacher, owe their
influence entirely to the force and character of the associations; and every habit and propensity illustrate
the law of association, from those of the epicure and
the anchorite to those of the saint and the philanthropist.

One very elegant production of an English divine
settled in Edinburgh deserves mention in connection
with the history and nature of the doctrine of association,—' Essays on Taste,' by Archibald Alison, father

of the modern historian. Alison seems to have considered Dugald Stewart as the writer who gave the
bias to his speculations; and with the unfailing practice of the coteries of Edinburgh, Adam Smith lauds
Alison and Alison lauds Smith. He has not mentioned the name of Hartley, but he has proved that
our emotions of the beauty and sublimity of the material world and of the human countenance and form are
resolvable into cases of association; and in the same
manner he might have proved, what he has only suggested, that our emotions of moral beauty and sublimity, our moral sentiments of every kind, are entirely
resolvable into the operation of the same great law,
namely, the law of sensible pleasures and pains passing gradually into intellectual and moral ones. The
Essays of Alison are a charming illustration of the
truth of the Hartleian chapters relating to imagination
and to sympathy.

Whatever is correct in Adam Smith's 'Theory of
Moral Sentiments,' a work of earlier date, deserving
much attention, easily falls in with the Hartleian theory. For what is that power of sympathy, of throwing ourselves into the situation of another, imagining
the feelings of others, and supposing ourselves spectators of our own conduct, but the renewal of the trains
of association,—but the application of notions and feelings, already gotten by experience, to new junctures
as they arise? The theory is obviously inadequate
for an explanation of all the phenomena of our moral
life, and for the formation of a wise rule. By making

present or popular sentiments the test of right and wrong, it affords no provision for the elevation and improvement of the popular standard of right.   It will not bear a close examination, since the sympathies of men with each other, and their no less real and important antipathies, are dependent on their educations, habits, interests, connections, tastes, society, party, and professed religion. But the book, full as it is of inconsistencies, of ill-considered and incorrect expressions, illustrates the value of one of the elements in forming the rule of life, namely, the common sentiments of mankind; and when it tells us that actions *of a beneficent tendency,* which proceed from proper motives, seem alone to require a reward; actions *of a hurtful tendency* seem alone to deserve punishment, it points in the right direction, and grows into harmony with the soundest and most thoughtful philosophy.

When we compare such writers as Locke, Cumberland, Law, Butler, Hartley, Tucker, Paley, Austin, and even Bentham together, we perceive them to agree in the following fundamental principles :—that the will of God is the fountain of moral obligation ; that the tendency of actions to ultimate happiness is an index to the tacit commands of God, or the chief guide to the knowledge of His will; that the Deity wills the happiness of his creatures, therefore the means of that happiness, therefore virtue, which is the employment of the means ; that the dictates of natural and revealed religion, and the dictates of right reason and the principles of utility, suggest the same rule of life, and coalesce in their instruction; that rational and refined self-interest, and the truths or principles of religion, natural and revealed, point to one and the same course of life, to the culture of the same private and public affections, the discharge of the same social obligations and duties; or, what is the same thing, the pursuit of the same end, namely, the happiness of mankind.

I have classed Butler with Paley, Law, and Hartley, that is, with those who may be called the religious utilitarians. He is not commonly considered of that school. But there is no substantial difference as to facts or principles. Repeated perusal has satisfied me that Butler is perfectly utilitarian, substantially Hartleian. He has not accounted nor attempted to account for the facts in the same way. He has not traced, with care and exactness, the phenomena of human affections to their ultimate principles or laws. He has not gone so deeply into the origin and formation of the several affections and moral feelings, nor deduced the rules of life with the same care and precision. His language is more vague and less consistent; still there is a harmony in general views and results. Examine, for instance, his three first sermons on Human Nature. He lays down what no one disputes, or is worth disputing with if he does, that (1.) " there is such a thing, in some degree, as real good-will in man to man ;" (2.) " that the several passions and affections contribute to public good as really as to private ;" (3.) " that there is a *principle of reflection* in men, by which they approve or disapprove their own actions;" " that conscience is this principle of reflection." These are the three points established in his first sermon; but he talks in it of self-love, as if there were an affection for self independent of, and distinct from, the particular gratifications and pleasures sought for, and of men violating their nature, as if their nature did not include everything done and every thought of the mind; as if propensities to evil were not as natural as propensities to good, forgetting the theology which teaches that propensities to evil alone are natural.   The second sermon is less happy, owing to this unadvised use of the terms nature and self-love.   The attempt to show the natural supremacy and sacred authority of conscience seems partly superfluous, since the subordination of other principles, passions, and motives of action, its office as regulator, is assumed in the definition or notion of it; and partly unsatisfactory, since, if conscience be but the principle of reflection, applied to our conduct, to actions, their motives, and their consequences, if the reflection turns on the conformity of actions to the rule, which is their rightness; the question, how we come by the rule, and what or who gives it authority, remains unanswered.

A similar error pervades the third sermon.   There is no value in the phrase of " man being a law to himself," every man being at liberty, and feeling himself at liberty, except where some law, the dictate of a power superior, restrains him.   However, in the con-

clusion of the whole argument which he is insisting
upon, Butler is eminently utilitarian, and as much an
advocate for a so-called selfish system in his view of
the foundation and end of morals, as Bentham himself.   Thus he says, " Conscience and self-love, *if we
understand our true happiness*, always lead us the
same way.   *Duty* and *interest* are perfectly coincident,
for the most part, in this world; but entirely and in
every instance, if we take in the future and the whole,
this being implied in the notion of a good and perfect
administration of things."   The concluding sermons
upon the love of our neighbour, the love of God, and the
ignorance of man, are in perfect and beautiful accordance with the Hartleian theory and principles; but they
are far less clear and determinate in their directions,
less full and abundant in their suggestions as to the
means and methods of improving the temper and
making the heart better, and " avoiding that general
wrong frame of mind, from which all the mistaken
pursuits and far the greatest part of the unhappi-
ness of life proceeds."   " He who should find out one
rule to assist us in this work, would deserve infinitely better of mankind than all the improvers of
other knowledge put together."   Now Hartley has
found out many rules, and his merits in this respect
are supreme.

I shall not touch at length upon Paley.   There is
little evidence of reading or of deep thought in his
' Moral and Political Philosophy.'   His clear forcible
style has done more for his popularity and influence than

his principles or arguments.   Tucker's ' Light of Nature ' was his favourite book.   Now Tucker's philosophy
is, with some exceptions, a sort of diluted Hartleianism.
Its loose and rambling method makes it rather painful than satisfactory to the logical reader, however
amusing and suggestive for an hour of vacancy.

If the most important phenomena of the mind and
the best portions of the best writers are comparatively
neglected, even among the few who, in England, may
be thought to have paid most attention to mental and
moral science, still less can the *literati* of Gemany
and France be supposed to know what is most valuable in the English masters.

In the scarce Latin tract by Hartley, reprinted in
the volume of ' Metaphysicians of the Eighteenth
Century ' prepared by Dr. Parr, there is a passage so
remarkable for its wisdom, that I cannot but sum up
and enforce the matter of these pages with truth so
valuable.   While it points to the quarter whence light
may be expected, it prophesies the darkness that must
continue till that light shall dawn.   Had not the English metaphysician been driven from his rightful place
of estimation by unhappy prejudices, hastily taken
up and sedulously propagated, the history of mental
science would have been brighter, its study more
agreeable, and the culture of it far more fruitful.   In
the translation, I drop the few phrases relating to vibrations, as not necessary to the principle.

" The doctrine of Association moreover is absolutely
necessary to form a true logic.   Nor will it be suffi-

cient for this purpose, that attention be given only to associations formed in mature life. We must attend to them in their very cradles. We must investigate, with the greatest care, the impressions and ideas which are joined by custom with single words and sentences, and thus at length arrive at a right determination concerning the nature of the ideas affixed to words, and the assent and dissent which are connected with propositions. When these things are physiologically treated, new light will forthwith dawn on the arts of thinking and discoursing. All are agreed in exclaiming with one voice, that the advancement of science is most impeded by the ambiguities and overwhelming mass of words; and that the strifes of the learned are, with scarcely an exception, nothing but vain logomachies. It is to be desired therefore, that the nature and use of words being carefully sifted, the useless be thrown aside, the vague be limited, and that the sciences themselves be advanced by tools more simple and more adapted for use. Now here the doctrine of Association, unless I greatly err, will afford excellent aid, and will conduce most powerfully, as well to root out altogether prejudiced opinions, as to build up the sciences in solid form, and to free them from the sophistries and subtleties of sceptics*."

* " Doctrina porro Associationis ad veram logicem condendam omnino necessaria est. Neque satis erit in hunc finem, ut quis persequatur associationes ætate maturâ factas. Ordiendum est ab ipsis incunabulis. Perquirendum accuratissimæ quænam Impressiones et Ideæ, i. e. vibrationes et vibratiunculæ cum singulis vocibus et sententiis usitato conjungantur; et sic demum rectè statuetur de na-

When we open a ' Critic,' or pretended examination
and analysis of the pure reason, and find such expressions as the *amphiboly* and *antinomy* of reason ; ' *external* and *internal intuition;*' 'analytical cognitions
à priori,' 'synthetical cognitions *à posteriori ;*' or when
opening Schelling's 'Transcendental Idealism,' we
stumble at the threshold on such a sentiment as " that
all knowledge consists in the agreement of the objective with the subjective;" a repetition of language
which we find in Norris's ' Intelligible World,' and by
him probably borrowed from the later Platonizing
schoolmen, and which means either the agreement of
ideas with realities, or has no meaning ;—when a peculiar knowledge of the mind, some rare insight into
its darkest recesses, is conceived to lie hid under such
phraseology, yet, after the closest attention, no new
facts, no principles in harmony with the rest of our
thoughts and feelings, capable of application to the

turâ Idearum vocibus affixarum, assensusque et dissensus, qui pro-
positionibus adhibentur. His autem physiologicè tractatis, novum
lumen protinus accedet artibus cogitandi et disserendi. Cordati
omnes uno ore clamant, augmentum scientiarum quam maximè im-
pediri verborum ambiguitatibus, et mole obruente ; litesque eruditorum fere universas esse nil nisi logomachias inanes. Optandum
est itaque, ut verborum naturâ et usu diligenter excussis, abjici-
antur inutilia, limitentur vaga, scientiæque ipsæ apparatu simpli-
ciore, et ad praxin accommodatiore, instruantur. Egregiam vero
hic operam præstabit, ni fallor, Doctrina Associationis, qualis à doctrina vibrationum nasci suprà ostensa est, simulque magnoperè con-
ducet, tum ad radices præjudicatarum opinionum penitus extirpandas,
tum ad scientias solidè ædificandas, expediendasque a Scepticorum
implicationibus et argutiis."

conduct of the understanding, suited to the wants
and business of life, can be discovered, it is evident
that we are driven back upon such truth as Hartley
expresses.   We are compelled to acknowledge that
the study of words, their etymology, their natural history, so to speak, as a guide to the associated sensations and ideas, must constitute one chief portion of
mental philosophy.   The English metaphysicians and
logicians alone appear to feel this.   Mr. De Morgan,
in his ' Formal Logic,' rightly conceives that the ultimate elements of logic lie wrapt up in whatever sound
truth can be arrived at respecting the relations of objects, ideas, and names.

    In regard to the common terms of logic, a refer-
ence to etymology readily suggests their appropriate
meaning.   Take the words, subject, copula, predi-
cate, premiss major and minor, proposition, analytic,
synthetic, conclusion, de-monstrate, e-vidence, in-fer-
ence, de-duction, in-duction; the scholar, knowing
their derivation from the Greek or Latin, easily discerns their meaning and the reason for their use.   It
is observable that almost all the terms common in
metaphysical books, significant of mental operations
and conditions, are of Latin or Greek origin.   Such
are sensation, perception, conception, conscious, conscience, with its associates and derivatives, abstraction,
intuition, imagination, fancy, memory, association, suggestion, attention, observation, apprehension, volition,
comprehension, discernment, recollection, etc.   For
the organs and operations of sense we have short

emphatic words, such as eye, head, ear, nose, smell, taste; and for the strong emotions and passions, such as love, hate, joy, grief, woe, which come to us generally more from the Saxon element of our language; although the connection even of these with the Latin is, in many cases, easily traceable; but for the abstractions of the mind, for what we may call the conditions and laws of thought, we have only such long classical terms as the above.   Now the so-called mental philosophers have turned for the most part to the mind itself, selecting arbitrarily its more obscure phenomena in order to fasten on these terms a meaning more precise than that of common use, and often inconsistent with it.   But if terms were used without much precision, loosely and interchangeably, by the writers from whom they have descended, such as Cicero and Plato, how vain seems the effort to seek for nicer distinction in later days and to hope that any distinction will be habitually observed!   How idle seems the attempt to assign to the mind as many distinct faculties, with separate functions and operations, as there are compound terms of Latin origin to express its complex affections and associations!   How much better to turn to etymology to find easy definitions, and meanings more accordant with the common acceptation, which meanings were likely to flow as by a kind of legitimate authority from the first examples, as a slight acquaintance with etymology teaches.   It is true that many terms come in time to change their meaning, and scarcely a trace of the original application is left in the adopted and existing sense. But this is less the case with terms of scientific use and with the compounds of classical origin than with words of constant application in the familiar uses and changing customs of common life, such as gate, city, wit, and the French *église*.

To the value of the *per* in per-ception I have already adverted. A similar observation holds in respect of *con* in con-ception. To conceive is to put ideas together. The expressions, ' I can easily conceive that,' or ' I could not have conceived that he would act in such a manner,' signify, either I can or cannot reconcile the new statement or idea presented to the mind with previous notions. To the etymology in the case of the word *conception*, the late Mr. Mill has adverted in his chapter on that subject. " It is applied," he says, " exclusively to cases of the secondary feelings; to the idea, not the sensation, and to compound, not to single ideas." " I conceive, that is, I take together a horse ; that is, the several ideas combined under the name, and constituting a compound idea." No doubt the terms conscious and conscience had reference originally to what two or more persons knew together, as Hobbes has suggested, and hence came easily to signify what was known confidently or intimately. Intuition from *intueor*, attention from *adtendo*, faculty from *facio*, abstraction from *abstraho*, are easily seen to draw their force from their fountains; the analogy of mental actions to material processes being always discernible in the expressions applied to the mind. So the participles right, just, absolute, infinite, abstract, concrete, and many others, have a clear and useful meaning when the force of the verbs from which they come is kept in view; and metaphysicians lose themselves by trying to fix a meaning on such participles and adjectives irrespective of those realities and particulars, whether objects of sense or conditions of human thought and action, to which alone they can be applied with meaning and advantage. After all, as Locke often suggests, a good dictionary is the best metaphysical treatise*.

When, by reference to etymology, or any other and better method, a definite and satisfactory meaning, a meaning significant of fact, shall be given to the terms employed in mental and moral science, the study will be cleared from the difficulties and obscurity now surrounding it, and the reasoning will become more satisfactory. The laws of the mind, like the so-called laws of material nature, will be perceived to be classes of facts, or the permanent order and succession of undisputed phenomena. In both cases the

* Mr. Samuel Bailey, the author of many excellent works on the mind, in a recent volume has dwelt on the value and distinction of the terms discerning, perceiving, and conceiving. He has gone over much of the ground touched in these pages, and with very striking agreement in the results of metaphysical study ; particularly in his remarks on the force of general and abstract terms, and in his view of the evils arising from the treatment of mental abstractions as real entities. He has not adverted to etymology as a useful and safe guide to the meaning of metaphysical terms. Perhaps his discussion of that meaning might sometimes have been cleared and simplified had he done so.

laws can only be derived from, and be verified by, observation and experience. If they do not rest upon these, and be not conformable to them, they are mere hypotheses or dreams. *Opinionum commenta delet dies; naturæ judicia confirmat.* When the mind is thus studied, its leading faculties, memory, imagination, and reason, will be found to work upon one simple principle, that of association, which, like the sap, or the element of nutrition to the vegetable kingdom, will be an ultimate principle, beyond which investigation cannot go. These faculties, aided by language, their chief instrument, will be seen fraught with use and beauty, God's choicest gifts. For by their aid, all the traces of beneficence that reign in nature become transfused into the mind, and again the pleasurable emotions of the mind become reflected in the forms of external nature, to which a new and permanent interest is given by their perceived connection with benevolent design, that is, with the happiness present or to come of sentient, intellectual, and active beings. Imbued with this principle, the mind, though it be but a dark cavern, echoes faintly the first mandate, " Let there be light;" or like a mirror, though it be broken, contorted, and foul with dust, it becomes capable of reflecting, in some humble measure, the divine conception, when " God saw all that he had made, and behold, it was very good !"

One great and inestimable advantage the disciple of Bacon, Locke, and Hartley must enjoy over the pupils of every other school. A philosophy, intelligible, consistent, and practical, will supply him with a number of rules available for constant self-regulation, improvement, and happiness. Sympathy with the pure and lofty spirit of the masters, and the constant study of their works, will mould the temper to a like heavenly frame. Through the purification of the heart the understanding will be cleared.   No fumes of prejudice and passion, of envy or malignity, will rise to dim the eye of the mind.   Curiosity, stimulated by the desire of good, will issue in truth and the attainment of useful knowledge.   All that is solid and instructive in science, all that is sublime and beautiful in the order of nature, graceful and sweet in poetry and the expression of human sentiment, all that is delicate, tender, consoling and elevating in common life and the instruction of Scripture, will mix with it and vanish into it, to enhance the radiance of the glory of God.   Teaching us that benevolence is the fountain and happiness the end of universal being, by attracting to itself all our pleasures, and by softening, if not subduing, all our pains, such philosophy will place us among the men who

> " With God himself
> Hold converse; grow familiar, day by day,
> With his conceptions; act upon his plan,
> And form to his the relish of our souls."

Then, in the exquisite language of Milton :—

> "How charming is divine Philosophy !
> Not harsh and crabbed, as dull fools suppose,
> But musical as is Apollo's lute,
> And a perpetual feast of nectar'd sweets,
> Where no crude surfeit reigns."

2 I

APPENDIX.

———◆———

I.

An Account of Locke's last hours, Death, and Character, translated from Le Clerc's Eloge of Locke (Bibliothèque Choisie, vol. vi. p. 395, 1705).

FOR more than a year before he died, his weakness became so great that he could not apply himself powerfully to anything, and could scarcely write a letter to one of his friends without pain. Hitherto he had written with his own hand everything which he had occasion to write, and as he was not accustomed to dictate, he could not avail himself of the services of a secretary. Although his frame became weaker, his temper did not change, and if his chest had permitted him to take part in conversation, he would have been still the same. A few weeks before his death, he foresaw that his time was not long, but it did not prevent him from being as gay as usual, and when surprise was expressed, he was wont to say, "Live, while you live."

The study of Holy Writ had produced in him a piety lively and sincere, though far removed from affectation. As he remained a long time unable to go to the church, he thought proper, some months before his death, to take the Lord's Supper at home, as is done in England, and two of his friends partook of it with him. When the minister began to officiate he said to him, "that his feelings were those of perfect charity towards all mankind, and of sincere union with the Church of Christ, by whatever name distinguished." He was too enlightened to take the Communion as a symbol of schism and division, as many ill-instructed people do, who, when they take the Communion in their church, condemn all other Christian societies. He was deeply penetrated with admiration of the wisdom of God in the manner in which he had willed the salvation of mankind, and when he conversed thereon, he could not refrain from exclaiming, " Oh the depth of the riches of the wisdom and of the knowledge of God!" He was persuaded that every one must be convinced of this by reading the Scriptures without prejudice; and to this he exhorted often those with whom he conversed towards the close of his life. His application to this study had given him an idea of the Christian religion more noble and more enlarged than that which he had before entertained; and if he had had sufficient strength to commence new works, there is much ground for thinking that he would have composed some designed to convey to the minds of others, in all its vastness, this great and sublime idea.

Some weeks before his death, as he could no longer walk, he had been carried in an arm-chair about the house; but Lady Masham having gone to see him the 27th of October, 1704, instead of finding him in his study, as usual, found him in bed. On her expressing surprise, he said to her, that he had resolved to stay in bed, as he had fatigued himself too much by rising the day before, that he could not sustain this fatigue, and that he knew not that he should ever get up again. He could not dine that day; and after dinner, those who loved his company, having gone into his room, proposed to him to read something to occupy his mind; but he declined it. Nevertheless, some one having brought some papers into his room, he wished to know what they were, and they read them to him; after which he said that what he had to do here must be done forthwith, and he thanked God for it. Thereupon they approached his bed, and he added his wish, "that they would remember him in the evening prayer." They said to him, that if he would like it, all the family would come into his room to offer prayer, and he consented. They then inquired if he thought himself about to die, and he replied, that perhaps it might happen that night, but that it could not be delayed three or four days. He had then a cold sweat, but recovered soon after. They offered him a little moum (a strong beer which is made at Brunswick), which he had taken with pleasure a week before. He thought it the least injurious of strong beverages, as I myself have heard him say. He took some spoonfuls of it, and drank to the health of the company, saying, " I wish you all happiness when I shall have departed." The persons who were in his chamber having gone out, except Lady Masham, who remained sitting by his bedside, he exhorted her to regard this world only as a state of preparation for a better, adding, that he had lived long enough, and that he blessed God for having passed his life happily ; yet that this life appeared to him as a mere vanity. After supper, the family went up into his chamber again to pray to God, and between eleven and twelve he appeared a little better. Lady Masham having wished to watch by him, he would not permit it, and said that perhaps he should sleep ; but that if he felt any change he would call her. He did not sleep ; but resolved to try to get up on the morrow, as he did. They carried him into his study, and placed him on a more comfortable chair, where he slept at intervals a considerable time. Appearing a little revived, he wished that they would dress him as he was accustomed to be, and asked for some small beer, which he very seldom tasted, after which, he entreated Lady Masham, who was reading the Psalms in a very low voice, to read aloud. She did so, and he appeared very attentive, until the approach of death prevented it. He then requested this lady to read no more, and a few minutes after, on the 28th of October, 1704, about three o'clock in the afternoon, in his seventy-third year, he expired.

Thus died one of the most excellent philosophers of our day, who, after having thoroughly examined all parts of philosophy, and having developed its most secret mysteries with uncommon penetration and exactness, happily turned his attention to the Christian religion. He examined it at the fountain, and, with the same freedom with which he had treated the other sciences, and he found it so reasonable and so beautiful, that he consecrated the remainder of his life to it, and endeavoured to impart to others that high esteem which he had conceived for it. He mingled with it no melancholy, no superstition, as sometimes happens to people who give themselves up to devotion only after disappointment (*chagrin*). The same light which had guided him in his philosophical studies, guided him in that of the New Testament, and lighted up in his heart a piety perfectly rational, and worthy of Him who has given us *reason*, to profit by revelation, and whose revealed will supposes the use of all the good faculties which he has given, to know, to admire, and to obey it.

It is not necessary here to eulogize the mind of Mr. Locke, nor to speak of its comprehensiveness, its penetration, its exactness. His works, which may be read in many languages, are the proof of it, and his eternal monument. I shall only give here the portrait received from an illustrious person to whom he was perfectly known.

" He was, she says (and I can confirm the testimony in great measure by what I have myself seen here), a profound philosopher, and a man fitted for great affairs. He had great knowledge of elegant literature, and manners full of politeness and most engaging. He knew something on almost every subject which can be useful to mankind, and searched to the bottom every subject which he had studied ; but he was superior in all these acquirements in this, that he did not appear raised in his own esteem on account of this illumination. No one wore less the air of a master, nor was less dogmatical than he, and he was by no means hurt when people did not enter into his opinions. There are however a species of squabblers, who, after having been often refuted, return again and again to the charge, and do nothing but repeat the same thing. He could not endure these people, and spoke of them sometimes with a little heat, but he was the first to recognize his idle disturbance.

" In the least affairs of life, as well as in speculative opinions, he was ready to give himself up to Reason, whoever it was that led him thither ; the faithful servant, or, if you will, the slave of Truth, whom he never abandoned, and loved for herself alone. He accommodated himself to the capacity of humbler minds, and in disputing with them, diminished not the force of their reasonings against himself, though they might not have been well expressed. He conversed with pleasure with persons of all sorts, and endeavoured to profit by their intelligence, which arose not only from the good manners imparted by his education, but from an opinion that there was scarcely a person from whom he could not learn something advantageous.

Hence he had learned so many things concerning the *arts and trade* that he seemed to have made these things his particular study, and they who pursued these things professionally, often profited by his knowledge and consulted him with pleasure.

" If there were anything to which he could not accommodate himself, it was bad manners, which filled him with disgust when he saw that they sprang, not from ignorance of the world, but from pride, barbarism, bad temper, brutal stupidity, and other such like vices. Yet he was very far from despising any one because he had a disagreeable exterior. He regarded civility not only as a thing agreeable and fit to gain affection, but as a duty of Christianity, which ought to be observed the more, as persons do not commonly attend to it. He recommended with this view a treatise by the gentlemen of Port Royal (Sur les Moyens de Conserver la Paix avec les Hommes), and he highly approved the sermons which he had heard from Dr. Whichcot on this subject, and which have since been printed.

" His conversation was very agreeable with all persons, and even to ladies; and no one was better received than he among persons of the highest rank. For he was by no means austere, and as the conversation of persons of condition is usually more easy and less formal, if Mr. Locke had not these talents naturally, he had acquired them by intercourse with the world; and this rendered him so much the more agreeable to those who, not knowing him, did not expect to find these manners in a man so much devoted to study. Those who sought the acquaintance of Mr. Locke, to learn from him whatever a man of his knowledge could teach, and who approached him with respect, were surprised to find in him, not only the manners of a man well-bred, but all the politeness which they could desire.

" He spoke often against ridicule, which requires delicate handling in conversation, and is dangerous if not well managed. He could employ raillery as well as most people; but he never said anything which could shock or injure any one. He knew how to soften whatever he said, and give it an agreeable turn. If he rallied his friends, it was for some considerable fault, or upon some point which would turn to their advantage when they knew it. As he was wonderfully civil, even when he commenced his raillery, they felt as well assured of something obliging as when he at length expressed it. He never ridiculed a misfortune or a natural defect.

"He was very charitable to the poor, provided they were not idle, vicious, nor such as never went to any church, but frequented the alehouse on Sunday. He had special compassion for those who, after having laboured as much as they had been able in youth, sank into poverty in their old-age. He would say it was not enough to save them from dying of hunger, but that we ought to help them to live with some comfort. Thus he sought opportunities of doing good to those who deserved it, and often in his walks he visited the poor of the neighbourhood, and gave them something wherewith to comfort them in their necessities, or to purchase the remedies which he prescribed for them if they were sick and had no doctor. He did not like anything to be wasted which might be useful; this was, in his opinion, to lose the treasure of which God has made us the economists. Thus he was a man of order, and one who kept exact accounts of everything.

"If he was subject to any passion, it was that of anger; but he mastered it by reason, and it rarely led him to any wrong. He saw perfectly its folly. He used to say that it availed nothing, neither in the education of children nor keeping servants in order, and that it tended to destroy the authority which might be exerted over them. He was kind towards his servants, and took pains to instruct them with gentleness as to the manner in which they were to serve him.

"Not only did he keep strictly a secret entrusted to him, but he never mentioned again what might be injurious, though he had not been warned to silence; nor did he at any time by indiscretion or inattention do mischief to his friends. He was particular in keeping to his word, and what he promised was sacred. He was scrupulous as to the recommendation of persons whom he did not know, and never could bring himself to praise those whom he thought not praiseworthy. When told that his recommendations had not the effect that was expected, he said, 'that it arose from this, that he never deceived any one by saying more than he knew; that whatever he was answerable for must be found such as he described; otherwise his recommendations would never have any weight.'

"His greatest enjoyment was that of conversing with intelligent persons, and he valued their society. He had all the qualities which could render his friendship delightful. He played cards only out of good nature, though being often in the company of persons who did so, he played not badly, when the occasion came. But he never proposed it, and said that it was only an amusement for those who had no conversation. In dress he was neat, without affectation, without singularity. He was naturally very active and always employed, as much as his health would permit. Sometimes he took pleasure in working in a garden, which he understood perfectly well. He loved a walk, but his weakness of chest not permitting him to walk much, he took exercise on horseback after dinner, and when he could not bear the fatigue of this, in a wheel-chair; and wished always to have company, though only that of a child, for he delighted in the conversation of children well brought up.

" The weakness of his health gave inconvenience to no one but himself, and the only pain which he occasioned was that of observing him to suffer. His mode of living was like that of others, except that he drank only water, and believed that this had preserved his life so long, in spite of his feeble constitution. He attributed to the same cause the preservation of his sight, which was very little injured at the close of his life, for he could read by candlelight books of all kinds, if the type was not very small, and he never used glasses. He had no other inconvenience but that of his asthma, except that about four years before his death he became very deaf. This lasted however scarcely more than six months. Finding himself deprived of the pleasure of conversation, he expressed his doubts in a letter to one of his friends whether it were not better to be blind than deaf. But he suffered very patiently his disadvantages."

We have here the portrait of this great man, drawn from nature and by no means flattered. I wish it were in my power not only to render the memory of him immortal, but still more to give his mind an eternal life, by inducing men of letters to seek truth, to love it, and defend it as he did. But better than all my praises and exhortations would be the study of his works; and I learn that he has left one on the conduct of the understanding in pursuit of truth, which will soon be given to the world. The bookseller who prints this ' Bibliothèque' will publish it in French with his other posthumous works.

On the 28th of October, 1853, the 149th anniversary of his death, I visited the tombs of Locke and of the Mashams in the churchyard of High Lever in Essex, in company with a learned friend, the Rev. Benjamin Mardon. The day was calm and bright. Instead of lamenting, with Bishop Law, the tomb's decay, we had the pleasure of finding it in excellent preservation, and of reading on the spot the beautiful and characteristic epitaph written by the philosopher himself.

II.

Examples of the Prevalence of the Opinion of Locke's Connection with Scepticism and with Hume.

" Mr. Hume's religious opinions chiefly appear in his ' Philosophical Essays.' In these he endeavours, on the system of Locke, who was a firm believer in Christianity, to rear a system of materialism. He advances sentiments which subvert the foundations of morality and religion, and aims wholly to set aside all proofs of a divine revelation."—HENRY A. ROWLAND, ' *On the common Maxims of Infidelity.*' New York. 1850.

The late Rev. JOSEPH MILNER, A.M., in section viii. p. 154, of his work entitled, ' *Gibbon's Account of Christianity considered, together with some Strictures on Hume's Dialogues concerning Natural Religion,*' A.D. 1781, thus severely animadverts on Mr. Locke's theological writings :—" Mr. Locke led the fashion in introducing a pompous parade of *reasoning* into religion ; from that time a *rational* religion has been the cant term with all who profess to be wiser than others. The proper humble subserviency of reason to Christianity as a very useful but submissive handmaid, has been discarded. He appears to know little or nothing of that divine faith which the Scripture describes ; from Locke down to Hume, that is to say, from a cold historical assent down to atheism itself, or to what is much the same, there has been a gradual melancholy declension from evangelical simplicity. Reason has impertinently meddled with the Gospel, and that with such overbearing sedulity as to darken it more and more ; and rivers of tears would not suffice to bewail the increase of moral misery which, since Mr. Locke's time, has pervaded these kingdoms."—*Quoted by the late* REV. R. WALLACE, ' *Antitrinitarian Biography,*' *under the article* ' *John Locke,*' vol. iii. p. 409.

Locke was vindicated from the attacks of Milner and another author, Mr. Kett, by Thomas Ludlam, of Leicester, who published, with his brother William, 1807, some useful essays, scriptural, moral, and logical, designed to promote attention to clearness of ideas, precision of expression, and accuracy of reasoning.

" Again, we think it quite legitimate to infer the character and tendency of any school of thought from the writers it has actually produced. And what has been the school that has grown out of the ' sensational' philosophy of Locke ? From this school has sprung the materialism of Priestley, the French school of Deism that preceded the Revolution, the atheism of Darwin, the utilitarian ethics of Bentham and of Paley. On the other hand, from the Cartesian idealism we derive, in direct descent, the devout (if somewhat exaggerated) spiritualism of Malebranche, of Bishop Berkeley, of Pascal, of Fénelon, to say nothing of the brilliant array of German thinkers—of Leibnitz, Kant, and Fichte—of Schelling and of Hegel, with the modern school of Cousin in France ; writers destined, we believe, to emancipate Christianity from the trammels of scholasticism, and to give it once more the Catholic character and spiritual power contemplated by its holy Founder."—*Westminster Review ; Article on Rogers's Reason and Faith*, vol. lvi. Oct. 1851. The author of the above did not condescend to spell quite correctly the names of some of the philosophers to whom he refers. A very different spirit pervades subsequent articles in the Review, such as that entitled ' *Iconoclasm in German Philosophy,*' *Review of Schopenhauer*, New Series, vol. iii. for April. ' *Universal Postulate,*' *Review of Metaphysical Works*, vol. iv. Oct. 1853.

" It may appear strange to say that sensationalism is conformable to Cartesian principles, and that Locke, Condillac, Diderot, with all their numerous and unhappy progeny, are legitimate descendants of Descartes; since he gives to his doctrines an air of the purest theism, and would establish on a solid basis the spirituality of human minds. But the theism of Descartes is wholly paralogistic; his doubt, methodical and absolute; and the endeavour to make inward feeling the basis of everything knowable, necessarily led to the negation of every material and sensible reality. He who starts from doubt can only end in doubt; because the summit of the scientific pyramid must resemble the foundation. He who sets out from fact cannot arrive at truth, since fact is contingent and relative; and truth in its radical character is necessary and absolute. Moreover sensationalism (*il sensismo*), despoiled of the contradictions of its partisans, and reduced to its true essence by the severe logic of David Hume, is peculiarly sceptical, terminating in a subjective play of the mind which is constrained to dally with appearances after removing all reality; and it manifests itself as the ultimate end of every doctrine which places the elements of knowledge in the sentiment of the individual mind. If Locke, and even Condillac, knew not how to avert this consequence, they showed themselves more prudent than Descartes, by rejecting the bold rationalism which the French philosopher had fabricated in the air; and if less sagacious, they appeared at any rate more judicious."— *Translated from the Italian of* VINCENZO GIOBERTI : ' *Introduzione allo Studio della Filosofia*, vol. i. pp. 139, 140. Brussels, 1844.

Gioberti gives the following estimate of English philosophy as compared with the French and German :—" English philosophy, of which we have not yet said a word, occupies a middle place between the French and the German, and partakes of the mixed genius of the present inhabitants of Great Britain, who are allied to the German race through the Anglo-Saxons, the Danes, the Normans, and some more ancient migrations, and to the Celtic through the remains of the Cimri and the Gauls. Hence arises that wonderful temperament of the English genius, and the civil greatness of the nation, whose manliness is the more striking in comparison with the childishness or decrepitude of the other European nations. The English genius is allied to the Positive, and most skilful in the studies and the business of exterior life; but it does not forget, on that account, that the true value of material things depends on the conceptions of the mind, and that practical sense cannot have place without morality and religion."

III.

A remarkable Passage from Sir Matthew Hale's ' Primitive Origination of Mankind' (1677, pp. 60, 61), showing the State of Opinion on Innate Ideas or Connate Principles before or about Locke's Time.

" I come now to consider of those rational instincts, as I call them, the connate principles engraven in the human soul, which, though they are truths acquirable and deducible by rational consequence and argumentation, yet they seem to be inscribed in the very *crasis* and texture of the soul, antecedent to any acquisition by industry or the exercise of the discursive faculty in man; and therefore they may be well called anticipations, prenotions, or sentiments characterized and engraven in the soul, born with it, and growing up with it, till they receive a check by ill customs or educations, or an improvement and advancement by the due exercise of the faculties. I shall show first what they are: secondly, what moves me to think that such are connatural.

" 1. Touching the former, I think those implanted and connatural anticipations are these: namely, that there is a God; that he is of greatest power, wisdom, goodness, and perfection; that he is pleased with good and displeased with evil; that he is placable; that he is to be feared, honoured, loved, worshiped, and obeyed; that he will reward the good and punish the evil; a secret sentiment of the immortality of the soul, or that it survives the body, to be capable of rewards and punishments, according to its deportment in this life; certain common notions of moral good and evil, of *decorum* and *turpe;* that faith and promises are to be kept; that a man must do as he would be done by; that the obscene parts and actions, though otherwise natural, are not to be exposed to public view, *obvelatio pudendorum;* that a man must be grateful for benefits received. These, and some such common notions or intimate propensions, seem to be connaturally engraven in the soul antecedently to any discursive rationication; and though they are not so distinct and explicit, yet they are secret biases, inclining the human nature primarily to what is useful and convenient for it in proportion to the state of an intellectual nature." . . . . He goes on to call them *certain rational instincts, a certain congenite stock of rational sentiments,* predisposing and inclining to the good and convenience proportionable to a rational and intellectual life.

" 2. And that which inclines me to believe this is, not only the congruity of the supposition to the convenience of the human nature, and the instance of the sensible instincts in the animal nature proportioned to their convenience, and the great importance of them to the convenience thereof; but also that which is observable in the attentive consideration of the manners of mankind in general, which seems to have those common sentiments in them, and to accord in them in a very great measure; and though evil customs and education much prevails among men, yet it doth not wholly obliterate these sentiments, at least from the generality of mankind."

IV.

Opinion of Hume by the Translator of Buffier's ' First Truths.'

" Hume is indeed a metaphysician of such subtilty, at least, that his *own* conceptions appear to have escaped the intelligence of himself. I have frequently analysed a multiplicity of his sentences, paragraphs, and pages: I have assiduously endeavoured to affix the properest idea to each word, and to consider the whole in all the points of view within my power; and yet without a possibility of comprehending his intention. Diffident of my own abilities, I have consulted men of distinguished eminence in metaphysical learning: these also have united in the previous conclusions. Of this fact I can adduce innumerable instances, that through his Essays, together with his usual unintelligibility, he has not only been guilty of introducing opinions which have no other tendency than that of levelling all distinction between virtue and vice, and of exterminating that supreme felicity which necessarily results from the exercise of religion and morality; but that he abounds with more flagrant self-contradictions than can be found in any writer whom I have read: for such is the truth, that men not only acquire reputation in metaphysical literature by the very means which would inevitably preclude it in all others, but they are more secure from the detection of that criticism which is generally within the reach of common understandings.

" Metaphysical researches in their nature include a difficulty of being comprehended: the readers, therefore, of such productions, whenever they encounter a passage unintelligible in itself, are inclined to suppose it to have sprung from the abstruseness of the matter, and kindly impute to an insufficiency in themselves, the want of comprehending that which the author himself had never conceived with any degree of ideal precision, nor expressed with intelligible perspicuity; and thus the latter acquires the reputation of being extremely refined, and deep in the knowledge of his subject, and beyond his reader's reach of thought, when, in fact, he was only truly incomprehensible, and not to be fathomed either by himself or even the most extensive line of the human intellect."

V.

Definitions of Virtue.

I have said that Hume nowhere attempts a definition of virtue. This is incorrect. He does attempt it; but not where we should most expect it. In the first appendix to his Essays concerning moral sentiments, he thus expresses himself:—

" The hypothesis which we embrace is plain. It maintains that morality is determined by sentiment. It defines virtue to be *whatever mental action or quality gives to a spectator the pleasing sentiment of approbation;* and vice, the contrary."

According to this definition there can be no virtue without a spectator, and the virtue is entirely dependent on the nature of a spectator's sentiments—his approbation or disapprobation.

Mr. Belsham has collected and discussed several definitions of virtue at the end of his 'Elements of the Philosophy of the Human Mind.' Henry Grove, in his 'System of Moral Philosophy,' (vol. ii. pp. 198, 199) gives others, from Aristotle downwards. I have collected many more. Gay's Dissertation contains a very important one. One of the worst accounts of virtue is that by Bishop Butler in the Dissertation on Virtue appended to the 'Analogy,' as follows:—

"It is that which all ages and all countries have made profession of in public; it is that which every man you meet puts on the show of; it is that which the primary and fundamental laws of all civil constitutions over the face of the earth make it their business and endeavour to enforce the practice of upon mankind; namely justice, veracity, and regard to common good."

The last words, "*regard to common good*," come the nearest to a rational account or idea of it.

VI.

I proposed (p. 266) to give in the Appendix an analytical view of the Essay on the Goodness of God, contained in the 'Theodicæa' by Leibnitz. On reflection, as this work is extended beyond the length originally contemplated, I consider it best to reserve for separate publication a translation of that Essay, already prepared, should there be encouragement to give it to the public.

CHRONOLOGICAL TABLE OF WRITERS ON MENTAL AND MORAL PHILOSOPHY, AND KINDRED SUBJECTS,

COMPILED WITH RELATION TO ITS PROGRESS IN ENGLAND, AND TO THE OPINIONS AND INFLUENCE OF LOCKE.

1597. Lord Bacon's Essays, or Counsells Civil and Moral.
1605. Bacon's Advancement of Learning, or First Part of the Instauratio.
1617. Campanella, Philosophiæ instaurandæ Prodromus.
1620. Bacon's Instauratio Magna. Second Part.

1623. Campanella, Realis Philosophia.
1624. Herbert (Lord) of Cherbury, De Veritate.
1624. Gassendi, Exercitationes Paradoxicæ adversus Aristoteleos.
1625. Grotius, De Jure Belli; its Introduction contains a statement of the principles of morals prevalent in Christendom.
1627. Hakewill's, George, Apologie of the Power and Providence of God in the Government of the World.
1637. Descartes' Discourse on Method; Dioptrics.
1637. Barlow, Dr. Thomas, Exercitationes aliquot Metaphysicæ de Deo, 4to, Oxon.
1638. Brerewood, Edward, Tractatus Logici.
1640. ——— Ethici.
1640. Anderson, Robert, Logica; a compendium of Aristotle.
1641. Descartes' Meditationes de Prima Philosophia.
1641. Crakanthorp, Logica.
1642. Hobbes, De Cive; a few copies.
1645. Herbert, Lord, De Causis Errorum; annexed to a third edition of De Veritate.
1646. Culverwell's Discourse of the Light of Nature.
1650. Hobbes' Treatise on Human Nature, and Elements of Policy, or of the Law.
1651. ——— Philosophical Rudiments of Government and Society; Leviathan; with his Life.
1655. ——— Elementa Philosophiæ.
1656. Ward, Seth, Exercitationes in Hobbii Philosophiam.
1656. Crellius, John, Prima Ethices Elementa; Ethica Christiana; Ethica Aristotelica ad S. L. Normanne emendata.
1658. Gassendi's Syntagma Philosophicum; Logic, Physics, and Ethics.
1661. Glanvil, Joseph, Vanity of Dogmatizing.
1663. Lucy, William (Bishop of St. David's), Observations on Hobbes' Leviathan.
1663. Charleton, Dr. W., Account of the Philosophy of Gassendi.
1666. Parker, S., Free and Impartial Censure of the Platonic Philosophy.
1667. Ward, Seth, Essays on the Attributes of God, Immortality of the Soul, etc.
1669. Ramus, Peter, Dialecticæ duo libri; a reprint by Dounam.
1669. De la Forge, De Mente Humanâ.
1670. Pascal, B., Pensées.
1670. Spinoza, Tractatus Politico-theologicus.
1670. Tenison, T., Creed of Mr. Hobbes Examined.
1672. Cumberland, R., De Legibus Naturæ.

2 K

1672. Puffendorf, De Jure Naturæ et Gentium. See Kennett's edition with Barbeyrac's Preface and Notes.
1672. Le Grand, Apologia pro Renato Descartes, an Answer to Parker.
1672. Milton, J., Artis Logicæ plenior Institutio, ad Rami metho dum concinnata.
1673. Ferguson, Robert, Discourse of Moral Virtue and Grace.
1674. Malebranche, Recherche de la Vérité.
1674. Tepelin, J., Historia Philosophiæ Cartesianæ.
1675. Institutio Philosophiæ secundum principia Renati Descartes, in usum Juventutis: much read in Cambridge.
1676. Clarendon's Survey of Errors in Hobbes' Leviathan.
1676. Glanvil, Joseph, Essays on several Subjects in Philosophy and Religion.
1677. Spinoza, Opera Posthuma.
1678. Parker, S., De Deo et Providentiâ.
1678. Bernier's Abrégé de la Philosophie de Gassendi.
1678. Burthogge's Organum; or, Discourse of Reason and Truth.
1678. Cudworth's Intellectual System.
1678. Edwards on the Will.
1679. More, Dr. H., Collected Works.
1681. Parker, S., Divine Authority of the Law of Nature.
1682. Baxter's Immortality of the Soul and Nature of Spirits.
1682. Rust, Dr., Discourse of Truth, with Glanvil's Lux Orientalis.
1683. Arnauld, A., Des vraies et des fausses Idées contre Malebranche.
1684. Whitby, D., Ethices Compendium, a text-book at Oxford.
1684. Leibnitz, Acta Eruditorum; Meditations on Knowledge, Truth, and Ideas.
1686. Horneck, Anthony, First Fruits of Reason.
1687. Wallis, Institutio Logicæ, ad communes usus accommodatæ.
1689. Locke's Essay on the Human Understanding. ϗ ᴛᴛ ɢ
1689. Regis, J. S., Système de la Philosophie.
1689. Huet, P., Censura Philosophiæ Cartesianæ.
1690. Aldrich, Compendium Artis Logicæ.
1693. Bentley, R., On the Folly of Atheism.
1694. Burthogge, R., On Reason, and the Nature of Spirits; Author of a Letter to Mr. Locke, 'On the Soul of the World and of particular Souls,' in Lord Somers' Tracts, vol. ii. p. 229.
1695. Toland's Christianity not Mysterious.
1695. Locke's Reasonableness of Christianity.
1695. Norris, J., Account of Reason and Faith, in reply to Locke.

1696. Leibnitz, Réflexions sur l'Essai de l'Entendement Humain de M. Locke.
1697. Bolde, S., Tract in Vindication of Locke.
1697. Collier, Jer., Essays on Moral Subjects.
1698. Lowde on the Nature of Man.
1699. Shaftesbury's Inquiry concerning Virtue; surreptitiously printed.
1700. Account of Mr. Locke's Religion; supposed to be by Atterbury.
1701. Norris, John, Essay towards the Theory of an Intelligible World, First Part; a Second Part in 1704.
1702. King, Archbishop, De Origine Mali.
1702. Lee, Henry, B.D., Anti-Scepticism; or, Notes upon each Chapter of Mr. Locke's Essay, etc.
1703. Broughton, John, Nature of the Soul.
1703. Leibnitz, Nouveaux Essais de l'Entendement Humain.
1704. Clarke, Dr. Samuel, Boyle Lectures on the Being and Attributes of the Deity, followed by Lectures on the Nature of Christianity.
1705. Le Clerc, Eloge de M. Locke; Bibliothèque Choisie.
1706. Bold, Samuel, Collected Tracts in Vindication of Locke.
1706. Cudworth, an Abridgment of his Intellectual System, by Thomas Wise.
1706. Layton's Search after Souls.
1706. Carroll, W., Dissertation on the Tenth Chapter of Locke's Essay, wherein that Author's Endeavours to establish Spinoza's Atheistical Hypothesis are confuted.
1709. Berkeley, Bishop, Theory of Vision.
1710. ———— Principles of Human Knowledge.
1711. Shaftesbury's Characteristics, in 3 vols., and Inquiry concerning Virtue.
1712. Crousaz, J. Peter, Système des Réflexions qui peuvent contribuer à la netteté et à l'étude de nos Connoissances.
1713. Collier, Arthur, Clavis Universalis; being a Demonstration of the Non-existence of an External World.
1713. Berkeley, Bishop, Dialogues between Hylas and Philonous.
1715. Collins, Anthony, Philosophical Inquiry concerning Human Liberty.
1717. Buffier, Père, Traité des premières Vérités.
1717. Green, Robert, Principles of Philosophy for Cambridge.
1718. Colliber, Samuel, Inquiry into the Existence of God; with Remarks on Dr. Clarke's Lectures on the Being and Attributes of God.

1720. Clarke, Dr. John, On the Origin of Evil, 2 vols., 8vo.

1722. Wollaston's Religion of Nature.

1723. Mandeville, Dr. Bernard de, Fable of the Bees; to which there were various answers the following year.

1724. Carmichael's, Dr. Gerscham, edition of Puffendorf De Officio Hominis et Civis, with Notes.

1724. Buffier, Elémens de Métaphysique.

1724. Lyon's Infallibility of Human Judgment.

1724. Watts, Dr. Isaac, Logic.

1725. Crousaz, Tentamen Novum Metaphysicum.

1726. Butler, Bishop, Sermons on Human Nature.

1726. Fiddes, Dr. Richard, General Treatise of Morality.

1726. Hutcheson, F., Inquiry into the Origin of our Ideas of Beauty and Virtue; first edition with his name.

1726. Balguy, John, A Letter to a Deist concerning the Beauty and Excellence of Moral Virtue, etc.

1726. Gretton's Review of the Argument à priori, in Reply to Dr. Clarke.

1728. Browne, Peter, Procedure, Extent, and Limits of the Human Understanding.

1728. Balguy, Foundation of Moral Goodness, in reply to Hutcheson. (2nd Part in 1733.)

1728. Innes, Dr. Alex., Inquiry into the Origin of Moral Virtue.

1729. Kennett's edition of Puffendorf's Law of Nature and Nations.

1730. Clarke, Dr. John, Demonstration of Newton's Philosophy.

1731. Cudworth's Eternal and Immutable Morality, edited by Chandler, Bishop of Durham.

1732. Law, Edmund, Translation of King, on the Origin of Evil. with Notes.

1732. Berkeley's Alciphron; or, Minute Philosopher.

1732. Watts, Dr. I., Philosophical Essays, with Remarks on Locke.

1733. Mosheim's Translation into Latin of Cudworth's Eternal and Immutable Morality.

1733. Campbell, Dr. Archibald, Inquiry into the Original of Moral Virtue.

1734. Berkeley's Analyst.

1734. Law's Inquiry into the Ideas of Space, Time, Immensity, and Eternity, with Waterland's Historical Dissertation on the Argument à priori.

1734. Ernesti; de Mente Humanâ, initia Doctrinæ solidioris.

1734. Colliber, Samuel, Free Thoughts concerning Souls, in four Essays.

1736. Butler, Bishop, Analogy of Religion, Natural and Revealed, to the Constitution and Course of Nature.

1736. Gravesande, Introductio ad Philosophiam, Metaphysicam, et Logicam. Follower of Leibnitz.

1737. Baxter, Andrew, Inquiry into the Nature of the Soul; a first edition without date; 4to in 1735.

1738. Warburton, Divine Legation of Moses.

1739. Hume, David, Treatise of Human Nature, 2 vols., a third in 1740.

1742. —— Essays, forming chiefly 1st volume of subsequent editions.

1743. Birch's edition of Cudworth's Intellectual System, with a Life of the Author, and translation of Mosheim's Notes.

1743. Cockburn, Catharine, Essay concerning the Foundation of Moral Duty; with a Defence of Locke, edited by Dr. Birch in 1751.

1744. Berkeley's Siris.

1744. Rutherforth's Essay on the Nature and Obligation of Virtue.

1744. Harris, James, Treatises.

1745. Condillac, on the Origin of Human Knowledge. Traité des Sensations.

1747. Hutcheson, F., Short Introduction to Moral Philosophy, translated.

1747. Burlamaqui, Principles of Natural Law.

1748. Hartley, David, Observations on Man.

1748. Maclaurin, Account of Sir I. Newton's Discoveries.

1748. Montesquieu, Esprit des Loix.

1748. Reid, Dr. T., Essay on Quantity, in Transactions of the Royal Society.

1749. Grove, Henry, System of Moral Philosophy.

1750. Baxter's (Andrew) Appendix to his Inquiry into the Nature of the Soul.

1751. Glover, Philips, Inquiry concerning Virtue and Happiness.

1751. Home, Henry (Lord Kames), Essays on the Principles of Morality and Natural Religion.

1751. Harris, J., Hermes; or, Philosophical Inquiry concerning Universal Grammar.

1752. Hume, D., Inquiry concerning the Principles of Morals.

1752. Burlamaqui, Political Law, translated by Nugent.

1753. Balfour, James, A Delineation of the Nature and Obligation of Morality, with Reflections on Hume.

1753. Some Thoughts on Self-Love, Innate Ideas, Free-will; occasioned by Hume and Bolingbroke. *Anon.*

1754. Bolingbroke's View of Philosophy, in Letters to a Friend.

1754. Rutherforth, Institutes of Natural Law.
1755. Hutcheson's Moral Philosophy, with Life, by Leechman, 2 vols. 4to.
1755. Taylor's Elements of Civil Law.
1756. Burke's Inquiry into the Origin of our Ideas of the Sublime and Beautiful.
1756. Hume, D., Essay on the Natural History of Religion.
1757. Price, Dr. R., Review of Morals.
1757. Warburton, W. (Bishop), Remarks on Hume's Natural History of Religion.
1758. Helvetius, De l'Esprit.
1758. Boscovich, Theoria Philosophiæ Naturalis.
1759. Smith, Adam, Theory of Moral Sentiments.
1759, Taylor (Dr. John, of Norwich), Examination of Hutcheson's Scheme of Morality.
1760. ———— Sketch of Moral Philosophy; or, Essay to demonstrate the Principles of Virtue and Religion.
1761. Home (Lord Kames), Introduction to the Art of Thinking.
1762. ———— Elements of Criticism.
1763. Tucker, Abraham, Free-will; part of the Light of Nature pursued, published in 4 vols. in 1765.
1764. Reid, Dr. Thomas, Inquiry into the Human Mind.
1765. Blackstone, Sir W., Commentaries on the Laws of England, 1st vol.
1766. Beccaria, Dei Delitti e delle Pene; translated into English.
1767. Ferguson, Dr. A., Institutes of Moral Philosophy.
1767. Price, Dr. R., Dissertations.
1767. Adams, Dr. W., Essay in reply to Hume.
1768. Oswald, Appeal to Common Sense.
1768. Priestley, Dr. Joseph, Essay on Government.
1770. Beattie, Dr. T., Essay on Truth.
1774. Priestley, Dr., Examination of Reid, Beattie, and Oswald.
1775. ———— Edition of Hartley, with Introductory Essays.
1775. Harris, James, Philosophical Arrangements.
1775. Powell, Dr. Wm. Sam., Discourses edited by Dr. Thomas Balguy; one 'On Public Virtue.'
1776. Smith, Adam, Inquiry into the Nature and Causes of the Wealth of Nations.
1776. Condillac, Course of Study.
1776. Campbell, Dr. A., Philosophy of Rhetoric.
1776. Bentham, Jeremy, Fragment on Government; Critique on Blackstone.
1776. Berington, Rev. Jos., Letter on Materialism and on Hartley's Theory.

1776. Philosophical Discourse on the Nature of Human Being; with remarks on Berkeley.

1777. Sharpe, Granville, Tract on the Law of Nature and Principles of Action in Man.

1779. Sharpe, Granville, Dialogues concerning Innate Principles. (See M. R. for year.)

1780. Buffier, First Truths, translated, with Preface.

1781. Tucker, Joseph, Treatise concerning Civil Government.

1781. Kant, Immanuel, Kritik der reinen Vernunft.

1782. Towers, Dr. Joseph, Vindication of Locke's Political Principles.

1785. Reid, Dr. T., Essays on the Intellectual Powers.

1785. Paley, Principles of Moral and Political Philosophy.

1786. Tooke, J. Horne, Epea Pteroenta.

1788. Reid, Dr. Thomas, Essays on the Active Powers.

1789. Bentham, J., Principles of Morals and Legislation.

1789. Cooper, Thomas, Ethical Tracts.

1790. Alison, Arch., Essays on Taste.

1790. Gisborne, Thomas, Examination of Paley.

1790. Trembley, Essai sur les Préjugés.

1792. Gregory, Dr. James, Philosophical Essays on the relation of Motive and Action, and that of Cause and Effect, etc.

1792. Stewart, Dugald, Elements of the Philosophy of the Human Mind.

1793. Crombie, Dr. A., on Philosophical Necessity.

1793. Godwin, W., Inquiry concerning Political Justice.

1794. Doddridge, Dr., Lectures on Pneumatology, Ethics, and Divinity, third edition, by Kippis.

1794. Darwin, Dr. E., Zoonomia; or, Laws of Organic Life.

1794. Morell, Thomas, Notes and Annotations on Locke, written by order of Queen Caroline.

1795. Intellectual Physics, believed to be by Governor Pownall, of Bath.

1796. Gilbert's Law of Evidence, with an Abridgment of Locke by C. Lofft.

1797. Croft, Dr., Defence of Paley's Moral Philosophy.

1798. Willich, Dr. A. F. M., Elements of Critical Philosophy, from Kant.

1798. Brown, Dr. Thomas, Observations on Darwin's Zoonomia.

1799. Monboddo, Lord, Ancient Metaphysics, 6 vols. 4to.

1800. Cogan, Dr. T., Philosophical Treatise on the Passions.

1800. Pearson, Dr., Two Pamphlets against Paley.

1801. Malmesbury, Lord, edition of Harris's Philological and Philosophical Works, with Life.

1801. Belsham, Thomas, Elements of the Philosophy of the Human Mind.
1806. Brown, Dr. T., Essay on Cause and Effect, second edit.
1806. Knight, R. P., Essay on the Principles of Taste.
1807. Cogan, Dr. T., Ethical Treatise.
1809. Kirwan, Richard, Metaphysical Essays.
1810. Stewart, Dugald, Essays on the Philosophy of the Mind.
1817. Cogan, Dr. T., Ethical Questions.
1832. Austin, John, the Province of Jurisprudence determined.
1835. Hampden, Dr. R. D., Lectures introductory to the Study of Moral Philosophy.
1842. Bowen, Francis, Critical Essays on Subjects connected with Speculative Philosophy. Boston, U.S.
1849. ———— Lectures on the Application of Metaphysical Science to the Evidences of Religion.
1850. Smith, Rev. Sydney, Elementary Sketches of Moral Philosophy.
1852. Whewell, Dr. W., Lectures on the History of Moral Philosophy in England.
1854. Outline of the Laws of Thought, by William Thomson, M.A.

To these should be added the modern works of highest repute on Logic, by Whately, De Morgan, and Mill; the dissertations on the History of Philosophy, by Stewart and Mackintosh, in the Encyclopædia Britannica; works on Physiology as connected with the Mind; and the books of Mr. S. Bailey; but with recent works well known I have been less particular as to the date of their appearance. A similar table might be compiled for France and Germany.

THE END.

JOHN EDWARD TAYLOR, PRINTER,
LITTLE QUEEN STREET, LINCOLN'S INN FIELDS.

Titles in This Series

7

Lee, Henry
*Anti-Scepticism: or, Notes Upon Each Chapter of
Mr. Lock's Essay Concerning Humane Understanding*
(London, 1702)

8

Lough, John
*Locke's Travels in France, 1675–1679; As Related in His
Journals, Correspondence and Other Papers*
(Cambridge, 1953)

9

MacLean, Kenneth
John Locke and English Literature of the Eighteenth Century
(New Haven, 1936)

10

Parker, Samuel
*A Demonstration of the Divine Authority of the Law of
Nature, and of the Christian Religion*
(London, 1681)

11

Polin, Raymond
La Politique morale de John Locke
(Paris, 1960)

12

Proast, Jonas
*The Argument of the Letter Concerning Toleration,
Briefly Consider'd and Answer'd*
(Oxford, 1690)

bound with

Proast, Jonas
*A Third Letter Concerning Toleration: in Defence of the
Arguments of the Letter Concerning Toleration,
Briefly Consider'd and Answer'd*
(Oxford, 1691)

bound with

Proast, Jonas
*A Second Letter to the Author of the Three Letters for
Toleration. From the Author of the Arguments of the Letter
Concerning Toleration, Briefly Consider'd and Answer'd*
(Oxford, 1704)

13

Sergeant, John
*Solid Philosophy Asserted, Against the Fancies of the Ideists:
or, the Method to Science Farther Illustrated. With Reflexions
on Mr. Locke's Essay Concerning Human Understanding*
(London, 1697)

14

Tagart, Edward
*Locke's Writings and Philosophy Historically Considered and
Vindicated from the Charge of Contributing to the
Skepticism of Hume*
(London, 1855)

15

Toland, John
Christianity Not Mysterious
(London, 1696)

16

Watts, Isaac
*Logick: or, the Right Use of Reason in the Enquiry After
Truth, With a Variety of Rules to Guard Against Error, in the
Affairs of Religion and Human Life, as Well
as in the Sciences*
(Second Edition, London, 1726)